Fun with the Family™ Illinois

Praise for the Fun with the Family™ series:

"Bound to lead you and your kids to fun-filled days, those times that help compose the memories of childhood."

—Dorothy Jordon, Publisher, *Family Travel Times*

Help Us Keep This Guide Up to Date

Every effort has been made by the author and editors to make this guide as accurate and useful as possible. However, many changes can occur after a guide is published—establishments close, phone numbers change, hiking trails are rerouted, facilities come under new management, etc.

We would love to hear from you concerning your experiences with this guide and how you feel it could be improved and be kept up to date. While we may not be able to respond to all comments and suggestions, we'll take them to heart, and we'll make certain to share them with the author. Please send your comments and suggestions to the following address:

The Globe Pequot Press
Reader Response/Editorial Department
P.O. Box 480
Guilford, CT 06437
Or you may e-mail us at: editorial@GlobePequot.com

Thanks for your input, and happy travels!

INSIDERS' GUIDE®

FUN WITH THE FAMILY™ SERIES

fun WITH the Family™ ILLINOIS

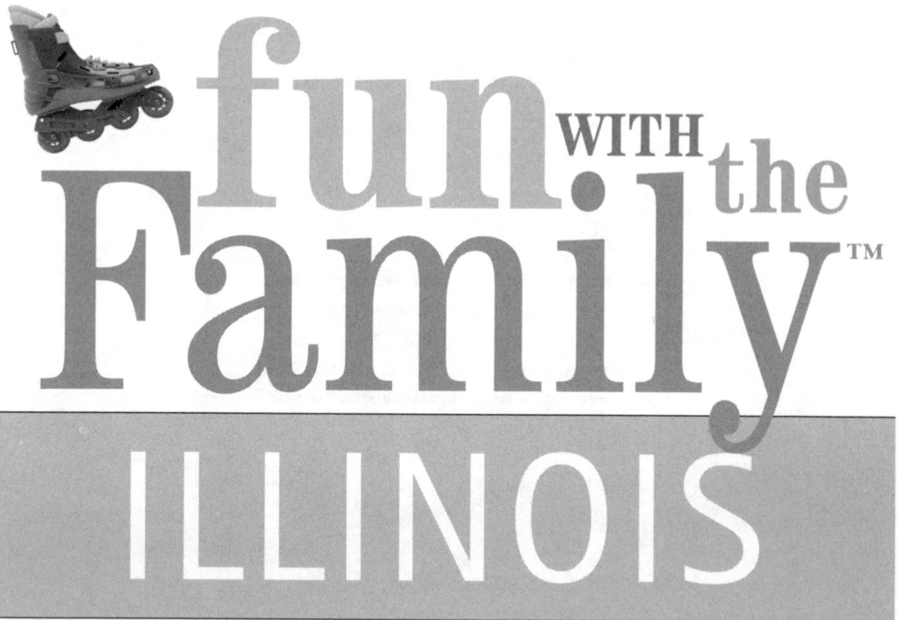

HUNDREDS OF IDEAS FOR DAY TRIPS WITH THE KIDS

LORI MEEK SCHULDT

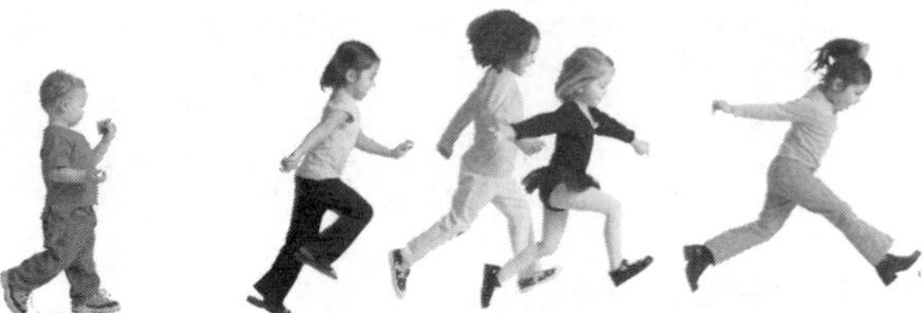

SIXTH EDITION

INSIDERS' GUIDE®

GUILFORD, CONNECTICUT
AN IMPRINT OF THE GLOBE PEQUOT PRESS

The prices, rates, and hours listed in this guidebook were confirmed at press time. We recommend, however, that you call establishments to obtain current information before traveling.

To buy books in quantity for corporate use or incentives, call **(800) 962–0973** or e-mail **premiums@GlobePequot.com.**

INSIDERS' GUIDE®

Text design by Nancy Freeborn and Linda R. Loiewski
Maps by Rusty Nelson © Morris Book Publishing, LLC
Spot photography throughout © Photodisc and © RubberBall Productions

ISSN 1546-3303
ISBN 978-0-7627-4547-0

Printed in the United States of America
10 9 8 7 6 5 4 3 2 1

To Michael and Rachel, who put the fun in my family.

ILLINOIS

Rockford
Northern Illinois
Chicag
Moline
Chicagoland
Peoria
Western Illinois
Bloomington
Champaign
Quincy
Springfield
Central Illinois
Effingham
Mount Vernon
Southern Illinois

Contents

Acknowledgments

I would like to thank the staff at The Globe Pequot Press for all their work. Special thanks to Mike Urban. Thanks also to the many others who have aided me, both professionally and personally, in the journey from idea to printed page. I appreciate all the suggestions and support I have received from friends and family, especially my parents, Bill and Dian Meek; my sister, Cindy, and her kids, Tyler and Sarah, who accompanied us on some of our "field research"; my loving sisters in P.E.O. Chapter KY; and all the others whom I may not have named specifically but who made their own unique contributions.

In the grand tradition of saving the best for last, I would like to thank Rachel P. Schuldt, my darling daughter, for her spirit of adventure in all our little family "vacations" (since 1995, when we began work on the first edition of this book) and her patience during the long process of writing about them, and Michael B. Schuldt, my sweet husband and partner in life, for his willingness to play pilot to my navigator during our travels, for his experienced editorial eyes in reading the manuscript, and for his constant love and reassurance in this and every other endeavor.

Introduction

Probably no other state serves as such a microcosm of the United States as Illinois does. Illinois is a marvelous melting pot of people—descendants of immigrants from Europe, Africa, Asia, and Latin America, plus a few Native Americans—whose homes are big cities, sprawling suburbs, small towns, and isolated farmsteads. The state's topography includes rivers, bluffs, hills, flatlands, forests, and a Great Lake as wide as an ocean. For those of us who live in Illinois, it's a great place to visit somewhere different without ever leaving the state: Downstaters can get energized by the hustle and bustle of the greater Chicago area, while city dwellers can escape to the south and reconnect with nature. Illinois is the perfect state for all kinds of family fun.

This book is designed to help you find places throughout the state that are of special interest to families, from educational attractions such as children's museums and zoos to recreational facilities such as water parks and miniature golf courses, keeping in mind that having fun is the number one goal. The guide is divided into six geographically based chapters: Chicago, Chicagoland, Northern Illinois, Western Illinois, Central Illinois, and Southern Illinois. The sections within each chapter also are arranged geographically so that you can find attractions that are close to one another. A regional map appears at the beginning of each chapter to help you get a better feel for the lay of the land. At the end of the book are a Restaurant Appendix and a Lodging Appendix that will familiarize you with some of the more family-friendly chains. And beyond the general index is an activities index that will help you find attractions by type, such as children's museums or water parks—plus one index of all the free attractions listed in this book.

Here are a few general guidelines to keep in mind. First, always call ahead to double-check that what you want to see is still there; some places may change location or shut down between the time this book goes to print and the time you want to visit. For family travel it's safest to stick with chain hotels and motels and to make your reservations in advance. This book places special emphasis on properties that have a swimming pool, because this amenity tends to keep the kids happier and gives them a place to burn off some of the energy that built up during the trip getting there. When possible, motels that allow pets are also pointed out for families who want to bring along four-legged members. In a similar vein, most of the restaurants mentioned are geared toward middle-of-the-road tastes: buffets, burgers, pizza, and meat-and-potatoes sorts of places. One last note: When admission to an attraction is by donation, you can usually gauge what the real expectation is by whether a specific dollar amount is suggested. If it is, you'll be more comfortable if you plan to pay that amount; if not, they'll be grateful for whatever you give.

The Illinois legislature in 2007 passed a law that as of January 1, 2008, bans smoking in all public places, in all workplaces, and within 15 feet of entrances to public facilities—which means just about every place covered in this book. The new law is likely to dramatically reduce the number of deaths in Illinois from secondhand smoke—currently about 2,900 annually—and provide a more healthful environment for children throughout the state.

Dollar symbols are used throughout the book to provide an idea of the cost for attractions, restaurants, and lodgings.

For attractions, prices represent the cost per person for admission, not including tax, or the average cost of the activity—for example, one line of bowling. Where the symbol "$+" appears, typically in listings for amusement centers, it means that although the price of a single activity—for example, one go-kart ride or one round of miniature golf—is $5 or less, you will probably want to do more than one thing at that place, and the cost will rise depending on how many activities you choose.

For restaurants, prices represent the cost of a single adult dinner entree, not including tax or tip. Total cost will vary depending on type and quantity of additional food and beverages ordered, such as appetizers, desserts, coffee, or wine. Lunches are usually cheaper than dinners.

For lodgings, prices represent the cost of a room with two double beds for one night. Most lodgings offer a range of pricing options based on the size of the room and the amenities. Prices do not include taxes, parking, phone usage, room service, or any other added-on costs.

The following three tables illustrate the price ranges the dollar symbols represent.

Rates for Attractions

$	$5.00 or less
$$	$5.01 to $9.99
$$$	$10.00 to $19.99
$$$$	$20.00 or more

Rates for Lodging

$	$50.00 or less
$$	$50.01 to $75.00
$$$	$75.01 to $100.00
$$$$	$100.01 or more

Rates for Restaurants

$	most entrees $10.00 or less
$$	most entrees $10.01 to $14.99
$$$	most entrees $15.00 to $19.99
$$$$	most entrees $20.00 or more

Many of the individual regions, towns, and sites included in this guide have a phone number you can call, an Internet Web site you can look up, or an address to which you can write to obtain more information.

For general information covering the whole state, you can contact the following:

- **Illinois Bureau of Tourism,** (800) 226-6632; www.enjoyillinois.com
- **Illinois Restaurant Association,** (312) 787-4000 or (800) 572-1086; www.illinoisrestaurants.org
- **Illinois Hotel and Lodging Association,** (217) 522-1231; www.stayillinois.com
- **Illinois Association of Park Districts,** (217) 523-4554; www.ilparks.org
- **Illinois Department of Transportation,** (217) 782-7820; www.dot.state.il.us or www.dot.il.gov
- **Illinois Tollway,** (630) 241-6800; www.illinoistollway.com

Note: The author and her family spent their own money for all the attractions they visited. The author did not identify herself as a writer; the Schuldts wished to be treated the same way as any other family so that a realistic experience could be reported. No one paid the author or the publisher to appear in this book.

Attractions Key

The following is a key to the icons found throughout the text.

SWIMMING	FOOD
BOATING / BOAT TOUR	LODGING
HISTORIC SITE	CAMPING
HIKING / WALKING	MUSEUM
FISHING	PERFORMING ARTS
BIKING	SPORTS/ATHLETICS
AMUSEMENT PARK	PICNICKING
HORSEBACK RIDING	PLAYGROUND
SKIING/WINTER SPORTS	SHOPPING
PARK	PLANTS / GARDENS / NATURE TRAILS
ANIMAL VIEWING	FARM

Chicago

Where does one start in describing the city of Chicago? There's so much to say. There's the history: the Fort Dearborn massacre of 1812, the incorporation of the city in 1833 with a white population of 150 and the subsequent ouster of more than 3,000 indigenous Indians, the industrial expansion in the mid-1800s that created the Union Stock Yards and the Chicago Board of Trade, Mrs. O'Leary's cow and the Great Chicago Fire of 1871, the World's Columbian Exposition of 1893, Al Capone and the gangster era of the 1920s, race riots throughout the 1900s, the political empire of Mayor Richard J. Daley. There's the architecture: risen from the ashes of the Great Chicago Fire by pioneers who created the Chicago School, it today includes what we Illinoisians consider the world's tallest building (the Sears Tower) and other skyscrapers that make the downtown skyline one of the most distinctive in the world, especially since the lakefront has been deliberately spared from development so that everyone may enjoy the beauty of its parks and beaches. There's the culture: an ethnic mixture that includes the largest Polish population of any city outside Poland, plus descendants of wave after wave of immigrants from Europe, Africa, Asia, and Latin America, giving the city a vitality in music, art, and food that few other places can match. There are the sports: professional baseball, basketball, football, and hockey teams. It's no wonder that singers have made the city famous as "Sweet Home Chicago" and "My Kind of Town"—whatever you're looking for is probably here.

But you may need help finding it. The Illinois listings for tourism, hotels, and restaurants in the introduction to this book include Chicago, but for the city specifically, contact:

Chicago Convention and Tourism Bureau
2301 South Lake Shore Drive
Chicago 60616
(312) 567-8500
www.877chicago.com

CHICAGO

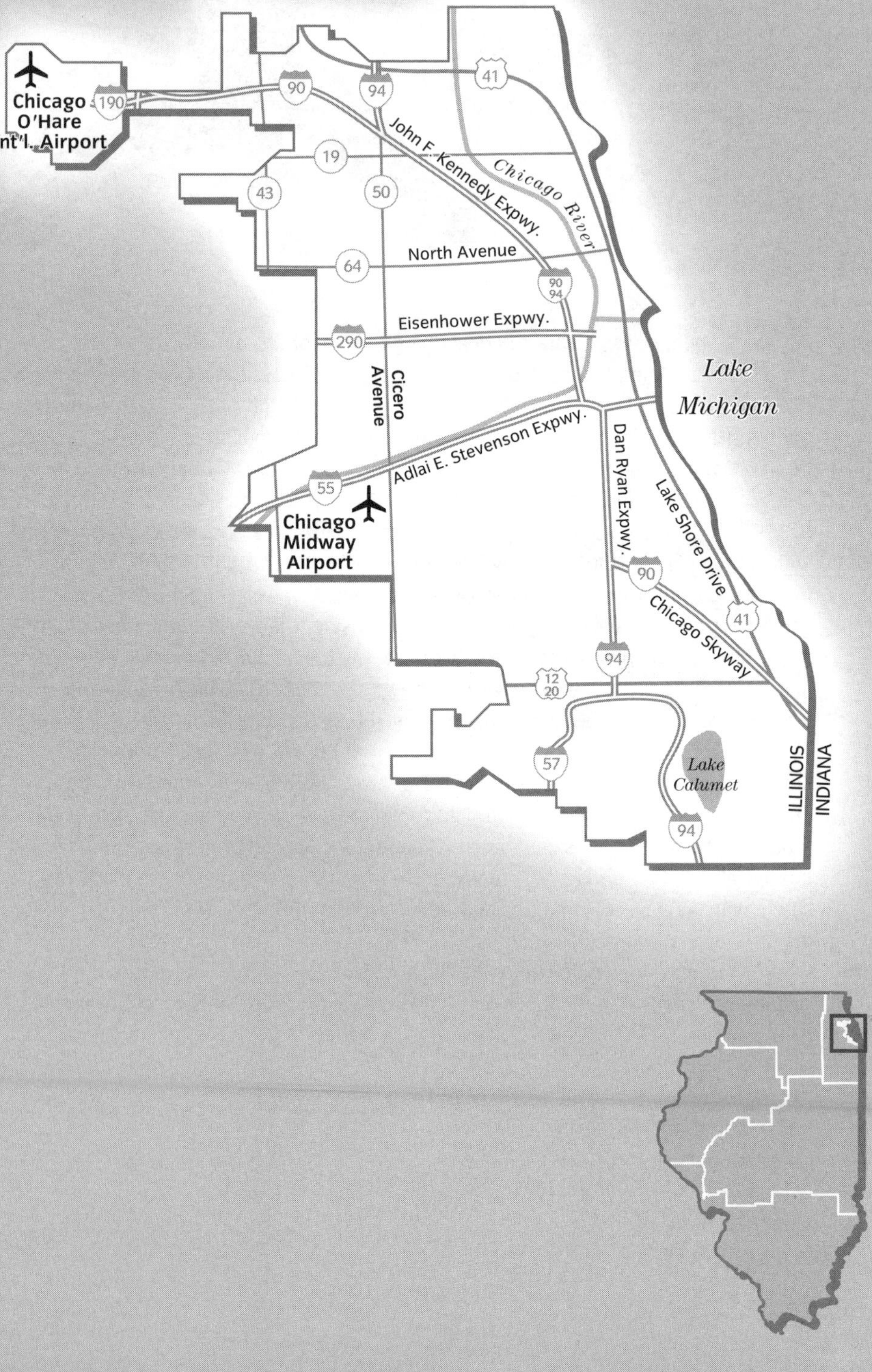

Chicago O'Hare Int'l. Airport
190
90
94
41
John F. Kennedy Expwy.
Chicago River
19
43
50
North Avenue
64
90 94
Eisenhower Expwy.
290
Cicero Avenue
Lake Michigan
Adlai E. Stevenson Expwy.
55
Chicago Midway Airport
Dan Ryan Expwy.
Lake Shore Drive
90
Chicago Skyway
41
94
12 20
57
Lake Calumet
94
ILLINOIS
INDIANA

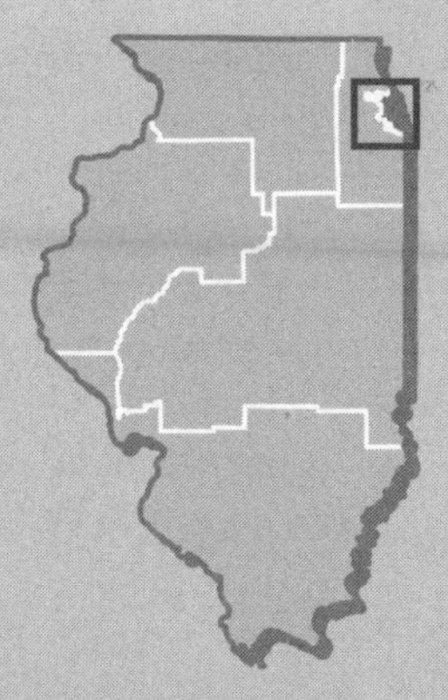

Getting to Chicago is no problem; there are so many choices. If you live in the suburbs, you can enjoy a comfortable ride in on a commuter train; the Metra rail system has about a dozen lines radiating outward from the city in all directions. You can reach Chicago from as far out as Fox Lake, Harvard, Elgin, Elburn, Aurora, Joliet, or University Park. For schedules, fares, and other information, contact Metra, 547 West Jackson Boulevard, Chicago 60661; (312) 322-6777; for the hearing impaired, TDD (312) 322-6774; www.metrarail.com. The downtown Metra passenger terminal, officially called the Richard B. Ogilvie Transportation Center and formerly the Chicago and Northwestern Station before Union Pacific took over, was remodeled in the early 1990s and today is an eye-catching gray-blue architectural work of glass, steel, and marble. The food court on the lower level rivals that of many shopping malls, and there are useful stores on the upper level where you can grab a newspaper and a cup of coffee, get your shoes shined, or buy flowers, candy, or other gifts.

Train service is available from other parts of the state and from out of state via Amtrak; call (800) 872-7245 or check www.amtrak.com for information on routes, schedules, and fares. Another economical choice for transportation is Greyhound bus lines; call (800) 231-2222; for the hearing impaired, TDD (800) 345-3109; for information in Spanish/Español, (800) 531-5332; or go online at www.greyhound.com. Both Amtrak and Greyhound have passenger terminals in downtown Chicago.

You can fly in and out of Chicago's two major airports. On the northwest side, O'Hare—one of the world's busiest airports—handles flights from all over the globe; the general airport numbers are (773) 686-2200 and (800) 832-6352; for the hearing impaired, TTY (773) 686-0000; Web site www.ohare.com. Smaller Midway, on the south side, services more domestic and regional carriers and is less congested; call (773) 838-0600. The Chicago Transit Authority (CTA) operates trains that can get you to and from either airport as well as trains and buses that go all around the city; call (312) 836-7000 or (888) 968-7282. For the hearing impaired, call (312) 836-4949. You can also check the CTA Web site www.transitchicago.com for information on service. Shuttle services and taxicabs also provide transportation from either airport to the city and suburbs.

Coming by car affords travelers the greatest degree of independence and flexibility, but unless you live somewhere bigger (for example, New York or Los Angeles—the only two larger U.S. cities—or London, Tokyo, or Mexico City, among about two dozen urban centers in the world that exceed Chicago's size), you'll be appalled at the traffic. No matter what thoroughfare you take, you'll have plenty of other vehicles whizzing around you, cutting you off, riding your bumper, and generally paying little heed to many rules of the road, including speed limits—all this while your kids are screaming in the backseat. Downtown amid the congested streets, you'll have to deal with aggressive cabs resenting your very existence, harried couriers on bicycles darting out in front of you, delivery vehicles suddenly double-parking, and maybe even an overzealous young entrepreneur giving your windshield an unsolicited washing for a solicited tip. Parking is hard to come by on the streets and expensive in the lots. For the amount of aggravation incurred, driving may not be your top choice.

If you nonetheless opt to drive, here's a little assistance with the expressway lingo. The major north-south thoroughfare of Interstate 94 is known as the Edens Expressway. Another interstate, Interstate 90, which starts out being called the Northwest Tollway and changes its name around Rosemont to the John F. Kennedy Expressway, heads in from the northwest. In the north around Irving Park Road, I-94 joins with I-90, and at about that point the joint interstate is called the Dan Ryan Expressway. I-90/94 splits off again south of downtown, where I-90 continues east into Indiana as the Chicago Skyway and I-94, which is still called the Dan Ryan, continues south to a junction with Interstate 80, at which point I-80/94 becomes known as the Kingery Expressway. A couple of key spurs off I-94 are Interstate 294, also called the Tri-State Tollway, and Interstate 394, also known as the Bishop Ford Freeway, formerly the Calumet Expressway. I-90's western spur, Interstate 290, is called the Dwight D. Eisenhower Expressway. A major artery coming into Chicago from the southwest is Interstate 55, which is known as the Adlai E. Stevenson Expressway. It has a spur, Interstate 355, which was built in the late 1980s to connect western suburbs from north to south and has been creatively dubbed the North-South Tollway. Lacking additional nomenclature is Interstate 57, which enters from the south. U.S. Highway 41 becomes concurrent with Lake Shore Drive as it skirts Lake Michigan. Farther out, U.S. Highway 30 has been dubbed Lincoln Highway, and Illinois Highway 50 is called the Dixie Highway. In June 2004 the section of Interstate 88 that stretches from I-290 westward to the Iowa border was officially named the Ronald Reagan Memorial Tollway in honor of the late president, a onetime resident of Dixon. All this jargon is helpful to know if you have to ask directions, because a native may well say, "Take the Stevenson down to . . ." or "Get on the Dan Ryan and . . ." or "Head out the Kennedy to . . ." and not even be sure which number goes with which name. Radio traffic reporters also use the names more than the numbers.

One other thing you should know about Chicago: Its many neighborhoods (officially there are 77) have their own names, which can be a bit confusing to visitors from outside the metropolitan area who don't know the difference between a neighborhood name and a suburb name. If you hear about something in Uptown, Bucktown, Austin, Bridgeport, Englewood, Lakeview, or Pullman, you're still in Chicago. Many neighborhoods have *Park* as part of their name: Hyde Park, Rogers Park, Wicker Park, Jefferson Park, Norwood Park, Portage Park, Brighton Park, and Morgan Park, for example. (Unfortunately, many suburbs also use the word: Oak Park, Franklin Park, Schiller Park, Melrose Park, Bedford Park, Evergreen Park, Park Ridge, and Park Forest, to name a few.) You can lock in more easily on street addresses, because all the numbers radiate outward from the intersection of State and Madison

Streets downtown. State Street runs north-south, so street addresses with *East* will be east of State, although not more than a mile or two because you run into the lake, and those with *West* run all the way to the city limits on the West Side. Madison Street runs east-west through the middle of the Loop, as the heart of downtown is called, so all the North and South addresses are relative to this point.

Now that you're finally here, let's examine what there is for families to see and do within the city limits of Chicago. We'll start downtown, then branch out to the North, West, and South Sides.

Downtown

You can get around downtown on a **free** trolley, a helpful option if you want transportation between key tourist attractions without the fuss of driving or the expense of a taxi or bus. These red trolleys have rubber wheels and roll along the streets like a bus; the original trolley tracks and lines are long gone. Get on at the street where you see the diamond-shaped FREE TROLLEY sign; there are stops near Union Station and the Ogilvie Transportation Center; near Sears Tower, the Field Museum, the Art Institute, Navy Pier, and Water Tower Place; and along Michigan Avenue, Wacker Drive, and State, Adams, Washington, Randolph, and Lake Streets, among others. The green line loops south to the museums, the red line goes north toward Water Tower, and the yellow line heads out to Navy Pier. The drivers liven up the ride with their own personal commentaries, some of them quite funny. Be nice and drop a dollar in the tip box when you get off. The free trolley operates daily during the summer and Saturday and Sunday only the rest of the year, about every 20 to 30 minutes between 10 a.m. and 6 p.m. For more information call (877) 244-2246 or, for the hearing impaired, TTY (866) 710-0294, or check www.877chicago.com or www.cityofchicago.org.

Chicago Trolley and Double Decker Company (all ages)

Pickup at various downtown locations; (773) 648-5000; www.coachusa.com/chicago trolley. Tours operate daily and run between 9 a.m. and 6:30 p.m. from mid-March through late October and between 9 a.m. and 5:30 p.m. the rest of the year. No service Thanksgiving Day, Christmas Eve, Christmas Day, or January 9. $$–$$$

You can get an overview of the downtown area aboard a red sightseeing trolley. The Chicago Trolley Company—not to be confused with the similar-looking free trolley service—offers a narrated tour a bit more than an hour long, and you can get on or off at any number of key spots, such as Water Tower Place, Navy Pier, Sears Tower, the Art Institute, and the Field Museum. Each trolley has an interior furnished with oak and brass trimmings and can hold 34 passengers at a time. The all-day pass allows an unlimited number of reboardings. The company also operates British-style red double-decker buses for tours.

Hit the **Beach**

The Chicago Park District manages the free public beaches along the city's 29 miles of lakefront. You can swim (in certain supervised areas at designated times), play volleyball, or go jogging, roller-skating, or biking. It's a pleasure just to sit and watch the waves roll in, even during winter. The park district also oversees the dozens of local swimming pools throughout the city. Just north of the downtown area is the popular Oak Street Beach. For general information about the lakefront areas, call the park district at (312) 742-7529 or see www.chicagoparkdistrict.com.

Hancock Observatory (all ages)

875 North Michigan Avenue, Chicago; (312) 751-3681; www.hancock-observatory.com. Open from 9 a.m. to 11 p.m. daily. $–$$

The John Hancock Center Observatory tower offers a panoramic view of the city from the 95th floor. Hang onto your stomach for the 40-second elevator ride that takes you to the top. You may want to give kids a piece of gum ahead of time or babies a pacifier to help keep their ears from popping. It's worth it once you get up there. It's true: On a clear day you can see forever.

American Girl Place (age 6 and up) 

111 East Chicago Avenue, Chicago; (877) 247-5223; www.americangirlplace.com. During the school year, hours are 10 a.m. to 7 p.m. Monday through Wednesday, 10 a.m. to 9 p.m. Thursday and Friday, 9:30 a.m. to 9 p.m. Saturday, and 9:30 a.m. to 7 p.m. Sunday. Summer hours are 9 a.m. to 7 p.m. Sunday through Wednesday and 9 a.m. to 9 p.m. Thursday through Saturday. Admission to the store is free. Theater tickets $$$$.

If your grade-school daughter is into American Girl dolls and books, she will be begging you to take her here. This three-story mecca just west of Michigan Avenue near Water Tower Place has it all: beautiful 18-inch American Girl dolls, accessories, books, and related merchandise (Bitty Baby, Angelina Ballerina), plus entertainment, food, and special services. Tickets for the stage show, *The American Girls Revue,* cost $28 per person, and reservations are required. No one younger than age 6 is admitted, and that includes babies, so hire a sitter rather than dragging your daughter's little siblings along. The food at the American Girl Cafe is pretty mainstream American; it's the atmosphere that's the real draw. You dine at a lovely table decorated with frills and flowers, and there's a special seat at the table *for your doll.* The food is delivered on a black-and-white trolley cart. You can enjoy breakfast, lunch, afternoon tea, or dinner; reservations are recommended. While you're waiting for your table or the show, you can wander through the free exhibit called Peek into the Past. It features human-size models of rooms from the homes of the American Girl characters, for example, Kirsten's log cabin, Samantha's Victorian parlor, and Molly's World War II-era living room. If your doll is having a bad hair day, you can take her to the Doll Hair Salon for a new do, at a cost of $10 to $20. There's even a Doll Hospital where you can drop off a patient and have her shipped home a couple weeks later once her wounds have been mended. American Girl Place, which opened in 1998, is an unabashedly commercial enterprise but one that knows how to satisfy its clientele. American Girl Place was scheduled to relocate to the first two floors of Water Tower Place (see next entry) by October 2008.

Water Tower Place (all ages) 

835 North Michigan Avenue, Chicago; (312) 440-3166; www.shopwatertower.com. Hours are 10 a.m. to 9 p.m. Monday through Saturday and 11 a.m. to 6 p.m. Sunday. Hours may be extended around Christmastime.

At the north end of the Magnificent Mile, as the famous shopping district is called, is Water Tower Place. Lord & Taylor and Macy's anchor this six-level enclosed shopping center built in 1976—reportedly the first vertical mall in the United States. The 125 or so stores encircle a central atrium, with lighted glass elevators and crisscrossing escalators to transport shoppers up and down. The original light brick water tower for which the mall was named stands at Michigan Avenue and Pearson Street, across the street. It looks rather puny compared to the skyscrapers that now surround it, but it was one of the few structures that survived the Great Chicago Fire of 1871, so give it some respect.

Jazz Showcase (age 5 and up) 

Chicago; (312) 670-2473; www.jazzshowcase.com. Shows run Tuesday through Sunday evenings plus a Sunday matinee. At press time, Jazz Showcase was in the process of moving; call or go online for current address and schedule. $$–$$$$ (accepts cash only)

Although Joe Segal's venerable downtown jazz club is generally geared toward adults, children are encouraged to attend the Sunday afternoon concerts. The venue is typically intimate enough that they'll get an up-close look at some of the finest jazz musicians in the business. Ellis and sons Branford, Delfeayo, and Wynton Marsalis have all played for the club; so have talented young trumpeters Roy Hargrove and Nicholas Payton, and numerous veterans, including saxophonists James Moody and Johnny Griffin, pianist McCoy Tyner, and drummer Roy Haynes. Portraits of Charlie Parker, Dizzy Gillespie, and other jazz greats adorn the walls, and the seating is at tables around the room. Club policy mandates that the entire venue be nonsmoking—a boon for those with sinus or allergy problems.

Navy Pier (all ages) 

600 East Grand Avenue, Chicago; (312) 595-7437 or, outside the Chicago area, (800) 595-7437; www.navypier.com. Open daily. Free, except for rides ($), minigolf ($–$$), Amazing Chicago ($$), Time Escape ($$), and Children's Museum. (See next entry for information on the Children's Museum.) The pier is accessible for wheelchairs; rentals are available on-site. Parking at the on-site garage is charged at a flat rate for the whole day: $19 Monday through Thursday or $23 Friday through Sunday and holidays.

The 1995 grand reopening of the renovated Navy Pier was big news for Chicago—and it will be good news for you, too, because there are lots of things here of interest to visiting families. The pier, which opened in 1916 but by the early 1970s fell into disuse, now has a vibrant atmosphere that promises to attract city dwellers and tourists alike for years to come. The pier extends a total length of about 3,300 feet, but most of the family attractions are at the closer end. The first building you come to after passing the Gateway Park fountain is called the Family Pavilion. It houses the Chicago Children's Museum (see next entry), a large-screen theater, and a couple dozen retail shops and restaurants. At the west end of the pavilion is the spacious, glassed-in Crystal Gardens, which is filled with palm trees, exotic plants, and fountains. There are benches you can sit on to soak up the ambience. Just east of this building is a shallow reflecting pool that turns into an ice rink in winter. Nearby are a colorful musical merry-go-round and a spinning aerial ride called the Wave Swinger. Next comes the most obvious feature at Navy Pier: the 150-foot-tall Ferris wheel. Even people who have trouble with motion sickness could safely ride it: One revolution takes almost eight minutes. Passengers travel in 40 glass-enclosed gondolas that each can hold up to six people (sit on the right side for the best view of the city; the Ferris wheel is accessible for wheelchairs). An 18-hole miniature golf course winds around the base of the Ferris wheel. In summer the carnival atmosphere is enhanced by vendor carts and authorized street performers. Near the middle of the pier is the charming Chicago Shakespeare Theatre (see subsequent entry). Continuing east, the soaring white rooftop of the Skyline Stage is reminiscent of the famous Sydney Opera House in Australia, but you probably won't see much opera here (the gorgeous Lyric Opera building on Wacker Drive has the corner on that market). The 1,500-seat outdoor theater does host a variety of performances, including music, dance, theater, and films. The remainder of the pier houses a fine-dining restaurant, a festival hall, a beer garden, and the Grand Ballroom. Indoors in the middle of Navy Pier are a couple of year-round attractions. Amazing Chicago (888-893-7300; www.amazingchicago.com) is a fun-house-style maze with a Chicago theme. The Time Escape 3D Thrill Ride uses virtual reality and a motion simulator to give you a 20-minute journey through Chicago's past, present, and future. A corridor of shops, kiosks, and fast-food eateries adds to the interest indoors. You can get to Navy Pier aboard the sightseeing trolley or double-decker bus or ride one of six Chicago Transit Authority (CTA) public bus lines that stop here (numbers 29, 56, 65, 66, 120, and 121). If you drive, there is a parking garage underground that can hold more 1,600 cars, but the prices are outrageous.

Won't You Let Me Take You on a **Sea Cruise?**

A unique way to tour the city is by boat. Two sightseeing cruise lines operate from the lower level of Michigan Avenue at Wacker Drive, near the white Wrigley Building with its jutting clock tower. The cruising season runs from mid-April to mid-October. Each boat plies the Chicago River, then heads out into Lake Michigan to give you a truly panoramic view of the city skyline and lakefront before returning one and a half hours later to where you started.

- **Wendella Sightseeing Boats,** 400 North Michigan Avenue (north side of the Michigan Avenue Bridge); (312) 337-1446; www.wendellaboats.com. This is arguably the more well known of the two cruise lines. Cruises sail daily at 10 and 11:30 a.m. and 1:15, 2, 3, 4:30, 6, 7, and 8:30 p.m. A two-hour cruise, which includes a stop at Buckingham Fountain, sails at 7:45 p.m. daily. $$–$$$
- **Mercury Cruiseline,** across the river from Wendella; (312) 332-1353. Cruises sail daily and depart at 10 and 11 a.m. and 1:30, 5:30, and 7 p.m., plus an 8:30 p.m. cruise with fireworks. An extra daytime sailing is offered Wednesday only at 4 p.m. For an extra $5 per day, you can take Fido with you on the Canine Cruise at 10 a.m. Sunday in July, August, or September. $$–$$$

A newer entry into the Chicago cruise business operates out of Navy Pier and puts a twist into the standard excursion by using a giant yellow speedboat:

- **Seadog Cruises,** Navy Pier; (312) 822-7200; www.seadogcruises.com. Operates from May through October; call for current schedule. These half-hour cruises technically are narrated, but it's hard to hear the guide over the noise of the twin 12-cylinder diesel engines. Bathing suits are welcome, although you are advised to bring a sweatshirt or jacket in case of cool lake air, and you may very well get wet, especially if you're seated near the outside. The 70-foot boat can carry up to 149 passengers and reach a top speed of 45 mph, which is a pretty good clip when skimming across the water. $$$

Chicago Children's Museum (ages 1 to 12) 

700 East Grand Avenue, Chicago; (312) 527-1000; www.chichildrensmuseum.org. Open year-round. Hours are 10 a.m. to 5 p.m. Sunday through Friday and 10 a.m. to 8 p.m. Saturday, with extended hours some summer evenings; open with free admission from 5 to 8 p.m. Thursday; free admission for anyone age 15 or younger on the first Monday of the month. The facility is accessible for wheelchairs. $$

Natural light pours in from the arched glass ceiling of the Great Hall to enhance the open, airy feel of this place. The centerpiece of the museum is a white three-story replica of a schooner, with rigging that kids can climb all the way up to the crow's nest. The lower level gives the impression of being underwater, thanks to aquariums filled with live freshwater fish. A black steel staircase wraps around the ship. The museum takes advantage of the building's twin-towered Headhouse with exhibits that use the full 50 feet of space from floor to tower ceiling. One tower has pipes, pumps, locks, and all manner of water propulsion. The other tower houses the Inventing Lab, where kids make their own flying machines and then test their creations' aerodynamics by cranking up a conveyor belt to hoist the machines to the top of the tower and letting them go. One of the more popular exhibits is the hospital. Youngsters can handle medical instruments, X rays, kid-size crutches, and a model skeleton. The cab of a real ambulance features a flashing light and a dispatch radio. In the excavation pit you can dig for dinosaur bones. A special play area called PlayMaze is reserved for kids age 6 or younger (plus accompanying parents). Its wooded rural setting contains a log cabin, with cast-iron stove and other furnishings, and a tree house. Nearby is a "baby pit" filled with soft toys and encircled by 2-foot-high padded walls, restricted to children no older than 18 months. An urban setting lets kids pretend to be shopkeepers.

Chicago Shakespeare Theatre (age 6 and up) 

800 East Grand Avenue, Chicago; (312) 595-5600; www.chicagoshakes.com. Call or check online for current productions and ticket prices. $$$$

This wonderful theater on Navy Pier was modeled after the famous playwright William Shakespeare's Globe theater of the 1600s, but it's totally state of the art in its production ability. The stage combines a traditional space framed by a proscenium arch at one end with a platform that juts out into and is surrounded on three sides by the audience seats on the main floor. Two levels of gallery seats wrap around this space as well, giving the theater a cozy intimacy and great acoustics. While the main season offerings here are full-length productions of the Bard's works, which would be beyond the grasp of most grade-schoolers, the theater does offer special shows during the summer that are geared toward children under its CST Family program. A perennial favorite is the abbreviated version of the comedy *A Midsummer Night's Dream,* perhaps Shakespeare's most accessible work. Although the language may sound a little odd to modern ears, the body language and the colorful costumes and action make the show easy to enjoy. Other summer kids' plays have included such non-Shakespearean shows as *Peter Pan, The Wizard of Oz, The Little Mermaid,* and the Aesop's fables musical *How Can You Run with a Shell on Your Back?* The theater has a gift shop with playbooks and nifty souvenirs.

Chicago Cultural Center (age 3 and up) 

78 East Washington Street (at Michigan Avenue), Chicago; (312) 744-6630 for the current schedule of events.

The Chicago Cultural Center is a National Historic Landmark. It's worth stopping in just for a glance at the golden Byzantine mosaic tiles on the curving arches. There are four galleries of art exhibitions, and you often can catch a free musical performance. You can also see a free informative multilingual video show called *Round and About the Loop.*

Art Institute of Chicago (age 5 and up) 

111 South Michigan Avenue (at Adams Street), Chicago; (312) 443-3600; www.artic.edu. Hours are 10:30 a.m. to 5 p.m. Monday through Friday and 10 a.m. to 5 p.m. Saturday and Sunday; closed Thanksgiving and Christmas. Except for the free day, Thursday, a monetary donation is required to enter. The suggested amount is $12 for anyone age 15 through 55 and $7 for kids age 6 through 14, students age 15 or older with an ID, and senior citizens age 56 or older. You can give less than these amounts, but you must give something and get a receipt from the cashier to enter. Children age 5 or younger are not expected to pay. In June, July, and August, the museum is also open from 5 to 9 p.m. Thursday and Friday with free admission thanks to sponsorship by Target. In 2007, the Art Institute offered free admission for the entire month of February. Backpack-style baby carriers, large bags, and video cameras are not allowed; you must check such items at a cost of $1 each before entering the galleries.

The Art Institute of Chicago is one of the city's most famous attractions, easily recognizable by the mammoth twin lions guarding the white building's pillared facade. It's also one of the world's premier art museums, with what's widely recognized as the finest collection of French impressionist paintings outside Paris. Georges Seurat's giant tableau *Sunday Afternoon on the Island of La Grande Jatte* holds a prominent place on display. Other galleries house fine collections of Oriental and "primitive" art. Medieval buffs will enjoy the glass cases filled with suits of armor and related paraphernalia. Most of the viewing rooms are spacious, and you can navigate a stroller through fairly easily, but please exercise good judgment in deciding whether to bring children younger than school age here. A quiet baby in a stroller is fine, but a chronically fussy one will disrupt others' peaceful enjoyment of these great artworks. Likewise, the average toddler will have little interest in the art and simply think the open spaces look like a great place to run, causing distraction to other patrons and also depriving you of the opportunity to appreciate what the museum has to offer. For older children, however, a visit to the Art Institute can open up a whole new world. There are art books and hands-on activities for kids in the Kraft Education Center downstairs; the restrooms are down there, too.

Taste the **Taste**

Taste of Chicago, or "the Taste," is one of the city's biggest and most popular annual events. It runs from late June through the Fourth of July and features about 70 booths that represent the city's finest foods (restaurateurs compete fiercely for a spot here). The food booths line Columbus Drive from Monroe to Balbo Drives, which are all blocked off from vehicular traffic. You buy tickets in strips of 11 for $7 at a booth near the entrance and then exchange them with the vendors for food and drink. Most dishes require three to nine tickets, so you'll spend roughly $2 to $6 per item—it adds up fast. You can find safe bets like pizza and corn on the cob, but this food fair also gives you a wonderful opportunity to sample ethnic cuisine you might not be willing to gamble on at a regular restaurant, such as Ethiopian beef, Thai chicken satay, Polish potato pierogies, or Jamaican jerk chicken. Save room for dessert—for example, Italian ice, fried dough, chocolate-dipped strawberries, or Eli's famous Chicago cheesecake. There are all sorts of music and dance performances to entertain you while you eat. Taste of Chicago does get pretty crowded, so if you can flex your schedule to come during the week in the late morning or midafternoon, you'll avoid competing with downtown office workers who come at lunchtime or after 5 p.m. during the week and with the throngs that surge in all weekend. On the evening of July 3, there is an Independence Day concert emanating from the Petrillo Music Shell and climaxing with a spectacular fireworks display to the *1812 Overture*. For information on this year's Taste, call (312) 744-3315.

Millennium Park (all ages) 

Michigan Avenue between Randolph and Monroe Drives, Chicago; (312) 742-1168; www.millenniumpark.org. Open from 6 a.m. to 11 p.m. daily. Free.

Just north of the Art Institute and across the street from the Chicago Cultural Center, the wonderful new Millennium Park opened in the summer of 2004 (OK, so it was a few years late for the actual millennium, but so it goes). In keeping with long-ago city planners' notion of preserving some green space along the lakefront for the public to enjoy, Mayor Richard M. Daley and a cast of thousands transformed a big, ugly pit of concrete and gravel along Michigan Avenue into a beautiful park full of green grass, multihued flowers, stunning sculptures, and—best of all—people of all sizes and colors. Here's a place downtown that doesn't cost anything to get into, a place where the kidlets can run around in open spaces and the older folks can rest their weary feet, a place where contentment prevails.

Entering the park at its center, off Michigan Avenue, the most eye-catching thing you see is "the Bean," a huge, round-sided, shiny silver steel sculpture that arches gently to resemble a giant bean (jelly bean, kidney bean, whatever you like). On a nice sunny day, its smooth surface dazzlingly reflects the blue sky and puffy white clouds, the surrounding skyscrapers, and the hundreds of people standing around and under it. Yes, you can walk underneath its central curve and look up into a vortex of humanity as the myriad reflections of you and everyone swirl inward and upward. The Bean stands 33 feet high and is 66 feet long. Its real name is Cloud Gate, and it was designed by the noted sculptor Anish Kapoor.

Another noted sculptor, Frank Gehry, designed the Pritzker Pavilion that is visible behind the Bean. Its arc of twisting steel panels framing the stage complements the Bean quite harmoniously. An overhead latticework of steel pipes encompasses the oblong area, which has 4,000 permanent seats facing the stage at one end and the rest a blanket of soft grass that can accommodate up to 7,000 more concertgoers. When no concert is in progress, it's simply a great big lawn on which to flop or play. The stage is enclosed by glass panels that slide open in nice weather and stay closed when it's not so nice, allowing it to be used year-round.

The park's silvery steel motif is carried out beyond the pavilion along the pedestrian bridge that snakes over Columbus Drive, connecting Millennium Park with Grant Park. Smooth steel shingles adorn the sides of the enclosed bridge, but the footpath is made of wooden planks, a charming throwback to earlier times. A security guard posted at the Columbus Drive end of the bridge directs visitors to other parts of the park and keeps an eye out for anyone who might try to disturb the peace.

Younger children adore the two towering rectangular fountains in the southeast corner of Millennium Park. These fountains stand 50 feet tall, spaced far enough apart on a black granite slab to create a reflecting pool between them, and the water cascades down their sides with varying intensity. Each tower is made of glass blocks behind which a full-wall electronic-display screen shows a nature scene or, more interestingly, the face of a Chicagoan (1,000 people modeled for this gig). The face changes expression, with the eyes blinking or the mouth widening into a smile. But watch out when the lips purse—then a jet of water spurts out from a horizontal fountain in the center of the mouth. Kids who are in the know eagerly anticipate this trick and squeal with delight as they get doused by the shower. The water never gets more than an inch or two deep, so it's relatively safe for even the youngest visitors. Also at the south end of the park is a lovely garden filled with perennial flowers and plants. Footpaths traverse the grounds for easy viewing.

At the north end of the park, closest to Randolph Drive, a fountain jet shooting straight up from the center of a round pool is surrounded by a semicircular arc of white limestone columns. This peristyle is a slightly smaller replica of one that stood in the same spot from 1917 to 1953, when it was torn down to make way for an underground parking garage (which is still there, hidden down below, where there are also train tracks for both commuter and freight lines). Two other attractions of interest are at the north end of Millennium Park. The starkly minimalist Harris Theater is the new permanent home of the Hubbard Street dance company, a troupe that presents an eclectic blend of ballet and other styles. Other Chicago musical and theatrical groups perform here as well. A two-level, glass-enclosed bicycle storage facility also has a locker room with showers so that commuters who bike into the city can freshen up.

Care was taken in the design of Millennium Park to provide for the comfort of visitors. Public restrooms on either side of the Pritzker Pavilion have numerous stalls, the walls and doors of which are made of a nubby hard plastic that resists graffiti. Several large stalls with doors wide enough to accommodate wheelchairs have fold-down wall-mounted changing tables. Soft drinks and snacks are sold from vending carts throughout the park, and there's a sit-down restaurant facing Michigan Avenue, down-

State Street, That Great Street

State Street has a long history and a variety of stores. The area regained some of its long-ago vitality in 1996 after a renovation that basically undid all the changes made in 1979, when the street was turned into more of a pedestrian mall and closed to all vehicular traffic except buses. That idea was a flop—why come to the city for a mall-like atmosphere when there are so many nice malls in the suburbs? No, you come to the city for the hustle and bustle, the traffic noise and smog, the crowded sidewalks, the gritty urban reality that makes you feel so alive! And if you buy stuff in the meantime, so much the better for the merchants. The renovation added some lovely old-fashioned touches that hark back to the street's heyday in the 1920s through 1950s, such as wrought-iron ornamental tree grates and fencing, historic lampposts, and art deco-style subway canopies.

Winter is a special time along State Street. The Marshall Field's (now Macy's) window in this area has elaborate Christmas displays during the holiday season, and you can buy hot chestnuts from a nearby pushcart vendor.

stairs from the Bean. During the summer the restaurant also has outdoor terrace seating. In the winter the terrace is flooded and frozen to create an ice-skating rink that's free and open to the public. Bring your own skates or shell out $5 to rent a pair.

Whatever the season, be sure to visit Millennium Park.

Sears Tower (all ages)

233 South Wacker Drive (at Adams Street), Chicago; (312) 875-9447; www.the-skydeck.com. The entrance is on Jackson Boulevard between Wacker Drive and Franklin Street. Hours are 10 a.m. to 10 p.m. daily from April through September and 10 a.m. to 8 p.m. daily from October through March. Visitors must sit through a short movie presentation before boarding the elevator. $$

The preschoolers you opted not to take to the Art Institute are more likely to be happy riding the elevator up to the Sears Tower Skydeck and looking out at the vast expanse of the city below from what is reportedly the highest observation deck in the world, on the 103rd floor. Renovation in 2000 made the skydeck more family friendly. The Knee-High Chicago diorama is only 4 feet high and covered with colorful pictures to appeal to young children. Changes in sound and lighting also enhanced the ambience, and new viewing telescopes allow a better look at the world outside. InfoVision kiosks offer information on the building and the city in your choice of English, Spanish, French, German, Polish, or Japanese.

Sears Tower was once universally recognized as the world's tallest building. Then the Petronas Towers building in Kuala Lumpur, Malaysia, was completed in 1996 and declared the world's tallest building, as measured from the sidewalk to the "structural top" of the building. Sears Tower representatives, not about to give up the title without a fight, argued that the only reason Petronas Towers measured taller was because it has a decorative spire atop each tower. In terms of occupied space, Petronas is only 88 stories high; Sears Tower is 110 stories high. (Similarly, the Taipei 101 building in Taiwan that was completed in 2004 is taller but is only 101 stories high.) So the Council on Tall Buildings, the organization that makes these official designations, then split the "tallest building" category into two categories, one for "structural top" and one for number of floors. Thus, Sears Tower remains, in at least one sense, the world's tallest building. Many of us would argue that there was never a doubt.

Buckingham Fountain (all ages)

Columbus Drive (301 East) at Congress Parkway (500 South) in Grant Park, Chicago; (312) 747-2200. Operates daily from April through October 1. Free.

Some of Chicago's best-known family attractions are clustered along Lake Shore Drive. One nearby is this huge outdoor fountain. The water shoots up and cascades down the ornate 1927 structure between 10 a.m. and 11 p.m. daily, the last hour with a dazzling display of colored lights added. And there's no charge to enjoy all this aquatic magic.

Field Museum (all ages) 

1400 South Lake Shore Drive (Roosevelt Road and Lake Shore Drive), Chicago; (312) 922-9410; www.fmnh.org. Hours are 9 a.m. to 5 p.m. daily. Visitors in wheelchairs may be dropped off at the west door. Wheelchairs and strollers are available for rent. $$–$$$

The star attraction at this Chicago institution was unveiled May 17, 2000. It is Sue the dinosaur, the largest and most complete Tyrannosaurus rex skeleton ever found. Named after Sue Hendrickson, the fossil hunter who unearthed the prehistoric treasure in South Dakota in 1990, the skeleton was painstakingly cleaned and reassembled from more than 200 bones. No one knows for sure whether Sue was female or male, because the dinosaur's organs and soft tissue were not preserved. Alive, Sue would have weighed about 7 tons—nearly a ton of that weight resting in the 5-foot-long skull that remains. The skeleton is about 45 feet long and 13 feet high at the hips. It is the centerpiece of an informative display that kids and adults alike will enjoy. The museum also has an extensive collection of Native American artifacts, including a re-created Pawnee earth lodge you can walk around in and authentic carved totems. Another fascinating structure is the Maori meetinghouse in the Pacific section. Other permanent exhibits focus on ancient Egypt and other parts of Africa. The Egyptian exhibit includes a replica of the tomb of Unis-ankh, a pharaoh who lived around 2200 BC. It includes real mummies of people, cats, and falcons, all dating from 3100 BC to AD 323. The other Africa exhibit takes visitors on a tour of the continent, both chronologically and geographically, using pictures, artifacts, music, and videos. It includes some hands-on features that make the information more relevant to kids. For example, they can operate a hand-pump bellows for an iron-smelting furnace or use a pulley to "draw" water from a deep well. There are lots of fascinating interactive question-and-answer displays as part of the exhibit. A section you could easily skip contains glass cases of taxidermy; these seem rather stale and dated in an era when many zoos have a wide variety of animals in live displays that imitate their natural habitat. Unless you just have to see the now-extinct passenger pigeon, spend your time elsewhere in the museum. Special displays periodically join the regular collection; call for details.

Shedd Aquarium (all ages) 

1200 South Lake Shore Drive, Chicago; (312) 939-2438; www.sheddnet.org. Open year-round. Hours from Memorial Day through Labor Day are 9 a.m. to 6 p.m. daily. Hours the rest of the year are from 9 a.m. to 5 p.m. Monday through Friday and 9 a.m. to 6 p.m. Saturday and Sunday. The last entry is allowed 45 minutes before closing time. Admission price allows access to all areas. There is a special entrance south of the main one for visitors in wheelchairs. Programs and services also are available for people with vision or hearing disabilities. $$–$$$

Kids of all ages will enjoy the Shedd Aquarium. The aquarium galleries branch off in all directions from a glass-domed central hall containing a huge circular tank that houses a living coral reef; big, colorful tropical fish; gray-brown nurse sharks; and sea tortoises that swim floatingly by. The main galleries are divided by regions of the world, but be forewarned that while the tanks are well lit, the overhead lighting is very dim and the walls and vaulted ceilings are painted dark—hang onto your little ones. There are some really neat specimens in these tanks, however, so do take the time to look. An appealing permanent exhibit featuring creatures of the Amazon River opened in 2000.

The bilevel Oceanarium section at the Shedd is spacious, airy, and light. A beautiful glassed-in arena overlooks Lake Michigan. From a certain angle it's hard to see the demarcation point between the water tank and the lake. This is where the dolphin shows are held, but you can see the dolphins and beluga whales in the water even without the show. A space on the upper level is reserved for special exhibits. Downstairs you can see penguins frolicking in a glass-enclosed colony. You also can see the bottom half of the tanks you viewed on the upper level as well as some hands-on exhibits.

The Shedd's newest permanent exhibit area, the underground Wild Reef, opened in 2003. Simulating a Philippine coral reef, its ingenious design places viewing tanks above as well as alongside visitors to give them a greater sense of being within this colorful marine environment. Kids are wowed by the crashing waves in the surge tank and by the two dozen or so sharks gliding through the water, among the 500 species of fish on display.

Restrooms are located throughout the facility. There are two restaurants and a gift shop on the premises.

Shoreline Sightseeing and Charters (all ages) 

Office is at 474 North Lake Shore Drive, Suite 3511, Chicago; (312) 222-9328; www.shorelinesightseeing.com. Operates from May through September. Departs from Shedd Aquarium about once an hour, between about 10 a.m. and 6 p.m. daily. $–$$

The Shedd Aquarium overlooks Monroe Harbor, one of downtown Chicago's most picturesque locations. You can see both the city skyline and the boats in the harbor, with Lake Michigan beyond. Some people bring a picnic basket and just hang out on the grassy slopes. Docked at this spot is the boat for Shoreline Sightseeing and Charters. You can hop aboard this double-level excursion boat for a narrated half-hour jaunt around the lake. The company has several other pickup spots.

Adler Planetarium and Astronomy Museum (age 4 and up) 

1300 South Lake Shore Drive, Chicago; (312) 922-7827; www.adlerplanetarium.org. Open from 9 a.m. to 6 p.m. daily from June 1 through Labor Day. Regular hours the rest of the year are 9:30 a.m. to 4:30 p.m. daily. Closing time extended to 10 p.m. the first Friday of the month. Closed Thanksgiving and Christmas. Sky Shows start at 10 a.m. daily and continue on the hour until an hour before closing time. Admission is free for everyone on Monday and Tuesday from mid-September through late December. Buildings are accessible for wheelchairs. You can park at Soldier Field and ride the trolley to Adler at no extra charge. Downtown CTA bus number 146 stops at Adler. $$$

The Adler Planetarium is a pleasing combination of old and new. Its centerpiece, the original domed Sky Theater inside a 12-sided building, dates from 1929. Wrapped in a C-shape around that edifice is the Sky Pavilion, an angular, glass-walled, two-story Art Moderne addition completed in 1999. The pavilion has seven general exhibit areas; one of the most interesting is a sphere dotted with holes through which you can see the constellations visible in the Chicago area. A permanent exhibit added in 2006, *Shoot for the Moon,* includes the Gemini 12 spacecraft flown by astronaut Jim Lovell (the one played by Tom Hanks in the 1995 movie *Apollo 13*) and some of Lovell's space-related memorabilia. There are special Sky Theater programs designed for children age 6 or younger; call to plan for one of these if you have small children. If your child gets scared of the dark, consider thoughtfully whether she or he is really ready for a planetarium show. Older kids and teens may enjoy the SonicVision digital animation show with sound track by Coldplay, U2, Radiohead, and Moby. Galileo's restaurant is open from 8:30 a.m. to 3:30 p.m. and serves sandwiches, salads, and snacks. There's also a gift shop with out-of-this-world souvenirs.

Museum of Science and Industry (all ages) 

5700 Lake Shore Drive (at 57th Street), Chicago; (773) 684-1414; for the hearing impaired, TDD (773) 684-3323; www.msichicago.org. Hours are 9:30 a.m. to 5:30 p.m. Monday through Saturday and 11 a.m. to 5:30 p.m. Sunday from late May through Labor Day. The rest of the year, hours are 9:30 a.m. to 4 p.m. Monday through Saturday and 11 a.m. to 4 p.m. Sunday. General admission is free on Monday and Tuesday from mid-September through Thanksgiving and in January and February. Rental strollers are available for $2. Wheelchairs are available at no charge. Parking in the museum's underground garage costs $12 per vehicle. CTA bus numbers 6 and 10 stop at the museum. $$–$$$

This is a bright, busy place with lots to see and do. Many of the exhibits have hands-on features for youngsters to enjoy. Visitors of all ages can walk through a 16-foot-tall replica of the human heart to better understand its workings (at least in the physical sense). The Petroleum Planet permanent exhibit that opened in 2000 puts you in the place of a hydrocarbon molecule, and as such you go through the process of distillation, transformation, pipeline travel, cleaning, "bump-through" chemical reaction (performed on punching bags), and finished fuel for a race car. In 2002 The Great

Train Story permanent exhibit replaced the 60-year-old model-train display with a bigger, more detailed, family friendlier layout. It features 34 HO-scale trains, 500 realistic-looking buildings including Chicago Loop landmarks, and 1,485 tiny people. Other permanent exhibits include the popular coal mine, the U-505 World War II German submarine, the commercial aviation display with a real Boeing 727 airliner, and the Henry Crown Space Center with the actual Apollo 8 spacecraft. Special changing exhibits vary. The museum also has an Omnimax theater that shows the kind of vivid big-screen films that seem to surround you. Call for the title of the current film.

Grant Park (all ages) 

Columbus and Jackson Drives, Chicago; (312) 744-3370 for festivals and special events. Park admission is free, but special-event tickets for the seating area in front of the band shell do cost some money.

Grant Park is the site of many of Chicago's biggest music festivals, for which admission to the park is free. Bring a chair or blanket and sit on the lawn to enjoy world-class talent performing at the park's Petrillo Music Shell. General dates are as follows: Chicago Blues Festival, early June; Chicago Gospel Festival, mid-June; Chicago Country Music Festival, late June; Viva! Chicago Latin Music Festival, late August; Chicago Jazz Festival, early September. The park also sponsors an ongoing series of concerts from mid-June through late August; call for details.

Where to Eat

You can't say you've really visited Chicago until you try some of the city's famous deep-dish pizza. Three downtown restaurants in the Michigan Avenue vicinity are widely considered the standard-bearers: Gino's East, Pizzeria Uno, and Pizzeria Due.

Gino's East, 633 North Wells Street; (312) 943-1124. Hours are 11 a.m. to 10 p.m. Monday through Thursday, 11 a.m. to 11 p.m. Friday and Saturday, and noon to 10 p.m. Sunday. Although it moved here in 2000 from its Superior Street location, this is the original Gino's East, which was a downtown institution for years before it sent satellites into the suburbs. You may have to wait for a table and you'll have an additional wait for the pizza, which takes longer to cook than a thin-crust pie, but it's worth it. $

Pizzeria Uno, 29 East Ohio Street; (312) 321-1000. Hours are 11 a.m. to midnight Sunday through Thursday and 11 a.m. to 1 a.m. Friday and Saturday. This pizzeria is in an inviting 3-story brick building at the corner of Wabash and Ohio Streets. It has a cleaner, brighter look than Gino's East and similarly delicious pizza. $

Pizzeria Due, Wabash and Ontario Streets; (312) 943-2400. Hours are 11 a.m. to 1 a.m. Sunday through Thursday and 11 a.m. to 2 a.m. Friday and Saturday. This is Uno's younger sibling. (In Italian, *uno* means "one" and *due* means "two.") Housed in a 3-story Victorian-style building with an outdoor seating area in front, this restaurant was established in 1955, whereas Uno dates from 1934. $

Lou Mitchell's, 565 West Jackson Boulevard; (312) 939-3111. Open from 5:30 a.m. to 3 p.m. Monday through Saturday and 7 a.m. to 3 p.m. Sunday. As you might guess by its hours, this landmark luncheonette in the Loop specializes in breakfast. Sit in a booth or at the counter and order up freshly squeezed orange juice and a hearty meal of eggs and hash browns or big fluffy pancakes with real maple syrup. $

Where to Stay

Let's be realistic. It's going to be tough to find anything for less than $100 in downtown Chicago, especially during summer. Do ask about specials or package deals at every hotel you call, however; you might get lucky.

Best Western River North, 125 West Ohio Street; (312) 467-0800 or (800) 727-0800. This 172-room hotel received a 3-diamond rating from AAA. Amenities include indoor pool, sauna, and exercise room. $$$$

Chicago Hilton and Towers, 720 South Michigan Avenue; (312) 922-4400 or (800) 445-8667. This hotel has 1,544 rooms plus an indoor pool and health club, and it's close to Grant Park. $$$$

Chicago Marriott, 540 North Michigan Avenue; (312) 836-0100 or (800) 228-9290; www.chicagomarriottdowntown.com. This huge hotel has 1,172 rooms. Amenities include an indoor pool, sauna, and fitness center. $$$$

Comfort Inn and Suites, 15 East Ohio Street; (312) 894-0900 or (877) 424-6423. This 15-story hotel has an ornate exterior and fancy art deco lobby. Indoor hot tub but no pool. Parking available on-site for $25 per night. Continental breakfast is included in the room rate. $$$$

Drake Hotel, 140 East Walton Place; (312) 787-2200 or (800) 553-7253; www.thedrakehotel.com. This 537-room hotel sits at the north end of Michigan Avenue at Lake Shore Drive. It's ritzy, but there are some activities for kids (no swimming pool, though). $$$$

Fairmont Hotel, 200 North Columbus Drive; (312) 565-8000 or (800) 441-1414. This 692-room hotel is popular with out-of-town visitors; you can swim in the indoor pool at the health club next door. Pets weighing 25 pounds or less allowed at extra charge. $$$$

Red Roof Inn, 162 East Ontario Street; (312) 787-3580 or (800) 733-7663. This budget chain property has 191 rooms. There's an exercise room but no pool. One small pet per room allowed. $$$$

Palmer House, 17 East Monroe Street; (312) 726-7500 or (800) 445-8667. Like the Drake, the gorgeous, 1,639-room Palmer House is a Chicago landmark. But unlike the Drake, the Palmer House does have an indoor pool and fitness center. The hotel is now part of the Hilton chain. Pets under 85 pounds are allowed. $$$$

North Side

Chicago's North Side is largely residential. In the town houses and high-rise apartments of the Near North Side, you'll find many yuppies, some of whom moved into the area in the 1980s and 1990s as singles but remained after they married and had children. Farther north are middle-class neighborhoods with brick bungalows and small apartment buildings. Nearly a quarter of the North Side's population is Hispanic, and less than one-tenth African American.

Garfield Park and Conservatory (all ages) 

300 North Central Park Avenue, Chicago; (312) 746-5100; www.garfield-conservatory.org. Open from 9 a.m. to 5 p.m. daily; closing time extended to 8 p.m. Thursday. Admission and parking are free.

Garfield Park is a pretty spot for a family visit. Its opulent conservatory was built in 1907 and features a series of connected greenhouses. The Palm House, where you enter from outside, features a white marble sculpture carved by the famous American sculptor Lorado Taft. The Show House is where you'll find the special floral displays. The Aroid House looks like a jungle, with tropical plants and hanging vines. The Cactus House provides a dry contrast. The sunken Fernery has two Taft sculptures at its entrance and features a waterfall cascading over fern-studded rock walls and down into a pool that empties into a stream. Stepping-stones in the stream allow you to cross. The Children's Garden, opened in 2000, features tropical plants and giant interactive displays. An on-site restaurant is open during park hours and features breakfast and lunch fare. There's also a gift shop on the premises.

Peace Museum (age 5 and up) 

Mailing address P.O. Box 803887, Chicago 60680; (773) 638-6450; www.peacemuseum.org. Call or check the Web site for current hours and exhibits. $

The Peace Museum is reportedly the only museum in the United States dedicated to promoting peace through the arts and humanities. At press time, the museum was in the process of relocating; call or check the Web site for the new address.

Polish Museum of America (age 5 and up) 

984 North Milwaukee Avenue, Chicago; (773) 384-3352. Open from 11 a.m. to 4 p.m. Friday through Wednesday; closed Thursday. $

Documents, photographs, and folk art trace Polish immigration to the United States and Chicago at the Polish Museum of America. The Polish community in Chicago is so large and influential that children have the day off school on October 11 for Pulaski Day, which celebrates the birth of Casimir Pulaski, a Polish noble and soldier who immigrated to America and served heroically in the Continental Army during the American Revolution.

Chicago Children's Theatre (age 5 and up) 

Business office at 1464 North Milwaukee Avenue, 2nd floor, Chicago; (773) 227-0180; www.chicagochildrenstheatre.org. Call or check online for current schedule and ticket prices. $$$$

This theater company debuted in 2006 and has staged its performances in such notable venues as the Goodman and Steppenwolf theaters as well as the Harris Theater in Millennium Park. Shows typically run no longer than 90 minutes. Productions have included *A Year with Frog and Toad, Dandelion Wine, 4-Ish, Honus and Me,* and *Go, Dog, Go!*

Lincoln Park Zoo (all ages) 

2001 North Clark Street, Chicago; (312) 742-2000; www.lpzoo.com. Open daily, year-round. Hours are generally 9 a.m. to 6 p.m. for the grounds and 10 a.m. to 5 p.m. for the buildings; closing times are about an hour earlier in winter and an hour later on summer weekends. Admission is free. Parking in a lot along Cannon Drive costs $14 for 3 hours or less, more for longer.

Lincoln Park Zoo, near Fullerton Avenue and the lakefront, is a major family attraction on the North Side. This 35-acre zoo contains about 2,000 animals, including big cats, primates, bears, birds, and seals. The African Journey exhibit displays meerkats, giant hissing cockroaches, and other exotic creatures in surroundings resembling their native habitats. The Farm-in-the-Zoo section is a treat for city kids who have never set foot near a barnyard. The Pritzker Children's Zoo, which opened near the west gateway along Stockton Drive in 2003, has special exhibits geared toward youngsters, and sometimes the handlers will have animals that kids can touch. The biggest attraction of the children's zoo is the 20-foot-high climbing apparatus with nets and wooden platforms. A new ape exhibit area opened in 2004. Another popular attraction at the Lincoln Park Zoo is the Endangered Species Carousel, which costs $2.50 a ride. A ride on the LPZoo Express "train" (it actually has rubber tires and doesn't run on tracks) costs $2. If you come to the zoo at Christmastime, you could join the group of carolers who sing to the animals. It's hard to say whether the animals really enjoy the serenade, but it always makes the local TV news. At the north end of the zoo is the Lincoln Park Conservatory, on the corner of Fullerton Avenue and Stockton Drive. This Victorian-style conservatory contains towering palm and fig trees and exotic plants from around the world. There's a waterfall here, too. Conservatory hours are 9 a.m. to 5 p.m. daily, and admission is free. At the south end of the zoo is a lagoon where you can rent a four-seater paddleboat for $12 per half hour or a two-seater swan boat (a paddleboat that looks like a giant swan) for $16 per half hour.

Peggy Notebaert Nature Museum (all ages) 

2430 North Cannon Drive (at Fullerton Avenue), Chicago; (773) 755-5100; www.nature museum.org. Open year-round. Hours are 9 a.m. to 4:30 p.m. Monday through Friday and 10 a.m. to 5 p.m. Saturday and Sunday. Closed Thanksgiving, Christmas, and New Year's Day. Everyone is admitted free on Thursday. Museum is accessible for strollers and wheelchairs. $–$$

This museum has a number of interesting permanent exhibits. The Butterfly Haven houses the winged wonders in a high-ceilinged greenhouse. A different Green House is the model home of the fictitious Green family, in which you can learn how to make your own home more environmentally friendly. The Water Lab explains an urban river system and lets visitors try to create one at the stream table. The Hands-on Habitat is designed especially for toddlers and preschoolers to explore wetland and prairie habitats, and it includes a Tree of Life they can actually climb. Be sure to check for special exhibits, which have ranged from giant bugs to magic tricks to chimpanzees.

Wrigley Field (all ages) 

1060 West Addison Street, Chicago; (773) 404-2827; www.cubs.com. Chicago Cubs season runs from early April through early October. The ticket office is open during baseball season from 9 a.m. to 6 p.m. Monday through Friday and 9 a.m. to 4 p.m. Saturday and Sunday (closed Sunday in May when the Cubs are on the road). You also can buy tickets over the phone at (800) 843-2827 within Illinois or (866) 652-2827 outside Illinois, or order online. $$$–$$$$

Ah, you can't beat fun at the old ballpark. . . . Your visit to the North Side wouldn't be complete without a trip to Wrigley Field. The Chicago Cubs play professional baseball here and consistently draw good crowds, even though the team hasn't made it to a World Series since 1945 and hasn't won one since 1908 (though the Cubs did take division titles in 1984, 1989, 2003 and 2007). It must be the ballpark itself, then, that holds some of the allure. The ivy-covered brick outfield walls do make the "friendly confines" more attractive, and the fans are usually a cheerful lot, accustomed as they are to being hopeless optimists. Despite the addition of stadium lights in 1988, Wrigley Field hosts most of its home games in the afternoon. Avoid the Terrace Reserved section if you want to see the full arc of a fly ball—the skyboxes that were added in the early 1990s partially obstruct the view in those seats, although TV monitors help make up for it.

Note: Although there are some shops and restaurants nearby, Wrigley Field is basically in the middle of a residential neighborhood and has no public parking lot of its own. If you drive, you'll crawl through dense traffic and be at the mercy of the local entrepreneurs who operate little lot-size parking lots. The CTA elevated train station on Addison is a block from Wrigley, and CTA buses stop at the ballpark as well, making mass transit an appealing alternative. For more information, call the CTA at (312) 836-7000 or (888) 968-7282; for the hearing impaired, TDD (312) 836-4949 or (888) 282-8891.

Silver Screens on the North Side

There are two unique movie houses on the North Side that are worth mentioning, but don't look for the latest Disney flick at either one.

- **Facets Multimedia,** 1517 West Fullerton Avenue; (773) 281-9075; www.facets.org. This theater in the Lincoln Park area shows many fine foreign films that you won't find anywhere else in the city. Most are subtitled in English, so don't take younger kids who can't read yet. Also check for ratings, and don't hesitate to ask about films that are not rated. (European films generally contain less graphic violence than American films, but you may see more flesh in love scenes.)
- **Music Box Theatre,** 3733 North Southport; (773) 871-6604; www.musicboxtheatre.com. Farther north, the Music Box is an older theater with classic decor. It shows more arty films and old black-and-white movies (such as Buster Keaton silent films with a live organist playing the score), plus some first-run features, and from time to time it hosts film festivals.

Waveland Bowl (age 4 and up) 

3700 North Western Avenue, Chicago; (773) 472-5900; www.wavelandbowl.com. Open 24 hours a day. Bumper bowling is available daily. Cosmic Bowling for kids is offered from 3 to 5 p.m. Friday, 2 to 4 p.m. Saturday, and 1 to 3 p.m. Sunday. $–$$

This North Side bowling alley has 40 lanes and will fill the gutters with soft bumpers for families upon request. Automated scoring makes it easy to keep track of the pins knocked down. The alley also has a children's theater, showing Disney movies on a big screen, an arcade, and concessions.

Where to Eat

Leona's, 3215 North Sheffield; (773) 327-8861; www.leonas.com. Open Sunday through Thursday from 11 a.m. to 11 p.m. and Friday and Saturday 11:30 a.m. to 12:30 a.m. After the ball game at Wrigley Field, walk south down Sheffield Avenue a few blocks for dinner at Leona's. This family-owned Italian restaurant has been around since the 1950s but underwent its most notable expansion during the 1990s. There are two floors of seating areas, plus an outdoor rooftop garden that's open during mild weather. Expect a wait on weekends. The pasta is homemade and can be topped with your choice of red or white sauces that are also prepared from scratch. Dinners are served with a crisp lettuce salad loaded with fresh vegetables. You'll also get a loaf of hot bread accompanied by cups of butter and ricotta-and-chive spread. The thin-crust pizza has a satisfying bite. The restaurant has its own private-label wine, Leona's Graffiti Red, that's made in California but evokes the flavor of a good Italian table wine. There is a children's section on the multipage menu. $$

Ann Sather, 929 West Belmont; (773) 348-2378. Hours are 7 a.m. to 3 p.m. Monday and Tuesday and 7 a.m. to 9 p.m. Wednesday through Sunday. Also not far from Wrigley Field, this restaurant bears the name of its Swedish founder and is famous for its exquisitely luscious cinnamon rolls. If you come for breakfast, you can get bacon and eggs to go with them, or you can try the Swedish pancakes with tart lingonberry preserves. Dinner entrees include Swedish meatballs, roast pork, meat loaf, and other hearty dishes. $

Where to Stay

Best Western Hawthorne Terrace, 3434 North Broadway Avenue; (773) 244-3434, (888) 675-2378, or (800) 937-8376. One long block west of Lake Michigan; a short cab ride or perhaps a half-hour walk to Wrigley Field. This 4-story, 59-room hotel has a sauna and whirlpool but no swimming pool. Pets kept in a carrying case are allowed. Room rate includes continental breakfast. $$$$

O'Hare Marriott Hotel, 8535 West Higgins Road; (773) 693-4444 or (800) 228-9290. If you are flying in and out of O'Hare airport for your Chicago visit, you might want to stay here to avoid scrambling too much for your return flight. The hotel has indoor and outdoor pools and a sauna, spa, and fitness center. Special rates on weekends and for tourists can lower the cost. $$$$

Flights of Fancy

In the northwest corner of Chicago, jutting out like an island surrounded by suburbs, is O'Hare International Airport. In the days before September 11, 2001, it was an interesting place to visit even if you weren't flying. Nowadays you can't get much farther than the front door unless you're a ticketed passenger. If you have a ticket, however, there are interesting things to see beyond the security checkpoints while you're waiting to board your flight. United Airlines Terminal One inherited the Field Museum's four-story mounted dinosaur model, Brachiosaurus, in 2000 after the museum cleared it out to make room for Sue (see Field Museum entry). The lower level of the two-part United terminal has a groovy display of wavy, multicolored neon patterns suspended above the people mover (moving sidewalk), and the International Terminal is decorated with flags and alive with the sounds of excited travelers chattering in foreign languages. As long as they aren't too sensitive to noise, little kids love watching the planes take off and land. In the late 1990s, the airport even added a kids' play area to keep young passengers occupied.

West Side

About half the residents of Chicago's West Side are African American, more than a quarter Hispanic, and slightly less than a quarter whites of European ancestry. The West Side was at one time a prime industrial district. In the latter half of the 1900s, however, many industries downsized or moved to the suburbs, hurting the economy of the area and its people. As a result, there are many decaying neighborhoods in this part of town. The neighborhoods on the Near West Side, however, have benefited since the opening of the United Center in 1994. Real estate investors began to take a closer look, and a massive redevelopment program began to reconnect isolated public housing with the surrounding area. Ugly high-rise buildings in the crime-ridden Henry Horner complex have been torn down and replaced with tidy brown-brick row houses to be split evenly between low-income and working-class families. Statistics in the 1990s reflected some improvement, showing an increase in employment and a decrease in crime.

United Center (all ages) 

1901 West Madison Street, Chicago; (312) 455-4000 for Bulls, (312) 455-7000 for Blackhawks.

Probably the biggest attraction on the West Side is the United Center. There's a one-ton bronze leaping figure of athlete extraordinaire Michael Jordan out front. This stadium opened in 1994 and is the home court for the Chicago Bulls, the National Basketball Association (NBA) team with which Jordan won six championships—in 1991, 1992, 1993, 1996, 1997, and 1998 (he spent 1994 and most of 1995 away from the Bulls playing baseball). Although MJ has long since retired, the championship banners remain to remind visitors of the Bulls' glory days. The Chicago Blackhawks of the National Hockey League (NHL) also play at the United Center; call for details about "cold steel on ice."

UIC Pavilion (all ages) 

525 South Racine Avenue (at Harrison Street), Chicago; (312) 413-5700. Call for current schedule of events.

The Near West Side was revitalized somewhat during the 1960s with the construction of the West Side Medical Center and the University of Illinois at Chicago. Old factories became artists' studios, and new apartments and houses were built in the area. The Pavilion schedules various special events, including music concerts as well as tennis tournaments and other sporting matches.

Museum of Holography (all ages) 

1134 West Washington Boulevard, Chicago; (312) 226-1007; www.holographiccenter.com. Hours are 12:30 to 5 p.m. Wednesday through Sunday. $

This facility claims to be the only museum in the United States devoted to holography. It has about 150 of the three-dimensional, laser-generated images on display in four galleries.

National Museum of Mexican Art (age 4 and up) 

1852 West 19th Street, Chicago; (312) 738-1503; www.nationalmuseumofmexicanart.org. Hours are 10 a.m. to 5 p.m. Tuesday through Sunday. Admission is free.

The National Museum of Mexican Art in the Pilsen neighborhood is the largest museum of its type in the United States and is the first and only Latino museum accredited by the American Association of Museums. Such stature is fitting for a city with more than a million residents of Mexican descent. The museum sees its mission not only as an affirmation of this group's rich cultural heritage but also as a forum for connections with other groups among Chicago's diverse community. For example, the recent special exhibit "The African Presence in Mexico" drew as many African American as Latino visitors. Permanent exhibits of contemporary and folk art by Mexican and Mexican-American artists remain on display year-round. Families can also enjoy making their own artworks together on Sunday afternoons; call ahead to reserve a place in the museum's weekly program. The museum hosts two performing arts festivals each year and a variety of other events. The gift shop offers Mexican pottery, jewelry, toys, and crafts.

Where to Eat

Billy Goat Tavern, 1535 West Madison Street; (312) 733-9132. Near the United Center. Hours are 6 a.m. to 9:30 p.m. Monday through Friday, 7 a.m. to 10 p.m. Saturday, and 10 a.m. to 4 p.m. Sunday. Don't let the *tavern* part of its name keep you away from the Billy Goat. This offshoot of the original Lower Michigan Avenue eatery specializes in the "cheezborger, cheezborger" made famous on the classic *Saturday Night Live* skit. It's a thin, greasy burger on a chewy Kaiser roll that may make you wonder what all the fuss is about, but it's a Chicago legend. Contrary to the "no fries—chips" part of the skit, you can get french fries with your burger. The menu also includes a grilled chicken sandwich, hot dog, steak, chili, and soup. Photos of sports stars and Hollywood celebrities decorate the walls. $

Leona's Neighborhood Place, 1936 West Augusta; (773) 292-4300; www.leonas.com. Hours are 11 a.m. to 11 p.m. Monday through Thursday, 11:30 a.m. to 1 a.m. Friday, noon to 1 a.m. Saturday, and noon to 10:30 p.m. Sunday. This Leona's in the Wicker Park neighborhood has the same sort of Italian menu as its Wrigleyville progenitor. It also has a special place for kids: the Jungle Room, which has a tropical rain forest motif and offers such attractions as climbing equipment, a ball pit, games, and finger painting. The Jungle Room is popular for birthday parties, however, so call ahead before coming to make sure it's available. $$

Where to Stay

The attractions listed in this section are not that far from downtown Chicago. It is recommended that you stay overnight there and take public transportation or a cab to the West Side.

South Side

Chicago's South Side has more people than either of the other two sections outside downtown and a greater mix of residential and industrial areas. The population is about 60 percent African American, with the balance composed of Hispanic, Asian, and white European communities. Although some areas are racially integrated, most are not.

U.S. Cellular Field (all ages) 

333 West 35th Street, Chicago; (312) 674-1000; www.whitesox.com. Chicago White Sox season runs from early April through early October. During baseball season the box office is open from 10 a.m. to 6 p.m. Monday through Friday and 10 a.m. to 4 p.m. Saturday and Sunday. You also can buy tickets over the phone at (312) 559-1212, or order online.

The 2006 World Series champion Chicago White Sox play major-league baseball on the South Side at a 40,000-seat ballpark that was renamed U.S. Cellular Field in 2003 after a cell-phone company signed a $68 million, 23-year agreement that put its name on the facility. But most Chicago fans still call the place Comiskey Park, the name they'd been using for 90-plus years, even after the original ballpark was torn down and this one erected a few blocks away in 1991. Whatever you call it, it's a nice place to watch a ball game. You can walk full circle around the diamond along the wide concrete main concourse, which is lined with both usual (hot dogs, popcorn) and unusual (churros, corn off the cob) ballpark fare. There is a family restroom on the main concourse in the outfield area. A scoreboard with giant video screen enlarges the on-field action. Fireworks shoot from the top of the scoreboard when a Sox player hits a home run and when the team wins the game. The upper deck is rather steeply sloped, and some fans have been heard to complain of vertigo, so you'll probably be more comfortable with seats in the lower deck. Above the main concourse, ultraposh skyboxes called "luxury suites" are held mostly by businesses but may be rented by groups if you've got the bucks. Unlike at Wrigley Field, the skyboxes do not hamper the view from any of the seats below.

DuSable Museum of African-American History (age 4 and up) 

740 East 56th Place, Chicago; (773) 947-0600; www.dusablemuseum.org. Hours are 10 a.m. to 5 p.m. Tuesday through Saturday and noon to 5 p.m. Sunday and holidays; closed Monday. Closed Easter, Thanksgiving, and Christmas. Admission is free for everyone on Sunday. No smoking, food, or beverages allowed. $

The DuSable Museum has cultural and art collections that represent the work of Africans and Americans of African descent. Of particular note are the permanent collections representing the Works Progress Administration (WPA) era of the 1930s and the civil rights movement of the 1960s. The museum sponsors an annual art festival and other special events. In July and August, the museum offers the Children's Penny Cinema film series on selected mornings at 10:30, with admission fee of one cent. The movies reflect the African-American experience, ranging from historical (*George Washington Carver*) to contemporary (*Akeelah and the Bee*).

Martin Luther King Jr. Park and Family Entertainment Center (age 4 and up)

1219 West 76th Street, Chicago; (312) 747-2602; www.usa-skating.com. Call or check the Web site for current roller-skating and bowling schedules. $

Roller-skating and bowling are offered at this facility, formerly called Hawthorne Park. An area in the middle of the roller rink is reserved for toddlers and beginners, while more experienced skaters zoom around the perimeter to top-of-the-pops tunes. The bowling alley has 32 lanes with automated scoring. For families, bumpers are available to block the gutters. A concession area offers pizza and snacks.

Chinatown

The Asian community of Chinatown, at the crossroads of Wentworth and Cermak Avenues, is one of the most active neighborhoods on the South Side. About 10,000 people live within a 10-block radius, and you'll find fabulous restaurants and shops here. There are many special events throughout the year. For detailed information about the area, contact the Chicago Chinatown Chamber of Commerce, 2169B South China Place, Chicago 60616; (312) 326-5320; www.chicagochinatown.org or www.chicago-chinatown.com. Chinatown is about a five-minute cab ride south of the Loop and is easily accessible by CTA elevated train or bus.

Other Things to See and Do

JANUARY

Chicago Winterbreak Celebration, various locations; (312) 744-3370

FEBRUARY

Chinese New Year Parade, Chinatown; (312) 225-6198

Chicago Auto Show, McCormick Place; (312) 791-7000

MARCH

St. Patrick's Day Parade, Downtown; (312) 744-3370

APRIL

Earth Day Celebration, Shedd Aquarium, Downtown; (312) 939-2438

MAY

Lakeview Mayfest, North Side; (773) 665-4682

JUNE

Festival of Ethnic Arts, Beverly Art Center, South Side; (773) 445-3838

Grant Park Music Festival Free Concerts Series, Downtown; (312) 744-3370

JULY

International Children's Fest, Navy Pier, Downtown; (312) 595-7437

AUGUST

Chicago Air and Water Show, North Avenue Beach, Downtown; (312) 744-3315

Bud Billiken Parade and Picnic, King Drive, Downtown; (312) 225-2400

SEPTEMBER

Celtic Fest Chicago, Downtown; (312) 744-3370

OCTOBER

Columbus Day Parade, Downtown; (312) 828-0100

Chicagoween, Daley Plaza, Downtown; (312) 567-8500

Boo Fest, Museum of Science and Industry, Downtown; (773) 684-1414

NOVEMBER

Christkindlmarket, Daley Plaza, Downtown; (312) 744-3315

Thanksgiving Parade, State Street, Downtown; (312) 781-5681

DECEMBER

Christmas Around the World, Museum of Science and Industry, Downtown; (773) 684-1414

Winter Wonderfest, Navy Pier, Downtown; (312) 595-7437

Ridge Historical Society (all ages) 

10621 South Seeley Avenue, Chicago; (773) 881-1675; www.ridgehistoricalsociety.org. Open from 2 to 5 p.m. Tuesday, Thursday, and Sunday. Admission is free, but donations are appreciated.

This museum has a number of exhibits for children that make history interesting and hands-on. They can crank the wringer of an old-fashioned washing machine, try on costumes from Granny Ridge's Trunk, use tools to make something in Grandpa Ridge's Workshop, or unearth an object in the archaeological exhibit called I Dig the Ridge Historical Society.

Where to Eat

Daley's Restaurant, 809 East 63rd Street, at Cottage Grove Avenue; (773) 643-6670. In the Woodlawn neighborhood, a few miles from the DuSable Museum and the Museum of Science and Industry. Open from 5 a.m. to 8:45 p.m. daily. No credit cards accepted. No relation to the Chicago mayor but instead named after the Irish immigrant who opened it in 1892, this establishment has since the 1960s been a haven for soul food, for example, catfish, pork chops, black-eyed peas, collard greens, buttery corn muffins. It also serves breakfast.

Dixie Kitchen and Bait Shop, 5225 South Harper Avenue; (773) 363-7723. In the Harper Court mall in the Hyde Park neighborhood. Open from 11 a.m. to 9:30 p.m. Sunday through Thursday and 11 a.m. to 11 p.m. Friday and Saturday. No, you can't buy fishing bait here, but the atmosphere is designed to evoke a roadside diner along the Mississippi bayou, complete with zydeco music. The food is Southern style, of course. The menu includes gumbo, jambalaya, red beans and rice, fried catfish, blackened chicken breast, bread pudding, and peach cobbler. $

Where to Stay

Holiday Inn Select Chicago-Midway, 6520 South Cicero Avenue; (773) 594-5500 or (800) 465-4329. This elegant 6-story, 202-room property near Midway Airport has a fitness center and an indoor swimming pool. $$$$

Ramada Inn Lake Shore, 4900 South Lake Shore Drive; (773) 288-5800 or (800) 237-4933. This 182-room property has an outdoor swimming pool. Pets are allowed. $$$$

Chicagoland

The Chicago metropolitan area extends for many miles beyond the city limits. The adjacent communities can easily be called suburbs, but the farther out you go, the harder it is to determine what's a suburb, an exurb, or simply a smaller town that happens to be within an hour or so's driving distance—and often one blends into the next with little more than a city limits sign to give you a clue that you've crossed a border. Complicating matters further is the fact that while some of these cities and towns are eager to be perceived as linked to Chicago, others shun such connections. Ultimately, no label or boundary will satisfy everyone, so the decision becomes rather arbitrary. For this book Chicagoland will be defined as everything in Lake, DuPage, Will, Kankakee, and Cook Counties outside the city of Chicago. We will move in a roughly counterclockwise sweep from north to west to south.

Lake County is sandwiched between the state line with Wisconsin and the concentrated population of Cook County. As such, it contains both rural areas dotted with parks and urban communities lying along the affluent North Shore of Lake Michigan. For general information about the county, contact the Lake County, Illinois, Convention & Visitors Bureau, 5465 West Grand Avenue, Suite 100, Gurnee 60031; (847) 662-2700 or (800) 525-3669; www.lakecounty.org.

Gurnee

Population: 28,834. This far-northern suburb along Interstate 94 has two of the Chicago metro area's biggest attractions—literally—Six Flags Great America and Gurnee Mills. At press time, a third huge attraction was in the works: Key Lime Cove Resort and Water Park, which was to include 400-plus hotel rooms and a 50,000-square-foot indoor water park. It was slated to open in 2008.

CHICAGOLAND

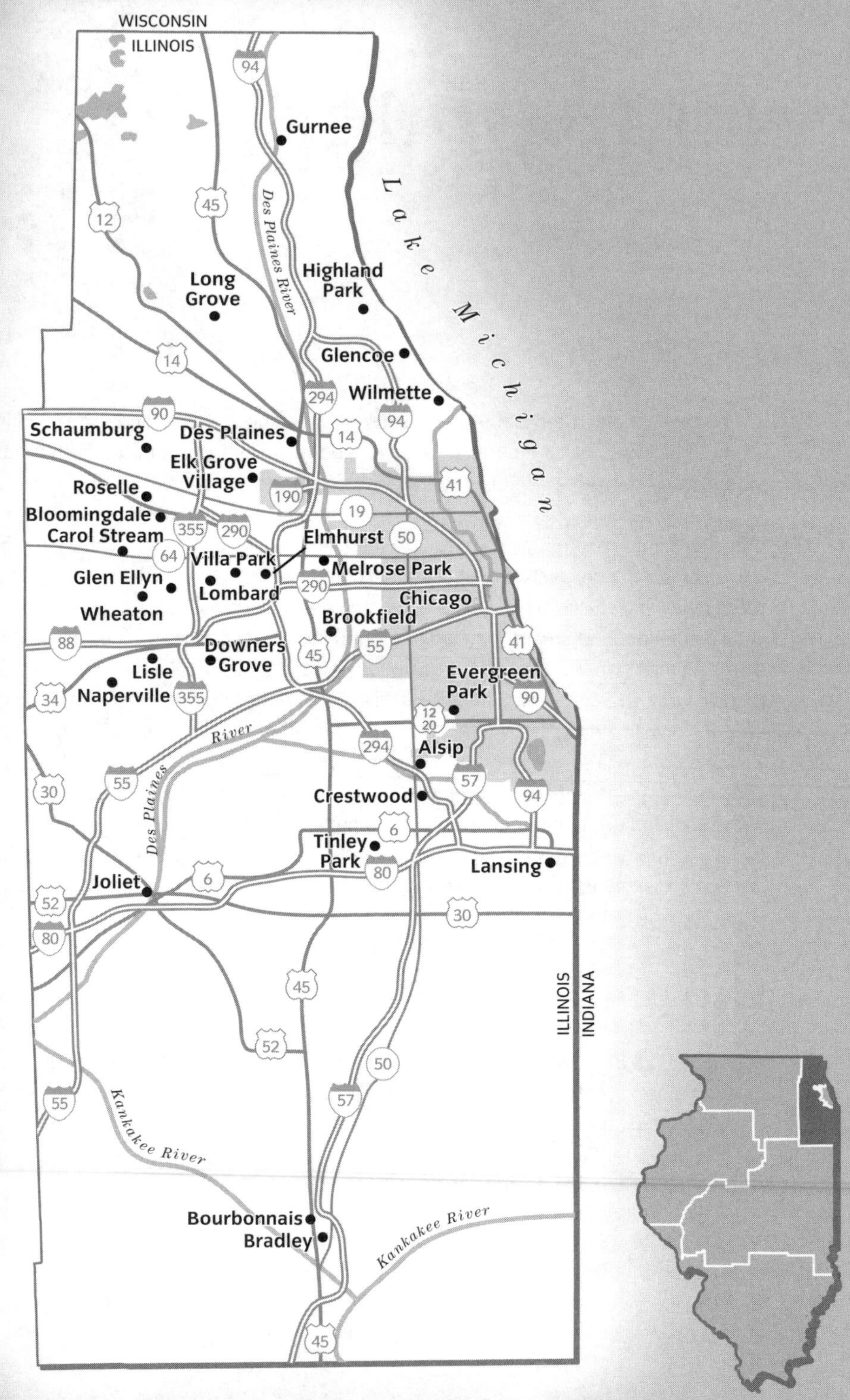

Six Flags Great America (all ages) 

I-94 at Illinois Highway 132, Gurnee; (847) 249-4625 or (847) 249-4636; www.sixflags.com/greatamerica. Opens in late April and closes in mid-September. From mid-June through late August, the park is open from 10 a.m. to 10 p.m. daily. Hours at the beginning and end of the season are more limited; call ahead of time and check. Also open on weekends in October for haunted house–themed Fright Fest. Admission price includes all the rides and shows (but not taxes, arcade games, souvenirs, or food and drink). Ask about special deals and season passes. Parking costs $10. The park is accessible for strollers and wheelchairs. $$$$

As you're driving along I-94 near its intersection with Highway 132 in Gurnee, you can't miss Six Flags Great America—you can see this sprawling amusement park from the road, beckoning you tantalizingly. This isn't one of those let's-stop-in-for-an-hour attractions; there's a lot to see and do here, and you'll pay a pretty penny for it, so plan for an all-day outing to get your money's worth. You might want to start with a 20-minute overview of the park on the Six Flags Great America Scenic Railway; that way you can scope out the rides you most want to try.

The Viper is an elegant wooden roller coaster patterned after the classic Coney Island Cyclone. But don't let the lovely latticework lull you into a false sense of security. After the cars ratchet up a 100-foot incline along a single track, you'll scream your head off as they plunge 80 feet downhill. You get 10 more drops and some whizzing turns in a ride that lasts just under two minutes. The American Eagle double-track wooden coaster remains a popular ride as well. If steel coasters are more your style, loop the loop on the Déjà Vu, twist like a human corkscrew on the spiraling Vertical Velocity, or ride standing up for a 90-foot drop and more loops on the Iron Wolf. Batman fans and big-time thrill seekers will want to try Batman the Ride, billed in all its stomach-churning glory as "the world's first suspended, outside looping thrill ride." In the Superman "megacoaster," you ride pretty much horizontally, with your arms and legs stretched out as if you're flying like the Man of Steel. The tallest, fastest, longest roller coaster at Great America is the Raging Bull, billed as "the world's first hyper-twister coaster." Use good parental judgment in determining whether your kids are ready for these thrill rides, some of which have height restrictions that would exclude many youngsters anyway.

Especially popular with families are the ornate double-decker Columbia Carousel and the motion simulator Space Shuttle America. The Games Gallery has a wide variety of arcade games. Children who are 54 inches tall or shorter can enter Wiggles World to ride the Big Red Cars, Big Red Planes, or Dorothy's Tea Cups. Other attractions here include Bouncin' with Wags, the SS *Feathersword* Play Ship, and Hen's Splish Splash Fountain. The Camp Cartoon Network area has kiddie rides and features strolling costumed characters such as Scooby-Doo and Fred Flintstone.

You can sit down for a while and take in a show. The wee ones will like the shows starring adult performers in full-body costumes as Bugs Bunny and other Warner Brothers classic cartoon characters. Wiggles World also has a show with songs and costumed characters based on the popular TV series. Kids also enjoy the Serpent Safari Animal Show with live critters. Then there are assorted song-and-dance shows, with music ranging from ragtime to country-and-western fare. Concession choices range from hot-dog stands to a sit-down restaurant, and there are plenty of tempting souvenirs to buy.

If it's a hot day, bring swimsuits and you can cool off in the adjacent Hurricane Harbor outdoor water park, free with Great America admission. There are showers and lockers at the water park. The 10 attractions here include giant water slides, a wave pool, and a huge water playground with fountains and spray jets.

Gurnee Mills (all ages) 

6170 West Grand Avenue (I-94 at Highway 132), Gurnee; (847) 263-7500; www.gurneemills.com. Open from 10 a.m. to 9 p.m. Monday through Friday, 10 a.m. to 9:30 p.m. Saturday, and 11 a.m. to 7 p.m. Sunday. The mall is accessible for strollers and wheelchairs.

Reportedly the world's largest outlet mall, Gurnee Mills has roughly 200 stores along a 2-mile-long, S-shaped strip, plus two food courts, each with about a dozen eateries, including a Rainforest Cafe. Major stores include Saks Fifth Avenue and JCPenney Outlets. Stock up on your toddler's play clothes at Carter's Childrenswear, Happy Kids, OshKosh B'Gosh, or the Children's Place. Kay-Bee Toys and Gamers Paradise have outlets here, too. Among the other types of stores are shops selling adult and teen apparel, shoes, jewelry, cosmetics, fashion accessories, sporting goods, books, and music and electronics. You can drop off your roll of film—with the Six Flags Great America pictures you took yesterday—at the Ritz Camera One Hour Photo, and they'll be ready when you're finished shopping. You can even catch a movie at the 20-screen Marcus Cinema.

Serpent Safari (age 2 and up) 

In Gurnee Mills outlet mall, 6170 West Grand Avenue, Gurnee; (847) 855-8800. Open from 10 a.m. to 9 p.m. Monday through Saturday and 11 a.m. to 7 p.m. Sunday. $–$$

This store has an exhibit area (accessible only by tour) with about 40 large reptiles, including the world's largest snake, according to the Guinness Book of World Records—a Burmese python 27 feet long, weighing 400 pounds.

Where to Eat

Culver's, 1505 Nations Drive; (847) 662-9666. Open from 10:30 a.m. to 10 p.m. daily. See Restaurant Appendix for description. $

Pizzeria Uno, 6593 Grand Avenue; (847) 856-0000. Across from Gurnee Mills. Hours are 11 a.m. to 11 p.m. Monday through Thursday, 11 a.m. to 1 a.m. Friday and Saturday, and 11 a.m. to 10 p.m. Sunday. This suburban cousin of the Chicago fixture offers the trademark deep-dish pizza as well as pasta dishes, sandwiches, chicken, and ribs. $

TGIFriday's, 6557 Grand Avenue; (847) 855-0007. Hours are 11 a.m. to midnight Sunday through Thursday and 11 a.m. to 1 a.m. Friday and Saturday. See Restaurant Appendix for description. $$

Where to Stay

Comfort Inn, 6080 Gurnee Mills Boulevard; (847) 855-8866 or (800) 424-6423. This 3-story chain property has 63 rooms and an indoor heated pool. Continental breakfast is included in the room rate. $$$$

Fairfield Inn, 6090 Gurnee Mills Boulevard; (847) 855-8868 or (800) 228-2800. This inn has 3 floors and 63 rooms. Amenities include indoor pool and whirlpool. Room rate includes continental breakfast. $$$$

Hampton Inn, 5550 Grand Avenue; (847) 662-1100 or (800) 426-7866. Across the street from Six Flags Great America. There are 134 rooms and an outdoor swimming pool at this 5-story inn. Room rate includes continental breakfast. $$$$

For More Information

Lake County Convention and Visitors Bureau, 5465 West Grand Avenue, Suite 100, Gurnee 60031; (847) 662-2700 or (800) 525-3669; www.lakecounty.org.

Highland Park

Population: 31,365. This upper-crust North Shore suburb has several attractions of interest to families.

Ravinia Festival (all ages)

1575 Oakwood Avenue, Highland Park; (847) 266-5100; www.ravinia.org. Call for current schedule. The festival runs from late June through early September. Parking is available on-site, at a cost of $7 for evening pavilion events and free at other times. $$$–$$$$

The Ravinia Festival has been around for more than 100 years. Nestled among 36 acres of wooded and landscaped grounds are an outdoor pavilion, an indoor recital hall, and numerous restaurants and high-class food stands (you'll think you've died and gone to heaven when you taste the cappuccino ice cream). The Chicago Symphony Orchestra provides the mainstay classical music that dominates the schedule, but you can also hear jazz and pop concerts, and there's a special series of concerts aimed at kids. Don't limit your family to the kids' concerts, however—jazz and classical music can be exciting even to the youngest listeners, especially when you get to have a picnic at the same time. There's a sprawling lawn section where you can bring in your own basket and spread out your blanket or set up your folding chairs. You see a real cross section of people here: families with baby strollers, groups of high school and college students, couples out for a romantic evening, and parties of well-to-do North Shore-ites whose "picnic" consists of haute cuisine entrees dished up on fine china and served on a low table covered with a linen cloth and set with silver utensils and candlesticks. But everyone pays the same price for a lawn ticket. If you want a better view of the concert, you can buy a seat in the pavilion. The park is just off Green Bay Road (a major north-south artery along the North Shore). From downtown Chicago you can take the Metra Union Pacific North Line train right to Ravinia's main entrance (call 312-836-7000 or check the Web site www.metrarail.com for schedule and fare information) or ride a chartered bus from selected hotels for about $15 round-trip (call the Ravinia number for details). This is a wonderful evening under the stars.

River's Edge Adventure Golf (age 3 and up) 

2205 Skokie Valley Highway, Highland Park; (847) 433-3422. Open from 8 a.m. to 10 p.m. Monday through Friday and 6 a.m. to 10 p.m. Saturday and Sunday during summer. $–$$

You can play 18 holes of miniature golf at this facility operated by the Park District of Highland Park. Nine of the holes are billed as "handicap accessible." The naturalistic layout features a lovely waterfall.

Hidden Creek Aqua Park (all ages) 

1220 Frederickson Place, Highland Park; (847) 433-3170. Open from 5:30 a.m. to 8 p.m. daily during summer. $$$

This facility has a zero-depth pool and a children's play area with water slides and a big sandbox. There are bigger slides for the bigger kids and adults, and there is a lap pool for those who want exercise as well as recreation. There is a concession area, too.

Where to Eat

Judy's Pizza, 1855H Deerfield Road (in Garrity Square strip mall); (847) 579-8330. Open from 11 a.m. to 9 p.m. daily; carry-out only. Double-decker pizza is the specialty here—sauce and cheese are sandwiched between two thin layers of crust and then covered with more sauce, cheese, and toppings. Take one with you to Ravinia. $

Good Tidings from Zion

About 20 miles north of Highland Park, Illinois Beach State Park is the only Illinois state park on Lake Michigan and has the state's only sand dunes. Naturally, there are beaches here for swimming, and you can also enjoy fishing, picnicking, hiking, and pedaling along the bike trails. The park is at Sheridan and Wadsworth Roads in Zion; (847) 662-4811. It's open from sunrise to 8 p.m. daily, year-round. Admission is **free.**

Where to Stay

Courtyard by Marriott, 1505 County Line Road; (847) 831-3338 or (800) 321-2211. The Courtyard chain is geared more toward business travelers than families, but you can sometimes get a bargain rate over the weekend, when the business people have gone home. This particular 3-story property has 149 rooms. Amenities include indoor swimming pool, whirlpool, and fitness center. $$$$

For More Information

Highland Park Chamber of Commerce, 508 Central Avenue, Suite 206, Highland Park 60035; (847) 432-0284; www.ehighlandpark.com.

Long Grove

Population: 6,735. Settled in the 1800s by a group of German farmers, this off-the-beaten-path Lake County town is centered around the historical village at the crossroads of Illinois Highways 53 and 83. Under Long Grove's Historic Landmark Ordinance, all new buildings at that crossroads must conform to the architecture of the early 1800s.

Long Grove Historical Village (all ages) 

3110 RFD, Long Grove; (847) 634-9440; www.longgroveonline.com. Open year-round. Regular business hours are 10 a.m. to 5 p.m. Monday through Saturday and 11 a.m. to 5 p.m. Sunday. Individual shop hours may vary slightly. Some buildings have stairs and are not accessible for wheelchairs or strollers.

This village is a collection of quaint shops and restaurants, all housed in historic one- and two-story buildings. They line the streets for a block or two along Old McHenry Road and Robert Parker Coffin Road, more commonly known as Illinois Highways 53 and 83. At this junction, however, the roads are only one lane wide in either direction, and the traffic usually isn't too bad. Everything is clustered together closely enough that the walking distances are easy for most people. You can stroll at leisure and browse the windows or go in if the merchandise particularly intrigues you. Among the shops most interesting to families with children age 12 or younger are the following.

- **Apple Haus,** (847) 634-0730. Apple pie, apple cider doughnuts, apple butter, and gooey caramel apples—yum!
- **Baby Baby and More,** (847) 821-9296; www.babybabyandmore.com. Clothes and gifts for children from newborn through size 4T in a "stroller-friendly" shop that once housed the village blacksmith.
- **Creative Hands,** (847) 634-0545. Beanie Babies, dough art, Cat's Meow Village, Wee Forest Folk, and miniatures that are sooo cute!

- **The Dog House,** (847) 634-3060. Collars, toys, beds, clothing, treats, and all manner of merchandise for your four-legged friend, who can come into the store with you.
- **Long Grove Confectionery Co.,** (847) 634-0080. An absolute must; handmade chocolates as beautiful as they are succulent.
- **Long Grove Popcorn Shoppe,** (847) 821-9101; www.longgrovepopcorn.com. All sorts of flavored popcorn and other crunchy munchies.
- **Long Grove Soap & Candle Co.,** (847) 634-9322. Fascinating soap-making demonstrations on weekends using hand-operated equipment (on the second floor, no elevator) and a sampling of the finished product as well as fancy soaps made elsewhere.
- **Nickelby's Rubber Stamp Emporium,** (847) 634-6552; www.nickelbys.com. A mind-boggling array of rubber stamps.
- **Pine Cone Christmas Shop,** (847) 634-0890. Year-round display of decorated Christmas trees and related holiday collectibles for sale.

Where to Eat

Seasons of Long Grove, in the historic village; (847) 634-9150; www.seasonsoflonggrove.com. Hours are 11 a.m. to 2:30 p.m. Tuesday through Saturday and 10 a.m. to 2:30 p.m. Sunday; closed Monday. This restaurant is a fairly formal, sit-down place. It isn't your best bet with toddlers but could be a treat for a school-age child who can be patient with the slower service and impressed by the fresh flowers and cloth napkins on the table. The children's menu is pretty pricey, however, especially since the selections include such fairly ordinary items as a burger, hot dog, pizza, and grilled cheese sandwich. Adults can enjoy the elaborate luncheon buffet or order an entree off the menu. $$

Where to Stay

There are no hotels or motels in Long Grove. Plan to make this community a day trip from wherever you live or are staying in the Chicago metropolitan area.

For More Information

Village of Long Grove, 3110 RFD, Long Grove 60047; (847) 634-9440; www.longgroveonline.com.

At this point we cross the boundary from Lake County into northern Cook County. A number of northern and northwestern suburbs share Cook County with the city of Chicago.

Wilmette

Population: 27,651. This posh North Shore suburb, founded in 1872, has a couple of interesting museums to check out.

Kohl Children's Museum (ages 1 to 8) 

2100 Patriot Boulvevard, Wilmette; (847) 832-6600; www.kohlchildrensmuseum.org. Hours are 9:30 a.m. to 5 p.m. Monday through Saturday and noon to 5 p.m. Sunday. $–$$

Founded in 1985, this children's museum draws about a quarter million visitors annually. The current location dates to 2005, but the museum remains the same in that it specializes in learning experiences for children ages 1 through 8—the formative years, according to many experts—but does so in such fun ways that it doesn't seem like "education." Some of the exhibits miniaturize real-life experiences, such as shopping at a Dominick's grocery store, making sandwiches at a Potbelly's, taking care of dolls at the day-care center, or donning a veterinarian's white coat and examining stuffed toy dogs in the pet clinic. Kids can create melodies and rhythms in the Music Makers area or wander through the maze, the walls of which are low enough that parents can spot their youngsters amid the layout. Especially appealing to the tinier tots is the Water Works play area. You may want to stuff a change of clothes in your carryall bag if your toddler is especially fond of splashing, pouring, and floating things, because there's a lot to do here. Even prewalking visitors have a spot to play at this facility. Four padded, enclosed baby play areas are strategically placed throughout the museum near exhibit areas designed for older children, with benches between the two types from which parents can more easily keep an eye on two youngsters of disparate ages simultaneously. There are also nursing alcoves for mothers who need to feed their infants.

Outdoors, the museum's Habitat Park is a big open field used for group activities for children age 8 or younger. At any given time, it may have a corn maze or a spider-web climbing net set up.

Wilmette Historical Museum (age 6 and up) 

609 Ridge Road, Wilmette; (847) 853-7706; www.wilmettehistory.org. Hours are 1 to 4:30 p.m. Sunday through Thursday; closed Friday and Saturday. Closed in August. Admission is free. The facility is accessible for wheelchairs. Call for details about current exhibits.

The building that houses this museum is itself a piece of history. The two-story Victorian structure was built in 1896 to serve as the Gross Point Village Hall. (The town of

Gross Point existed from 1874 to 1924.) It was named to the National Register of Historic Places in 1991. Inside are exhibits chronicling the history of the area, including the original jail cells. The permanent Fire House exhibit includes a hands-on activity area for children. A three-story addition to the original building provides additional exhibit space.

Where to Eat

Walker Brothers Original Pancake House, 153 Green Bay Road; (847) 251-6000. Open from 7 a.m. to 10 p.m. daily. There's a special kids' menu, and the silver-dollar pancakes are just the right size. $

Bakers Square, 200 Skokie Boulevard; (847) 256-6080. Hours are 7 a.m. to 11 p.m. daily. See Restaurant Appendix for description. $

A Natural Attraction

Commune with nature in the Chicago Botanic Garden, which is actually quite a ways north of the city but still in Cook County, in the North Shore suburb of Glencoe. The entrance is on Lake-Cook Road about half a mile west of Green Bay Road and half a mile east of I-94. The spacious grounds are a riot of color in spring and summer, yet there's a pristine beauty to them even in winter, when the snow covers everything. In fall the flowers are goners, so the surrounding trees pick up the slack by trotting out their best red-yellow hues. Three greenhouses on the grounds were built in the 1870s and contain a variety of interesting flora. The main building has a collection of plants that kids are actually supposed to touch, plus another group of useful plants such as cotton, pineapple, coffee, and cacao. There may also be a temporary display of art or craft items, such as prints or quilts. The grounds are open from 8 a.m. to sunset daily, year-round. Admission is **free,** but parking costs $15 per car. Tram tours of the grounds—daily from late April through October and on weekends only the rest of the year—run on the half hour between 10 a.m. and 3:30 p.m. and cost $5 for adults, $4 for seniors, and $3 for children. One tram is wheelchair accessible. You can get a bite to eat in the Garden Cafe, open from 8 a.m. to 5 p.m. Monday through Friday and 8 a.m. to 5:30 p.m. Saturday and Sunday. Souvenirs are available in the Garden Shop, and there's also a library. Restrooms are available in the main building. For further information, contact Chicago Botanic Garden, 1000 Lake Cook Road, Glencoe 60022; (847) 835-5440; www.chicagobotanic.org.

Where to Stay

There are no hotels or motels in Wilmette. See entry for Highland Park.

For More Information

Wilmette Chamber of Commerce, 1150 Wilmette Avenue, Wilmette 60091; (847) 251-3800; www.wilmettechamber.org.

Des Plaines

Population: 58,720. The Des Plaines River runs along the eastern edge of this Cook County suburb just north of O'Hare International Airport. Interstate 294 and Interstate 90 skirt the eastern and southern edges of town and Highway 83 the western edge. Illinois Highway 58 runs through the northern part, and U.S. Highways 14 and 12/45 crisscross in the middle. About a block north of Lee Street (the main drag for the small downtown) on the west side of River Road is a little re-creation of the first McDonald's burger joint, complete with big golden arches. You can peek in the windows at the mannequins posed at the counter, but you can't go inside.

Mystic Waters Family Aquatic Center (all ages) 

2025 Miner Street, Des Plaines; (847) 391-5705; www.desplainesparks.org/facilities/mystic_waters.asp. Open from mid-June through late August. Hours are 11 a.m. to 9 p.m. Monday through Friday and 11 a.m. to 8 p.m. Saturday and Sunday. $$

This community swimming pool was remodeled in 1996 to become a family-friendly water park. The pool now has a zero-depth end where tiny tots can frolic. Kids also like the sand play area and the "splash playground" added in 2004. There are three kinds of slides: twisty water slides, drop slides, and a dolphin slide. If you don't feel like swimming, you can just float along a "river" in an inner tube. Concessions are available, and there is a changing station in the women's restroom.

Where to Eat

ChooChoo Grill, 600 Lee Street; (847) 391-9815. Hours are 10:30 a.m. to 8 p.m. Monday through Friday, 7 a.m. to 3 p.m. Saturday; and 10:30 a.m. to 3 p.m. Sunday. This little diner's claim to fame is the miniature railroad track that runs along the counter. If you sit on a stool at the counter, the choo-choo will deliver your plate of toast. $

Perry's X-press, 1065 East Oakton Street; (847) 823-4428. Open from 11 a.m. to 11 p.m. Monday through Thursday, 11 a.m. to midnight Friday and Saturday, and noon to 9 p.m. Sunday. This local Italian restaurant occupies a building that was once a bank. Both pan pizza and "panzarotti" (in which the crust is folded over to encase the toppings, sort of like a big turnover) are popular, and you can order a variety of pasta dishes. $

Where to Stay

Comfort Inn O'Hare, 2175 East Touhy Avenue; (847) 635-1300 or (800) 424-6423. About 2 miles from O'Hare International Airport; a free courtesy car will take you to and from the airport. The inn has 145 rooms with coffeemakers. The property has a workout room and whirlpool but no swimming pool. Pets are allowed for an extra $20 per night per pet. The room rate includes continental breakfast. $$

For More Information

Des Plaines Chamber of Commerce, 1401 East Oakton Street, Des Plaines 60016; (847) 824-4200; www.dpchamber.com.

Elk Grove Village

Population: 34,727. This suburb is easily accessible from I-90, Interstate 290, Interstate 355, and Highway 53. If you're flying in and out of O'Hare airport or planning to shop till you drop at Woodfield Mall just up the road in Schaumburg, you may get a better motel rate if you stay in Elk Grove Village.

Pirates' Cove (ages 2 to 10) 

901 Leicester Road, Elk Grove Village; (847) 439-2683 or (847) 690-1129; www.parks.elkgrove.org/pages/piratescove.asp?id=257. Open mid-June through mid-August. Hours are 11 a.m. to 4 p.m. Monday through Friday and 10 a.m. to 4 p.m. Saturday; closed Sunday. Good accessibility for strollers and wheelchairs. Restrooms have fold-down changing tables. From I-290, I-355, or Highway 53, exit at Biesterfield Road and head east, and then turn south onto Leicester Road and follow the signs. From I-90 or Illinois Highway 72, exit south onto Arlington Heights Road and continue a few miles to Biesterfield Road. Turn right, heading west on Biesterfield, and then south onto Leicester Road. Signs direct you to the entrance building, with its salmon-pink, Mediterranean-style facade. $$

This pint-size amusement park is a cute place to take your tiny tots and younger grade-schoolers. Administered by the Elk Grove Park District, the facility has a clean, attractive appearance. Brick walkways wind through the landscaped grounds, with beds of marigolds, geraniums, and other flowers lending a splash of color. Trees are tall enough to afford some shade, and there are benches where the adults can sit to wait for the kids. The admission price, verified by a colorful wristband, covers unlimited use of about a dozen attractions. Admission is charged only for the kids; accompanying adults and teens get in free. Children must be able to ride by themselves—parents are not allowed on the rides, and it's easy to see why. Even kids as old as 8 or 9 may feel a bit oversize on some of them. A unique ride is a little train that is powered by the kids themselves. They each get their own private locomotive, and they crank a handle as vigorously as possible to make it go around the track, which passes under a couple short tunnels. A merry-go-round with 20 horses is also popular. There are two water rides, the Bumper Boats and the Jungle Cruise, both of which are very gentle. Cute animal puppets at the end of the cruise make it a memorable ride. Behind a castle wall is a free-form playground with ladders, platforms, nets, tires, and a slide that forms the back of a green dragon that puffs steam out its nostrils. Older kids will enjoy the cable ride or the 20-foot climbing wall. The pirate ship in the center of the park has tables and chairs on the upper level and ice cream and souvenirs on the lower. You can bring your own picnic or buy food from a concession shop that sells pizza, drinks, and other goodies.

Rainbow Falls Waterpark (all ages) 

200 Reverend Morrison Boulevard, Elk Grove Village; (847) 228-2860; www.parks.elkgrove.org/rainbowfalls.asp.?id=451. One block east of Arlington Heights Road, behind Elk Grove High School. Season runs from mid-June through mid-August. Hours are 11 a.m. to 8 p.m. Monday through Friday and 11:30 a.m. to 6 p.m. Saturday and Sunday. Accessible for strollers and wheelchairs. From I-290, I-355, or Highway 53, exit at Biesterfield Road and turn right onto Biesterfield, heading east a mile or so. Turn left, heading north, onto Arlington Heights Road, following it around a curve, and then turn right onto Elk Grove Boulevard and right again onto Reverend Morrison Boulevard (formerly Lions Drive). From I-90 or Highway 72, exit south onto Arlington Heights Road; turn left onto Elk Grove Boulevard and then right onto Reverend Morrison Boulevard. $$

This facility, operated by the Elk Grove Park District, has something for everyone. For the tinier tots there's a shallow "adventure pool" with a turtle fountain, a little slide, and squirt guns. For the older family members, the park has a swimming pool, giant water slides, a waterfall, and a 300-foot floating inner-tube ride. If you're really adventurous, try the "cliff" diving off one of two high platforms. A miniature golf course winds among the falls and fountains; $3 extra charge to play. The three-story family fun house resembles an amusement park fun house, only with water stuff. You can exit the fun house down the "space bowl slide," which is a bit like being flushed down a toilet, albeit a clean, chlorinated one. The park has an on-site concession stand, but you're allowed to bring your own lunch if you choose, as long as you don't pack any glass containers or alcoholic beverages.

Where to Eat

Le Peep, 130 Biesterfield Road; (847) 439-7337. In a strip mall on the north side of the road. The curb in front could pose a problem for wheelchairs from the parking lot, but the restaurant is on one level and negotiable. Hours are 6:30 a.m. to 2:30 p.m. Monday through Friday and 7 a.m. to 2:30 p.m. Saturday and Sunday. This airy restaurant with crisp white walls, dark green carpeting, and burgundy accents is a comfortable place for a hearty breakfast or lunch. The specialty dish is a skillet, a ceramic dish shaped like its namesake and filled with a mixture of diced potatoes, onions, and cheese, topped with two sunny-side-up eggs; you can also get it with other ingredients added. A Schuldt favorite is the crepe stuffed with seafood, mushrooms, and broccoli and slathered in hollandaise sauce. The children's menu items are priced from $2.99 to $3.95, not including drink. Kids can choose pancakes, French toast, grilled cheese sandwich, burger, or chicken strips. $

Giordano's, 1800 South Elmhurst Road; (847) 290-8000. Open from 11 a.m. to 10 p.m. Sunday through Thursday and 11 a.m. to 11 p.m. Friday and Saturday. See Restaurant Appendix for description. $

Portillo's, 1500 Busse Highway; (847) 228-6677. Hours are 10:30 a.m. to 8 p.m. Monday through Friday and 10:30 a.m. to 5 p.m. Saturday; closed Sunday. See Restaurant Appendix for description. $

Where to Stay

Best Western Chicago West, 1600 Oakton Street; (847) 981-0010, (800) 482-3887, or (800) 937-8376. This chain property has 159 rooms on 3 floors, with elevator. Amenities include a domed atrium with indoor pool, whirlpool, and steam room. Restaurant on premises. Some pets allowed with prior approval from manager. $$$$

Comfort Inn International, 2550 Landmeier Road; (847) 364-6200. This 3-story chain motel has 102 comfortable rooms but not much in the way of amenities; no pool. Room rate includes a full hot breakfast. $$$

Days Inn O'Hare West, 1920 East Higgins Road; (847) 437-1650. A basic chain property, the motel has 78 rooms with cable TV; no pool. Pets are allowed. Room rate includes continental breakfast. $

Holiday Inn Elk Grove, 1000 Busse Road; (847) 437-6010 or (800) 465-4329. This 4-story hotel has 159 rooms and features indoor pool, sauna, and fitness center. Pets allowed. Room rate includes full breakfast. $$

For More Information

Elk Grove Chamber of Commerce, P.O. Box 756, Elk Grove Village 60009; (877) 355-4768; www.elkgrovechamber.org.

Schaumburg

Population: 75,386. This suburb's Woodfield Mall has made it a commercial mecca. The village and the mall are accessible off I-290 (a spur off I-90) and Highways 53, 58, and 72. There's other family fun here, too.

Woodfield Mall (all ages) 

Golf Road (Highway 58) and Highway 53, Schaumburg; (847) 330-1537 or, outside the Chicago metro area, (800) 332-1537; www.shopwoodfield.com or www.gowoodfieldmall.com. Regular mall hours are 10 a.m. to 9 p.m. Monday through Saturday and 11 a.m. to 6 p.m. Sunday. Holiday hours vary, so call ahead to check. The mall is accessible for strollers and wheelchairs. No smoking inside the mall.

Woodfield is the world's largest mall in terms of retail space. (The Mall of America in Minnesota covers more total space but includes a huge indoor amusement park in

Reigning Cats and Dogs

The three-story glass-enclosed concourse at Arlington International Racecourse is the spacious venue for the annual Chicagoland Family Pet Show in mid- to late March. The weekend event normally runs from 2 to 7 p.m. Friday, 9 a.m. to 8 p.m. Saturday, and 10 a.m. to 5 p.m. Sunday, so it's easy to work around toddlers' nap times. Cats and dogs are the kings and queens of this show, but you'll find small areas with such exotic pets as rats, ferrets, hedgehogs, snakes, turtles, and assorted smaller reptiles. More than 300 booths with all sorts of pet-related merchandise and services fill one whole huge section of the concourse. It's a wonderful place to spend a few hours. (Concessions are available if you want a snack or a meal, but frankly, the food is overpriced and generally mediocre.)

In the cat section hundreds of gorgeous felines rest in fancy cages or in their owners' arms, awaiting their turn to compete for a blue ribbon. To prevent the spread of germs, touching or petting the animals is prohibited, and the owners of these expensive show cats do not take kindly to people who disregard that rule, so have a talk with your little one beforehand and then stay close enough to make sure the child obeys. Some of the professional breeders who bring cats to the show also bring kittens for sale. You might be able to take one home for a mere $400.

The dogs are not on display like the cats, but you'll still be able to find a few wandering about—on leashes, of course—or resting in one of the booths with its owner. Some owners will let kids pet their animal, and others prefer not to, so always ask before you touch. The dogs are paraded into a show ring for judging, and when there's a lull in the competition, there's usually some form of canine entertainment. You'll see "dancin' doggies," Frisbee-catching pooches, and guard dogs.

Arlington Racecourse is located at 2200 West Euclid Avenue, east of Highway 53, in Arlington Heights. Ticket prices for 2008 were set at $9 for anyone age 13 or older and $6 for kids age 3 through 12, with tots age 2 or younger admitted free. Discount coupons are available online and at many area Dominick's grocery stores. Parking costs $6, or you can take the Metra Union Pacific Northwest Line train and get off at the nearby Arlington Park stop and walk over. The concourse is accessible for strollers and wheelchairs, and there are elevators as well as escalators between floors. Smoking is not allowed. For further information contact Tower Show Productions at (630) 469-4611, ext. 203; www.towershow.com or www.petchicago.com.

addition to the retail stores.) Woodfield has 235 stores, anchored by JCPenney, Lord & Taylor, Macy's, Nordstrom, and Sears. This two-and-a-half-story mall is made for serious shoppers, too, without a lot of obstacles to impede foot traffic—the few aesthetic touches here include glass elevators and a fountain in the central courtyard. The lack of numerous kiosks and much decorative greenery makes the walkways more navigable for baby strollers and wheelchairs as well. It's hard to imagine something you couldn't buy at Woodfield; there are so many different kinds of stores—clothing, books, music, electronics, home furnishings, wacky gifts, you name it. Stores appealing to kids include Kay-Bee Toys and the Disney Store. Unlike many other malls, Woodfield has no food court. Instead, restaurants and snack shops are scattered throughout (McDonald's is in the small middle level sandwiched between the expansive upper and lower levels). The most popular spot to eat is the Rainforest Cafe on the lower level. You'll pay inflated prices for burgers and other casual fare, but the place makes up for it with its vividly entertaining atmosphere. Often there's a line to get in, so don't wait until you're on the brink of starvation to wander over there. The parking areas are fairly well marked, as are the access points along the ring road encircling the mall.

Medieval Times Dinner and Tournament (age 5 and up) 

2001 Roselle Road, at I-90, Schaumburg; (888) 935-6878; www.medievaltimes.com. The dinner program starts at 7:30 p.m. Wednesday, Thursday, and Friday; 4 p.m. and 7 p.m. Saturday; and 2 p.m. and 5 p.m. Sunday; closed Monday and Tuesday. Reservations are required. The price includes both the meal and the pageantry. Advertisements in the newspaper frequently have coupons that may allow you to save money off the regular prices, sometimes even admitting a child free. Souvenirs, including the aggressively hawked photographs, cost extra. Tickets for the Dungeon exhibit cost $2. The Great Hall area (including restrooms) and the back of the arena area are accessible for wheelchairs. Smoking is not allowed. There are no changing tables in the restrooms, and the paper-towel dispenser is mounted too high on the wall to be easily reached by children or by people in wheelchairs. $$$$

Looking for a change of pace? Here's "joust" the thing. Inside a climate-controlled castle, you'll feast on a hearty dinner while watching colorfully clad "knights," mounted on real horses, put on a two-hour show in the arena below. The moment you enter the castle—well, after you pay the admission and in return receive a table number and a paper crown in one of six colorful designs—you are cheerfully greeted by lavishly costumed actors in the role of king and queen. A photograph is taken of your party upon arrival. You will later be offered a package for $20 consisting of two 6- by 8-inch photos and a key chain. Onward you proceed into the Great Hall, an open, high-ceilinged room with wooden chandelier and a balcony from which royal proclamations are issued. Everyone stays out here until the doors to the arena are opened. In the meantime you can wander around and, the management hopes, spend a lot of money. The souvenir counter has a tantalizing assortment of wooden weapons, golden goblets, and colorful costumes, plus mugs and T-shirts. At the very least you'll want to spend a couple bucks per kid on a "cheering pennant" to wave during the show. Prices for the individual items are not too bad, but the cost adds up fast if you have more than one child or buy more than one thing. If you're willing to spend $15, your boy or girl can be officially knighted, receiving a photograph of the king touching the sword to the kid's shoulder, plus an inscribed scroll. Even adults sometimes opt for this feature.

You may have purchased tickets at the admission booth for the Dungeon, which is located down a hallway off the Great Hall. Be forewarned that this display is far too disturbing for many children and some adults. (The ticket sellers don't tell you that, and by the time you see the NOT SUITABLE FOR SMALL CHILDREN sign by the door, you've already bought the tickets.) It is a room filled with replicas of medieval instruments of torture, accompanied by written descriptions, some sketches, and a mannequin or two. Although you may think that doesn't sound so bad, wait until you find out how some of these things actually were used—slowly tearing muscles, rupturing internal organs, or asphyxiating the victim in an excruciating manner. Often the alleged crime or the punishment involved the sexual organs. Do you really want to get into all that with a child? No thanks. While it could be argued that the Dungeon is only for entertainment and shouldn't be taken so seriously, the truth is that this kind of hideous torture really did happen in human history and is not some make-believe thing that can merely be wished away—just read today's headlines and you know that torture is not simply a thing of the past. In the vernacular: You don't want to go there.

Once the doors to the arena open, the real magic begins. Guests are ushered in, grouped according to the design of their crowns, and seated at long tables in six sections around the perimeter of the oval arena. The table assignments are first come, first served, so the earlier you arrive, the closer you'll sit to the action (but the longer you'll have to wait around in the hall; it's a trade-off). The tables are stair-stepped so that everyone gets a clear view of the arena floor. Plexiglas walls prevent flying dirt from getting into your food after the meal is served. You start with soup and garlic bread, followed by roasted chicken, barbecued ribs, and twice-baked potato, and conclude with a flaky apple pastry. All the food is eaten without silverware, in the style of the Middle Ages, but napkins and, later, wet washcloths are provided to control the mess. For mass-produced food, the fare is surprisingly tasty—hot, flavorful, and fun to eat. Two servings of Pepsi are included in the price of the meal, but additional soft drinks or alcoholic beverages may be ordered at extra charge from the roving "wenches."

The show begins once everyone has their first course, with a parade down the middle of the arena featuring the king and queen, six handsome young men dressed in knightly regalia, and all the members of the "court," including your waiters. The show has a bit of a story line, but mainly the spectacle consists of the six knights competing on horseback in various contests of skill and eventually going one-on-one with weapons. The fights are choreographed, but even so, there remains an element of risk that makes them thrilling to watch. Grade-schoolers will think it's all "really cool," but the action and the dim lighting might make the experience too intense for younger children.

Clearly, all the expenses beyond the basic admission price make Medieval Times the kind of attraction you probably can't afford very often. But try to save your money and go at least once. The pageantry is worth it.

Schaumburg Waterworks (all ages) 

505 North Springinsguth Road, Schaumburg; (847) 490-2505; www.parkfun.com/dir/ww/wtrwks.html. From I-290/355 South, take the Elgin-O'Hare Expressway and exit at Irving Park Road. Turn right onto Springinsguth Road and continue about half a mile; Waterworks is at the corner of Springinsguth and Schaumburg Roads. Open year-round. Hours during the school year are 5:30 to 8 p.m. Monday through Thursday, 4 to 8 p.m. Friday, and noon to 5 p.m. Saturday and Sunday. Hours are expanded in the summer. $$

This indoor water park has a zero-depth pool, a lap pool, a diving pool, a whirlpool, and three water slides. A nursery and a family changing room provide added convenience to families with young children, but the facility also welcomes teenagers.

Schaumburg Flyers (age 4 and up) 

Games are played at Alexian Field, 1999 Springinsguth Road, Schaumburg; (847) 891-2255; www.flyersbaseball.com. A phone recording provides good driving directions. Season runs from late May through late August. Parking is free in an adjacent paved lot. Facility is accessible for wheelchairs and strollers. $–$$

Minor-league baseball of the independent Northern League is what you'll see at this beautiful redbrick ballpark that opened in 1999 with a team managed by former Chicago White Sox outfielder Ron Kittle. Little planes flying overhead toward the nearby Schaumburg regional airport were the inspiration for the team's name and pilot-head logo. The cute mascot, Bearon, is a huge teddy with aviator hood and goggles who charms kids and adults alike. As at other minor-league ballparks, at each game the mascot races a kid around the bases (and of course comes in second). Other gimmicks include skill contests with Wiffle bats, golf clubs, hula hoops, and two couples dancing on the dugout roofs. The wide concrete aisles of the main concourse are easy to navigate. Restrooms are evenly spaced along the length of the concourse, one of them a "family" restroom that alleviates the father-daughter/mother-son issue of which one to use. The lawn sections at either end of the first- and third-base sides have a rather steep slope. The reserved seats are surprisingly narrow for a newer ballpark; expect a bit of a squeeze if you're at all overweight. The cup holders are a handy touch, however. Skyboxes are placed above and behind the reserved seats, so no one's view is blocked. Concessions are reasonably priced, although the cups for tips seem inappropriate at this sort of facility. Popcorn, peanuts, pretzels, cotton candy, and Cracker Jack are among the snack offerings. For heartier appetites there are hot dogs, bratwurst, Italian beef, and chicken sandwiches. For the more health conscious, a fruit or veggie plate or a cold deli sandwich is a nice alternative. Souvenirs sporting the team's navy and orange colors include caps, shirts, mugs, pens, stuffed toys, soft baseballs, and miniature bats; some of the smaller items can be purchased for less than $5 each.

Where to Eat

Portillo's, 611 East Golf Road; (847) 884-9020. Hours are 10:30 a.m. to 10:30 p.m. Monday through Thursday, 10:30 a.m. to 11 p.m. Friday and Saturday, and 11 a.m. to 9:30 p.m. Sunday. See Restaurant Appendix for description. $

Red Lobster, 680 North Mall Drive; (847) 843-2743. Near Woodfield Mall. Hours are 11 a.m. to 10 p.m. Sunday through Thursday and 11 a.m. to 11 p.m. Friday and Saturday. See Restaurant Appendix for description. $$

Where to Stay

Hampton Inn, 1300 East Higgins Road; (847) 619-1000. This chain motel has 128 comfortable rooms but no swimming pool. The room rate includes continental breakfast. $$$$

Hyatt Regency Woodfield, 1800 East Golf Road; (847) 605-1234 or (800) 233-1234. Hyatt is a more upscale chain that's typically beyond a family budget, but if you can afford to pamper yourselves a bit, give this one a try. It has 469 rooms and is loaded with amenities, including indoor and outdoor pools, whirlpool, and fitness center. There is a restaurant on the premises. $$$$

La Quinta Motor Inn, 1730 East Higgins Road; (847) 517-8484 or (800) 531-5900. This budget chain property has 121 rooms and an outdoor swimming pool. Pets are allowed. The room rate includes continental breakfast. $$

For More Information

Greater Woodfield Convention and Visitors Bureau, 1430 North Meacham Road, Suite 1400, Schaumburg 60173; (800) 847-4849; www.visitgw.com. Thirteen communities in the northwest suburbs form the Greater Woodfield area, which encompasses Woodfield Mall, Medieval Times, and numerous restaurants, hotels, and motels.

Our sweep of Chicagoland now reaches DuPage County in the west. For general information about this region, contact the DuPage Convention and Visitors Bureau, 915 Harger Road, Oak Brook 60523; (630) 575-8070 or (800) 232-0502; www.dupagecvb.com.

Roselle

Population: 23,115. This suburb has several family-oriented attractions all within a mile or so of one another along or just off Lake Street, also known as U.S. Highway 20. The area is just east of Gary Avenue, a few miles north of Bloomingdale's Stratford Square Mall.

Brunswick Zone (age 2 and up) 

1100 West Lake Street, between Gary Avenue and Bloomingdale Road, Roselle; (630) 351-2100. Open year-round except for miniature golf, which is an outdoor course open only in summer. Call ahead to check current hours for open bowling and Cosmic Bowling. Game room generally open from 3 to 8 p.m. daily. No street shoes allowed on the lanes. Bumpers available at no extra charge. $

This facility has three main parts. The **game room** in front has games for tots and teens alike. The wee ones will have fun using a big padded mallet to clobber things that pop up in the RoboBop and Whak A Mole games, while the teens will find air hockey, pinball, and video games to attract their interest, and everyone can try the Skeeball. Games spit out tickets at the end of a round of play, and those can be redeemed for brightly colored plastic prizes when you leave. Additional games are downstairs.

Around to the east side downstairs, with its own entrance, is a 32-lane Brunswick **bowling alley** where you can try Cosmic Bowling, which will push your senses to the limit. You bowl in black light (ultraviolet), so wear white if you really want to glow. Multicolored lights flash, and three big screens above the lanes carry dance-style music videos. Automated scoring on video screens means you don't have to count pins or remember how to add a spare, and you can request a lane with bumpers that fill the gutters to make it easier for everyone to hit some pins. The lightest ball available weighs six pounds, so make sure your youngster is strong enough to heft it—probably about age 4 or 5—to get the most pleasure out of the experience. Basic snacks and drinks are available to keep you fueled; budget a few extra bucks. Cosmic Bowling is aptly named and a lot of fun.

The third section is the outdoor **miniature golf course,** in back and off to the east side but visible from the road. This eye-catching 18-hole course has a castle, a Victorian mansion, and numerous waterfalls and fountains set amid landscaped grounds with colorful flower beds. But think twice before bringing younger children here—the course is much trickier than it looks, and even adults may have trouble making par. The water hazards will cost you an extra dollar if you knock your ball in and can't get it back out, which happens a little too easily.

Coachlite Roller Skating Center (age 5 and up) 

1291 Bryn Mawr Avenue, at Lake Street, Roselle; (630) 893-4480; www.coachlite skate.com. Hours vary; call ahead for current schedule. You may bring your own (clean) skates. $–$$

Inside this plain brick building is a lively spot for some family recreation. Kids of all ages are allowed, but many don't have the necessary strength and balance until about kindergarten—you be the judge of your own child's capabilities so that the experience will be safe as well as fun. Also keep in mind that even if your youngster whizzes around the neighborhood on Rollerblades, he or she will be surprised on the first visit to an indoor rink like this one at how slippery the smooth parquet floor is. But once they get the hang of it, wheeee! During summer the center offers a two-hour session with organ music for old-fashioned fun. Other sessions have a disc jockey playing the tunes and calling for occasional special restrictions, such as girls-only, boys-only, couples, or backward skate. You'll also get a chance to do the hokey-pokey and the chicken dance on wheels. The painted rainbow that runs along the back wall reflects the flashing multicolored lights overhead that pulse to the beat of the music. Skate pickup is at the far end of the rink; you trade your shoes for the skates. There are 50-cent lockers along the wall for stowing other stuff. The concession area has soda, candy, hot dogs, and pizza, with many items under $2. A game room and a gift shop can siphon off a bit more of your money.

Where to Eat

Skippy's Gyros, 1322 Lake Street, at Bryn Mawr; (630) 894-9960. Open from 10:30 a.m. to 9 p.m. Monday through Thursday, 10:30 a.m. to 10 p.m. Friday and Saturday, and noon to 6:30 p.m. Sunday. This little eatery is in a strip mall just north of Coachlite Roller Skating Center. A gyro, the signature Greek sandwich, features seasoned roasted lamb or chicken packed in pita bread with onion, tomato, and cucumber sauce, and is a bargain at less than $4. For more conventional tastes the menu contains hamburgers, hot dogs, fried chicken and shrimp, and barbecued ribs. $

Where to Stay

There are no hotels or motels in Roselle. The Holiday Inn on Gary Avenue in Carol Stream is about 5 miles south of the attractions listed for Roselle; see entry for Carol Stream.

For More Information

Roselle Chamber of Commerce and Industry, 81 East Devon Avenue, Roselle 60172; (630) 894-3010; www.roselle chamber.com.

Bloomingdale

Population: 21,675. This town reportedly dates back to the early 1800s. The Old Town section just west of Bloomingdale Road, between Lake Street and Schick Road, is rather like historic Long Grove, only on a smaller scale. But for the most part, Bloomingdale blends into the amalgamation of suburbs sprawling out to the west of Chicago.

Stratford Square Mall (all ages) 

Corner of Gary Avenue and Army Trail Road, accessible from either, Bloomingdale; (630) 539-1000; www.stratfordmall.com. Hours are 10 a.m. to 9 p.m. Monday through Saturday and 11 a.m. to 6 p.m. Sunday. Accessible to strollers and wheelchairs; strollers available for rent. No smoking inside the mall or any of its stores.

Stratford Square is one of the most pleasant indoor shopping malls in the entire state for families with small children. It offers a storytime for kids during summer, and the Back-to-School train typically runs from late July through mid-August to make the obligatory fall pilgrimage more palatable to the wee ones. The mall is laid out roughly in a T-shape, with upper and lower levels that are connected via escalators and a glass elevator that kids love to ride. Skylights augment and soften the artificial light so that the place usually looks bright and airy. Several ponds with fountains add character and an aura of tranquillity. (All the fountains accept penny-pitched wishes.) There are five anchor department stores to suit a wide range of tastes and budgets, from the economical Sears to the midrange Kohl's, JCPenney, and Carson Pirie Scott to the tonier Macy's. There are also some stores of particular interest to kids, such as the Disney Store and Kay-Bee Toys. If you set clear budgetary limits beforehand, they can enjoy themselves just looking around. Gymboree and Gap Kids are among a handful of specialty children's clothing stores at the mall. Providing a productive outlet for children's energy, the Kids' Cartowne play area contains brightly colored fiberglass cars that kids can play on—and which are regularly wiped down with disinfectant by mall employees. The centralized food court on the first floor—with a geyserlike fountain that toddlers simply adore—features such kid-pleasing fare as pizza, burgers, and hot dogs, plus baked potatoes or Chinese food for children with broader tastes. Have a deliciously gooey cinnamon roll for dessert at Cinnabon on the second floor. If you want to make a full day of it, you can take in a movie at the theater complex at one end.

Where to Eat

Red Lobster, 391 West Army Trail Road; (630) 529-0097. Near the mall. Open from 11 a.m. to 10 p.m. Sunday through Thursday and 11 a.m. to 11 p.m. Friday and Saturday. See Restaurant Appendix for description. $$

Popeyes Chicken, 405 Army Trail Road; (630) 893-1070. Near the mall. Open from 10 a.m. to 10 p.m. daily. See Restaurant Appendix for description. $

Old Country Buffet, 154 South Gary Avenue; (630) 529-5056. Near the mall, in an outdoor strip plaza called Stratford Promenade Shopping Center. Hours are 11 a.m. to 8:30 p.m. Monday through Thursday, 8 a.m. to 9 p.m. Friday and Saturday, and 8 a.m. to 8 p.m. Sunday; breakfast on weekends only, lunch and dinner daily. See Restaurant Appendix for description. $

Where to Stay

Indian Lakes Resort, 250 West Schick Road; (630) 529-0200. This deluxe facility has 308 rooms and lots of amenities: indoor and outdoor pools, indoor whirlpool and sauna, outdoor miniature golf course, tennis court, volleyball, two 18-hole regular golf courses, and two restaurants. The expansive grounds feature landscaping and ponds. Book a room here when you want more than just a place to sleep. $$$$

For More Information

Bloomingdale Chamber of Commerce, 107 South Third Street, Bloomingdale 60108; (630) 980-9082; www.bloomingdalechamber.com.

Carol Stream

Population: 40,438. This suburb is mainly an industrial and residential area, but you can find some fun things to do with the kids here. At the corner of Gary Avenue and Lies Road is a large fountain that marks the lovely Town Center park, completed in 1998.

Brunswick Zone (age 4 and up) 

170 West North Avenue, Carol Stream; (630) 682-0150. Regular hours are 11 a.m. to midnight Sunday through Thursday and 11 a.m. to 2 a.m. Friday and Saturday. Call for current Cosmic Bowling hours. No street shoes allowed on the lanes. Bumpers available at no extra charge. Check for package deals. $

This bowling alley is similar to the one in Roselle but costs slightly less. It, too, has the funky Cosmic Bowling by black light, with big-screen music videos pumping up the volume and multicolored lights splashing color all around. Automated scoring displayed on video screens and bumpers in the gutters take the frustration out of playing. A food court offers snacks to keep you going.

Carol Stream Ice Rink (age 5 and up) 

540 East Gunderson Drive, Carol Stream; (630) 682-4480; www.carolstreamicerink.com. Session times vary; call or go online to check current schedule. $

This indoor facility offers public ice-skating year-round. Bring your own skates or rent them there. Vending machines provide the only concessions.

Where to Eat

Pizza Hut, 333 South Schmale Road; (630) 682-4020. Hours are 11 a.m. to 11 p.m. Sunday through Thursday and 11 a.m. to midnight Friday and Saturday. Dine in or carryout. See Restaurant Appendix for description. $

Carol's Garden, 515 South Schmale Road (just north of Geneva Road); (630) 260-0303. Open from 6 a.m. to midnight daily, serving breakfast, lunch, and dinner. The extensive menu at this family-oriented restaurant features salads, sandwiches, and entrees including beef, chicken, seafood, and pasta. The children's menu has the usual favorites. A bonus here is the glass-walled ice-cream case with about a dozen flavors to choose from. The pastry case is tempting, too. $$

Where to Stay

Holiday Inn Carol Stream, 150 South Gary Avenue, just south of North Avenue (Illinois Highway 64); (630) 665-3000 or (800) 800-6509. This attractive 4-story chain property has 198 rooms with cable TV. Amenities include indoor pool, Jacuzzi, fitness room, and game room. Restaurant on premises. $$$

For More Information

Carol Stream Chamber of Commerce, 150 South Gary Avenue, Carol Stream 60188; (630) 665-3325; www.carolstreamchamber.com.

Wheaton

Population: 55,416. You would expect this western suburb, home of the Billy Graham Center at Wheaton College, to have plenty of wholesome family activities, and it does. Railroad tracks run along Front Street downtown, and the area has been developed with brick walkways and fountains into a pleasant place to hang out on a nice day. Wheaton also has numerous well-maintained parks throughout the city.

DuPage County Historical Museum (age 4 and up) 

102 East Wesley Street, Wheaton; (630) 682-7343; www.co.dupage.il.us/museum. Hours are 10 a.m. to 4 p.m. Monday, Wednesday, Friday, and Saturday and 1 to 4 p.m. Sunday; closed Tuesday and Thursday. Call for information on current special exhibits and programs. $

The first historical thing you'll encounter at this museum is the building it's in. Designed by noted Chicago architect Charles Sumner Frost and constructed in 1891, it has a light brick facade, Gothic windows, a steep roof, and a tower at one end. The museum arrived in 1965. A highlight here is the model railroad, which is part of an exhibit that also includes artifacts and photographs chronicling the history of railroading in DuPage County. Other ongoing exhibits invite visitors' participation. There are enjoyable free programs for adults and children throughout the year, among them demonstrations of games and toys from the 1800s. In 2007, the DuPage County Historical Museum was named one of the "150 Illinois Great Places" by the American Institute of Architects, Illinois Council.

Kelly Park (all ages) 

South off Roosevelt Road (Illinois Highway 38) on Main Street, a block west of Naperville Road, Wheaton; (630) 665-4710. Open from dawn to dusk daily. Free.

Women have been in the majority on Wheaton's park district board, and it's probably no coincidence that this community has a better-than-average collection of kid-friendly local parks. An easy one to reach is Kelly Park, on Main Street at the intersection with Elm Street in a residential neighborhood. There are separate play areas for tiny tots and for older kids, each with colorful, modern, metal-and-plastic playground equipment. A paved bicycle path surrounds and passes between the playgrounds. Children of all ages like to climb the "spider" of red nylon webbing that reaches a height of about 10 feet. There's a drinking fountain near the picnic tables, and in warmer weather there's usually a portable toilet available.

Cantigny (all ages)  

1S151 Winfield Road, Wheaton; (630) 668-5161; www.cantigny.org. Cantigny is accessible off Roosevelt Road (Highway 38) from the north or Butterfield Road (Illinois Highway 56) from the south and is well marked by brown signs. Parking costs $7 per car (or $4 evening only), but everything else is free. Grounds are open from 9 a.m. to sunset Tuesday through Sunday; closed Monday. Museum hours are 10 a.m. to 5 p.m. Tuesday through Sunday; closed Monday. The museum stays open an hour later in the summer. Grounds, mansion, and museum are closed in January.

One of the more notable landmarks in Wheaton is this 500-acre estate of the late Colonel R. R. McCormick, former editor and publisher of the *Chicago Tribune*. You can stroll through 10 acres of landscaped gardens and have a picnic on the grounds. Sometimes you can catch a musical concert at the gazebo. There are three buildings to visit, too. The visitor center has a large map of the grounds embedded in the floor.

Here you can also view a 10-minute orientation film. You can get a bite to eat in the Tack Room Cafe, where toddlers can sit in a saddled high chair. There's also a gift shop. Full-length tours of the three-story R. R. McCormick Mansion depart every 15 minutes, the first at 10:15 a.m. and the last at 4:15 p.m., and take about 45 minutes. The second and third floors are accessible by stairs only. A 30-minute tour covers the first floor only, and the five-minute "Just a Peek" tour shows you just four main rooms on that floor. The First Division Museum uses life-size dioramas and exhibits to tell the story of the First Infantry Division of the U.S. Army.

Wheaton Rice Pool (all ages) 

1777 South Blanchard Road, Wheaton; (630) 653-8884; www.wheatonparkdistrict.com/pgs/parks/aquatics/rice_pool.htm. East off Naperville Road a mile or 2 north of Butterfield Road (Highway 56). Hours are 12:30 to 8 p.m. Monday through Friday and noon to 8 p.m. Saturday and Sunday. $$–$$$

The swimming facility is outdoors behind the Wheaton Park District Community Center, a modern redbrick building. In addition to the main pool, it has a kiddie pool with a waterfall and a sand play area for children. Unlike other pools, Wheaton Rice Pool charges extra to ride the water slides: $2 for a 10-ride wristband.

Cosley Zoo (all ages) 

1356 Gary Avenue, Wheaton; (630) 665-5534; www.cosleyzoo.org. Open year-round. Hours during peak season from April through September are 9 a.m. to 5 p.m. daily. Admission is free, but much-appreciated donations may be slipped into the unobtrusive box near the train station.

This small zoo operated by the Wheaton Park District is a pleasant place to pass a few hours. Bring your own lunch and sit at the picnic tables in a partially shaded area next to a vintage train car that kids can play in. You can wheel the stroller along a paved walkway next to a duck pond and go into a barn filled with horses, cows, sheep, goats, pigs, chickens, and other farm animals. The zoo also displays some native Illinois wildlife, such as foxes, coyotes, deer, owls, and hawks. The re-created train station houses exhibits, a gift shop, and restrooms.

Where to Eat

Muldoon's, 133 West Front Street; (630) 668-8866. Open from 11 a.m. to 10 p.m. daily. This Irish-themed corner restaurant in downtown Wheaton serves lunch and dinner. Entrees include steaks, chicken, seafood, pasta, and nightly specials. The children's menu includes burgers, chicken nuggets, and the like. $$

Boston Market, 625 South County Farm Road; (630) 871-0100. A few miles from Cosley Zoo or Cantigny. Open from 10:30 a.m. to 9 p.m. daily. See Restaurant Appendix for description. $

Outback Steakhouse, 50 East Loop Road; (630) 462-8850. Near Wheaton Rice Pool. Hours are 4 to 10 p.m. Monday through Thursday, 4 to 11 p.m. Friday, 3:30 to 11 p.m. Saturday, and 12:30 to 9 p.m. Sunday. This family-friendly sit-down chain serves steak, chicken, seafood, and pasta dinner entrees and burgers with an Australian flair. Some of the food is a bit on the spicy side, but it's tasty. Call-ahead seating and curbside take-away service offer extra convenience for families.

Where to Stay

There are no hotels or motels in Wheaton. See listings for Carol Stream, Glen Ellyn, and Naperville.

For More Information

Wheaton Chamber of Commerce, 108 East Wesley Street, Wheaton 60187; (630) 668-6464; www.ewheaton.com.

Glen Ellyn

Population: 26,999. This west suburban town dates back to the mid-1800s. It has an old-fashioned downtown with specialty stores, boutiques, coffee shops, restaurants, and a movie theater that shows second-run and foreign films.

Lake Ellyn Park (all ages) 

645 Lenox Road, Glen Ellyn; (630) 858-2462; www.gepark.org. Open from dawn to dusk daily. Free.

One of the prettiest community parks for families in the suburbs is Lake Ellyn Park, nestled in a wooded area with a small lake behind Glenbard West High School (take Park Boulevard or Main Street north of downtown and turn east onto Hawthorne; you'll see the park on the left as Hawthorne dead-ends behind the high school). The children's playground is of modern design but in shades of green, tan, and brown that blend in with the surrounding trees, which provide merciful shade on hot sunny days. There's a nearby but separate area for littler kids, plus tables where you can have a snack you brought or simply set down the diaper bag. The park's boathouse has restrooms and an outdoor drinking fountain. You can fish off the deck in summer. In winter you can ice-skate on the frozen lake.

Willowbrook Wildlife Center (age 3 and up) 

525 South Park Boulevard, at Fawell Boulevard (formerly 22nd Street), Glen Ellyn; (630) 942-6200 or (630) 933-7683; TDD (800) 526-0857; www.dupageforest.com/education/willowbrook.html. Open year-round from 9 a.m. to 4 p.m. daily (until 5 p.m. during the summer); closed Thanksgiving, Christmas Eve, Christmas, and New Year's Day. Admission is by donation; suggested amount is $1 per person, all ages.

The center is a haven for animals that have been permanently disabled and are incapable of living in the wild. A 10-minute video explains how the staff treat and care for injured animals, and there are indoor and outdoor exhibits of critters. The Baby Nursery has, you guessed it, baby animals. The center's hands-on museum for children has animal puppets and a stage for creating their own nature shows. Outdoors there are picnic tables, a butterfly garden, and a nature trail.

Harold D. McAninch Arts Center at College of DuPage

(all ages)

Fawell Boulevard (formerly 22nd Street) between Park Boulevard and Lambert Road, Glen Ellyn; (630) 942-4000; www.cod.edu/ArtsCntr. Call or go online for current schedule of events.

The Arts Center, which opened in 1986, is home to five resident professional ensembles but attracts big-name concert performers and theatrical productions as well. There are periodic special shows geared toward children, including the popular "Kid Jazz," and a group of College of DuPage thespians puts on cute adaptations of children's stories outdoors in the courtyard during summer.

Where to Eat

Alfie's, 425 Roosevelt Road; (630) 858-2506. Open from 11 a.m. to 11 p.m. Monday through Saturday and 11 a.m. to 10 p.m. Sunday. This local favorite calls itself "The Camelot of Glen Ellyn" and has a suit of armor standing guard in the waiting area. But it's not a fancy place at all; the specialty "Sir Alfie Loinburger," a big, juicy hamburger served with fries and a pickle, comes in a plastic basket. The restaurant also serves chicken, shrimp, barbecued ribs, and large salads. The kids' menu features many of the same items on the regular menu, only in smaller sizes and at lower prices. $

Biking the Prairie Path

The 45-mile Illinois Prairie Path extends from Maywood to Aurora, but some of the prettiest stretches are through Villa Park, Glen Ellyn, and Wheaton, where the communities have done landscaping or created a parklike setting for the trail. Surfaced with crushed limestone in some parts and paved with asphalt in others, the path is favored by bicyclists, who outnumber walkers and runners about three to one. Motorized vehicles are prohibited on the Prairie Path. Police on bicycles patrol the path in some communities, and the incidence of vandalism or other crime has remained low.

Beijing, 404 Roosevelt Road; (630) 469-1535. Hours are 11:30 a.m. to 9:30 p.m. Sunday through Thursday and 11:30 a.m. to 10:30 p.m. Friday and Saturday. At this charming restaurant owned by Johnny and Bee Chen, family groups are always welcome. The Chinese cuisine here includes Hunan, Mandarin, and spicy Szechwan styles. If you want to go all-out, call ahead and order a succulent Beijing duck, which will feed a family of four quite generously. You can try some Chinese beer with your meal or order a round of Singapore Slings and Shirley Temples. $$

Where to Stay

Super 8, 677 Roosevelt Road; (630) 469-9200 or (800) 800-8000. This budget property has an indoor pool. Pets are allowed. Continental breakfast is included in the room rates. $$

For More Information

Village of Glen Ellyn, 535 Duane Street, Glen Ellyn 60137; (630) 469-5000; www.glen-ellyn.com.

Lombard

Population: 42,322. Like many of the western suburbs, this one traces its roots back into the 1800s. Wear purple if you visit Lombard during a couple special weeks in May—that's **Lilac Time.** The centerpiece of the action is Lilacia Park downtown, where hundreds of bushes are in bloom. During the festival the village charges a few dollars to walk through the park; at other times admission is free. Stores have special sales, and a portable carnival sets up to offer rides and concessions to visitors. A Sunday parade down Main Street is another Lilac Time highlight. The parade usually features about 150 units, including themed floats, marching bands, and antique cars, and attracts about 10,000 spectators.

Enchanted Castle (all ages) 

1103 South Main Street (at Roosevelt Road/Highway 38), Lombard; (630) 953-7860; www.enchanted.com. Hours are 10 a.m. to 10 p.m. Sunday through Thursday and 10 a.m. to midnight Friday and Saturday. Package deals offer a combination of attractions and are a good value. The Web site also includes coupons. $–$$

This is one of the larger family amusement centers in the area. Everything is indoors, under one roof, and there are recreational activities for all ages. Smaller children can frolic in the Kids Quest, a playground with tubes, slides, and the like. There are also kiddie rides with miniature cars, trucks, trains, and ponies, plus a pint-size Ferris wheel and a cute little roller coaster with a dragon head at the front. Older kids may want to play Q-Zar laser tag or try out one of the simulation rides. For these rides, you sit in a seat similar to an amusement park ride, facing a movie screen. The seat rocks and sways in time with the action shown on the screen. The Rage Theatre offers six different simulated adventures. Enchanted Castle also has bumper cars, a

Which Main Is Main?

A helpful hint for visitors: Wheaton, Glen Ellyn, and Lombard all have a Main Street that runs from north to south, and these three towns run consecutively from west to east, so be sure you're in the right one for the Main Street you want.

nine-hole miniature golf course, and about 280 arcade games. An intriguing attraction here is Bowlingo, which is like bowling but not quite. You use a wooden ball 16 inches in diameter and without holes, and you stand in one place to roll it down the lane rather than taking gliding steps as you release it. The score is kept automatically by the alley computer. Dine on pizza, pasta, and salad in the Enchanted Theatre on-site restaurant; Toby the Birthday Dragon, Wally the Wizard, and their entourage of animated puppets will keep you company. If you're an uninhibited sort, grab the mike and belt out a song during free karaoke time some evenings.

Yorktown Center (all ages) 

Highland Avenue and Butterfield Road, Lombard; (630) 629-7330; www.yorktowncenter.com. Easily accessible off Interstate 88. Hours are 10 a.m. to 9 p.m. Monday through Saturday and 11 a.m. to 6 p.m. Sunday. Accessible for wheelchairs and strollers.

Yorktown is one of the more appealing shopping malls in the western suburbs. This brightly lit, two-level indoor mall has wide walkways and an open central area where youngsters can ride a three-car choo-choo around a circular track. The train ride is part of the enclosed Treehouse Adventure Play Area, which has a tall artificial tree and colorful plastic tot-size houses to play in. Admission is **free.** The anchor department stores are Carson Pirie Scott, JCPenney, and Von Maur. Stores of particular appeal to children include Kay-Bee Toys and the Disney Store. Gap Kids and Gymboree sell children's clothes. Older kids and teens should check out Dave and Jerry's for funky T-shirts. The Love from Chicago store features all sorts of Windy City souvenirs. The food court has a generous seating area surrounded by restaurants that offer Chinese, Japanese, Mexican, and Italian foods, plus baked potatoes, big soft pretzels, ice cream, crepes, and lusciously gooey cinnamon rolls. Oh, there's a McDonald's, too.

Moran Water Park (all ages) 

433 East St. Charles Road, Lombard; (630) 627-6127; www.lombardparks.com/moranwaterpark.htm. Open daily throughout summer. Hours are generally 11:30 a.m. to 8 p.m. Monday through Thursday, 11:30 a.m. to 7 p.m. Friday and Saturday, and 11:30 a.m. to 6 p.m. Sunday. Scheduled for renovation summer 2008. $$

This water park is a family-friendly facility. The separate children's area has two pools that are zero-depth for the entire circumference, connected by a rock waterfall structure between them. There's a sand play area for children, too. The larger pool has diving boards at the deeper end and a play area about 4 to 5 feet deep at the other end that appeals especially to older grade-schoolers. Teenagers flock to the sand volleyball court, and everybody likes the two 210-foot winding water slides. A concession area provides snacks and tables.

Where to Eat

Jonathan's, 667 West Roosevelt Road; (630) 627-3300. Hours are 11 a.m. to 10:30 p.m. Monday through Thursday, 11 a.m. to 11 p.m. Friday, 3:30 to 11:30 p.m. Saturday, and 11:30 a.m. to 9 p.m. Sunday. This local favorite serves delicious steaks, seafood, chicken, and pasta. The prime rib and the chicken marsala are particularly good. The children's menu costs about $4, including fries and beverage; kids can choose a burger, chicken nuggets, fried shrimp, fish sandwich, grilled cheese sandwich, or pasta of the day. $$

Old Country Buffet, 551 East Roosevelt Road; (630) 916-8809. Open from 11 a.m. to 8:30 p.m. Sunday through Thursday and 11 a.m. to 9:30 p.m. Friday and Saturday. See Restaurant Appendix for description. $

Where to Stay

Hampton Inn, 222 East 22nd Street; (630) 916-9000 or (800) 426-7866. This inn has 128 rooms. Rates include continental breakfast. No pool. $$$$

For More Information

Lombard Area Chamber of Commerce, 225 West St. Charles Road, Lombard 60148; (630) 627-5040; www.lombardchamber.com.

Villa Park

Safari Land (all ages) 

701 West North Avenue (Highway 64), Villa Park; (630) 530-4649; www.safari-land.com. Open noon to 10 p.m. Monday through Thursday, 11 a.m. to midnight Friday and Saturday, and 11 a.m. to 10:30 p.m. Sunday. Package deals can cut the per-item cost. $+

This jungle-themed indoor amusement center was designed to be a place where parents as well as their kids would have fun things to do, and it succeeds in striking that balance. From the minute you walk past the big, colorful giraffe and elephant statues guarding the front door, you can see that the place is geared for more than the Sponge Bob and Barney crowd. You could bring your teen as well as your toddler here. The carpeting practically glows with the bursts of hot pink, orange, neon green, purple, and blue splotched against a black background, and black lighting supplements regular fluorescent lighting to make the colors even more vivid. Safari Land boasts the largest indoor roller coaster in Illinois, the 22-foot-tall Tiger Terror, on which children shorter than 3 feet are not even allowed. There's also an adult-oriented go-kart track with faster cars and a longer route than the kid-scale version. Parents and older kids can enjoy the bumper cars and the Tilt-A-Whirl. The 12-lane bowling alley offers "Jungle Bowl" sessions. Like Cosmic Bowling, they feature black light illumination, fluorescent balls, and loud rock music. All that said, however, tiny tots are indeed welcome and abundant here as well. For them, the fenced-off Lion's Den is a multilevel playland of tubes, nets, and a ball pit, along with cute kiddie rides. Arcade games include one section geared toward children and another for teens and adults. To play these games, you insert a prepaid Adventure Card, which can be programmed to block access to the more "mature" or violent video games you wouldn't want to expose your youngsters to. The on-site concession area is more like a real restaurant, with appetizers, soups, salads, a nice variety of sandwiches, pizza, and dinner entrees, the latter of which are mostly under $6. You can even get beer or wine with your meal. Safari Land is a place for the whole family to play.

Where to Eat

Chuck E. Cheese's, 200 West Roosevelt Road; (630) 833-6212. Near Motel 6. Hours are 10 a.m. to 10 p.m. Sunday through Thursday and 10 a.m. to 11 p.m. Friday and Saturday. See Restaurant Appendix for description. $$

Portillo's, 635½ North Avenue; (630) 530-8440. Near Safari Land. Hours are 10:30 a.m. to 10 p.m. Monday through Saturday and 11 a.m. to 9 p.m. Sunday. See Restaurant Appendix for description. $

Fusion Fire, 123 East St. Charles Road; (630) 832-8900. Hours are 4 to 9:30 p.m. daily. The fusion here is between Brazilian and Italian cuisine, and the specialty here is meat, meat, meat—10 kinds, each seasoned, grilled on a skewer, and sliced tableside onto your plate by *churrascarias,* handsome waiters in long-sleeved shirts, gaucho pants, and boots. The lively atmosphere with all these cheerful guys scurrying around makes it very family-friendly. The all-you-can-eat adult price of $25, which also includes a huge salad and pasta buffet, is about half of what comparable places in the area charge. You also can buy a pasta dinner for under $10 and skip the meat, but unless you're a vegetarian, you'll be sorry. $$$$

Where to Stay

Motel 6, 10 West Roosevelt Road (just east of Highway 83); (630) 941-9100 or (800) 466-8356. This budget motel, renovated in 2004, has an outdoor swimming pool and allows pets. $$

For More Information

Village of Villa Park, 20 South Ardmore Avenue, Villa Park 60181; (630) 834-8500; www.invillapark.com.

Elmhurst

Population: 42,672. Elmhurst has a pleasant downtown with lots of attractive shops and restaurants, including a fudge shop and an ice-cream parlor on either side of the cool old movie theater. In the warmer months, the streets in the evening often are lined with "classic" cars, some of which don't look *that* old to parents who grew up in the 1970s or 1980s. The Metra station at the south end of the downtown allows you to easily hop a train for a half-hour ride into Chicago. York Road is the main north-south street.

York Theatre (age 3 and up) 

150 North York Road, Elmhurst; (630) 834-0675; www.classicccinemas.com. Call or go online to check for current films and times. Children age 5 or younger not admitted to R-rated films after 6 p.m. Restrooms have diaper-changing stations. When you buy your ticket, be sure to get a free Classic Cinemas Director's Club Free Movie Ticket card, a little paper card with seven squares that they fill with ink stamps for each ticket sold, and then your eighth ticket at any Classic Cinemas theater is free. $$

Built in 1924, back in the days of silent films, this movie theater has undergone much renovation since its 1982 acquisition by Classic Cinemas, the same local outfit that owns the Tivoli in Downers Grove and 10 other cinemas in the Chicago metro area. Classic used deep mustard-yellow paint and black wrought-iron lighting sconces to return the interior to its original warm "Spanish-style" decor. Upgrades and expansion continued over the next quarter century to bring it to its present-day total of nine screens plus a couple of party rooms. But the prices remain a bargain—about $2 per ticket lower than any other first-run theater around—and refills on all sizes of popcorn and soda are free. There's always at least one movie for children playing, and in the summer the chain also runs a weekly series of Wednesday morning kid flicks for $1 a ticket.

Lizzadro Museum of Lapidary Art (age 4 and up) 

220 Cottage Hill Avenue, Elmhurst; (630) 833-1616; www.lizzadromuseum.org. From downtown, go south on York Road a couple miles to St. Charles Road; turn right and head west a few blocks to Prospect Avenue; turn right and continue north another couple blocks to the entrance to Wilder Park on the west side at Cottage Hill Avenue; turn in and look for the blocky white building. Open from 10 a.m. to 5 p.m. Tuesday through Saturday and 1 to 5 p.m. Sunday; closed Monday. Free admission on Friday. $

Lapidary is the art of cutting and polishing colored stones, which includes both sparkly, multifaceted gemstones and such smooth, translucent stones as jade. It was green Chinese jade that first attracted the Italian-born Elmhurst resident Joseph Lizzadro to the art in the 1930s. He became both a carver and a collector, and he opened this museum in 1962 to display the pieces. Although he died 10 years later, his family has kept the museum going. The collection may appeal to kids with varying interests, for example, those who are into rocks, those who like three-dimensional art, and those who like animals, as many of the pieces are carved in animal shapes and displayed in cute little dioramas. This isn't hands-on stuff, though, so bring children who can be content just to look. The museum has a gift shop if you're looking for souvenirs.

Mayan Adventure Indoor Waterpark at Holiday Inn

(all ages)

624 North York Road, Elmhurst; (630) 279-1100 or (800) 972-2494; www.mayanindoor waterpark.com. Coming off I-290, turn left onto York Road, go north a block to the first stoplight at Industrial Road, and then make a U-turn back onto York Road heading south. At midblock, turn right at the hotel parking lot entrance—don't miss it or you'll end up turning right onto the westbound I-290 entrance ramp! This one access off southbound York Road is the only way to get in; York Road has a high median, so you can't make a direct left turn into the entrance. The water park is open from 9:00 a.m. to 10:00 p.m. daily. No pets allowed at the hotel or water park. $$$$

This is a great place for families from afar who want to spend a few days visiting the Chicago metro area. Located near O'Hare Airport just off I-290, this 4-story, 210-room hotel with attached indoor water park is also less than 5 miles from downtown Elmhurst—a straight shot down York Road—where you can park near the station, board a Metra train into Chicago, and not have to worry about the traffic or the expensive and scarce parking in the city. You can spend one day seeing the sights there but then stay put the next day and still have lots of fun playing at the water park. If you live in the area, this is an ideal spot for an overnight minivacation, especially in the dead of winter. The water park, the first of its kind in the Chicago metro area, is huge—at 24,000 square feet, it occupies the full 4 stories of space, with many of the hotel rooms overlooking it. The south and west walls are mostly glass, letting in a lot of natural light that makes it seem more like being outdoors in the tropics; the sky-blue ceiling and the potted palm trees enhance that effect. Anyone who is at least 3 feet, 6 inches tall may ride the two high, twisting, hot pink and sea green water slides that actually loop part of the way outdoors (though sealed against the elements) and wind back in for the splashdown. Active older kids are drawn to the water basketball hoops. Littler kids adore the zero-depth pool with multilevel, multicolored water play apparatus studded with spray jets everywhere. High above, a giant brown bucket decorated to look like a "Mayan" head carving slowly fills with water and then, as a warning beep sounds, overturns to douse anyone standing below. Those who want a more leisurely experience can grab a single or double inner tube and float around the circumference of the main section of the water park along the "Oogaboo River" (yeah, like that's a real Mayan name—not), but be aware that there are spray jets along the route. Lifeguards patrol the water park, but they're not baby-sitters; please remember that parents remain responsible for their children at all times. Along the north wall running parallel to the water park is an enclosed arcade full of brightly flashing electronic and skill games. The Island Breeze Bar and Grill at the east end of the water park provides burgers, hot dogs, pizza, salads, appetizers, and beverages at surprisingly reasonable prices, so you don't have to leave when you're hungry unless you want to. The Holiday Inn itself also has a hotel restaurant/bar off the lobby. The hotel's tan hallway walls and patterned carpets in Southwestern hues of clay, turquoise, and tan are designed to carry out the Mayan motif. Check-in time is 4:00 p.m., but the wristband you get with the water park package is good through 3:00 p.m. on the day you check out, several hours longer than the room checkout time. During the summer the hotel also offers a $20 day pass to anyone who wants to use the water park without staying at the hotel; call (630) 279-1100 for details.

Where to Eat

Walk around the heart of downtown Elmhurst and you'll find a dozen appealing places to eat. Here's one among the many.

Two Brothers from Italy Ristorante and Pizzeria, 128 West Park; (630) 833-0415. Across from the train station on the south side of the tracks. Opens at 4 p.m. Tuesday through Saturday and at 2 p.m. Sunday; closing time varies, but get there by 9 p.m. to be safe; closed Monday. The Battaglia family opened this restaurant in 1976, and it's still going strong 30+ years later. Choose which kind of pasta with which of about a dozen sauces you'd like; the menu also includes steak, chicken, seafood, and sandwiches. Children's menu for ages 12 or younger includes chicken, perch, or pasta, each no more than $5. $$

Where to Stay

Of course the Holiday Inn is the recommended place to stay. But if you can't leave Fido behind, here's a motel that allows pets.

Quality Inn, 933 South Riverside Drive; (630) 279-0700. This 2-story property has an indoor pool. Pets are allowed in smoking rooms only, for an extra $25 per pet per stay. $$$$

For More Information

Elmhurst Chamber of Commerce and Industry, 113 Adell Place, Elmhurst 60126; (630) 834-6060; www.elmhurstchamber.org.

Downers Grove

Population: 48,724. This town, which was settled in the 1800s, makes several historical claims: It was a stop on the route of the first railroad; it was a transfer point on the Underground Railroad; and in 1892 it was the site of the nation's first 18-hole golf course, 9 holes of which are still in use today. But for families, the most interesting spot of historical significance may well be the old-fashioned cinema downtown. In August the city is overrun with wheels for the annual International Criterium In-Line

Skating and Cycling Championships. Entertainment and family activities accompany the weekend event. A downtown redevelopment program in the late 1990s and early 2000s made the area even more appealing.

Tivoli Theatre (all ages) 

5021 Highland Avenue, Downers Grove; (630) 968-0219; www.classiccinemas.com. Call or check online for titles and show times; matinees on Saturday and Sunday; organist plays before shows Friday and Saturday nights. The theater is accessible for wheelchairs. No smoking. From the main stretch of Highland Avenue that slices through downtown, turn east at Warren Street near the railroad station and jog over 1 block. There's a very small parking lot next to the theater, and you can park on the street in the surrounding neighborhood. $

One look at this place and you'll think you've stepped through a time warp. The three-story brick building has rounded marble arches carved with leafy scrollwork, and the glowing marquee looks just as it did in 1928, when the Tivoli opened on Christmas Day. Four thousand people lined up to buy tickets for this 1,000-seat theater, reportedly the second cinema in the United States designed and built for "talking movies." Buy your tickets—priced at less than half the matinee rate of the local multiplexes—get your popcorn, and then walk across the burgundy-patterned carpeting through the lavishly appointed lobby, with its chandeliers, tall potted palms (fake but realistic looking), wing chairs, and golden-framed wall mirror through one of five entry doors to the cavernous auditorium. The interior walls and ceiling are painted in shades of sky blue and burgundy with gilded ornate trim. Lamps in wrought-iron sconces provide gentle lighting, and a red-lit dome draws your eyes upward in the center of the theater. There are 29 long, long rows of seats, and the floor slants downward so that the views are fairly unobstructed. A square clock with illuminated dial is placed over the exit sign on one side. Reasonably priced concessions are pretty basic—popcorn, sodas, and candy—and include free refills. The theater was renovated in 2002 and 2003 with comfier, high-backed seats (with cup holders), new carpet, and porcelain tile replacing the cracked terrazzo. None of these upgrades significantly altered the character of the theater, which is protected by its historic landmark status. In fact, in 2007, the Tivoli was named one of the "150 Illinois Great Places" by the American Institute of Architects, Illinois Council. The biggest improvement was to the restrooms. Formerly inaccessible for wheelchairs because you had to climb steps to get inside, they are now entered right off the lobby by a wide, gently sloping ramp. The new sinks and toilets operate by sensors, and both the women's and the men's rooms have pull-down diaper-changing tables.

Tivoli Lanes Bowl (age 4 and up) 

938 Warren Avenue, Downers Grove; (630) 969-0660; www.tivolibowl.com. Hours vary; call for open bowling hours and rates. The bowling alley is around the corner from the Tivoli Theatre, but its basement location down a narrow flight of stairs makes it inaccessible for wheelchairs. $

This cozy little alley has just 12 lanes, but automated scoring on video screens has brought the place into the modern era. The small snack bar has cold drinks and munchies.

Downers Grove Ice Arena (age 5 and up) 

5501 Walnut Avenue, Downers Grove; (630) 971-3780; www.downersgroveicearena.com. Open year-round; public skating hours vary. $

If you're looking for something different to do to escape summer heat, how about ice-skating? This indoor facility is open year-round, and while there may be a line out the door during winter, you and the kids may have the rink nearly to yourselves in summer. Just make sure you bring long pants, a sweatshirt, and maybe even gloves, because the temperature stays pretty cool to keep the ice frozen. Glide along to easy-listening music and imagine your favorite Olympic ice dancer.

Where to Eat

Downers Grove has tons of restaurants and fast-food franchises. Here are but a select few; for more, contact the Visitors Bureau (see For More Information) or check the local yellow pages.

Joe's Crab Shack, 1461 Butterfield Road; (630) 960-2033. Hours are 11 a.m. to 10 p.m. Sunday through Thursday and 11 a.m. to 11 p.m. Friday and Saturday. Opened in 1996, Joe is giving nearby Red Lobster a run for the money. This funky restaurant has a casual atmosphere. The young waitstaff wear bright tie-dyed T-shirts, and strings of multicolored lights brighten the kitschy interior. But the real draw for families is the outdoor porch area with its adjacent sand playground. Come in summer and sit out here, where Mom and Dad will have a chance to linger over coffee and adult conversation while the kids have a blast playing. The menu features crab, of course, and other standard seafood dishes plus chicken and steaks. Entrees on the kids' menu cost about $4, including a drink and a dish of ice cream, and feature both seafood and nonseafood items, such as tasty fried chicken "fingers." The breading for all the fried dishes is a bit on the spicy side, so you may need extra ice water. Adults may enjoy the wide selection of beers to accompany their meal. $$

Red Lobster, 3001 Finley Road, at Butterfield Road; (630) 515-0565. Open from 11 a.m. to 10 p.m. Sunday through Thursday and 11 a.m. to 11 p.m. Friday and Saturday. See Restaurant Appendix for description. $$

Olive Garden, 1211 Butterfield Road; (630) 852-4224. Hours are 11 a.m. to 10 p.m. Sunday through Thursday and 11 a.m. to 11 p.m. Friday and Saturday. See Restaurant Appendix for description. $

Portillo's, 1500 Butterfield Road; (630) 495-9033. Hours are 10:30 a.m. to 9:30

p.m. Sunday through Friday and 10:30 a.m. to 10:30 p.m. Saturday. See Restaurant Appendix for description. $

Where to Stay

Comfort Inn, 3010 Finley Road, off Butterfield Road; (630) 515-1500 or (800) 424-6423. This 3-story property has 120 rooms with cable TV. Amenities include an outdoor heated pool, an indoor whirlpool, and a sundeck. Restaurants nearby. Room rates include continental breakfast buffet. $$$

Doubletree Suites, 2111 Butterfield Road; (630) 971-2000. This is an all-suite hotel with 251 rooms. Amenities include indoor heated pool, whirlpool, sauna, and fitness center. The room rate includes full American breakfast. $$$$

Holiday Inn Express, 3031 Finley Road; (630) 810-0059 or (800) 465-4329. This 3-story property has 123 rooms with cable TV and free in-room movies. No pool. The room rate includes continental breakfast buffet. $$$

Red Roof Inn, 1113 Butterfield Road; (630) 963-4205 or (800) 843-7663. Rooms have cable TV and free in-room movies. No pool. Small pets allowed. Restaurants nearby. $$

For More Information

Downers Grove Area Chamber of Commerce and Industry, 1015 Curtis Street, Downers Grove 60515; (630) 968-4050; www.downersgrove.org.

Lisle

Population: 21,182. If you visit Lisle during late June and early July, look up—it's the **Eyes to the Skies** Festival of hot air balloons. The four-day event at Lisle Community Park features a balloon launch at about 5:30 each morning, with the rest of the festival events starting at noon. If you're not an early riser, you can catch a second launch at about 6:30 in the evening on three of the four days. Games and contests, arts and crafts, carnival rides, food booths, and musical performances are all part of the festival. Admission costs $10 a day for anyone age 13 or older and $2 a day for kids ages 5 through 12. Children age 4 or younger get in free. Parking is free, with free shuttle buses providing transportation from the more remote lots. Area businesses near the festival also offer parking—for a price, usually $4 to $6. For the current year's schedule of events, call (630) 575-9798 or check the Web site www.eyestotheskiesfestival.com.

Morton Arboretum (all ages)  

4100 Route 53, Lisle; (630) 968-0074 or (630) 719-2465; www.mortonarb.org. Off Highway 53 near I-88. Grounds are open year-round from 7 a.m. to 7 p.m. daily. Admission $, tram tickets $.

Here is a lovely place to commune with nature. It's been around since 1922, plenty of time for some of the trees to get nice and big. The trees and other woody plants—

more than 3,000 kinds in all—cover the 1,500-acre tract, and 25 miles of hiking trails wind throughout. Some specially maintained areas, such as a field of daffodils, will have you waxing poetic. The Children's Garden gives children a place to walk up a boardwalk that extends 20 feet up into a real tree. It also includes a pond and a model farm field. Not everything here is natural, however—the arboretum has a visitor center with restrooms, a restaurant, and a gift shop. During summer you can ride an open-air tram for a tour of the arboretum. Buy your tickets at the visitor center and pick up the tram in the main parking lot. It departs at 10:45 a.m., noon, and 1:15 and 2:30 p.m. daily. The ride takes 50 to 60 minutes and covers about 8 miles. In 2007, Morton Arboretum was named one of the "150 Illinois Great Places" by the American Institute of Architects, Illinois Council.

Lisle Station Museum (all ages) 

921 School Street, Lisle; (630) 968-0499; www.lisleparkdistrict.org/museum.htm. Two blocks south of Ogden Avenue and 2 blocks east of Main Street. Open from April through December. Hours are 1 to 4 p.m. Tuesday, Saturday, and Sunday or by appointment other times. Admission is free.

This 1874 train station was built in the Federal style of architecture. It was a working station for 104 years, but now it houses a museum with ticket office, waiting room, station master's living quarters, and exhibits on Lisle's history. Just west of the depot is the Netzley-Yender farmhouse, which has been restored to show what rural life in 1850 was like.

Sea Lion Aquatic Park (all ages) 

1825 Short Street, Lisle; (630) 964-3410; www.lisleparkdistrict.org/slp.htm. Open from noon to 5:30 p.m. and 6:30 to 9 p.m. Monday through Friday and noon to 5:30 p.m. and 6:30 to 9 p.m. Saturday and Sunday. $$

The Sea Lion Aquatic Park has four drop slides, which launch swimmers into the air before they splash into the water. The pool here has zero-depth entry, and there's a separate fenced-in, zero-depth tot pool with kiddie slide. The sand volleyball court and separate play pool appeal to teens, and an adult deck with hot tubs soothes weary parents. There is a concession area, too. The facility underwent renovation in 2004 that expanded some areas and upgraded others.

Lisle Lanes (age 4 and up) 

4920 Lincoln Avenue, Lisle; (630) 968-1300; www.bowlfoxvalley.com/Centers/lisle.htm. On Highway 53 just south of Ogden Avenue. Hours are 10 a.m. to 2 a.m. daily, but call ahead to check on availability of open bowling. $

Kids can enjoy bumper bowling (with long inner tubes placed in the gutter so that the ball stays in the lane) at Lisle Lanes. You should call ahead so they can get the bumpers set up for your arrival. The alley has 32 lanes. Concessions are available.

Where to Eat

Country House, 6460 College Road; (630) 983-0545. Open from 11 a.m. to 10 p.m. Monday through Thursday, 11 a.m. to 11 p.m. Friday and Saturday, and noon to 10 p.m. Sunday. Serving lunch and dinner. The adult menu features steaks, pork chops, burgers, barbecue beef sandwiches, soups, and salads. Children's menu entrees are in the $3 to $4 range and include burgers, chicken nuggets, spaghetti, and fish and chips. $

Where to Stay

Lisle isn't the place to look for a cheap motel. Its major hotels are at the deluxe end of the lodging spectrum, so give up and indulge yourselves if you want to stay overnight in this town.

Wyndham Lisle, 3000 Warrenville Road; (630) 505-1000. This luxury hotel has 242 rooms. The huge spa and fitness center includes an indoor pool, whirlpool, and racquetball court. The on-site restaurant is in a 7-story atrium. $$$$

For More Information

Lisle Convention and Visitors Bureau, 4746 Main Street, Lisle 60532; (800) 733-9811; www.stayinlisle.com.

Naperville

Population: 128,358. Naperville is a fairly convenient and hospitable place to stay overnight. It is easily accessible off I-88, which links up farther east with north-south thoroughfares such as I-355 and I-294, eventually merging into I-290, heading east into Chicago. On July 4, 2000, the city dedicated the Millennium Carillon at the base of Rotary Hill by the Riverwalk. The tower stands 155 feet high and houses 72 bells.

DuPage Children's Museum (age 10 and under) 

301 North Washington Street, Naperville; (630) 637-8000; www.dupagechildrens museum.org. Coming down Washington Street from the north, take an immediate right after passing under the railroad bridge. Regular hours are 9 a.m. to 5 p.m. Tuesday through Saturday (until 8 p.m. Thursday) and noon to 5 p.m. Sunday. Monday hours are restricted to members only, except for certain school holidays; call to check. The building is wheelchair accessible. $$

Although the DuPage Children's Museum was founded in 1987, its location changed several times before 2001, when it reopened in what is expected to be its permanent home. Brightly painted in red, yellow, and blue on the outside and boasting 20,000 square feet of exhibit space on the inside, this three-story building is a delight for families with young children.

Most of the hands-on exhibit areas are on the ground floor, which is divided into five main sections: Creativity Connections, Make It Move, Build It, AirWorks, and WaterWays. It's easy to pass from one section into the next—in fact, almost too easy.

You'll have to keep a watchful eye on wandering tots. The action also is monitored by museum workers called Play Facilitators, some of whom are paid staff, others volunteers. One of the most appealing attractions is a wall of sliding plastic pegs. Stand on one side of the wall and press your hand against the pegs, then walk around to the other side and see a raised handprint. It gets really wacky when there are half a dozen people standing on both sides, simultaneously pushing and watching as the pegs zip in and out. Another cool exhibit is like a giant Lite Brite board, with foot-long fluorescent pegs that glow under black light. The museum has giant Tinkertoys, too. Preschoolers have fun in a darkened circular room where they can chase colored lights dancing on the floor while a glitter ball above throws further splashes of color against the wall. The Build It section is like Grandpa's workshop, with hammers, saws, drills, and other tools with which to mangle chunks of wood. Young children especially enjoy making giant soap bubbles and playing in the WaterWays section, which features fountains, sprinklers, PVC faucets, and plastic toys, all pouring into a circular trough. The plastic aprons don't keep rambunctious youngsters from getting rather soaked, but they can dry off fast in the nearby wind tunnel. Also in the AirWorks section are tubes and PVC pipes through which kids can blow or shoot foam balls or gauzy squares of cloth. On the main floor, high ceilings lined with acoustic tiles help absorb some of the noise generated by the throngs of visitors (about 300,000 a year), and benches on the sidelines provide a welcome resting spot for accompanying parents and grandparents.

The upper and lower floors are quieter. The upper floor houses mostly program rooms (used by school groups and for birthday parties) and staff offices, but there are a few exhibits, such as a model train layout on a surrealistic landscape, real mice in cages, and a big-screen TV with closed-circuit camera facing the viewer—a great spot for budding ballerinas. The lower level has a wonderful play area for babies, where they can crawl around and find appealing things at their own eye level; as a parent, you have to practically lie on the floor to truly appreciate it. Also on the lower level are a snack room with vending machines and microwaves (for popcorn) and a private area set aside for nursing mothers. Restrooms on all three floors have wide doors and changing tables. The main floor also has one family restroom with adult and child-size toilets.

The museum gift shop is, unfortunately for parents, placed just inside the main entrance. Kids are liable to be distracted by the toys there before they even get into the museum itself. At least the stuff is of decent quality and reflects the themes of the exhibits. In the coat room, you can hang up your coat for free or pay 50 cents to store your gear in a small locker.

A Cool Pool

The Bolingbrook Recreation and Aquatic Complex actually has two pools to offer year-round swimming. The indoor pool has a zero-depth end with spraying fountains and a section of lap lanes. The larger outdoor pool has a zero-depth end, two twisting water slides (one for inner tubes), and a kids' Sprayground with waterfall. The center is at 200 South Lindsey Lane, near Naperville Road; (630) 739-1700; www.bolingbrookparks.org/facilities/brac/index/shtml. Hours are 8:30 a.m. to 10 p.m. Monday through Friday and 9 a.m. to 5 p.m. Saturday; closed Sunday. Concessions are available. $$

Naper Settlement Museum Village (all ages) 

523 South Webster Street, Naperville; (630) 420-6010; www.napersettlement.org. Museum village is open from April through October. Hours are 10 a.m. to 4 p.m. Tuesday through Saturday and 1 to 4 p.m. Sunday. $–$$

Enjoy a bit of living history at the Naper Settlement Museum Village. This 12-acre site contains 25 historic homes, businesses, and public buildings, all peopled by costumed interpreters portraying life during the period from 1831 to 1900. Children may be able to get a hands-on feel for the ways things used to be done by writing with a quill pen, churning butter, or carrying buckets of water with a yoke. Special events include Civil War Days in May and Christmas Memories in December.

Skating Away at Seven Bridges

The suburb of Woodridge has one of the largest ice-skating facilities in the United States, with three rinks: one Olympic, one collegiate, and one conforming to National Hockey League (NHL) standards. **Seven Bridges Ice Arena** prides itself on its computerized control system that keeps the air fresh (of course, smoking is not allowed) and the ice the right temperature for the best possible skating experience. To keep yourself in good shape off the ice as well, there's a fitness center staffed with professional trainers who can help you work out. There's also a glass-enclosed children's playroom. Open skating times vary. Skate rental costs $3 per person, all ages. Call (630) 271-4400 or check www.sevenbridgesicearena.com for the current open-ice times and fees. The arena is on Double Eagle Drive, north off Hobson Road west of Highway 53. $$

Brunswick Zone Entertainment Center (age 2 and up)

1515 West Aurora Avenue, Naperville; (630) 355-7622. Hours are 9 a.m. to midnight Sunday through Thursday and 9 a.m. to 2 a.m. Friday and Saturday. $+

Billed as the largest indoor amusement center in Illinois, this spacious complex features a full-size classic carousel and four other rides. Younger kids also can frolic in the Fun Playhouse, with its tubes, slides, and ball pits. There's an arcade with more than 200 video games, most just a quarter. The center has 40 lanes of bowling, and you can try the Cosmic Bowling here at selected times. That's when you bowl by black light and the balls and pins glow, while lively music and flashing lights jazz up the atmosphere.

All Seasons Ice Rinks (age 5 and up) 

31W330 North Aurora Road, Naperville; (630) 851-0755. Family skate is from 3:30 to 5 p.m. Sunday. Public skate sessions are from 11:30 a.m. to 12:30 p.m. Monday through Friday and 3:30 to 5 p.m. Saturday. $

This indoor facility is open year-round. Two ice-skating rinks offer public or family skating sessions every day. Even if it's a hot summer day, you'll want to bring along a sweatshirt to ward off the chill of the ice. Bring your own skates or rent some here.

Odyssey Fun World (all ages) 

3440 Odyssey Court (I-88 and U.S. Highway 59), Naperville; (630) 416-2222; www.odysseyfunworld.com. Driving directions posted on Web site. Hours are noon to 10 p.m. Sunday, 10 a.m. to 10 p.m. Monday through Thursday, and 10 a.m. to 11 p.m. Friday and Saturday, with the outdoor area opening an hour later than the indoor. Exploration Adventure admission costs $5 for kids age 1 through 12, with accompanying parent admitted free. Wristband deals offer various combinations of attractions that allow unlimited use for a fixed price. Coupons available online. $$–$$$

This facility, a newer cousin to the Odyssey Fun World in Tinley Park, offers both indoor and outdoor family recreation. The spacious indoor area includes an FX simulator, bumper cars, and two other rides for both children and adults, Dizzy Clown and Frog Hopper. It also features arcade games you can play to earn prize tickets for accumulation and redemption. Kids age 8 or older may opt to play laser tag. Younger kids will want to check out the Exploration Adventure, a four-level "soft playland" with equipment to climb on, jump in, go through, slide down—you name it. The children must wear socks to play here. The dining room features singing and dancing robotic characters and serves Connie's Pizza, a Chicagoland favorite. The outdoor recreation area has a paintball arena (for those age 10 or older), batting cages, and two go-kart tracks. For the latter, riders must be at least 4 feet tall and drivers at least 4 feet, 10 inches.

Where to Eat

Connie's Pizza, 1170 Iroquois Drive; (630) 357-8807. Hours are 11 a.m. to 9 p.m. Monday through Thursday, 11 a.m. to 11 p.m. Friday and Saturday, and noon to 9 p.m. Sunday. Some people swear that this chewy, cheesy pizza is the best in Chicagoland. If you didn't go to Odyssey Fun World, you can get some at this pizzeria. $

Lou Malnati's Pizzeria, 131 West Jefferson, downtown; (630) 717-0700. Hours are 11 a.m. to 11 p.m. Monday through Thursday, 11 a.m. to midnight Friday and Saturday, and noon to 10 p.m. Sunday. Another local favorite. $

Olive Garden, 620 Route 59; (630) 355-2818. Hours are 11 a.m. to 10 p.m. Sunday through Thursday and 11 a.m. to 11 p.m. Friday and Saturday. See Restaurant Appendix for description. $$

Where to Stay

Courtyard Chicago Naperville, 1155 East Diehl Road; (630) 505-0550 or (800) 321-2211. The 3-story inn has 147 spacious rooms with cable TV. Amenities include indoor swimming pool, whirlpool, and minigym with exercise equipment. This chain in the Marriott family actually is geared toward business travelers, but you often can get a good rate for a Friday or Saturday night when most of them have gone home for the weekend. $$$

Holiday Inn Select, 1801 Naper Boulevard; (630) 505-4900 or (800) 465-4329. This 7-story hotel has 426 rooms with coffeemaker, hair dryer, and iron and ironing board. Amenities include indoor swimming pool, fitness center, and game room. $$$

Sleep Inn, 1831 West Diehl Road; (630) 778-5900 or (800) 424-6423. This white, 3-story chain property has 69 comfortable rooms. TV has VCR. No swimming pool. Room rate includes continental breakfast. $$$

For More Information

Naperville Area Chamber of Commerce, 400 South Eagle Street, Naperville 60566; (630) 420-6111; www.naperville.il.us.

Naperville Convention and Visitors Bureau, 212 South Webster Avenue, Naperville 60566; (630) 305-7701 or (877) 236-2737; www.visitnaperville.com.

Across the DuPage County borderline in the west are the Cook County communities of Melrose Park and Brookfield, both of which have key family attractions—a longtime children's amusement park and the state's biggest zoo.

Melrose Park

Population: 23,171. Highway 64, also known as North Avenue, slices right through Melrose Park. The town's major family attraction is along this thoroughfare.

Megamovie Mania

In the late 1990s there was an explosion of megamovie complexes in the Chicago suburbs. These huge theaters encompass more than a dozen screens—over two dozen, in some cases—and feature a new concept in comfort: stadium seating. What that means is that the floor is stair-stepped so that each row of seats is several feet higher than the one in front of it, allowing clear sight lines looking down and across at the large screen. Cup holders in the armrests prevent spillage of soda pop kicked over on the floor. Some theaters also have love seats, which are sofalike seats wide enough for two people to sit together with no armrest between them. Less obvious at first glance are the technical improvements in the sound and projection systems, but you'll notice those once the film starts. Most chain theaters in the Chicago metro area are now hooked into a telephone system using the local area code and the number 444-FILM, or 444-3456. By punching in a code for the theater you want, you can hear a recorded listing of current show titles and times and can even buy the tickets over the phone with a credit card. Theater locations and show times also are published in area newspapers.

Kiddieland (ages 2 to 10) 

8400 West North Avenue, Melrose Park; (708) 343-8000; www.kiddieland.com. At the corner of North and First Avenues. Opens in mid-April and closes at the end of October. Peak summer hours are 11 a.m. to 9 p.m. Sunday through Thursday and 11 a.m. to 10 p.m. Friday and Saturday. Hours are more restricted earlier and later in the season; call ahead or go online to check for the day you want to visit. The Web site offers information on discount coupons available through certain companies and local businesses. Admission price includes free soda; serve yourself from a soda fountain. Stroller rental is available for $5. $$$

This old-fashioned amusement park has been around since 1929 and remains a favorite for many Chicago-area children. The park is situated at the corner of a busy intersection, and heavy traffic whizzes by beyond the gates, but no one notices that inside. The small scale makes Kiddieland especially inviting for little kids in the 3-to-6 age range, and most kiddie rides are reserved for children who are no taller than 4 feet, 6 inches. Aside from the choo-choo train, most of the kiddie rides are the vehicular kind that go round and round. The little boats even float atop a few inches of real water. There are rides with cars, helicopters, airplanes, and flying saucers.

The Mushroom is a tame, pint-size Scrambler, and the tiny Ferris wheel has six cages, so there's no chance of falling out. The Lava Run is a child-size go-kart track, and the Volcano play area next to it has a rope to climb and a slide to slip down. The roller coaster is the traditional variety—it runs on a double-rail track in a white wooden framework—just up and down, no loop-de-loops. The most charming of the children's rides, however, is the German carousel. Scenes from Grimm's fairy tales are painted along the top outer panels, and painted figurines of musicians stand in the center. Kids sit on motorcycles or in little cars, a bus, or a fire truck. One area of the park has rides for bigger people, such as a full-size carousel, a regular Ferris wheel, bumper cars, a Tilt-A-Whirl, a Scrambler, and a Galleon. An arcade features Skeeball, pinball, video games, and skill games. Another section has two water rides. The Log Jammer flume ride floats you gently along, but watch out when you come to the bridge. Someone standing on the bridge can put a token into a machine and trigger water jets that squirt the riders below. The Pipeline is billed as "a high speed water coaster full of quick turns and drops, in the dark," and that pretty well describes it. While it resembles the sort of twisting water slide you see at many suburban swimming pools, it is totally enclosed and indeed very dark. Pairs of riders zip through on a yellow inflated raft, sliding along a long, open flume at the end. You do get rather wet on this ride, so save it for last if you don't want to walk around the rest of the park soaked. The surface at Kiddieland is all asphalt, so rolling along in a stroller or wheelchair is easy. A centrally located brick building contains restrooms, a first-aid station, and concessions. Both the women's and men's restrooms have a diaper-changing table. Concessions include soft drinks and an assortment of snacks—the cotton candy is especially flavorful—plus hot dogs and pizza. Prices are better than at most amusement centers. Compared to Six Flags Great America or to carnivals where you pay by the ride, Kiddieland offers good value for the money. If you come around Halloween, you'll find a fairly mild haunted house and a place for hayrides in a horse-drawn wagon, plus seasonal food like brats, corn on the cob, and caramel apples.

Where to Eat

Chuck E. Cheese's, 1314 North Avenue; (708) 343-1224. Hours are 10 a.m. to 10 p.m. Sunday through Thursday and 10 a.m. to 11 p.m. Friday and Saturday. See Restaurant Appendix for description. $

Where to Stay

Days Inn, 1900 North Mannheim Road; (708) 681-3100 or (800) 325-2525. This 2-story, no-frills budget property has 120 rooms with cable TV but not much else; no swimming pool. Room rate includes continental breakfast. $$

For More Information

Melrose Park Chamber of Commerce, 1718 West Lake Street, Melrose Park 60160; (708) 338-1007; www.melroseparkchamber.org.

Brookfield

Brookfield Zoo (age 1 and up) 

First Avenue and 31st Street, Brookfield (accessible from Illinois Highway 39 [Roosevelt Road], Illinois Highway 43 [Harlem Avenue], US 45 [Mannheim Road], and Interstate 55 and I-290); (708) 688-8000; www.brookfieldzoo.org. Open year-round, 9:30 a.m. to 6 p.m. daily from Memorial Day weekend through Labor Day and 10 a.m. to 5 p.m. daily the rest of the year. Closing time is 7 p.m. Sunday from mid-June through July. Free on Tuesday and Thursday from October through February. Children age 2 or younger always free. Parking fee $8 per car. Basic admission $$, with additional charges for certain amenities. You can buy a slightly higher-priced $$$ ticket that includes 3 of the special attractions or opt for the $$$$ all-in-one ticket that covers all the extras except food and souvenirs.

Brookfield Zoo is the largest zoo in Illinois and a premier Chicago-area attraction where you can easily pass an entire day.

Wide, paved avenues throughout the zoo accommodate both foot and wheeled traffic. If your kids are small enough to fit in a stroller, bring it along—even peppy young grade-schoolers may wear out from the amount of walking needed to cover the expansive but beautiful grounds (flower beds and a central fountain are among the touches that add aesthetic appeal). You can rent a stroller, a little red wagon (holds two or three small children), or an adult pushchair. You can also relieve your feet by hopping aboard the Motor Safari open-air tram; a ride costs $3 for adults and $2 for kids and seniors.

The wee ones will want to visit the children's zoo, where they can mingle with the goats, pet an exotic animal held by a zoo handler, or watch a cow or goat being milked. Small mammals, birds, and farm animals are the dominant creatures here. Admission to the children's zoo costs $1.50 for adults and $1 for kids and seniors.

The Hamill Family Play Zoo is kind of like a children's museum with animals. Kids can do a variety of zoo-related crafts, and there are bunnies, guinea pigs, and other touchable critters to play with. Admission here costs $3.50 for adults and $2.50 for kids and seniors.

Another premium attraction is the entertaining dolphin show, which costs $3 for adults and $2.50 for kids and seniors. Hour-long shows are scheduled from late morning through midafternoon; check for exact times. Outdoor pools nearby contain seals, sea lions, and walruses.

A charming, old-fashioned wooden carousel opened at the zoo in 2006. It features 72 hand-carved and painted animals and a calliope in the middle. Rides cost $2.50.

Finally, you'd better budget a few extra dollars for the irresistible Mold-O-Rama figurines. The machines that press these animal figures out of hot plastic are located throughout the zoo (the dolphin one is by the Dolphin House, the koala by the Australia House, and so on) and cost $1 each. Let each child pick one favorite animal and mold it.

So what is included in the basic admission price? About 2,500 animals in settings designed to resemble their natural habitats. Outdoor exhibit areas for elephants, bears, apes, and big cats are family favorites. In the Fragile Desert building near the big cats, a glass exhibit wall extends all the way to the floor to afford a full view of the playful meerkats, chasing one another around or piling into a heap as if in a scrum. There are plenty of creepy-crawlies in the Reptile House, and you'll have a g'day waltzing through the Australia House. The Habitat Africa! area has a watering hole for giraffes, zebras, and antelope of the savanna. The huge Tropic World building contains three spacious rooms, each representing a tropical rain forest of South America, Asia, and Africa and containing native plants and animals. Spanish moss hangs from the ceiling in the building housing The Swamp, home of some river otters that are a favorite of families. The Living Coast has some really nifty things to see. The moon jellies are fascinating; these gelatinous white globules float suspended in water like blobs in a lava lamp. Humboldt penguins and brown pelicans play in their habitat area. And then there's "the wave." In Quest to Save the Earth, visitors walk along a life-size game board and have to choose between the easier "throwaway society" approach or the more responsible environmental awareness in actions that will preserve the planet for all its life-forms. The newest exhibit area, Salt Creek Wilderness, is a marshland environment.

Brookfield Zoo also has a free children's playground area with swings, slides, and climbing equipment in case your kids get tired of watching the animals have all the fun. There are picnic tables here, too, where you can eat your own home-packed lunch (a good way to economize). Restrooms are scattered throughout the zoo, so you shouldn't have to run too far if your toddler announces, "I have to go potty!"

Concession and souvenir stands are scattered throughout the zoo grounds. The former provide anything from an ice-cream treat to a complete meal, while the latter range from cheap kitsch to finely crafted artworks with animal motifs.

Where to Eat

Villa Maria Ristorante, 9237 West Ogden Avenue; (708) 485-6010. Open from 3 to 10 p.m. Monday through Friday and noon to 10 p.m. Saturday and Sunday. This family-friendly restaurant a few miles from the zoo serves steak, chicken, pasta, burgers, and other familiar favorites. $

Where to Stay

There are no chain motels in Brookfield, but you might want to give this local property a try.

Colony Motel, 9232 Ogden Avenue; (708) 485-0300; www.colonymotelbrookfield.com. A few miles from Brookfield Zoo and within walking distance of Villa Maria and other restaurants, this 2-story tan brick motel has 36 clean, very basic rooms. There are few amenities (no pool, no breakfast), but the prices are much better than anywhere else in the surrounding area, so it will do just fine if all you really need is a place to sleep after a full day at the zoo. $$

For More Information

Brookfield Chamber of Commerce, 3724 Grand Boulevard, Brookfield 60513; (708) 485-1434; www.brookfieldchamberofcommerce.org.

Southern communities in Will and suburban Cook Counties are represented by the ***Chicago Southland Convention & Visitors Bureau,*** *2304 173rd Street, Lansing 60438; (708) 895-8200 or (888) 895-8233; www.cscvb.com.*

Another source of regional information is the ***Heritage Corridor Visitors Bureau,*** *81 North Chicago Street, Joliet 60432; (800) 926-2262; www.heritagecorridorcvb.com.*

Alsip

Population: 19,725. I-294 runs through this southern suburb that borders the South Side of Chicago.

Fun Time Square (age 4 and up) 

11901 South Cicero Avenue, Alsip; (708) 388-3500. Opens in April and closes in September. Summer hours are 10 a.m. to midnight daily. $+

This outdoor facility has plenty of things to keep a family busy for a few hours. Play a round or two on the 18-hole miniature golf course, and then take a ride on the bumper cars, bumper boats, or go-karts, whee!

Where to Eat

Bakers Square, 4839 West 111th Street; (708) 636-0212. Hours are 7 a.m. to 11 p.m. Sunday through Thursday and 7 a.m. to midnight Friday and Saturday. See Restaurant Appendix for description. $

Where to Stay

Baymont Inn, 12801 South Cicero; (708) 597-3900. This hotel has 102 comfortable rooms but no swimming pool. Pets are allowed. Room rate includes breakfast. $$

For More Information

Alsip Chamber of Commerce, 12159 Pulaski Road, Alsip 60658; (708) 597-2668; www.alsipevents.com.

Bronzeville Children's Museum

This museum is dedicated to teaching kids in a fun way about the heritage and contributions of African Americans. Exhibits change periodically and include hands-on activities. The recent interactive two-part exhibit Food Becomes You and African-Americans in the Food Industry helped kids understand the connections among food, exercise, and health and showed the importance of African-American workers in the food industry. The Bronzeville Children's Museum is located in the lower level of the Evergreen Plaza shopping center at 96th Street and Western Avenue in Evergreen Park. Hours are 10 a.m. to 4 p.m. Tuesday through Saturday; closed Sunday and Monday. Tours are given at 10 and 11 a.m. and 1, 2, and 3 p.m. The museum is popular with school groups. For more information, call (708) 636-9504 or check the Web site www.bronzeville childrensmuseum.com.

Crestwood

Population: 11,251. This southern Cook County suburb lies to the southwest of Alsip. There are two popular family attractions here.

Hollywood Park (all ages) 

5051 Cal Sag Road, Crestwood; (708) 389-7275. At 131st Street, behind Target. Open year-round. Summer hours are 10 a.m. to midnight daily. During the school year the hours are 11:30 a.m. to 10 p.m. Monday through Thursday, 11:30 a.m. to midnight Friday, 10 a.m. to midnight Saturday, and 10 a.m. to 10 p.m. Sunday. $+

Indoor and outdoor recreational activities are available at Hollywood Park. Kids age 10 or younger enjoy Playland. This indoor playroom has tunnels, ball pits, and slides. Kids must wear socks, and the park will sell you some if they come without. Also indoors are bumper cars, a rock-climbing wall, a large game room, and the Hollywood Cafe & Pizzeria, where you'll find a robotic talking tree. Outdoors you can enjoy the giant slide or play miniature golf on one of two 18-hole courses. This place hosts a lot of birthday parties, so don't expect to have it all to yourself.

Windy City ThunderBolts (all ages) 

Games are played at Hawkinson Ford Field, 14100 South Kenton, Crestwood; (708) 489-2255; www.wcthunderbolts.com. Season runs from June through August. Most games are in the early evening. Regular box office hours are 9 a.m. to 5 p.m. Monday through Friday, with Saturday hours from 10 a.m. to 2 p.m. added during baseball season. $$

The Windy City ThunderBolts play minor-league baseball in the independent 12-team Frontier League, which includes several other Illinois ball clubs: the Rockford River-Hawks, the Gateway Grizzlies, and the Southern Illinois Miners. The ThunderBolts' home field is located in an industrial area, and tall electrical towers stand watch beyond the ballpark along the first and third baselines. The stadium is a utilitarian tan-and-clay brick building with dark green seats, and the outfield scoreboard offers simply a line score of the game. Hawkinson Ford Field does have one neat thing many small parks lack, however—an upper deck. Concessions are located at either end of the concourse, and there is a large area with long tables near the one on the first-base side. "Picnic parties" are offered that include unlimited soft drinks and beer for 90 minutes before the game. Unfortunately, this deal encourages some people to drink too much of the latter, making the overall atmosphere less family friendly than at some other minor-league ballparks around the state. The entertainment between innings is also weak compared to some other minor-league parks: witness the between-innings spectacle of two giant pairs of men's underpants racing on the field, propelled by scrambling groups of children holding them up.

Where to Eat

IHOP, Cal Sag Road and Cicero Avenue; (708) 824-1886. Open 24 hours a day. See Restaurant Appendix for description. $

Portillo's, Highway 83 and Cicero Avenue; (708) 385-6400. Hours are 10:30 a.m. to 10:30 p.m. Monday through Thursday, 10:30 a.m. to 11 p.m. Friday and Saturday, and 10:30 a.m. to 10 p.m. Sunday. See Restaurant Appendix for description. $

Where to Stay

Hampton Inn, 13330 South Cicero Avenue; (708) 597-3330 or (800) 426-7866. This 123-room property has a fitness center and an indoor pool. Free shuttle transportation to and from Midway Airport is available. Pets are allowed. Room rate includes continental breakfast. $$$$

For More Information

Village of Crestwood, 13840 Cicero Avenue, Crestwood 60445; (708) 371-4800; www.villageofcrestwood.com.

Tinley Park

Population: 48,401. Tinley Park is a southern suburb in Cook County, just north of the border with Will County. Highway 43 runs through the town, and U.S. Highways 6 and 45 skirt it to the north and west, respectively.

Odyssey Fun World (all ages) 

19111 Oak Park Avenue, at 191st Street (near I-80 and Harlem Avenue), Tinley Park; (708) 429-3800; www.odysseyfunworld.com. Driving directions posted on Web site. Hours are noon to 10 p.m. Sunday, 10 a.m. to 10 p.m. Monday through Thursday, and 10 a.m. to 11 p.m. Friday and Saturday, with the outdoor area opening an hour later than the indoor. Exploration Adventure admission costs $5 for kids age 1 through 12, with accompanying parent admitted free. Wristband deals offer various combinations of attractions that allow unlimited use for a fixed price. Coupons available online. $$–$$$

Odyssey Fun World offers both indoor and outdoor family recreation. The huge indoor area covers more than an acre, with a Ferris wheel, bumper cars, and the Himalaya roller coaster, plus arcade games you can play to earn prize tickets for accumulation and redemption. Kids age 8 or older may opt to play laser tag. Younger kids will want to check out the Exploration Adventure, a four-level "soft playland" with equipment to climb on, jump in, go through, slide down—you name it. The children must wear socks to play here. The dining room features singing and dancing robotic characters and serves Connie's Pizza, a Chicagoland favorite. The outdoor recreation area covers more than a dozen acres. Choose from among bumper boats, paddle boats, batting cages, and two 18-hole miniature golf courses, one of them ominously titled Whitewater Doom. Anyone age 10 or older can form or join a team to play paintball. There's a special Kids' Adventure Park section with rides for youngsters age 8 or younger.

Tinley Park Roller Rank (age 5 and up) 

17658 Oak Park Avenue, Tinley Park; (708) 532-4021. Call for current schedule and prices. $–$$

Another place for family fun in this suburb is the Tinley Park Roller Rink. You can bring your own skates or Rollerblades or rent them there.

Centennial Lanes (age 4 and up) 

16050 Centennial Circle, at 159th Street and South Harlem Avenue, Tinley Park; (708) 633-0500; www.centenniallanes.com. Call or go online to check open bowling times and rates. $+

This bowling alley has 32 lanes, all with automatic scorekeeping. You can get the soft bumpers to fill the gutters so that littler kids (and parents) won't throw any gutter balls. There is a concession area for drinks and snacks to keep you going.

Where to Eat

Old Country Buffet, 16060 South Harlem Avenue, in the Park Center Plaza; (708) 614-0202. Regular hours are 11 a.m. to 8:30 p.m. Monday through Thursday, 11 a.m. to 9 p.m. Friday, 8 a.m. to 9 p.m. Saturday, and 8 a.m. to 8:30 p.m. Sunday. See description in Restaurant Appendix. $

Where to Stay

Sleep Inn, 18420 Spring Creek Drive; (708) 342-1700 or (800) 424-6423. This 4-story redbrick hotel is about 4 miles from Odyssey Fun World. No pool. The room rate includes continental breakfast. $$$$

For More Information

Tinley Park Chamber of Commerce, 17316 South Oak Park Avenue, Tinley Park 60477; (708) 532-5700; www.tinleychamber.org.

Lansing

Population: 28,332. This southern suburb lies in Cook County at the Indiana border. Interstate 80/94 slices through the northern part of town, and US 6/Highway 83 runs along its western edge.

Wrights Barnyard (age 4 and up) 

2635 Bernice Road, Lansing; (708) 474-8989. Hours are 10 a.m. to midnight daily. $+

This indoor-outdoor recreation facility is a sister to Hollywood Park in Crestwood. Like that one, it has a Playland for kids age 10 or younger. This one also has more than 100 arcade games and a 1950s-style restaurant indoors. Outdoors you'll find two 18-hole miniature golf courses, go-karts, and batting cages.

Where to Eat

IHOP, 16851 Torrence Avenue; (708) 474-2240. Across from Home Depot, north of I-80. Open from 6 a.m. to midnight daily. See Restaurant Appendix for description. $

Where to Stay

Comfort Suites, 2235 West 173rd Street; (708) 418-3337 or (800) 424-6423. This 3-story motel has 65 suites with coffeemaker, microwave, and refrigerator. Amenities include an indoor pool and whirlpool. Room rate includes continental breakfast. $$$

Super 8, 2151 Bernice Road; (708) 418-8884 or (800) 800-8000. This budget chain motel has 50 rooms with cable TV. No pool. Continental breakfast is included in the room rate. $$

For More Information

Lansing Chamber of Commerce, 3404 Lake Street, Lansing 60438; (708) 474-4170.

Joliet

Population: 76,836. Joliet is the largest community in Will County. I-80 skirts the southern edge of town, and numerous other roadways crisscross through, among them U.S. Highways 6, 30, and 52 and Illinois Highways 7, 53, and 171.

Joliet Jackhammers (age 4 and up) 

Silver Cross Field, 111 East Jefferson Street, Joliet; (815) 726-2255; www.jackhammer baseball.com. From Highway 53, turn east onto Washington Street, which curves northeast, and then turn east onto Jefferson Street. Season runs from late May through early September. Ballpark is accessible for strollers and wheelchairs. $$

The Joliet Jackhammers, a minor-league baseball team affiliated with the Northern League, debuted in 2002. They play in the newly constructed Silver Cross Field, a 6,675-seat ballpark of traditional brick and wrought iron, much like the Schaumburg Flyers' Alexian Field (it was designed by the same people). The field is nestled in downtown Joliet, near the castlelike Joliet High School and about a block from Union Station. You might consider taking the train, because there is very little parking around the ballpark. An elevator from the ground floor to the concourse is available for those who have difficulty climbing stairs. Inside, the ballpark has wide walkways, adequate restrooms including a "family" one, and moderately priced concessions featuring such usual fare as hot dogs, burgers, popcorn, ice cream, sodas, and beer. A multicolored playground off the left-field side appeals to little kids with energy to spare. There are picnic tables in the outfield area. An upper level of air-conditioned skyboxes rises above the main concourse. An electronic scoreboard with video display screen in center field helps fans follow the action. The Jackhammers mascot, Jammer, is a big blue thing that somewhat resembles the Philly Phanatic. Jammer circulates around the stadium and at one point does a wheelbarrow race with a kid on the field. Another amusing between-inning entertainment is the "hamster ball" race with two human contestants rolling along inside giant Plexiglas balls along the baselines.

Haunted Trails Family Amusement Park (all ages) 

1423 North Broadway Street, Joliet; (815) 722-7800. Open year-round, but outdoor attractions are closed during winter and inclement weather. Hours are 10 a.m. to 11 p.m. Sunday through Thursday and 10 a.m. to midnight Friday and Saturday. $+

Haunted Trails Family Amusement Park provides active family recreation. Visitors of all ages can play miniature golf on an 18-hole course and enjoy the Monster Himalaya ride. Older and bigger kids can ride the go-karts. Little Leaguers can get some extra practice in the batting cages. Video and skill games in the arcade take 25-cent tokens and dispense reward tickets that can be collected and later redeemed for prizes. There is a restaurant on the premises, serving meals and snacks.

Pilcher Park Nature Center (all ages) 

2501 Highland Park Drive, Joliet; (815) 741-7277; www.jolietpark.org/facilities/pilcher park.shtml. Open year-round. Hours are 9 a.m. to 4:30 p.m. daily from June through August and 9 a.m. to 3 p.m. daily from September through May. Admission is free. The building is accessible for wheelchairs and strollers.

This indoor-outdoor facility allows visitors to connect with nature. The building has observation windows that will please bird-watchers, and there are large aquariums and indoor turtle ponds that will delight toddlers. Display rooms feature hands-on exhibits. Outdoors the grounds have picnic areas, playgrounds, and hiking trails.

Where to Eat

Chuck E. Cheese's, 1965 West Jefferson Street; (815) 725-2044. Hours are 10 a.m. to 10 p.m. Sunday through Thursday and 10 a.m. to 11 p.m. Friday and Saturday. See Restaurant Appendix for description. $

Old Country Buffet, 2811 Plainfield Road; (815) 254-0045. Hours are 11 a.m. to 8:30 p.m. Monday through Friday and 8 a.m. to 8:30 p.m. Saturday and Sunday. See Restaurant Appendix for description. $

Where to Stay

Comfort Inn North, 3235 Norman Avenue (off Interstate 57 at exit 257); (815) 436-5141 or (800) 424-6423. This 2-story chain property has 48 rooms, 16 suites, and an indoor pool. Continental breakfast is included in the room rate. $$$

For More Information

Heritage Corridor Convention and Visitors Bureau, 81 North Chicago Street, Joliet 60432; (815) 727-2323 or (800) 926-2262; www.heritagecorridor cvb.com.

The far-southern part of Chicagoland is Kankakee County. For general information about the area, contact the **Kankakee County Convention & Visitors Bureau,** One Dearborn Square, Suite 521, Kankakee 60901; (800) 747-4837; www.visitkankakee county.com.

Bourbonnais

Population: 15,256. This town just north of the Kankakee River is easily accessible off I-57, US 45, or Illinois Highway 102. Here you'll find some pleasant family activities.

Kankakee River State Park (all ages) 

Highway 102 and DeSelm Road, P.O. Box 37, Bourbonnais 60914; (815) 933-1383. Hours are 6 a.m. to 10 p.m. daily, year-round. Admission is free. No alcoholic beverages allowed.

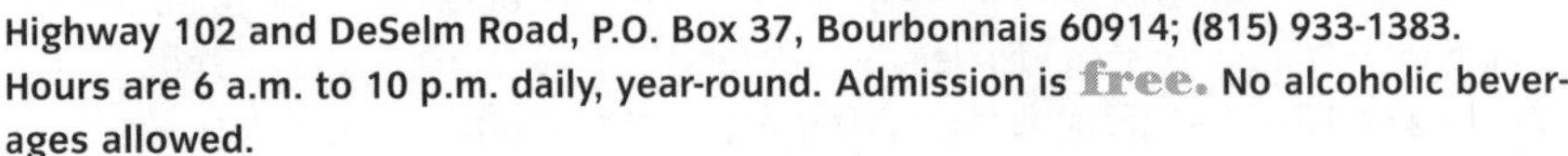

This is a lovely park with big, shady trees. Picnic tables, some with shelters, and playground equipment are scattered throughout. The smooth black asphalt bike trail is inviting; bring your own bicycles or rent them at the park. You can also rent a canoe if you want to try paddling along Rock Creek. A bridge over the creek affords a scenic view of the shallow water below, with anglers fishing from the banks. The park also has a designated Handicap Fishing Pier, a wooden platform slightly overhanging the water that could be used by someone in a wheelchair. (There's no place for swimming here, however.) For comfort and convenience, there's a spot with restrooms, a pay phone, and a soda machine. Outhouses are placed in other locations for those whose needs are too urgent to wait for a trek to the restroom that has plumbing. You can get burgers, pop, ice cream, and candy at a small concession building adjacent to the one for bike and canoe rentals.

Kankakee River State Park Riding Stables (age 6 and up) 

In Kankakee River State Park, off DeSelm Road, Bourbonnais; (815) 939-0309. Open year-round, weather permitting; horses will not be taken out in extreme heat or cold or if it's raining. Hours are 10 a.m. to 5 p.m. Tuesday through Sunday; closed Monday. Anyone age 6 or older and 43 inches (3 feet, 7 inches) tall or taller is allowed to ride the horses on the guided trail rides. A child age 3 through 6 may ride a gentle horse around the arena next to the stable, but a parent—not a stable employee—must walk along and lead the pony. This facility is not well equipped to serve persons with disabilities. Reservations required. $$$

Here is a good place to introduce your grade-schooler to the pleasures of horseback riding. Headed by a feisty mother hen named Mary, the friendly and knowledgeable staff at this stable will help novices learn how to mount one of the gentle horses for a short ride through the woods. Mary and her staff try to match riders' size and ability to the temperament of the horses, so trust them and take whichever one you're given. Each outing is led by a guide on horseback, and you'll be glad for that as you wind through dense forest along unmarked dirt trails. Although the foliage is trimmed back regularly, you'll avoid poison ivy and scratches and generally be more comfortable if you wear long pants. The horses are familiar with the trails and don't need much reining in, so even a first-time rider is likely to settle in and enjoy the slow-paced ride. In summertime the sound of insects and birds will lull you along. Or try an outing in fall

I Canoe—**Can You?**

Sure you can! In the Bourbonnais-Bradley area, you can go paddling down the Kankakee River, courtesy of **Reed's Canoe Trips** at 907 North Indiana Avenue (Illinois Highway 50) in Kankakee; (815) 932-2663; www.reedscanoetrips.com. Look for the corrugated metal building off Highway 50; there will probably be several of the company's yellow trucks in the big parking lot. This outfit will take you to the river and pick you up at the end of your journey. Six different trips are offered, ranging from a couple of hours to a couple of days. The shortest one, about two to three hours, covers 6 miles and costs $52 for two adults, with an additional cost per person of $10 for anyone age 13 or older. Children age 3 through 12 ride free. Tots age 2 or younger are not allowed in the boat. A $10 deposit is required. Each canoe seats a maximum of two adults and two small kids. Such tours depart at 10:30 and 11:30 a.m. and 12:30 and 1:30 p.m. daily in season. Reservations are not required but are a good idea, especially on Saturday. Reed's is open from 8 a.m. to 5 p.m. daily from mid-April through mid-October.

One final note about safety: If you want to try one of these trips, make sure that you and the kids are *good* swimmers (capable at least of doing several pool laps of the crawl stroke in water over your head) before you attempt it. You'll have life jackets on, of course, but you shouldn't depend on those alone to save you if you tip over. River currents can be tricky, and you don't want anyone to panic. The more confident you are in the water, the more relaxed you'll be, and the more fun you'll have. Also be sure to wear comfortable clothing and rubber-soled shoes.

when the trees are a palette of yellows, reds, and browns, or perhaps a winter trek through a quiet blanket of snow. There are just two caveats. First, be aware that the horses *walk* the trail—this is not the place for people with visions of some wild gallop like one they've seen in a movie, nor is it the place for skilled equestrians to show off their English riding skills; it's just a simple horsey ride. Second, the stable area has very little in the way of amenities: picnic tables, an outhouse, and a can of pop you can buy at the office. Go to the main area of the park if you want more.

Exploration Station . . . A Children's Museum (ages 2 to 10) 

1095 West Perry Drive, in Perry Farm Park, Bourbonnais; (815) 933-9905; www.btpd.org/exploration_station.htm. Summer hours are 10 a.m. to 5 p.m. Monday through Saturday and 1 to 5 p.m. Sunday. During the school year the museum is closed Monday. No smoking. Ramps and wide doors help make the facility easily accessible for strollers and wheelchairs. $

This is one of the most visually appealing children's museums in the state. Its vivid colors and varied shapes start on the outside—a yellow converted grain silo in front of an angular barnlike building painted with bright red and white stripes and slate-blue accents—and continue throughout the interior rooms. The masterpiece of the museum is a multilevel medieval castle with towers, a dungeon, and a fabric drawbridge that can be raised (rolled up, actually) using a hand-operated chain pulley. There are dress-up clothes inside that enable kids to become kings, queens, princesses, and knights. Nearby are some fun-house-style mirrors that will evoke a few giggles. Another large display is a wooden ship with red trim. Some kids could spend half an hour or more in the little post office, whipping dummy letters and postcards through a hand-cranked canceling machine and then sticking them into the space of their choice in a wall full of mail slots. An airplane display features a "cockpit" with computer simulator and real airline seats for "passengers," who can watch a video of a flight on a TV monitor. The medical room has a real ambulance that kids can sit inside and play in, plus real equipment such as crutches, an intravenous fluid bag, a gurney, and a light board with X ray. A computer here is equipped with role-playing software that enables a would-be doctor to diagnose a patient. The Wet Room is filled with water and PVC pipes to play with and lives up to its name—bring an extra set of clothes if you want to let your kids go in there. Glass display cases show off collections of fossils, model airplanes, and dolls dressed in foreign costumes. Near the entryway is the Make It and Take It room, the name of which pretty much says it all. A low, round table is stocked with markers, glue, scissors, and bits of paper, yarn, cloth, and Styrofoam for kids to create their own souvenir. There is also a small gift shop off to one side with toys, books, and costumes that tie in with the exhibits. The restrooms here are exceptionally well equipped for families. Not only is there a changing table for babies, but there are also tiny toilets and a low sink and paper-towel dispenser that preschoolers can reach. A box of tissues on the counter also is much appreciated. Most families can spend at least an hour here, some perhaps a whole afternoon.

Where to Eat

Aurelio's Pizza, 12 Heritage Plaza, just off US 45 on John Casey Road; (815) 935-1212. Hours are 11 a.m. to 9 p.m. Sunday through Thursday and 11 a.m. to 11 p.m. Friday and Saturday. This place claims the distinction of being voted "#1 pizza in the Chicago Southland five years in a row!!" You be the judge. $

Bakers Square, 1315 Armour Road; (815) 933-2042. Open from 6 a.m. to 11 p.m. Sunday through Thursday and 6 a.m. to midnight Friday and Saturday. See Restaurant Appendix for description. $

Where to Stay

Motel 6, 1311 Illinois Highway 50 North; (815) 933-2300. This basic motel has 96 rooms and outdoor pool. Small pets allowed. $$

Fairfield Inn, 1550 Highway 50 North; (815) 935-1334. This 3-story inn has 49 rooms, 8 suites, and indoor pool. Room rates include continental breakfast. $$$

Hampton Inn, 60 Ken Hayes Drive; (815) 932-8369. This motel has 59 rooms and indoor pool. Room rates include continental breakfast. $$$

Holiday Inn Express and Suites, 62 Ken Hayes Drive; (815) 932-4411 or (800) 465-4329. This 3-story property has 74 rooms and 18 suites. Rooms have coffeemaker and iron and ironing board. Suites also have microwave and refrigerator, and there is a door separating the living room and bedroom areas—a real plus for families with young children. Rates for both include continental breakfast. Amenities include indoor pool, whirlpool, and fitness center. $$$ (room), $$$$ (suite)

For More Information

Bourbonnais-Bradley Regional Chamber of Commerce, 1690 Newtowne Drive, Bourbonnais 60915; (815) 932-2222.

Bradley

Population: 12,784. This town is a next-door neighbor to the south of Bourbonnais. It has a couple of commercial attractions of interest to families.

Northfield Square Mall (all ages) 

Ken Hayes Drive (Highway 50, off I-57 at exit 315), Bradley; (815) 937-4111. Hours are 10 a.m. to 9 p.m. Monday through Saturday and 11 a.m. to 6 p.m. Sunday.

This indoor shopping mall has about 75 stores, anchored by JCPenney, Carson Pirie Scott, and Sears department stores. It also features a food court and a 10-screen movie theater.

Hidden Cove Family Fun Park (age 3 and up) 

70 Ken Hayes Drive (Highway 50), behind JCPenney store of Northfield Square Mall, Bradley; (815) 933-9150; www.thehiddencove.com. General park hours during the summer are 4 to 8 p.m. Monday through Thursday, 4 to 10 p.m. Friday, 11 a.m. to 10 p.m. Saturday, and 1 to 8 p.m. Sunday. Open only Friday through Sunday during the school year. For activities, pay at the register; the receipt becomes your ticket. Parts of the facility are not easily accessible for strollers and wheelchairs. $+

Other Things to See and Do

JANUARY

Ice Sculpture Festival, Downers Grove; (800) 934-0615

Winterfest, Itasca; (630) 773-5572

FEBRUARY

Ice Carnival, Bensenville; (630) 594-1190

MARCH

Kankakee Model Railroad Club Show; (815) 929-9320

APRIL

Youth Art Exhibit, Kankakee; (815) 939-4506

MAY

Rose Festival, Roselle; (630) 980-2000

JUNE

Elmfest, Elmhurst; (630) 834-6060

Kankakee Valley Strawberry Festival, Kankakee; (800) 747-4837

Highland Games and Scottish Festival, Oak Brook; (708) 447-5092

Oswego Prairiefest; (630) 554-1010

JULY

Wauconda Championship Rodeo; (847) 526-5580

Joliet Waterway Daze; (815) 740-2216

West Chicago Railroad Days; (630) 293-2200

Summerfest, Glendale Heights; (630) 260-6000

Most communities have a Fourth of July celebration, and many county fairs are in July and August.

AUGUST

Bartlett Summerfest; (630) 830-0324

Grayslake Summer Days Festival; (847) 223-6888

Momence Gladiolus Festival; (815) 472-6730 or (800) 747-4837

Westmont Summerfest; (630) 963-5252

SEPTEMBER

Arts and Crafts Faire, Antioch; (847) 395-2233

Carol Stream Multicultural Festival; (630) 871-6250

Harvest Fest, Hanover Park; (630) 372-4200

Winfield Good Old Days; (630) 682-3712

OCTOBER

Night at the Firehouse, Downers Grove; (630) 434-5896

Boo! at the Zoo, Brookfield; (708) 485-0263

Will County Pioneer Crafts Festival, Lockport; (815) 838-5080

NOVEMBER

Turkey Trot, Palos Park; (708) 361-1535

Countryside Christmas, Long Grove; (847) 634-0888

DECEMBER

Gallery of Trees, Kankakee; (800) 747-4837

Polar Express Santa Train, Lisle; (630) 769-1000

This indoor-outdoor family amusement center has a variety of activities for family fun. Indoors you'll find an arcade on the upper floor with games for younger children such as Bozo Buckets and Hungry Hungry Hippos, plus a giant Fun Jungle of tubes, nets, slides, and a plastic ball pit. Downstairs are video games for adolescents, pool tables, and air hockey. The major attraction down here, however, is a huge sky-blue roller rink. Colored lights and glitter balls hang from the high ceiling and swing into action during a skating session. Observation windows upstairs allow parents to watch older kids down on the rink while the littler ones play upstairs. Next to the roller rink is a small room with a half-dozen bumper cars. Both indoor levels have concession areas with tables where you can enjoy pizza or munchie snacks and sodas. The indoor area is open year-round. The outdoor area, which is open all summer and at other times as weather permits, has seven activities: an elliptical go-kart track, batting cages (baseball and softball at varying speeds), a golf driving range, two 18-hole miniature golf courses, a climbing wall, a bungee-cord apparatus, and paddleboats (moored in a little lagoon off the six-acre artificial lake). The centerpiece of the miniature golf is a wooden twin-masted pirate ship. The two courses wind through landscaped grounds dotted with flowers, fountains, rocks, and evergreens. One course is designed for amateurs, the other for players with more experience.

Where to Eat

Old Country Buffet, 1690 North Illinois Highway 50; (815) 932-9777. Open from 11 a.m. to 8:30 p.m. Monday through Thursday, 11 a.m. to 9 p.m. Friday, 8 a.m. to 9 p.m. Saturday, and 8 a.m. to 8:30 p.m. Sunday. See Restaurant Appendix for description. $

Where to Stay

Quality Inn, 800 North Kinzie Avenue; (815) 939-3501. This 160-room property has an indoor pool and hot tub, plus game room, laundry facility, and on-site restaurant. Continental breakfast is included in the room rate. Parking for trucks and RVs is available. $$

For More Information

See listing for Bourbonnais.

Northern Illinois

Perhaps the most varied of the state's six regions, 14-county Northern Illinois stretches across the top, from the fringe of the Chicago suburbs westward to the Mississippi River boundary with Iowa. In between you'll find state parks, historic towns, and—surrounded by an ocean of farmland—the largest city in Illinois beyond Chicagoland: Rockford.

Our exploration will follow a path from east to west, using a number of major arteries: (1) U.S. Highway 14, (2) Interstate 90 and U.S. Highway 20, (3) Illinois Highway 64, (4) Interstate 88, and (5) Interstate 80.

Crystal Lake

Population: 38,000. US 14 cuts straight through this rapidly growing town. At press time, a developer was putting together a proposal to build a $26 million sports complex on the McHenry County College campus in Crystal Lake that would serve as home field for a baseball team in the independent Frontier League. The hope was that the facility would be ready in time for the 2009 season.

Xtreme Wheels (age 5 and up) 

691 Virginia Road, Crystal Lake; (815) 356-8705. Call for current schedule of public skating sessions, generally offered during the early evening several times a week and in the afternoon on weekends. Admission prices depend on session time and length. You may bring your own skates or rent them here. $–$$

This rink opened in a brand-new building in the late 1990s. It has a large, natural maple wood floor and cheery decor in yellow, green, and white. Matinee sessions feature top pop tunes and include special skates in the dark with flashing multicolored lights. Arcade games and concessions are available.

NORTHERN ILLINOIS

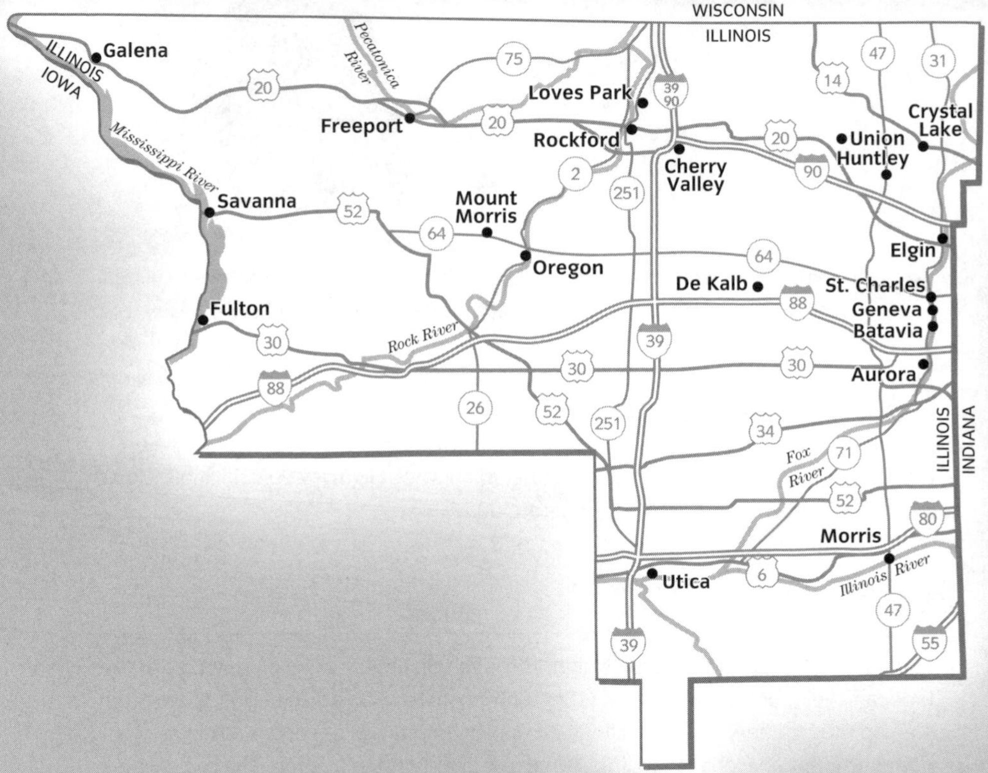

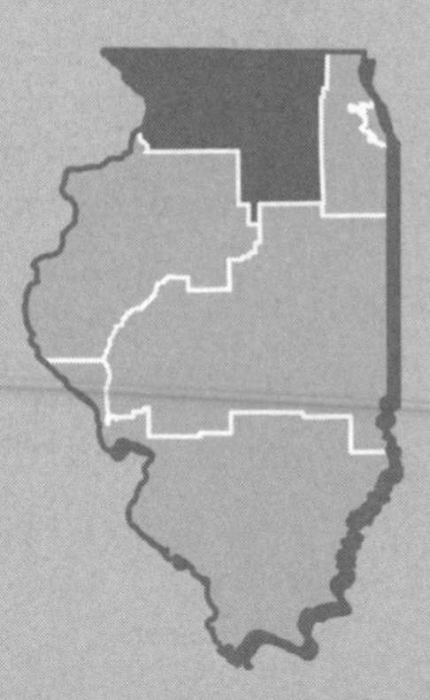

Art Works (age 3 and up) 

130 Washington Street, Ingleside (north of Crystal Lake; off U.S. Highway 14, take the Illinois Highway 59 exit and then at the second traffic light, turn right onto Washington Street); (847) 587-7882. Hours are 10 a.m. to 6 p.m. Tuesday through Saturday; closed Sunday and Monday. Scheduled to move in spring 2008; call to confirm location. $

At this hands-on children's museum, kids of all ages can create a variety of arts and crafts, play with puppets, or dress up in costumes.

Where to Eat

Bakers Square, 5689 Northwest Highway (US 14); (815) 477-9480. Open from 7 a.m. to 11 p.m. Sunday through Thursday and 7 a.m. to midnight Friday and Saturday. See Restaurant Appendix for description. $

Old Country Buffet, 6322 Northwest Highway (US 14); (815) 356-0355. Hours are 10:30 a.m. to 8:30 p.m. Monday through Thursday, 10:30 a.m. to 9 p.m. Friday, 8 a.m. to 9 p.m. Saturday, and 8 a.m. to 8:30 p.m. Sunday. See Restaurant Appendix for description. $

IHOP, 6606 Northwest Highway (US 14); (815) 356-3965. Open from 6 a.m. to 10 p.m. Sunday through Thursday and 6 a.m. to 11 p.m. Friday and Saturday. See Restaurant Appendix for description. $

Where to Stay

Holiday Inn Crystal Lake, 800 South Route 31 (Illinois Highway 31 at US 14); (815) 477-7000 or (800) 465-4329. This 6-story, 196-room property has an indoor swimming pool, whirlpool, and fitness center. There is a restaurant on the premises. $$$$

Super 8, 577 Crystal Point Drive (off US 14 about 1 mile west of Highway 31); (815) 788-8888 or (800) 800-8000. This budget motel has 59 rooms with cable TV. Pets are allowed for a $5 fee. No pool. $$$

For More Information

Greater Crystal Lake Area Chamber of Commerce, 427 Virginia Street, Crystal Lake 60014; (815) 459-1300; www.clchamber.com.

Now let's return to the eastern edge of Northern Illinois and head west along I-90 and US 20. These two thoroughfares run sort of parallel, although US 20 starts out south of I-90 but then intersects it and continues north of it along a similar northwesterly course into Rockford. At Rockford, I-90 veers straight north toward Wisconsin, and we'll continue west on US 20 alone to the Illinois border at Galena. Our first stop on this route is Elgin, north off I-90 at Illinois Highway 25.

Elgin

Population: 94,487. Accessible off I-90 or US 20 is Elgin. This community has a lot of downtown redevelopment projects going on, so the city continues to improve as an

Illinois tourism destination. Elgin also has numerous festivals throughout the year. **The Fox River Trail** follows Riverside Drive through the downtown district. Elgin is about the halfway point for this bike trail, which runs north to south for 35 miles from Crystal Lake to Aurora.

Lords Park Zoo (all ages) 

In Lords Park, east off Highway 25, Elgin; (847) 931-6120. Open from 10 a.m. to 5 p.m. daily during summer. Free admission.

This cute little zoo has half a dozen buffalo, plus deer, elk, pigs, cows, goats, and chickens. There's a petting area where kids can have some hands-on time with the goats. Lords Park also has picnic areas and playgrounds scattered around its three lagoons.

Hemmens Cultural Center (all ages) 

150 Dexter Court, downtown Elgin; (847) 931-5900. Call for performance schedule and ticket prices.

The Children's Theatre of Elgin and the Fox Valley Youth Theatre Company stage regular plays here. The Performing Arts for Young People series of productions brings stories based on popular book characters and real-life heroes to the stage. A recent musical was *If You Give a Mouse a Cookie.*

Clang, Clang, Clang **Went the Trolley**

At the **Fox River Trolley Museum,** you can ride an electric trolley car on a scenic 3-mile round-trip along the west bank of the Fox River. The line traces its history back to 1896. The museum also houses more than two dozen pieces of railway equipment from the early 1900s. There are all sorts of special events throughout the year, too, such as the Trolleyfest in August and Fall Caboose Days in early October. The address is 361 South LaFox Street, South Elgin (Highway 31, 3 blocks south of the State Street traffic light); (847) 697-4676; www.foxtrolley.org. Hours are 11 a.m. to 5 p.m. on Saturday from late June through early November and on Sunday from Mother's Day through late October. Children age 2 or younger ride **free.**

Elgin Area Historical Museum (age 4 and up) 

360 Park Street, Elgin; (847) 742-4248; www.elginhistory.org. Open from March through December, hours are noon to 4 p.m. Wednesday through Saturday. Accessible for wheelchairs. $

The Elgin Area Historical Museum, more commonly known as Old Main, is housed in a historic three-story building with a white cupola. Here you'll find old tools, a whole room full of articles from the Elgin National Watch Company, and memorabilia from the Elgin National Road Race.

Where to Eat

IHOP, Lake Street and Randall Road; (847) 289-4801. Open from 6 a.m. to 10 p.m. Monday through Thursday and then from 6 a.m. Friday until 10 p.m. Sunday. See Restaurant Appendix for description. $

Steak n Shake, 290 South Randall Road; (847) 741-0679. Open 24 hours a day. See Restaurant Appendix for description. $

Where to Stay

Days Inn Elgin, 1585 Dundee Avenue; (847) 695-2100 or (800) 654-2000. This 96-room budget chain property has an indoor swimming pool. Continental breakfast is included in the room rate. $$

Holiday Inn Crowne Plaza, 495 Airport Road (off Highway 31 north of I-90); (847) 488-9000 or (800) 227-6963. This 8-story, 243-room hotel opened in 1999. It features an indoor heated pool, whirlpool, game room, and exercise room. Room rate may or may not include continental breakfast. $$$

For More Information

Elgin Area Convention and Visitors Bureau, 77 Riverside Drive, Elgin 60120; (847) 695-7540 or (800) 217-5362; www.enjoyelgin.com.

Huntley

Population: 5,730. Moving westward on US 20, a jog north up Illinois Highway 47 takes you to Huntley. This town is seeing some growth in its tourist business as a result of the outlet mall built in the mid-1990s.

Prime Outlets at Huntley (all ages) 

11800 Factory Shops Boulevard, Huntley; (847) 669-9100 or (888) 545-7222. Off Highway 47 just north of I-90. Hours are 10 a.m. to 8 p.m. Monday through Saturday and 11 a.m. to 6 p.m. Sunday.

This outdoor factory outlet mall is very visible from I-90. Light gray stone buildings have awnings in green and white stripes with yellow accents. The green-domed food court stands in the center and offers fast-food fare. Stores feature clothing, housewares, and such special items as books, music, and chocolates. The Carter's store is great for babies' and children's clothes. OshKosh B'Gosh has good bargains, too.

Tom's Farm (all ages) 

10214 Algonquin Road, Huntley; (847) 669-3421. East off Highway 47 north of the outlet mall. Open in summer and fall. Hours are 9 a.m. to 6:30 p.m. Monday through Friday and 9 a.m. to 5 p.m. Saturday and Sunday.

A giant strawberry takes the place of the letter O in the word *Tom's* on the barn roof, and you can buy them here fresh in June on 21 acres. (You used to be able to pick them yourself, but not anymore.) Throughout summer you'll find a variety of fresh fruits and vegetables. Tom's also is a fun place to visit in fall, as many school groups do. You can go out in a field and pick your own Halloween pumpkin or some decorative gourds, and a farm stand offers fresh apples and other produce for sale. Kids have fun wandering through a giant maze made out of bales of straw—stacked round bales in front sport colorful flags, giving the entrance the appearance of a castle.

Stingray Bay Family Aquatic Center (all ages) 

12219 Main Street, Huntley; (847) 515-7665; www.huntleyparks.org. Open summer only. Hours are 11 a.m. to 7 p.m. Monday through Thursday, 11 a.m. to 8 p.m. Friday, and noon to 6 p.m. Saturday and Sunday. $$

This sprawling water park was carved out of the surrounding farmland. For little kids you'll find a zero-depth swim area with two tot slides and a sand play area. (Wee ones must wear a snug-fitting "aqua diaper," and there are no "flotation devices"—including water wings and inner tubes—allowed in the pool.) Older kids and teens can enjoy two water slides, two diving boards, a lap-swimming area, and a volleyball court. Concessions are available on-site.

Where to Eat

Parkside Restaurant, 11721 East Main Street; (847) 669-8496. Restaurant hours are 11 a.m. to 10 p.m. Monday through Saturday and 9 a.m. to 6 p.m. Sunday. This local favorite offers outdoor seating in the milder seasons. Enjoy a juicy burger or order from the extensive menu of sandwiches. Friday night also features a "fish boil," and Saturday you can get barbecued ribs. $

Where to Stay

Huntley has no hotels or motels (yet, emphasizes the chamber of commerce); see entries for Elgin or Rockford.

For More Information

Huntley Chamber of Commerce, 11419 Route 47, Suite 104, P.O. Box 157, Huntley 60142; (847) 669-0166; www.huntleychamber.org.

Union

Population: 576. There's not much to see in this tiny McHenry County town just off US 20; however, two outlying attractions that bear its name as an address are major draws for family fun in Northern Illinois during spring, summer, and fall.

Illinois Railway Museum (all ages) 

Off Olson Road, Union; (815) 923-4000 or (800) 244-7245; www.irm.org. Open from 10 a.m. to 4 p.m. Monday through Friday from Memorial Day through Labor Day, 10:30 a.m. to 5 p.m. Saturday from May through October, and 10:30 a.m. to 5 p.m. Sunday from April through October. Closed from November through March. All admission rates include unlimited rides on all trains running that day. Admission is always free for children age 4 or younger. Call to hear a recording detailing which trains will run on which days. Most parts of the facility are accessible for strollers and wheelchairs. From I-90, take the exit for US 20/Marengo. Off the exit turn left, heading west, and continue about 4½ miles. Turn right, heading north, onto South Union Road. Keep going until South Union Road dead-ends at West Union Road and then turn right, heading east. (There are signs to help guide you.) Continue east through downtown Union (don't blink or you'll miss it) and then soon afterward turn right, heading south, onto Olson Road. Once you've crossed the railroad tracks, look to the left for the gravel road heading into the grassy parking lot. Ironically, there are no trains that run from Chicago or the suburbs to Union. For a brochure with complete directions, schedules, and prices, contact Illinois Railway Museum, P.O. Box 427, Union 60180. $–$$

This museum, a nonprofit organization founded in 1953 and moved to Union in 1964, is a marvelous work in progress. There are things you can do and see today, but there will be new things the next time you visit as the collection constantly expands and equipment is restored. The station near the entrance has display cases of memorabilia, and it's also where you'll find the restrooms (the women's has a changing table). Parked near the station are two railway cars containing a gift shop and a bookstore with some really nifty souvenirs. Beyond them you can wander the grounds and walk through about half a dozen large "barns"—more like huge metal airplane hangars, really—to get a closer look at various types of engines, railway cars, and streetcars. Other locomotives stand outside. Signs tell you where you may or may not climb or enter. Some trains have ramps, and visitors in wheelchairs can maneuver inside, but others are accessible only by climbing narrow metal stairs. The grounds are manageable to walk for able-bodied adults and older children, but little kids' feet will likely tire if they don't get a break. You can bring a stroller and have no trouble on the paved sidewalks; just watch out for the trolley tracks. In summer you'll find several spots where you can stand under a nozzle that emits a fine spray of cool mist, aaaah. Concessions are pretty limited—soft drinks, hot dogs and brats, potato chips, and ice-cream bars—but are reasonably priced and enough to keep you going. Alternately, you can bring your own picnic (no grilling and no alcoholic beverages) and eat at one of several sites furnished with picnic tables.

The people who operate the working trains are all volunteers, and their love of railroading is evident in the wealth of information they are able to share. The most charming of the museum's vintage vehicles is the trolley, an electric streetcar from the early 1900s that travels in a loop around the perimeter of the grounds. It makes stops at several of the barns, where you can get off and look around, and then reboard the trolley on its next pass. It's so much fun just to ride the trolley that you won't want to get off. Chicago reportedly once had the largest streetcar system in the United States, with more than 1,100 miles of track, before the trolleys stopped running there in the late 1950s. You can also take a short ride on an electric trolley bus that was built in 1951 and used on the streets of Chicago until the Chicago Transit Authority abandoned the system in 1973—right about the time of a major oil crisis, go figure.

On the railroad's main line, you can board an electric, steam, or diesel train (the type available varies) for a 9-mile round-trip through Northern Illinois farmland filled with corn and soybean fields, wild plants, prairie grasses, and trees. (A special wheelchair lift is available on the platform to help board passengers who have disabilities.) In this pastoral setting, the relaxing chug-a-chug-a of the wheels could lull you to sleep. The mournful wail of a 1916 steam engine's whistle evokes a sense of a bygone era; it sounds quite different from the sharp, whiny blast of a modern Chicago commuter train. Inside the passenger cars are many original fixtures, including lamps, rotary fans, and advertising billboards, mostly for cleaning supplies and medical products.

The barns house a variety of interesting equipment. Barn 7, for example, has the oldest artifact, a cute little horse-drawn streetcar (sans horse, of course), along with a three-wheeled red velocipede from 1890 and a yellow lever-powered handcar like the kind you see in funny old black-and-white movies or "Roadrunner" cartoons. Barn 9 has some of the biggest trains. The gleaming silver Nebraska Zephyr of 1940 would have looked like a speeding bullet flying down the rails. In 1995 the museum acquired its largest piece, No. 2903, a 1943 mammoth black steam locomotive of the Atchison, Topeka & Santa Fe Railway that had previously been on display for more than 30 years at the Museum of Science and Industry in Chicago. (Yes, you'd better believe it was tricky to transport this 340-ton, 121-foot-long nonworking behemoth from downtown Chicago out to Union.) You'll marvel at its sheer size. Its largest wheels, about 6 feet in diameter, are probably taller than you—stand next to one and compare. Barn 3 has the most elegant artifact, an 1889 Pullman passenger car with dark wood interior and furnished with a brass bed, a manual typewriter on a writing desk, and a dining table set with fine china, crystal, and linens. Only the wealthiest travelers could afford such finery, of course, but we can always dream.

Donley's Wild West Town (ages 2 to 12) 

8512 South Union Road, just north of US 20, Union; (815) 923-9000; www.wildwesttown.com. Hours are 10 a.m. to 6 p.m. daily from Memorial Day through Labor Day and 10 a.m. to 6 p.m. Saturday and Sunday only during the months of April, May, September, and October. Closed from November through March. Most parts of the facility are accessible for strollers and wheelchairs. From I-90, take the exit for US 20/Marengo. Off the exit turn left, heading west, and continue about 4½ miles. Turn right, heading north, onto South Union Road. Look to the right for the four bronze cowboys on horseback. $$$

Hey, pardners, this here's a right fine place to bring your young'uns for a safe taste of the Old West. And if they don't behave, you can get the sheriff to throw them in jail. (Don't worry—he won't lock up anyone who's truly unwilling, and they can usually make bail by singing some kiddie ditty.) Three features of this theme park, all of which are included in the admission price, are not to be missed: pony rides, panning for gold, and the gunfight. The pony rides are especially good for kids age 3 through 6; those age 10 or older probably would feel a bit silly sitting on such a small mount, and for those in the 7-to-9 range, it depends on the kid. The ponies walk a roughly elliptical path around a fenced-in corral, led by youthful cowboys and cowgirls. Panning for gold takes place at the Sweet Phyllis Mine. There's no underground section to this mine, just a series of wooden troughs filled with water and pebbles. Would-be miners pick up a black plastic pan shaped like a pie tin, dip it into the cloudy but chlorinated water, and pull up a load of stones. Careful sifting will net you a few tiny nuggets of pyrite, a glittery but inexpensive mineral that looks enough like gold to please the kids. Parents enjoy this activity, too. Piped-in fiddle and banjo music helps set the mood. For the gunfight, spectators are ushered into an arena and seated on bleachers. A split-rail fence separates them from the staging area, which has open space in front and a movielike facade of a Wild West town in back. A young actor in cowboy costume comes out to address the audience before the show, explaining how it's all pretend and that although the guns used are real, they shoot something called blanks, which have gunpowder that makes a bang but no metal tip to penetrate a victim. A demonstration with an aluminum can gives the audience a chance to hear the bang before the show and also see that even a blank fired at close range can dent the can—so don't try any of this at home. This warning at the beginning is not only a responsible thing to do in a society in which children armed with guns are increasingly making headlines, but it also helps reassure the wee tots that this live performance is make-believe. The show itself is quite funny, involving a lot of jokes and pratfalls as well as some entertaining stunts with bad guys getting shot off the rooftops.

You won't forget that this facility is a commercial enterprise, however. To enter the museum or the grounds, you have to pass through a well-stocked gift shop, and most of the other shops in the town carry a price tag as well: toy shop, ice-cream parlor, rock shop, Native American "trading post," saloon (where you can get root beer or real beer, including Lone Star from Texas), and photography studio with Old West costumes and props (about $20 for an 8-by-10-inch portrait). Unless you're a real fiduciary hard-liner, you'd better bring along extra money.

Finally, do be sure to spend some time in the indoor museum portion, either before or after going outside into the town. This is where the Larry Donley family started their enterprise in 1975, and the real stuff on display here is definitely worth a look. Along one wall is a wonderful collection of vintage phonographs, circa 1900, and related equipment. If Grandma and Grandpa are along for the visit, they may have some recollections of their own grandparents' homes that will personalize the exhibit. Other glass cases contain Western memorabilia including guns, housewares, American Indian clothing, and the death masks and ball-and-chain shackles of criminals.

Where to Eat

Donley's Old West Steakhouse, 8512 South Union Road; (815) 923-8000. Just north of US 20, adjacent to Donley's Wild West Town. Open from 11 a.m. to 9 p.m. Monday through Thursday, 11 a.m. to 10 p.m. Friday and Saturday, and 11 a.m. to 8:30 p.m. Sunday. You can get a hearty meal at this sit-down restaurant featuring soups, salads, and burgers as well as entrees of ribs, chicken, seafood, and steaks. The kids' menu items cost $3 to $4, not including drink; choose from burger, hot dog, chicken nuggets, grilled cheese, or spaghetti. $$

Where to Stay

There are no hotels or motels in Union (see entries for Elgin or Rockford if that's what you want), but if you don't mind roughing it a bit, try this:

KOA Kampground, 8404 South Union Road; (815) 923-4206 or (800) 562-2827; www.koakampgrounds.com. Just north of US 20, adjacent to Donley's Wild West Town. Open from April 15 through October 15. Bring an RV, a trailer, or a tent to camp here. The facility has an outdoor pool, a game room, basketball, volleyball, and bicycles. $

Cherry Valley

Population: 2,191. This little suburb just east of Rockford along US 20 has several of the area's major attractions.

Magic Waters Waterpark (all ages)

7820 North Cherry Vale Boulevard/Bell School Road, Cherry Valley; (815) 396-6244 or (800) 373-1679; www.magicwaterswaterpark.com. Magic Waters is open from Memorial Day through late August and on Labor Day weekend. Hours are 10 a.m. to 6 p.m. daily. $$$

Along Bypass 20, near the junction with Interstate 39, is Magic Waters. Even from the highway you can see the water slides looming like giant intestines at this 35-acre water park. There are three of them, each about five stories tall, boasting the ability to propel a human body at speeds up to 30 miles per hour. The wave pool here is reportedly the largest in Illinois, with churning waves that reach up to 5 feet in height—definitely do not take your tiny tots in here, or even your grade-schoolers unless they're very good swimmers. The Little Lagoon is the place for the younger set. Decorated with figurines of aquatic creatures, it has fountains and slides. Nearly everyone can enjoy floating in an inner tube along the 1,200-foot-long Splashmagic River Ride. But the centerpiece of this water park is Splashmagic Island, which rises to a height of 50 feet with its fountains, slides, and giant water pail that tips over to dump a thousand gallons of H_2O down the slide and onto the people in the pool below. The Splash Blaster thrill ride, added in 2003, is a cross between a flume ride and a roller coaster—all on a rubber raft. New for 2004 was the Abyss, a tall, twisting, completely enclosed (and thus very dark) water slide. If you need a break from the watery stuff, there are concessions, a video arcade, and a gift shop on the grounds. Teens might enjoy the beach volleyball and the basketball court.

CherryVale Mall (all ages) 

7200 Harrison Avenue, at Perryville Road, Cherry Valley; (815) 332-2440. Hours are 10 a.m. to 9 p.m. Monday through Saturday and 11 a.m. to 6 p.m. Sunday. Accessible for strollers and wheelchairs.

This is the biggest and best indoor shopping mall in the greater Rockford area. Its 110 stores are anchored by Macy's, JCPenney, Bergner's, and Sears department stores. Cyberstation, on the lower level, has arcade games and virtual-reality games. The mall has a food court.

Cherry Valley Golf and Game (age 3 and up) 

7282 CherryVale Mall Drive, Cherry Valley; (815) 332-3399. Open from April 1 through October 31. Hours are 10 a.m. to 10 p.m. Monday through Saturday and 11 a.m. to 9 p.m. Sunday. The facility is accessible for strollers and wheelchairs. $+

Near the mall, this outdoor entertainment center has an 18-hole miniature golf course with a castle and a stream. You'll also find bumper boats, batting cages, an arcade, and a concession stand.

Where to Eat

TGIFridays, 2408 South Perryville Road; (815) 332-5355. Open from 11 a.m. to 10 p.m. Sunday through Thursday and 11 a.m. to 11 p.m. Friday and Saturday. See Restaurant Appendix for description. $

Where to Stay

Exel Inn, 220 South Lyford Road; (815) 332-4915 or (800) 356-8013. Near Cherry-Vale Mall and Magic Waters. This 2-story property in the midwestern regional chain has 101 rooms, each equipped with coffeemaker, hair dryer, and iron and ironing board. No pool. Cribs available free on request. Pets 25 pounds or smaller allowed. Room rate includes continental breakfast. $$

See also entries for Rockford.

For More Information

Village of Cherry Valley, 806 East State Street, Cherry Valley 61016; (815) 332-3441; www.cherryvalley.org.

Rockford

Population: 150,115. US 20 splits as it enters Rockford from the east. If you want to go into the heart of the city, look for the BUSINESS 20 sign. If you want to skirt the edge of town (maybe you're on the way to somewhere else and don't want to stop this time), you'll need Bypass 20. This distinction will be clearer if you get a Rockford map ahead of time.

Discovery Center Museum (ages 1 to 12) 

711 North Main Street, Rockford; (815) 963-6769; www.discoverycentermuseum.org. Hours are 10 a.m. to 5 p.m. Monday through Saturday and noon to 5 p.m. Sunday, extended to 7 p.m. Thursday during the summer; closed Monday during the school year except for school holidays. Accessible for wheelchairs. No smoking. $

Science is the emphasis at the family-oriented Discovery Center Museum in Riverfront Museum Park. Among the things you can do: make your hair stand on end with an electrostatic generator, walk through an "infinity tunnel," or manipulate an assortment of levers, pulleys, and gears. A planetarium will let you explore the stars, and the Body Shop has displays and demonstrations on the workings of the human body. Children age 5 or younger can play in the Tot Spot, which has a variety of sturdy plastic toys and a water area. A unique feature of the Discovery Center Museum is the outdoor science park, a two-story wooden maze that looks like a playground but sneaks in entertainingly educational exhibits about weather, water, sound, and caves.

Rockford Art Museum (age 5 and up) 

711 North Main Street, Rockford; (815) 968-2787; www.rockfordartmuseum.org. Hours are 10 a.m. to 5 p.m. Monday through Saturday (extended to 7 p.m. Thursday), and noon to 5 p.m. Sunday. The building is accessible for wheelchairs. Everyone gets in free on Tuesday. $

You'd expect the second largest city in Illinois to have an art museum, and this is a respectable one. As an established Regional Arts Institution, it carries many pieces by artists from around the Midwest. The annual Stateline Vicinity Exhibition includes paintings, photographs, and sculptures by regional artists. Contemporary art is also a specialty. For example, the museum's permanent collection includes Alexander Calder's 1973 lithograph *Balloons.* Another ongoing exhibition features brilliant glass pieces. A particularly interesting section of the museum contains works by self-taught African-American artists. About a dozen different exhibitions are displayed at the Rockford Art Museum each year, and since 1938 the museum has hosted an annual art fair in downtown Rockford in late September.

Forest City Queen and Track Trolley Car 36 (all ages) 

324 North Madison Street, Rockford; (815) 987-8894. *Forest City Queen* sails at 2, 3, and 4 p.m. Wednesday and Friday and at noon, 1, 2, 3, and 4 p.m. Saturday and Sunday. The trolley departs at noon, 1, 2, 3, and 4 p.m. Thursday, Saturday, and Sunday. Accommodations are made for passengers with disabilities. $

Cruise the Rock River on the *Forest City Queen* sightseeing boat or take a trip on a reproduction open-air trolley along the historic riverfront through Sinnissippi Gardens.

Midway Village and Museum Center (age 3 and up) 

6799 Guilford Road, Rockford; (815) 397-9112; www.midwayvillage.com. The village and museum are open from April through October. Village hours are 11 a.m. to 4 p.m. Tuesday through Sunday (but closed Tuesday and Wednesday in May and October); closed Monday. Museum hours are 10 a.m. to 5 p.m. Tuesday through Saturday and 11 a.m. to 5 p.m. Sunday; closed Monday. Thursday is Donation Day, when you pay an amount of your choice. Visitors are requested to call ahead to verify hours and fees before coming. The facility is accessible for wheelchairs. $

Midway Village is a re-creation of a typical town from the late 1800s and early 1900s. The buildings contain authentic furnishings, and interpreters in period costumes help visitors understand what life was like during that time. There are some hands-on activities available, such as churning butter. The Museum Center contains galleries chronicling Rockford's history. Among the contemporary displays is one about the rock band Cheap Trick, which started out in Rockford. You won't want to miss the full-size airplane in the aviation exhibit.

Riverview Ice House (age 4 and up) 

324 North Madison Avenue, Rockford; (815) 963-7465. Open daily, but public skating hours vary; call for current times and prices.

There are two ice-skating rinks at this indoor facility. It offers public skating sessions year-round, an unusual way to beat summer heat.

Rockford Lightning (age 3 and up) 

Lightning home games are played at the MetroCentre, 300 Elm Street, Rockford; (815) 874-4232; www.rockfordlightning.com. Season runs November through March. Call for current schedule and ticket prices. $$–$$$

You can see minor-league sports action on the basketball court with the Rockford Lightning. This team belongs to the Continental Basketball Association, the official developmental league of the National Basketball Association (NBA).

Klehm Arboretum and Botanic Garden (all ages) 

2715 South Main Street, Rockford; (815) 965-8146; www.klehm.org. Open daily year-round. Hours are 9 a.m. to 8 p.m. from Memorial Day through Labor Day and 9 a.m. to 4 p.m. the rest of the year. Admission is free. The site is accessible for strollers and wheelchairs.

Paved pathways wind for a mile through a lovely array of flowers, bushes, and trees. The Nancy Olson Children's Garden has a maze. You can strike off on your own or make a reservation ahead of time to take a guided tour. The 155-acre site is a joint development project of the Northern Illinois Botanical Society and the Winnebago County Forest Preserve, so expect it to look better each visit.

Tinker Swiss Cottage Museum (age 5 and up) 

411 Kent Street, Rockford; (815) 964-2424; www.tinkercottage.com. Tours are given at 1, 2, and 3 p.m. Tuesday through Friday and Sunday and last 1 hour; closed Monday and Saturday. The building is accessible for wheelchairs. $

Atop a limestone bluff, this 20-room cottage was built in 1865 in the style of a Swiss chalet. Painted murals adorn the walls and ceilings, and the home is filled with fancy furniture, porcelain, and artworks. The museum may be visited by tour only; you can't just go in and wander around. Due to the length of the tour and the number of delicate objects that must not be touched, this attraction is not recommended for children age four or younger.

Where to Eat

Bing's Drive-In, 3613 South Main; (815) 968-8663. Open from 11 a.m. to 8 p.m. daily from late spring through the first week of September. This is an old-fashioned place with carhops who deliver your order. You can eat in your car or at picnic tables set up along with a little playground on the restaurant grounds. Sandwiches include barbecued beef, breaded pork, hamburgers, and hot dogs, with french fries or onion rings if you choose. But the biggest treat is the soft-serve ice cream, which you can order in cones, sundaes, or shakes. The latter come in some yummy flavors, such as lemon and black raspberry. The orange shake tastes just like a Dreamsicle. $

Old Country Buffet, 6403 East State Street, at Mulford Road; (815) 394-1702. Hours are 11 a.m. to 8:30 p.m. Monday through Friday and 8 a.m. to 8 p.m. Saturday and Sunday. See Restaurant Appendix for description. $

Giordano's, 333 Executive Parkway, off Mulford Road; (815) 398-5700. Open from 11 a.m. to midnight Monday through Thursday, 11 a.m. to 1 a.m. Friday and Saturday, and noon to midnight Sunday. See Restaurant Appendix for description. $

HomeTown Buffet, 525 South Perryville Road, at State Street; (815) 227-1770. Hours are 11 a.m. to 8:30 p.m. Monday through Friday and 8 a.m. to 8:30 p.m. Saturday and Sunday. See Restaurant Appendix for description. $

Where to Stay

Clock Tower Resort and Conference Center, 7801 East State Street (I-90 and Business 20); (815) 398-6000. This resort offers 243 rooms of lodging in a facility with indoor and outdoor pools, sauna, whirlpools, volleyball and basketball courts, indoor tennis, planned kids' activities, and an adults-only fitness center. There are 4 restaurants and lounges on the premises. No pets allowed. The resort offers a variety of accommodation packages that include golf at the adjacent 18-hole course or a dinner-theater performance. $$$$

Comfort Inn, 7392 Argus Drive (along Business 20); (815) 398-7061 or (800) 424-6423. This 3-story chain property has 64 rooms. Amenities include indoor heated pool and whirlpool. Continental breakfast is included in the room rate. Minimum 2-night stay required. $$$

Hampton Inn, 615 Clark Drive (along Business 20); (815) 229-0404 or (800) 426-7866. There are 122 rooms in the inn. Amenities include indoor pool and whirlpool and Nordic Track room. The room rate includes continental breakfast. $$$$

Holiday Inn, 7550 East State Street (I-90 and Business 20); (815) 398-2200 or (800) 383-7829. This 7-story hotel has 198 rooms and lots of amenities, including heated indoor pool and Jacuzzi, fitness center, putting green, and table tennis. The on-site restaurant specializes in prime rib. The hotel also has a gift shop, a beauty salon, and a Hertz car rental office. $$$$

Howard Johnson Lodge, 3909 Eleventh Street (along Illinois Highway 251 South); (815) 397-9000 or (800) 446-4656. This property has 148 rooms, each with a coffeemaker, and 12 apartments. Amenities include an indoor pool, whirlpool, sauna, exercise room, and game room. $$

For More Information

Rockford Area Convention and Visitors Bureau, 102 North Main Street, Rockford 61101; (815) 963-8111 or (800) 521-0849; www.gorockford.com.

Loves Park

Population: 20,044. This suburb to the north of Rockford has several attractions of interest to action-oriented families.

Ski Broncs Water Ski Show (all ages) 

In Shorewood Park, 5000 Forest Grove, at Evelyn Avenue, Loves Park; (815) 322-7155. Shows are at 7 p.m. Wednesday and Friday from mid-May through Labor Day. Free.

Just show up at the park and find a spot near the water to enjoy this waterskiing spectacle. The Ski Broncs have been ranked third in the nation for their performances, which combine athletics with theatrics. Bring along a picnic, or partake of on-site concessions.

Carlson Arctic Ice Arena and Playworld (age 1 and up) 

4150 North Perryville Road, Loves Park; (815) 969-4069 for main facility, (815) 969-4082 for Playworld. Call for current public skating times. Bring your own skates, or rent them here. Playworld hours are 10 a.m. to 8 p.m. Monday through Saturday and noon to 5 p.m. Sunday. Playworld admission is half price on Tuesday. $

This family recreation complex is open year-round. Public skating sessions are offered at the ice rink. Maybe one parent can take the grade-schoolers there while the other parent monitors the younger kids' activity in the Playworld, a three-story apparatus with tubes, slides, nets, and ball pits. You can come to the Playworld even when the ice rink is closed or off-limits to the public while lessons are going on. The facility has a video arcade and concessions as well.

Rockford Raptors and Rockford Dactyls (age 3 and up) 

Games are played at Wedgebury Soccer Complex, 8800 East Riverside Boulevard, Loves Park; (815) 885-4848; www.rockfordraptors.org. Season runs from April through early September. Call for current schedule and ticket prices.

The Raptors are a men's "professional" soccer team and the Dactyls a women's "amateur" soccer team; the main difference in the designations is that the men get paid to play and the women do not. The teams belong to the United States Intercontinental Soccer League (USISL) and the U.S. Intercontinental Women's Soccer League (USIWSL), respectively. You can watch live soccer action and shout "Gooooooooooal!"

Where to Eat and Stay

See entries for Rockford.

Freeport

Population: 26,443. Continuing west from Rockford on US 20 brings you to Freeport. At Douglas and State Streets stands a statue of Abraham Lincoln that marks the site of the second debate between Lincoln and Stephen Douglas in 1858.

Silver Creek and Stephenson Railroad (all ages)

Corner of Lamm and Walnut Roads, Freeport; (815) 232-2306, (815) 235-2198, or (800) 369-2955. Excursions run on selected weekends from May through October; call for exact schedule. Accommodations are made for passengers with disabilities. $

Take a 4-mile ride on a 1912 Heisler steam locomotive with three antique cabooses and a covered passenger flatcar. You'll cross a bridge 30 feet above Yellow Creek on this short but scenic journey.

Krape Park (all ages)  

1799 South Park Boulevard near Empire Street, Freeport; (888) 851-1556. The park is open year-round, from dawn to 10:30 p.m. daily, and park admission is free. Miniature golf hours are noon to dusk daily during summer. Minigolf, canoe rental, paddleboat rental each $.

Krape Park has lots of family activities. You'll find a playground, a picnic area, a duck pond, a waterfall, tennis courts, and some hiking trails. You can even ride on an old-fashioned carousel (four rides for $1). The park also has an outdoor miniature golf course. Paddleboat and canoe rentals are available if you want to go up a creek with a paddle. In winter you can go ice-skating on Yellow Creek or sledding down Bandshell Hill.

Pecatonica Prairie Path (all ages) 

Hillcrest and East River Road, Freeport; (815) 233-0814 or (800) 369-2955. Open from sunrise to sunset. Free.

This scenic 20-mile nature trail goes between Freeport and Rockford. Its surface is a hard-packed dirt called "railroad ballast." The path is used by hikers, mountain bikers, horseback riders, and, in winter, cross-country skiers. It goes across the Pecatonica River on a 250-foot double-span trestle bridge. You can stop en route in Pecatonia for a picnic in Sumner Park, where there's a playground if you're carrying young passengers who need a chance to stretch their legs.

Smile and Say "Cheese"!

While in Lena, not far beyond Freeport to the west of US 20, remember that you are only about a dozen miles south of the Wisconsin border. Then it won't seem unusual to find two specialty cheese shops in a community of fewer than 3,000 people.

- **Kolb-Lena Cheese Company** is south off US 20 at 3990 North Sunnyside Road; (815) 369-4577. This outlet store offers daily specials and samples; the Delico baby Swiss cheese is a specialty. Hours are 10 a.m. to 6 p.m. daily; closed Sunday in January and February.
- **Torkelson Cheese Company** is off Illinois Highway 73 at 9453 Louisa Road; (815) 369-4265. Specialties here are Muenster and brick cheeses and heavy cream (bring your own jar). Hours are 8 a.m. to 3 p.m. Monday through Friday and 8 a.m. to 1 p.m. Saturday; closed Sunday.

Where to Eat

Cannova's, 1101 West Empire Street; (815) 233-0032. Hours are 5 to 9 p.m. Tuesday through Thursday, 5 to 11 p.m. Friday and Saturday, and 5 p.m. to "whenever we close" (?!) Sunday; closed Monday. This Italian restaurant has been a Freeport tradition since 1921. In addition to pasta and pizza, you can get chicken or fish entrees. $

Golden Corral, 1404 West Galena Avenue; (815) 235-7036. Open from 11 a.m. to 10 p.m. Monday through Friday and 7:30 a.m. to 10 p.m. Saturday and Sunday. Children's menu available. Order a steak, chicken, or seafood entree and then pick your own side dishes at the all-you-can-eat buffet. $

Pizza Hut, 1428 West Galena Avenue; (815) 235-3733. Open from 10:30 a.m. to 11 p.m. Sunday through Thursday and 10:30 a.m. to midnight Friday and Saturday. See Restaurant Appendix for description. $

Where to Stay

Freeport Ramada, 1300 East South Street; (815) 297-9700 or (800) 272-6232. This 90-room property features indoor pool, whirlpool, and exercise facilities. Pets allowed for extra $6 per night. Room rate includes continental breakfast. $$$$

For More Information

Stephenson County Convention and Visitors Bureau, 2047 AYP Road, Freeport 61032; (800) 369-2955; www.stephenson-county-il.org.

Galena

Population: 3,460. The picturesque town of Galena, near the Mississippi River, does an exceptionally high volume of tourist business, given its size; about a million visitors come through town each year, mostly from June through October. Galena reportedly started out as a boomtown during the nation's first mineral rush. Ulysses S. Grant was born here in 1822 and spent most of his life here, when he wasn't fighting the Civil War or serving as president. By 1900 lead production was declining and so was the town. Galena began its resurgence in the 1950s, cashing in on its historical appeal. The Illinois Department of Resources is hoping to build a bike path between Galena and Savanna, to the south, which would be a key link in the planned **Grand Illinois Trail** to circle the northern part of the state in a 500-mile network of trails for biking, hiking, and horseback riding.

If you intend to visit the downtown area, stop first at the visitor center 2 blocks north of US 20 on the east bank of the Galena River, which runs through the center of town. Housed in an old train depot, the center is stocked with maps and brochures and staffed with helpful people to answer your questions. It's open from 9 a.m. to 5 p.m. Monday through Thursday, 9 a.m. to 7 p.m. Friday and Saturday, and 10 a.m. to 5 p.m. Sunday. The center also has a big parking lot across the railroad tracks, and it would be a good place to leave your car if you plan to wander around downtown for more than a couple hours; parking along the narrow streets there is hard to come by and has a two-hour limit.

Main Street is more than just a name in Galena. Here you'll find the concentration of shops for which the town has become famous. There's a multitude of antiques shops, the biggest claim to fame, but you'll have better luck saving the antiques browsing for a time when the kids are staying at Grandma and Grandpa's. Instead look for spots that may be of particular interest to youngsters, such as the shops that sell dolls, teddy bears, toy soldiers, and sweets.

Here Comes the Fudge

Fudge lovers will travel for miles to find a mouthwatering morsel of the creamy confection. Here are a couple of area shops that have been favorably compared to those of the renowned mecca of Mackinac Island, Michigan.

- **Galena's Kandy Kitchen,** 100 North Main Street, Galena; (815) 777-0241. Reportedly owned and operated by the son of the guy who invented Chuckles gumdrop-style candy, Kandy Kitchen offers pick-your-own candies and jelly beans, along with numerous chocolate creations, including five kinds of fudge, all made with a 40 percent butterfat cream. You can watch some of the candy making in progress (the fudge maker hides in back, sorry). Hours are 10 a.m. to 9 p.m. daily from May through October and 10 a.m. to 5 p.m. daily from November through April.
- **Rocky Mountain Chocolate Factory,** 207 South Main Street, Galena; (815) 777-3200 or (800) 235-8160. This shop is one in a nationwide chain of more than 200 stores. Choose from among hand-dipped chocolates, truffles, chocolate chip cookies, frozen chocolate-covered bananas, and brownies, along with the fudge that is made out front. Try the specialty Oreo or black walnut fudge. Hours are 10 a.m. to 5:30 p.m. Sunday through Thursday and 10 a.m. to 9 p.m. Friday and Saturday.

Skiing in the Galena Area

If you're visiting the area in winter and your kids are old enough, consider going skiing. Both downhill and cross-country are offered here.

- **Chestnut Mountain Resort,** 8700 West Chestnut Road; (815) 777-1320 or (800) 397-1320; www.chestnutmtn.com. Illinois doesn't have a lot of downhill skiing, but you'll find some here. The resort has 17 runs, the longest of which is 3,500 feet. The biggest vertical drop is 475 feet. Chairlifts (including a quad lift), rope tows, equipment rental, and lessons are available. The lodge is on top of a bluff overlooking the Mississippi River, offering spectacular views. The facility is open from Thanksgiving Day through St. Patrick's Day. Rates for lift tickets and ski rental vary with time of day, day of the week, and number of days you plan to ski. Call for an exact quote.
- **Eagle Ridge Resort,** 444 Eagle Ridge Drive (US 20 East); (815) 777-2500; www.eagleridge.com. Here you can go cross-country skiing along 34 miles of trails through the woods and around the lake.

Ulysses S. Grant Home State Historic Site (age 7 and up) 

500 Bouthillier Street, Galena; (815) 777-3310. Hours are 9 a.m. to 5 p.m. Wednesday through Sunday; closed Monday and Tuesday. Admission is free, but donations are encouraged. The suggested amount is $3 for adults and $1 for young people age 18 or younger. The site is accessible for wheelchairs.

The Ulysses S. Grant Home State Historic Site is one of the most famous places to visit in Galena. The Italianate house was built in 1860 and presented to General Grant when he returned from the Civil War in 1865. Today it is owned and operated by the Illinois Historic Preservation Agency, which has taken pains to maintain the home as it appeared in Grant's time. It has many original furnishings.

Galena Post Office (all ages) 

110 Green Street, Galena; (815) 777-0225. Hours are 9 a.m. to 4:30 p.m. Monday through Friday (sometimes closed over the noon hour) and 9 a.m. to noon Saturday. The building is closed Sunday. Free.

Mail a postcard to a friend and see another bit of history at the same time when you stop in at the Galena Post Office. The Renaissance Revival building was constructed from 1857 to 1859 under the supervision of Ely Samuel Parker, a Seneca Iroquois Indian who was General Grant's military secretary during the Civil War (1861–1865). Parker would go on to become a brigadier general in 1867 and then be appointed

U.S. commissioner of Indian affairs in 1869 by President Grant. The Galena Post Office is one of the oldest continuously operating post offices in the United States.

Vinegar Hill Lead Mine and Museum (age 4 and up) 

8885 North Three Pines Road, Galena; (815) 777-0855. About 6 miles north of US 20 off Illinois Highway 84. Open from 9 a.m. to 5 p.m. daily from June through August and 9 a.m. to 5 p.m. Saturday and Sunday only in May, September, and October; closed November through April. Admission price includes the tour. Children age 5 or younger get in free. $–$$

Founded in the early 1800s by John Furlong, an Irish soldier, and passed down through subsequent generations, the underground mine is maintained as a tourist attraction by Mark Furlong, John's great-great-great-grandson. You can take a half-hour tour that starts in the museum with an explanation of the tools and methods used, then don a hard hat and descend into the mine.

Alice T. Virtue Memorial Pool and Water Park (all ages) 

North of town, on Stagecoach Trail, in Recreation Park, Galena; (815) 777-0802. Open daily during summer. Hours are noon to 7 p.m. Sunday through Friday and noon to 8 p.m. Saturday. $

The water park has a pool with zero-depth shallow end plus a separate wading pool and a 131-foot water slide. Recreation Park itself has picnic areas with grills and shelters, a playground, a horseshoe pit, a sand volleyball court, diamonds for baseball and softball, and a concession stand. Admission to Recreation Park alone is free.

Shenandoah Riding Center (age 8 and up) 

200 North Brodrecht Road, Galena, about 8 miles east of town, in the Galena Territory; (815) 777-2373; www.shenandoahridingcenter.com. Open from 8:30 a.m. to 4:30 p.m. daily. Children age 7 or younger are not allowed on the trail. Reservations are required. $$$$

Here you can take a one-hour or two-hour guided trail ride. The path includes wooded areas and open fields, even meandering along a creek for a while. The center also can offer you a hayride, or—in winter—a sleigh ride.

Where to Eat

Log Cabin, 201 North Main Street; (815) 777-0393. Open from 4 to 10 p.m. daily. Reportedly Galena's oldest restaurant, the Log Cabin offers a menu of soups, salads, sandwiches, steaks, and seafood—plus Greek specialties. Try some saganaki, the flaming cheese appetizer. *Opah!* $$

Happy Joe's Pizza and Ice Cream Parlor, 9919 US 20 East; (815) 777-1830. Open from 7 a.m. to 10 p.m. Sunday through Thursday and 7 a.m. to midnight Friday and Saturday. Here is a good place for a family meal. The kids can watch a model train travel its course while waiting for their pizza. At lunchtime there's a smorgasbord with salad bar. Just be sure to save room for dessert—ice cream, of course, prepared in a variety of tasty ways. $

Where to Stay

Forget about finding a cheap motel around here. Plan to stay overnight when you can splurge on a luxury resort, stay in the historic downtown hotel, or perhaps try a quaint bed-and-breakfast.

Eagle Ridge Inn and Resort, US 20 East; (800) 892-2269; www.eagleridge.com. You can't get anywhere near Galena without seeing signs for the Eagle Ridge Inn and Resort, off US 20 about 8 miles east of town. In summer you'll see golfers aplenty on the 4 championship 18-hole courses. From November through March the resort's winter activities are open to the public, including sleigh rides, ice-skating, sledding, snowshoeing, and cross-country skiing. There is a trail fee, and there are other charges for renting equipment. Lodging at the resort comprises 80 inn rooms and more than 300 other accommodation units, including houses, town houses, condos, and golf villas. Guests may enjoy the indoor pool, whirlpool, sauna, fitness center, game room, indoor golf center, and children's playroom. There are lots of package deals offered. $$$$

Chestnut Mountain Resort, 8700 West Chestnut Road; (815) 777-1320 or (800) 397-1320; www.chestnutmtn.com. This resort sits atop a high bluff overlooking the Mississippi River, 8 miles southeast of town. Guests may enjoy the indoor pool, whirlpool, and sauna, along with numerous other amenities that are also open to the public. For example, play miniature golf or, for a real adventure, try the Alpine Slide, where you ride a wheeled sled down a 2,500-foot-long, toboggan-like track—whee! The resort has a restaurant on the premises that serves breakfast, lunch, and dinner daily, with a special Sunday brunch offered from May through October. The specialties are fresh catfish and barbecued ribs. $$$$

Amber Creek's Territory Lodging can help you find a place to stay. This outfit manages such vacation rentals as furnished cottages, town houses, and houses, some of which can accommodate as many as 12 people—a boon for larger families. Rental prices vary greatly depending on when and where you stay; they range from $75 to $400 a night. Call (815) 777-9320 or (800) 781-9530 for details, or browse online at www.ambercreek.com.

DeSoto House Hotel, 230 South Main Street; (815) 777-0090 or (800) 343-6562; www.desotohouse.com. This 3-story brick building dates back to 1855 and is listed on the National Register of Historic Places. But don't let the period decor fool you: The 55 rooms have central air and cable TV. There's no swimming pool, though. If you stay during the week or in the less temperate off-season time, you'll get a lower rate. The hotel also offers a variety of package deals that include meals, downhill skiing, or entertainment with the room. $$$$

Best Western Quiet House Suites, U.S. 20 East; (815) 777-2577 or (800) 937-8376. Rated 3 diamonds by AAA. This lovely 2-story motel has 42 rooms. Those that face outdoors have little balconies. Amenities include indoor and outdoor swimming pools, whirlpool, and fitness center. Pets are allowed for $15 per night but must be attended. $$$$

B&Bs. Many bed-and-breakfast places don't cater to families and thus are generally not listed among lodging choices in this book. However, the Galena area is an exception. Jo Daviess County has become known as the "B&B capital of the Midwest" for its abundance of bed-and-breakfast houses and inns. Not all of the 50-plus B&Bs in the area accept children (some do so only with age restrictions such as "over 10" or "over 12"), but some do advertise themselves with "children welcome." Ask for a list of B&Bs (see For More Information section that follows).

For More Information

Galena/Jo Daviess County Convention & Visitors Bureau, 101 Bouthieller Street, Galena 61036; (877) 464-2536; www.galena.org.

Let's return to the eastern border of Northern Illinois and head west along Highway 64. We'll start in St. Charles, right along the Fox River.

St. Charles

Population: 27,896. When the city of St. Charles paved its Main Street (Highway 64) in 1928, it created a direct route west from Lake Street in Chicago. The city hosts a number of events throughout the year. The Pride of the Fox RiverFest takes place in June. Come to St. Charles in mid-October to catch the annual **Scarecrow Festival.** You'll see handcrafted scarecrows and can even try making your own. Costumed characters, including a scarecrow on stilts, liven up this family-oriented event. There are kiddie rides, puppet shows, a petting zoo, and a special haunted house just for kids. Live bands, concessions, and an arts and crafts show round out the offerings.

St. Charles Belle* and *Fox River Queen (age 3 and up)

Cruises depart from Pottawatomie Park, on the east bank of the Fox River about 1½ miles north of Highway 64, St. Charles; (630) 584-2334; www.stcharlesparks.org/links/paddlewheelriverboats.htm. Season runs from May through mid-October. Sailing times for June through August are 3:30 p.m. Monday through Friday and 2, 3, and 4 p.m. Saturday and Sunday. In May, September, and October, departures are at 2, 3, and 4 p.m. Saturday and Sunday only. $

You can catch a ride up the Fox River on one of two double-decker paddle wheelers, the *St. Charles Belle* and the *Fox River Queen.* Weekday sightseeing cruises last one hour, weekend cruises 50 minutes. You should be aware that there's a $5-per-car entrance fee to get into Pottawatomie Park. The fee is waived if you're coming in for the riverboat ride, and you can do other things in the park afterward, such as play miniature golf.

River View Miniature Golf (age 3 and up) 

In Pottawatomie Park, on the east bank of the Fox River about 1½ miles north of Highway 64, St. Charles; (630) 584-1028. Open daily from Memorial Day through Labor Day and weekends only in May, September, and October. Hours are 11 a.m. to 10 p.m. Sunday through Friday and 11 a.m. to 11 p.m. Saturday. $

This 18-hole outdoor miniature golf course has a waterfall, ponds, and gardens. It's a fun place to play after a riverboat ride.

Tekawitha Woods Nature Center (all ages) 

35W076 Villa Marie Road, St. Charles; (847) 741-8350. Hours are 9 a.m. to 4 p.m. Monday through Thursday and noon to 4 p.m. Saturday and Sunday; closed Friday. Admission is free, but donations are appreciated. The center is accessible for strollers and wheelchairs.

The namesake woods are at the big bend of the Fox River, making a scenic setting for this hands-on nature center. The "discovery corner" is especially for children, and there is a wildlife observation room. Exhibits and nature programs vary.

Pheasant Run Resort and Spa (all ages) 

4051 East Main Street, St. Charles; (800) 474-3272; www.pheasantrun.com. Call for current rates; be sure to ask about package deals.

About 500 people work here to keep this sprawling complex operating and the guests happy. The accommodation section has 473 rooms. Amenities include indoor pool and game room. Kids Klub offers supervised activities for children. On the weekends entertainment at the resort is provided by a magician, a clown, and a caricature artist. Ask about the Splash Bash Family Get-Away package.

The resort has a beauty salon, a golf shop, and several other shops full of gifts and souvenirs. The conference center, modestly named the Mega ExpoCenter, covers 39,000 square feet. Add in the 42 meeting rooms and the total space jumps to about 100,000 square feet.

There is a newly renovated theater in the complex, but most of the productions are geared toward adults. The occasional comedy or musical might appeal to older children, so check to see what's on the current schedule.

Charlestowne Mall (all ages)

3800 East Main Street, St. Charles; (630) 513-1120; www.charlestownemall.com. At Highway 64 and Kirk Road. Hours are 10 a.m. to 9 p.m. Monday through Saturday and 11 a.m. to 6 p.m. Sunday. Free wheelchair and stroller rentals are available in the office beside the arcade.

This attractive, two-story indoor shopping mall has about 120 stores, anchored by department stores Carson Pirie Scott, JCPenney, Kohl's, and Sears. The mall has an open, airy feel. Pastel green steel beams frame the glass-paneled ceiling above the corridors and a central atrium with a glass elevator and fountain. Floor tile is in light earth tones: tan, heather green, soft burgundy. The aisles are wide and unobstructed, so much so that two strollers can comfortably wheel along side by side without totally blocking everyone behind. Stores of interest to kids include the Disney Store and a handful of gift shops that carry Beanie Babies, Yu-Gi-Oh, and Sponge Bob merchandise. There are upscale clothing stores and shops full of art prints for more adult tastes.

The highlight of Charlestowne is its double-level carousel, which was custom-made in Italy for the mall's 1991 opening and is showcased in a glass-walled, skylit atrium facing the back of the mall. Painted scenes on the ceiling and around the top outer edge depict Venice, each framed in ornate, creamy gold. White lights outline the exterior. A few of the gilded horses pump up and down in the traditional manner, but most rock gently forward and back. There are teacups and bench seats for riders who want a flatter surface to sit upon. Tickets for the carousel cost $1. Children age 5 or younger must be accompanied by an adult age 18 or older. In this case, the adult does not have to pay; only the child needs a ticket. Restrooms and a food court are located near the carousel.

Another attraction of interest to families opened in December 2003. Located on the lower level near Sears, the Heartland Miniature Golf facility features an 18-hole indoor course that attempts to re-create the great outdoors through its sky-blue ceiling, garden-themed murals, and a layout that includes trees, flowers, and ponds. Cost for a round of minigolf is $5 per person, all ages.

Norris Cultural Arts Center (age 3 and up) 

1040 Dunham Road, St. Charles; (630) 584-7200; www.norrisculturalarts.com. North off Highway 64. Call for current schedule and prices.

This modern, brick arts-center complex offers a variety of family-oriented dramatic and musical performances. St. Charles East High School also puts on its plays here; *Peter Pan* was a recent production.

The Market (age 5 and up) 

12 North Third Street, St. Charles; (630) 584-3899. Hours are 10 a.m. to 6 p.m. Monday through Wednesday, 10 a.m. to 9 p.m. Thursday, 10 a.m. to 5 p.m. Friday and Saturday, and 11 a.m. to 5 p.m. Sunday.

This enclosed minimall has about two dozen shops—stalls, actually—under one roof. There are antiques, but kids may be more interested in Beanie Babies, Gund bears, rubber stamps, beads, American Girl books and dolls, and whimsical ceramic mugs with cats and characters from Disney and *Star Wars*. There are too many tempting things for toddlers to grab at, and the narrow aisles are not very handy for strollers, so please don't bring children younger than grade-school age.

Arcada Theatre (age 3 and up)

105 East Main Street, St. Charles; (630) 845-8900. Showing live entertainment and bargain-rate second-run feature films; call for current show titles and times.

Built in 1926 in an ornate style called Venetian Spanish, this theater was designed by architect Elmer F. Behrns, the same guy who did the Chicago Theatre and the Tivoli in Downers Grove. Today the original decor, balcony, and stage are intact. Outside is a big, blazing marquee. Inside, the auditorium has light peach-colored stucco walls and a wraparound balcony with a black wrought-iron railing. Arches and columns below the balcony frame the back of the theater. Hanging lamps with matching wrought iron lend soft illumination to the cavernous interior, which is capped by a domed ceiling painted with blue sky and puffy clouds. Dark wooden crossbeams in the ceiling are adorned with fancy designs in deep reds and greens. There is a curtained, columned balcony on either side of the stage. The proscenium arch frames a gigantic screen, and speakers all around pump out state-of-the-art sound that is an acceptable modification of the original system. The red plush seats also are acceptably modern, with cup holders. Some spaces are left open for theatergoers in wheelchairs. There is also a special accessible restroom with changing table. On Friday and Saturday before the first evening show, the huge pipe organ rises up from the orchestra pit, and an organist plays a little concert.

Where to Eat

Rookies Sports All-American Pub and Grill, 1545 West Main Street; (630) 513-0681; www.rookiespub.com. Hours are 11 a.m. to 1 a.m. Sunday through Thursday and 11 a.m. to 2 a.m. Friday and Saturday. The large family-oriented dining area in front offers good views of the TVs posted all around, tuned to sports, of course. One of Michael Jordan's jerseys hangs in a frame on the wall, along with autographed photos and other memorabilia. The horseshoe-shaped bar is in back. Cheesy thin-crust pizza is the house specialty, but you can also order barbecued ribs, a huge burger, or other sandwiches. Rookies has an extensive kids' menu, and on Thursday two kids per adult eat **free.** $

Gino's East, 1590 East Main Street; (630) 513-1311. Hours are 11 a.m. to 10 p.m. Monday through Thursday, 11 a.m. to 11 p.m. Friday and Saturday, and noon to 9 p.m. Sunday. This pizza place specializes in the same deep-dish kind that you can get at its parent restaurant in downtown Chicago, but you can get the thin-crust type, too. $

Bakers Square, 1510 East Main Street; (630) 584-2737. Hours are 7 a.m. to 11 p.m. Sunday through Thursday and 7 a.m. to midnight Friday and Saturday. See Restaurant Appendix for description. $

Where to Stay

Best Western Inn, 1635 East Main Street; (630) 584-4550 or (800) 937-8376. There are 53 rooms at this 2-story brick motel between Charlestowne Mall and downtown. All rooms are nonsmoking and have cable TV. Amenities include heated outdoor pool, indoor whirlpool, and fitness room. The room rate includes continental breakfast. $$$

Days Inn, 100 Tyler Road; (630) 513-6500. This 3-story, tan-and-brick property was remodeled in 1998. It has 82 rooms, including 1-room and 2-room suites, plus an indoor pool and fitness center. Continental breakfast is included in the room rate. Pets are allowed for an extra $10 a night. $$$

Holiday Inn Express, 1600 East Main Street; (630) 584-5300 or (800) 465-4329. This 2-story property has 122 rooms. Amenities include outdoor pool, fitness center, and laundry room. The room rate includes continental breakfast. $$

Super 8, 1520 East Main Street; (630) 377-8388 or (800) 800-8000. This 3-story Tudor-style budget motel has 67 rooms, but that's about all. No pool. Pets allowed at extra charge with advance permission. The room rate includes continental breakfast. $$$

For More Information

St. Charles Convention and Visitors Bureau, 311 North Second Street, Suite 100, St. Charles 60174; (800) 777-4373; www.visitstcharles.com.

Geneva

Population: 19,515. Just south of St. Charles is Geneva, sort of a sister city to St. Charles (extensive development over the past decade or two makes a boundary between the two cities nearly indistinguishable). Highways 25 and 31 and a number of local north-south streets link Geneva and St. Charles. The easiest entry into Geneva from east or west is Illinois Highway 38 (Roosevelt Road). Northwest Highways 25 and 31 also link up with Highway 38. Off I-88, exit north at the Farnsworth-Kirk exit and proceed north to Highway 38. Geneva is near the end of the line for the Union Pacific Metra West Line commuter service from downtown Chicago.

In the downtown area Geneva has lots of historic homes dating back to the mid-1800s. Many of them have been converted to specialty shops featuring apparel, art prints, pottery, jewelry, woodworking, wine, cheese, crafts, toys and games, and restaurants. For a free brochure containing a map and a complete list of shops with their addresses and phone numbers, write to the Third Street Merchants Association, P.O. Box 95, Geneva 60134.

Graham's Fine Chocolates and Ice Cream (all ages)

302 South Third Street, Geneva; (630) 232-6655. Hours are 10 a.m. to 9 p.m. Monday through Thursday, 10 a.m. to 10 p.m. Friday and Saturday, and noon to 8 p.m. Sunday.

This downtown shop deserves special mention. You can watch candy making and chocolate dipping in action here, and then buy some handmade chocolates and gourmet ice cream.

Kane County Cougars (all ages) 

Games are played at Philip B. Elfstrom Stadium off Highway 38 (you can see it from the highway) at 34W002 Cherry Lane, Geneva; (630) 232-8811; www.kccougars.com. Season runs from April through early September. Most weekend games are in the afternoon, most weekday games in the early evening. Call for the current schedule and prices. During the season the box office is open from 9 a.m. to 6 p.m. Monday through Friday and 10 a.m. to 4 p.m. Saturday; hours are shorter the rest of the year. On game days the box office stays open through the end of the game. $$

The Kane County Cougars are one of the state's most popular minor-league baseball clubs. The Cougars are the A-level affiliate of the Oakland Athletics. A 1998 renovation expanded the stadium's original 1991 capacity to about 9,200 seats, including some red box seats with cup holders and a row of spaces for wheelchairs behind the last row of stands. Some of the additional seating space was taken from the lawn sections along the outfield foul lines. There's still plenty of room in those sections if you want to bring a blanket and sit there; just be aware that there's a fairly steep slope to the turf. There are no awnings or overhangs, so use plenty of sunscreen for day games. A big outfield video screen displays player stats, crowd shots, and advertisements. The concourse behind the seating areas is wide and navigable for wheelchairs and strollers. Restrooms, including one for families, are adequate and well spaced. Concessions are abundant and varied, including fruit-flavored ices and grilled sandwiches as well as the usual ballpark fare. In the souvenir shops you'll find numerous items in Cougar and A's green. Cougars games include entertaining stunts and promotions such as the human bowling ball. A volunteer from the crowd is secured inside a metal-framed ball, which is then rolled down a ramp toward a set of giant plastic bowling pins. In the Mascot Dash, a child volunteer races Ozzie the Cougar around the bases (somehow Ozzie always comes in second).

Fox River Trail (all ages) 

Along the Fox River, Geneva; (630) 232-5980. Open from sunrise to sunset daily. Free.

This paved, 32-mile trail for hiking and biking passes through scenic parks with picnic areas and playgrounds.

Where to Eat

Inglenook Pantry Restaurant, 11 North Fifth Street; (630) 377-0373. Hours are 11:30 a.m. to 4 p.m. Tuesday through Saturday and 11 a.m. to 4 p.m. Sunday; closed Monday. This family-oriented downtown restaurant serves buffet-style food at lunchtime in a historic house. $

Where to Stay

Comfort Inn, 1555 East Fabyan Parkway; (630) 208-8811 or (800) 424-6423. This 3-story motel has 90 rooms and 42 suites. Amenities include indoor pool, hot tub, and exercise room. Room rate includes continental breakfast. $$$$

For More Information

Geneva Chamber of Commerce, 8 South Third Street, Geneva 60134; (630) 232-6060; www.genevachamber.com.

Oregon

Population: 4,060. Oregon is the seat of Ogle County. This town along Highway 64 has a number of attractions that will help you enjoy the natural beauty that surrounds you.

Lowden-Miller State Forest (all ages) 

River Road, Oregon; (815) 732-7329. Open year-round from dawn to dusk daily. Free.

Heading north off Highway 64 on River Road leads you to Lowden-Miller State Forest, a 207-acre tract situated on a bluff across the Rock River from Oregon. Towering above the park is a 48-foot-tall statue completed in 1911 by the famous sculptor Lorado Taft, who named the piece *Eternal Indian,* but everyone calls it Black Hawk, after the Sauk Indian leader. Picnicking, hiking, fishing, and boating are among the activities you can enjoy here.

Pride of Oregon (age 3 and up) 

1469 Route 2 North, Oregon; (815) 732-6761 or (800) 468-4222. Lunch and dinner cruises offered Monday through Saturday; lunch cruise boards at 11 a.m., dinner cruise at 6:30 p.m. Cruises depart a half hour after boarding time and last about 2 hours. $$–$$$

Another river attraction is the *Pride of Oregon.* This elegant paddle wheeler is 102 feet long, with the upper deck open for sightseeing and the lower deck enclosed by glass windows and reserved for dining. Board at the Maxson Manor dock, off Illinois Highway 2 north of Highway 64, for a two-hour cruise, with or without a meal.

Castle Rock State Park (all ages) 

1365 Castle Rock Road, Oregon; (815) 732-7329. Open year-round from dawn to dusk daily. Free.

Highway 2 south of Oregon winds through Castle Rock State Park, named for its sandstone butte along the Rock River. A stairway to the top of the butte affords visitors a fabulous view of the river. This is strictly a day-use park—there's no camping—with about 2,000 acres for picnicking, hiking, fishing, and boating during the milder months and ice fishing and cross-country skiing during winter.

Summer Fun Recreation 

5097 West Pines Road, Oregon; (815) 732-7004. Open in summer from 10 a.m. to 7 p.m. daily. $+

Continuing west on Highway 64 from Oregon, you can pick up the pace a bit at Summer Fun. The larger "maxi" go-kart track is a quarter-mile long and restricted to people who are at least 9 years old and 4 feet, 6 inches tall. There's a separate "mini" track for younger, smaller kids. Players of all ages can putt on the 18-hole miniature golf course, which has lots of moving obstacles to maneuver around. The facility also has a shooting gallery.

Where to Eat

Red Apple, 400 Highway 64; (815) 284-4549. Hours are 6 a.m. to 8 p.m. Tuesday through Saturday and 6 a.m. to 3 p.m. Sunday; closed Monday. Serving breakfast, lunch, and dinner. Steaks and chicken are the chief dinner entrees. Children's menu features chicken, fish, and hot dogs. $

Pizza Hut, Highway 64; (815) 732-4444. Hours are 11 a.m. to 10 p.m. Sunday through Thursday and 11 a.m. to 11 p.m. Friday and Saturday. See Restaurant Appendix for description. $

Where to Stay

Chateau Lodge, 1326 Highway 2 North (1 mile north of Highway 64); (815) 732-6195; www.chateaulodge.com. Wood-paneled rooms in this 1-story brick motel have a rustic look but include such modern conveniences as telephone and cable TV. $

Paddle Wheel Inn, Highway 2, north of Highway 64; (815) 732-4540; www.paddlewheelinn.com. This 2-story motel is situated on the Rock River, across the river from Lowden-Miller State Forest. The *Pride of Oregon* paddle wheeler docks at the on-site restaurant here. Amenities at the inn include spa and sauna but no pool. Room rate includes continental breakfast. $$$ (standard room), $$$$ (luxury riverview suite)

Hansen's Hideaway Ranch, Highway 2; (815) 732-6489. Drive 5 miles west of Oregon on Pines Road, and then turn south onto Harmony Road and continue about 1 mile. This family campground has a ranch atmosphere. Campsites have water and electrical hookups, and there's a shower building that also has flush toilets. Amenities include outdoor swimming pond, playground, game room, snack bar, and firewood. $

Lake LaDonna Family Campground, 1302 South Harmony Road; (815) 732-6804. Drive 5 miles west of Oregon on Pines Road, and then turn south onto Harmony Road. This facility has 3 rental cabins with kitchen and bath, plus campsites with water and electrical hookups and showers. The spring-fed Lake LaDonna has 2 docks, one with a slide and the other with a rope swing. Other amenities include basketball court, volleyball courts, and horseshoe pits. $$

For More Information

Oregon Chamber of Commerce, 303 West Washington, Oregon 61061; (815) 732-2100; www.oregonil.com.

Mount Morris

Population: 3,013. Eight miles west of Oregon along Highway 64 is Mount Morris. Many places here have "White Pines" in their name. So guess what kind of trees you'll see a lot of? You got it—white pines.

White Pines Forest State Park (all ages) 

6712 White Pines Road, Mount Morris; (815) 946-3717. Open year-round from 8 a.m. to sundown daily. Free.

You can turn off Highway 64 to the south for White Pines Forest State Park. Here you'll find what is reportedly the southernmost stand of virgin white pine in the United States. Seven well-maintained hiking trails wind through the trees so you can get a good look. You also can have a picnic or fish here. In some parts of the park, you can play "speedboat" when you drive splashingly across the concrete fords that span the streams of Pine Creek. The Chicago-Iowa trail that borders the south side of this 385-acre park once was a main east-west road through Illinois.

White Pines Roller Skating Center (age 5 and up) 

6929 West Pines Road, Mount Morris; (815) 946-9988; www.skatingfun.com. Open year-round from 7 to 10 p.m. Friday and Saturday and 1 to 4 p.m. Sunday. Parents get in free with a paid child. You may bring your own skates or rent them here. $

This local rink near White Pines Forest State Park offers a change of pace from the great outdoors. The facility has a game arcade and snack bar.

Where to Eat

White Pines Inn, 6712 West Pines Road; (815) 946-3817; www.whitepinesinn.com. Open daily from March through December. The lodge dining room is open to the public for dinner and Sunday Cornhusker Buffet. Fresh fish, baked chicken, and barbecued ribs are among the featured entrees, all served with freshly baked bread. Save room for homemade red raspberry pie, peach cobbler, or a chocolate dessert. Or combine food with entertainment in the White Pines Dinner Theatre. $$

Where to Stay

White Pines Inn, 6712 West Pines Road; (815) 946-3817; www.whitepinesinn.com. Open from March through December. Here you'll find 25 1-room log cabins that were built in the 1930s by the Civilian Conservation Corps. Each cabin sleeps up to 4 people. Package plans are available. The lodge restaurant, which maintains the knotty pine decor, is open for breakfast, lunch, and dinner. $$

For More Information

Mount Morris Village Hall, 105 West Lincoln, Mount Morris 61054; (815) 734-4525.

Savanna

Population: 3,542. If you continue west on Highway 64 all the way to the Mississippi River, you'll reach the town of Savanna. The Grand River Trail for biking goes between Savanna and Moline, roughly along the Great River Road (Highway 84) route.

Mississippi Palisades State Park (all ages)

16327A Highway 84 North, Savanna 61074; (815) 273-2731. Open year-round from 9 a.m. to sunset daily. Admission is free.

Highway 84 runs through Savanna. If you head north, you'll come to Mississippi Palisades State Park. This park has some fascinating rock formations that were carved by erosion. You can have a picnic or go fishing or hiking over 13 miles of trails during summer or go cross-country skiing in winter. There's also a camping area with electrical hookup if you want to stay overnight.

Where to Eat

Pizza Hut, 701 North Main Street; (815) 273-2233. Hours are 11 a.m. to 10 p.m. daily. See Restaurant Appendix for description. $

Where to Stay

Lake Wood Resort and Gardens, 6577 Mill Hollow Road; (815) 273-2898. One mile north of Mississippi Palisades State Park. The campground here has water and electrical hookups, flush toilets, and showers. There's also a primitive camping area "among the wildflowers." Stroll among the annuals and perennials in the gardens or hike in the woods. Guide service is available for the best fishing spots. Hunting is allowed in designated parts of the 140-acre grounds in season with a guide. $

Savanna Super 8, 101 Valley View Drive; (815) 273-2288 or (800) 800-8000. This white, 2-story motel has 46 rooms plus indoor pool and whirlpool. Room rate includes continental breakfast. $$$

For More Information

Savanna Chamber of Commerce, 51 South Main Street, Savanna 61074; (815) 273-2722; www.savanna-il.com.

Fulton

Population: 3,881. Highway 64 goes into Savanna, where it picks up Highway 84, also known as the Great River Road. To reach Fulton from Savanna, travel south on Highway 84 to about where it intersects with U.S. Highway 30. The city's annual Dutch Days festival is held the first weekend in May. Fulton claims to have the only authentic, working Dutch windmill in Illinois. Shipped from the Netherlands and dedicated in

2000, the windmill is open daily from May through September; admission is **free,** but donations are appreciated. You can buy stone-ground flour made on-site at the windmill's gift shop. Call (815) 589-3371 for more information about the windmill.

Great River Bike and Hike Trail (all ages) 

Throughout the town of Fulton; (815) 589-4545. Open daily from sunrise to sunset. Free.

This 20-mile paved section includes a 6-mile loop in and around Fulton. The section forms part of the Great River Trail that stretches 62 miles between Savanna and the Quad Cities and will connect to the Grand Illinois Trail under construction across northern Illinois.

Heritage Canyon (all ages) 

515 North Fourth Street, Fulton; (815) 589-2838. A little over a mile west of Highway 84. Open from April through mid-December. Hours are 9 a.m. to 5 p.m. daily. Admission is free, with suggested donation of $2 per person.

This 12-acre wooded area in the heart of a former rock quarry is the site of a re-created 1860s town, complete with house, log cabins, school, church, doctor's office, and blacksmith shop.

U.S. Lock and Dam 13 (all ages)

4999 Lock Road, at the river off Highway 64, Fulton; (815) 589-4545. Open daily for viewing at any time. Guided tours are given at 1 p.m. Sunday between Memorial Day and Labor Day. Viewing and tours are both free.

You never know what you'll see in the lock when you visit here, but chances are there will be a huge barge in the vicinity. Tours help visitors understand how the system works.

Where to Eat

Sunrise Family Restaurant, 927 Fourteenth Street; (815) 589-4880. Hours are 6 a.m. to 9 p.m. Monday through Saturday and 7 a.m. to 9 p.m. Sunday. This casual eatery serves breakfast, lunch, and dinner. Items on the children's menu cost about $3.25 and include chicken, spaghetti, and "pigs in a blanket"—sausages wrapped in pancakes. $

Where to Stay

Pine Motel, 19020 13th Street; (815) 589-4847. This cozy local property has 9 rooms in the main building and 1 cottage. All are equipped with air-conditioning, telephone, cable TV, and kitchenette with refrigerator and microwave. No pool. $

For More Information

City of Fulton, 415 Eleventh Avenue, Fulton 61252; (815) 589-2616; www.cityoffulton.us.

We'll return one more time to the eastern border of Northern Illinois and make a sojourn west along I-88.

Batavia

Population: 23,866. Batavia lies along Highway 31 between Highway 64 and I-88, so we'll make a quick stop here first. The Windmill City Festival in mid-July features a parade, a carnival, family activities, and food.

Fermilab (age 5 and up)

Kirk Road and Pine Street, Batavia; (630) 840-3351; www.fnal.gov. Grounds are open from 6 a.m. to 8 p.m. daily. Free admission. Enter through the Pine Street gate at the west end of the site and pick up a visitor's pass.

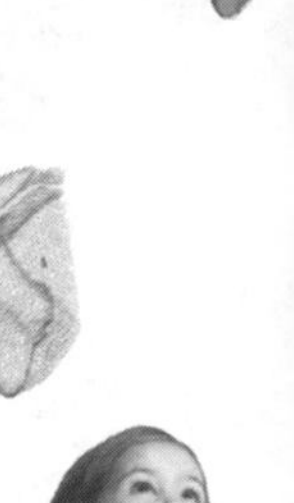

Perhaps the biggest claim to fame in Batavia is the Fermi National Accelerator Laboratory, more commonly called Fermilab, the physics research facility that has the Tevatron, the highest-energy particle accelerator in the world. After the terrorist attacks of September 11, 2001, stricter security measures were established, and the only building still open to the public now is the Leon Lederman Science Education Center. But you can have a guide who can answer your questions and take you through some of the restricted areas; call (630) 840-5588 in advance to arrange this type of free tour. The expansive grounds also encompass a hiking trail through restored tallgrass prairie and a pasture populated by about 75 buffalo. Casey's Pond has mallard ducklings in the water.

Batavia Depot Museum (age 4 and up) 

155 Houston Street, Batavia; (630) 406-5274. Open from March through November; closed December through February. Hours are 2 to 4 p.m. Monday, Wednesday, and Friday through Sunday; closed Tuesday and Thursday. Admission is free, but donations are welcome.

You'll find a variety of railroad and local history exhibits in the Batavia Depot Museum. The bed and dresser used by Mary Todd Lincoln during her stay at Bellview Sanitarium also are on display in this 1854 building. Of particular interest to a writer's family is the display of old typewriters, adding machines, and other office equipment. The Early Woodlands Indian statue at the staircase between the two floors of the museum is an attention-getter. The museum is staffed by volunteers. Near the museum is the Batavia Riverwalk park and boardwalk, where you can take a leisurely stroll through a wildflower garden.

Funway Entertainment Center (age 2 and up) 

1335 South River Street (Route 25), Batavia; (630) 879-8717; www.funwaybatavia.com. Open from April through October. Outback Park and Arcade hours are 11 a.m. to 10 p.m. Sunday through Thursday, 11 a.m. to 11:30 p.m. Friday, and 10 a.m. to 11:30 p.m. Saturday. Package deals can reduce individual attraction costs. Kids Towne, designed for children age 2 through 8, is open from 10 a.m. to 2 p.m. Saturday only. Roller-rink sessions include matinee skates from noon to 3 p.m. Wednesday and Friday and 12:30 to 3:30 p.m. Saturday and Sunday. Family Night skate session runs from 6:30 to 9 p.m. Tuesday. Bowling available from noon to 11 p.m. Sunday through Thursday, noon to midnight Friday, and 11 a.m. to midnight Sunday. $+

Funway Entertainment Center has a plethora of indoor and outdoor activities for families. Indoors you'll find a bowling alley; a roller rink with a cool, sky-blue floor; and a video arcade with bumper cars, for which kids must be at least 52 inches tall to ride. Numerous other activities are outdoors. For the regular go-kart track, you have to be 52 inches tall to ride alone. Special kiddie go-karts are available for youngsters age 6 through 9. These karts use the same track but not at the same time as the bigger ones. The 12 bumper boats (one- or two-seater; height restriction to ride alone is 45 inches) splash around in a pool that also has a jet-stream fountain. The 18-hole Western Trails miniature golf course has a fairly simple layout decorated with flowers, shrubs, rocks, waterfalls, and a cute trail wagon. Batting cages, Jumpshot Basketball, and two huge inflated enclosures—a giant slide and a dinosaur-themed area for jumping, crawling, and sliding—are other attractions outdoors. The outdoor activities shut down in rainy weather and over winter. Pizza, hot dogs, and snacks are available in the Outback Cafe outdoors and in the roller rink indoors.

Also at the Funway Entertainment Center, but with its own entrance, is Kids Towne, a complete little village geared toward children age 2 through 8. The various areas are furnished with props, and the kids supply the imagination. They can sit at a desk or write on the chalkboard in the schoolroom; shop in the grocery store, placing the items on a belt and ringing them up at the register; count play money at a teller window in the bank; mail a letter in the post office; or put on a performance in the theater. There's also a mural wall the kids can write on, and they can play with toys such as sponge puzzles and giant Lego blocks. Although the regular hours are on Saturday only, you can reserve a time Sunday through Friday if you have at least 10 kids; this option is exercised by a number of parent-tot play groups, but it could work for a family reunion as well.

Red Oak Nature Center (all ages) 

Highway 25, 1 mile north of Illinois Highway 56, Batavia; (630) 897-1808. Open from 9 a.m. to 4:30 p.m. Monday through Friday and 10 a.m. to 3 p.m. Saturday and Sunday. Admission is free.

Learn more about the Fox River Valley at this nature center filled with native plants. Naturalists in the facility's interpretive center can explain about the plants, insects, and birds in the area. There are trails for hiking and biking, the shortest being a quarter mile and the longest a mile and a half.

Harold Hall Quarry Beach (all ages) 

400 South Water Street, at Union Street, Batavia; (630) 406-5275. Open from late May through late August. Hours are 12:45 to 8 p.m. daily. $$

Here is a fun summer spot for families. This former rock quarry has a sandy beach, a swimming area with a straight tunnel drop slide (plus a smaller slide for the little kiddies), sand volleyball courts, a playground, and a picnic area where you can bring your own basket (no glass containers or alcoholic beverages allowed) or eat what you buy from the concession stand on the premises. The pool's 1.5 million gallons of water come from far underground, but the water is filtered and chlorinated to meet health safety standards. Much of the shoreline is shallow enough for toddlers to enjoy—within arm's reach of Mom or Dad, of course.

Where to Eat

Chili's, 491 North Randall Road; (630) 761-4479. Hours are 11 a.m. to 10:30 p.m. Sunday through Thursday and 11 a.m. to midnight Friday and Saturday. This chain restaurant features baby-back ribs, burgers, hot and cold sandwiches, soups, and salads. The low-fat Guiltless Grill entrees include lean meats and lots of veggies. Kids' menu entrees for those age 12 or younger cost about $4, including drink and fries. Choose the burger, corn dog, Chicken Crispers, pizza, grilled cheese, or mac and cheese. A kid-size order of the specialty ribs is $5.99. $

Where to Stay

There are no hotels or motels in Batavia. See subsequent entry for Aurora.

For More Information

Batavia Chamber of Commerce, 106 West Wilson Street, Batavia 60510; (630) 879-7134; www.bataviachamber.org.

Aurora

Population: 142,990. Just south of I-88, between Illinois Highways 59 on the east and 47 on the west, is the city of Aurora. There are lots of things for families to see and do here all year long, covering interests from sports to arts to science to history.

Fox Valley Center (all ages) 

Off Highway 59 at New York Street, Aurora; (630) 851-7200. Hours are 10 a.m. to 9 p.m. Monday through Friday, 10 a.m. to 7 p.m. Saturday, and 11 a.m. to 6 p.m. Sunday. No smoking inside the mall.

This two-story indoor shopping mall has about 180 stores, anchored by Macy's, Carson Pirie Scott, JCPenney, and Sears department stores. The mall was renovated in 1998, and skylights that were added give the place a brighter, more cheerful atmosphere. Gently sloping ramps with wooden handrails offer easy access from one level to another for visitors in strollers or wheelchairs. Square clay bricks surface the floors. Kids may gravitate toward the Disney Store, Gamers Paradise, Waldenkids, or Kay-Bee Toys. Yet despite the presence of these stores, the overall impression is that this mall doesn't cater as strongly to families with younger kids as some other malls do. It feels a little more teen oriented, judging by the clientele and by the abundance of stores carrying clothes, shoes, CDs, videos, and novelties. There is a centralized food court on the lower level, but there are also restaurants all along the ring road that encircles the mall. Signs around entrance and exit points off that road are pretty good at helping you find the street you want.

Phillips Park Family Aquatic Center (all ages) 

828 Montgomery Road, Aurora; (630) 851-8686. Open from June through the first week of September. Hours are noon to 7 p.m. Sunday through Friday and 10 a.m. to 5 p.m. Saturday. $$

This is the place for outdoor summer action. It has five pools, four water slides, beaches, and even hot tubs. You can zip down a body slide or a tube slide. Teens may head for the sand volleyball court while their younger siblings enjoy a separate sand play area. The pool has a kids' play area with a waterfall and a kiddie slide. The center has a concession area, so you can spend the better part of a day here if you bring enough sunscreen.

Parkside Lanes (age 2 and up) 

34W185 Montgomery Road, Aurora; (630) 898-5678. Hours vary; call ahead to check for open bowling times. $

With 54 lanes, this is one of the largest bowling alleys in the state. It's a popular venue for families, because it carries small shoe sizes, lighter balls, and bumpers to fill up the gutters to make it easier and more enjoyable for younger children to play. Computerized scoring makes it easier for Mom and Dad to relax and have fun, too. On occasion, usually a weekend evening, the facility offers "Glow Ball" bowling in which the overhead lighting is by black light and the lanes, pins, and balls become luminescent. Rock music plays and laser lights flash. It's funk-a-delic! There is a snack bar as well as the Tiffany's Pizza place to satisfy your hunger.

Paramount Arts Centre (age 3 and up) 

23 East Galena Boulevard, Aurora; (630) 896-6666; www.paramountarts.com. Call or check online for current schedule. The center is accessible for wheelchairs.

This 1930s movie house was restored in 1978 and now hosts a variety of musical and dramatic productions, many of them appropriate for families. A new lobby was added to the building in 2006.

SciTech (all ages) 

18 West Benton Street, downtown Aurora; (630) 859-3434; www.scitech.mus.il.us. Hours from Labor Day through Memorial Day are 10 a.m. to 5 p.m. Monday through Saturday (until 8 p.m. Thursday) and noon to 5 p.m. Sunday. Hours the rest of the year are noon to 5 p.m. Tuesday, Wednesday, Friday, and Sunday; noon to 8 p.m. Thursday; and 10 a.m. to 5 p.m. Saturday; closed Monday. Online coupon gives you $1 off admission. $$

SciTech brings principles such as light, motion, magnetism, and chemistry to life with more than 200 exhibits and hands-on activities. Encase yourself in a giant soap bubble. Walk through a tornado. Launch a balloon to the ceiling. Look for sunspots through the solar telescope. Speak into a microphone and watch the needle jump on the connected volume meter. Make a shadow on the wall that stays behind after you move. These are the sorts of interactive activities you'll find in this high-ceilinged downtown building that years ago was a post office.

Fox River Bicycle Trail (all ages) 

Along the Fox River; (630) 897-5581 for information or (800) 477-4369 for a map. Open from dawn to dusk daily. Accessible for strollers and wheelchairs. Free.

This paved, 42-mile bike trail starts in Aurora and heads north along the Fox River to Crystal Lake. It can also be used for walking.

Blackberry Farm–Pioneer Village (all ages) 

100 South Barnes Road, Aurora; (630) 892-1550; www.foxvalleyparkdistrict.org. Open daily from late April through Labor Day and Friday through Sunday only from the day after Labor Day until mid-October. Hours are 9:30 a.m. to 3:30 p.m. Monday through Friday and 11 a.m. to 5 p.m. Saturday and Sunday. The park reopens for special events around Halloween and Christmas; call for details. Snacks and souvenirs are available. $$

The city's Fox Valley Park District operates the Blackberry Farm–Pioneer Village at West Galena Boulevard (US 30) and Barnes Road. Set on 54 acres of pastoral countryside, this place offers a glimpse of pioneer life of the 1840s. There's a working farm, and on certain weekends you can also see people in period costumes shearing sheep, working in the blacksmith shop, or making craft items. Visit the redbrick schoolhouse to hear a storyteller impart a folktale of the time. Kids can pet farm animals in the Discovery Barn. If your youngsters crave a bit more action, they can whirl around on a beautifully decorated old-fashioned carousel, ride a real pony in the little corral, traverse the grounds in a horse-drawn open wagon, or board the miniature train.

Splash Country Aquatic Center (all ages) 

Adjacent to Blackberry Farm–Pioneer Village, west of Barnes Road and north of Prairie Street, Aurora; (630) 906-7981. Open during summer from noon to 7 p.m. Sunday through Friday and 10 a.m. to 5 p.m. Saturday. $$

This water park has a swimming pool with zero-depth end. The deeper part has lap lanes. You can ride inner tubes down one of the water slides or along the 1,100-foot "lazy river" course.

Where to Eat

Papa Bear Family Restaurant, 2340 North Farnsworth Avenue; (630) 851-1055. Open from 5 a.m. to 11 p.m. daily. Serving breakfast, lunch, and dinner. Entrees include beef, pork, chicken, and pasta dishes, including some Greek food. Children's menu items include burgers, hot beef sandwich, spaghetti, chicken, hot dog, and grilled cheese sandwich, all in the $4 to $5 range, not including drink. $$

Fuddruckers, 4250 Fox Valley Center Drive; (630) 851-9450. Open from 11 a.m. to 9 p.m. Sunday through Thursday and 11 a.m. to 10 p.m. Friday and Saturday. This casual eatery serves juicy, gigantic, made-to-order burgers. $

Red Lobster, 4435 Fox Valley Center Drive; (630) 898-5782. Open from 11 a.m. to 10 p.m. Sunday through Thursday and 11 a.m. to 11 p.m. Friday and Saturday. See Restaurant Appendix for description. $$

Where to Stay

Aurora Fox Valley Inn, 2450 North Farnsworth Avenue; (630) 851-2000. Formerly affiliated with Best Western, this independent 2-story motel has 114 rooms. Amenities include fitness center and outdoor pool. Cribs are available for an extra $5, roll-away beds for $10. $$

Comfort Suites, 111 North Broadway; (630) 896-2800 or (800) 424-6423. This 3-story hotel has 82 suites, each with coffeemaker, refrigerator, and microwave. There is no door separating the living and sleeping areas. Cribs are available upon request. Amenities include indoor swimming pool, hot tub, and kiddie play center. No pets. Continental breakfast is included in the room rate. $$$$

Motel 6, 2380 North Farnsworth Avenue; (630) 851-3600. This budget motel has 119 rooms. Small pets are allowed. $$

For More Information

Aurora Area Convention and Visitors Bureau, 43 West Galena Boulevard, Aurora 60506; (630) 897-5581 or (800) 477-4369; www.enjoyaurora.com.

DeKalb

Population: 39,018. DeKalb is the home of Northern Illinois University, and there are some interesting activities connected with the school. Probably the biggest annual event in town is the DeKalb Cornfest, which rolls around in August and features entertainment as well as enormous quantities of freshly picked sweet corn.

Apple Orchards in the DeKalb Area

Here are a couple of apple orchards in the vicinity of DeKalb for a few hours of family fun that will last even longer in the form of applesauce, pies, and so on.

- **Honey Hill Orchard,** 11747 Waterman Road, Waterman; (815) 264-3337. From DeKalb head south on Illinois Highway 23 about 15 miles. Turn west onto US 30, and Waterman is about a mile farther. This unpretentious orchard is open during early September through October 31. Hours are 9 a.m. to 5:30 p.m. daily. You can pick your own apples here, too, plus raspberries and pumpkins in season. Kids think it is so cool to be able to pluck the apples right off the trees, and to sample produce this fresh is to taste a bite of sunshine. Be sure to take home some of the namesake honey. Apple products for sale include fresh cider, pie, and doughnuts. There is a **free** farm petting zoo here, and sometimes hayrides are offered. For a hot meal or just ice cream after apple picking, head east a few miles on US 30 to **Dairy Joy** in nearby Hinckley (815-286-7701). It's open from 11 a.m. to 9 p.m. daily from early March through late October.
- **Kuipers Family Farm,** 1N318 Watson Road, Maple Park; (815) 827-5200. East of DeKalb off Highway 38, turn south onto Watson Road, a dirt road, and proceed 1 or 2 miles until you come to the farm on the west side of the road. Hours are 9 a.m. to 6 p.m. Tuesday through Friday and 10 a.m. to 6 p.m. Saturday and Sunday in September and October and 10 a.m. to 5 p.m. Tuesday through Sunday from November until a few days before Christmas. This operation is far more commercialized than Honey Hill. It started out with a pumpkin patch in 1998 and then in 2002 bought out the older Pine-Apple Orchard across the street. That's where you pick the apples, usually on Saturday and Sunday only, and where you'll find Christmas trees to cut. The complex on

the original Kuiper property has a section of attractions for entertainment. Offered for a per-person admission fee of $4.50 Wednesday through Friday or $5.50 Saturday and Sunday (with children age 1 or younger **free**), they include a straw maze, a cornstalk tunnel, a tame "haunted forest," pedal tractors, and a petting zoo. On weekends in October kids can take a pony ride for an extra $2.25 each, or the family can ride in a horse-drawn hay wagon for an extra $1 per person. The on-site bakery cranks out tasty apple cider doughnuts and apple and pumpkin pies. More food is available in the Corncrib Cafe, added in 2003. Shops at both the orchard and the pumpkin patch have produce, jellies, and souvenirs for sale. This is a busy place and as such lacks the peaceful atmosphere conducive to the simple pleasure of picking apples.

Huskies Basketball (age 2 and up) 

Games are played at the NIU Convocation Center on West Lincoln Highway, off Annie Glidden Road to the west on the NIU campus, DeKalb; (815) 753-0353 or (800) 332-4695; http://niuhuskies.cstv.com. Season runs from early November through mid-March. Call for a current schedule. Children age 3 or younger admitted free. Parking is $3 per vehicle. $$–$$$

If you want to root for the team in black and red but can't afford Bulls tickets, the Northern Illinois University Huskies are the team for you. The snazzy Convocation Center, opened in 2002, even looks a little like the United Center inside, with a four-sided Jumbotron electronic scoreboard in the center ceiling. Player introductions are made Bulls-style, with spotlights dancing across the darkened arena as an animated video pumps up the fans and the announcer calls out the names. Actually, there are two basketball teams, a men's and a women's, both of which play in the Mid-American Conference. Their quality of play tends to be fairly high; the Huskies have made some NCAA tournament appearances in recent years. It's especially exciting for sports-minded girls to be able to see women players in action, and they often make better three-point shots than the men do. For the Schuldts an ideal outing is when the two teams play on the same day. We catch the afternoon game, go eat supper at Pizza Villa, and then return for the evening game. In addition to the basketball, there is entertainment at halftime, including a spirited dance routine by the Silverettes, accompanied by the NIU band. The Huskies attract fans of all ages. The Convocation Center carries a full line of concessions, including popcorn, cotton candy, hot dogs, pizza, chicken tenders, sandwiches, fries, sodas, and ice cream. Prices for most items are in the $2 to $3 range. Video monitors help you keep an eye on the game while you wait in line. Restrooms are ample; there's even a family one: a single large room, big enough to accommodate a stroller or wheelchair, with toilet and pull-down changing table. The on-site gift shop features caps, T-shirts, and other NIU memorabilia.

Hopkins Park Aquatic Center (all ages) 

1403 Sycamore Road, DeKalb; (815) 758-8853; www.dekalbparkdistrict.com/aquatic_center.html. Enter the pool through the park building at the west end. Open from 11 a.m. to 8 p.m. Sunday through Friday and 11 a.m. to 6 p.m. Saturday. Wading pool opens at 10 a.m. daily. $$

This local swimming facility has been around for many years but was upgraded in the 1990s. The original pool is a big, extra-wide rectangular one that can accommodate a lot of bodies without feeling overcrowded. A long, twisty water slide was added in the center, where the water below is 4 to 5 feet deep, and a shorter, straighter water slide was placed at the shallower end, where it's about 3 to 4 feet deep. There is a separate deepwater diving pool nearby. The newer kiddie pool area is off to one side and enclosed by a fence. It's about 1 foot deep at the edge and 2 feet deep in the middle. Fountain jets spray water inward from the edges, and a little water slide lets the toddlers have their own splashdown. There is a fenced-in concession area with tables if you want to go get a snack.

Egyptian Theatre (age 3 and up) 

135 North Second Street, DeKalb; (815) 758-1215. Call for current schedule of events.

This historic old theater, built in 1929, was renovated in 1980 to recapture its past glory. The tall, light-brick facade has figures of pharaohs gazing out from the corners and a sphinx head above the main entrance. Inside, the stage accommodates live theatrical performances, concerts, and movies.

Ellwood House (age 6 and up) 

509 North First Street, at Augusta Avenue, DeKalb; (815) 756-4609; www.ellwoodhouse.org. Open from March through early December. Guided tours are given at 1 and 3 p.m. Tuesday through Friday and 1, 2, and 3 p.m. Saturday and Sunday. Not recommended for children age 5 or younger. Only the first floor is accessible for wheelchairs. $

This Victorian mansion was once the home of Isaac Ellwood, who made a fortune with his revolutionary fencing material, barbed wire. You must take a half-hour guided tour to see the place; you can't just drop in and wander around. The elegant furnishings reflect the period from the 1870s through the 1920s. The grounds have gardens, a carriage museum, and an 1890s playhouse. The eight-acre site has been declared a National Historic Site. Sometimes there are special events, such as an arts and crafts fair or an ice-cream social, on the grounds.

X Marks the Spot for Trains

Worth a slight detour off I-88 about 15 miles west of DeKalb is the **Rochelle Railroad Park.** Here double sets of tracks from two major freight-train lines, the Burlington Northern and the Union Pacific, make an X as they cross. In a 24-hour day, about a hundred trains thunder through this intersection. (On a recent visit we counted four within 15 minutes!) The park sits on the strip of land inside the X to the east of its convergence point. An open-air shelter with a roof above and picnic tables inside overlooks the X. Old railroad men and little kids alike love to watch the trains as they approach. Children can climb on a nearby scale-model train. The adjacent gift shop is loaded with genuine railroad memorabilia—such as old dining-car dishes and conductors' caps—and model-train paraphernalia. You can buy chips, candy, and sodas, but that's it for concessions. Restrooms are in the gift shop building but have outside access doors; no changing tables. To get to the park from I-88, exit at Highway 251 and head north a few miles. Turn left onto Highway 38 and head west. The road curves south as Ninth Street; continue about 10 blocks through a residential area. You'll know you're there when you reach railroad tracks. The shelter and restrooms are open year-round, 24/7, and are accessible for wheelchairs and strollers. Gift shop hours are 10 a.m. to 5 p.m. Monday through Friday and 10 a.m. to 6 p.m. Saturday and Sunday. For more information, contact Rochelle Railroad Park, 124 North Ninth Street, Rochelle 61069; (815) 561-1231; www.rochellerailroadpark.org. **Free.**

Where to Eat

Pizza Villa, 824 West Lincoln Highway; (815) 758-8116; www.pizzavilla.com. Hours are 4 to 10 p.m. daily. This family-owned restaurant, which has been around since 1956, is a favorite with college students and families alike. The thin-crust pizza is cheesy and to die for. You can also get pasta dinners, sandwiches, and tasty "broasted" chicken. The decor here is rustic, and kids will like the arcade on the lower level. Bring a quarter for the silly machine that dispenses multicolored plastic eggs filled with trinkets; it has a chipped plaster Fred Flintstone perched above the eggs, and the machine shouts "Yabba-Dabba-Doooo!" when the egg rolls down the chute. (Don't ask what the correlation between Fred Flintstone and colored eggs is—it sure attracts the kids.) The entire restaurant is nonsmoking. One caveat: The owner has the audacity to take a week or two off for vacation in summer and simply close the place, so call ahead before driving out there, to avoid the heartbreak of disappointing your taste buds. $

Tom & Jerry's, 215 West Lincoln Highway; (815) 758-1675. Open from 10:30 a.m. to 2 a.m. daily. Named after the TV cartoon cat and mouse, this casual eatery serves a variety of sandwiches and light meals. $

Where to Stay

Travelodge, 1116 West Lincoln Highway; (815) 756-3398 or (800) 578-7878. This budget chain motel has 111 rooms and an outdoor pool. Ask about Sleepy Bear's Den rooms. Pets are allowed. Continental breakfast is included in the room rate. $$

Super 8, 800 West Fairview Drive; (815) 748-4688 or (800) 800-8000. This 2-story 44-room property, unlike most in the chain, has an indoor pool. Continental breakfast is included in the room rate. $$

For More Information

DeKalb Area Chamber of Commerce, 164 East Lincoln Highway, DeKalb 60115; (815) 756-6306; www.dekalb.org.

Returning to the eastern edge of Northern Illinois one last time, we'll make our final foray westward along I-80.

Morris

Population: 11,928. Dropping south on Highway 47 from I-80, the first town we come to is Morris. Two state parks are in this area.

Gebhard Woods State Park (all ages) 

401 Ottawa Street, west of Highway 47, Morris; (815) 942-0796. Open from 8 a.m. to 4 p.m. daily. Free. Dulcimer Festival held here in July.

This 30-acre state park extends along the historic Illinois & Michigan (I & M) Canal and is one of the state's more popular parks. You can have a picnic beneath the shade of a maple, sycamore, or eastern cottonwood tree or go hiking or canoeing. There is a park interpreter on-site. Camping is available for a fee. Call ahead to check availability.

Goose Lake Prairie State Natural Area (all ages)   

5010 North Jugtown Road, Morris; (815) 942-2899. Southeast of Morris on Pine Bluff/Lorenzo Road, midway between Interstate 55 and Highway 47. Open from sunrise to sunset daily. Free. Visitor center is open from 10 a.m. to 4 p.m. Monday through Friday and noon to 4 p.m. daily.

This site covers 2,600 acres, much of it prairie as it was in the mid-1800s. It's reportedly the biggest chunk of prairie left in the state. If you're into identifying plants, look for big bluestem, Indian grass, switchgrass, and wildflowers. Have a picnic or take a hike. You can fish in Heidecke Lake. There is a park interpreter on-site. The visitor center has exhibits of fossils and a display explaining the prairie ecosystem.

Where to Eat

Maria's Ristorante, 1591 Division Street; (815) 942-3351. Hours are 11 a.m. to 11 p.m. Sunday through Thursday and 11 a.m. to 11:30 p.m. Friday and Saturday. Serving lunch and dinner. Pizza and Italian dishes are a specialty here, but you can also get steak, chicken, seafood, and sandwiches, plus salad bar. The children's menu features pasta, fried shrimp, fried cod, pork chop, hot dog, and grilled cheese, at prices in the $4 to $5 range, not including drink. $$

Where to Stay

Comfort Inn, 70 West Gore Road; (815) 942-1433. Near the intersection of I-80 and Highway 47. This 2-story, 50-room inn was renovated in 2001 and has an indoor heated swimming pool. Pets are allowed. Continental breakfast is included in the room rate. $$$

Holiday Inn, 200 Gore Road (I-80 and Highway 47); (815) 942-6600 or (800) 465-4329. This 2-story motel has 120 rooms with cable TV and coffeemaker. Amenities include indoor pool with whirlpool. Pets allowed. $$$

For More Information

Grundy County Chamber of Commerce and Industry, 909 North Liberty Street, Morris 60450; (815) 942-0113; www.grundychamber.com.

Utica

Population: 848. Utica is south of I-80 along Illinois Highway 178. A devastating tornado in April 2004 killed eight people and destroyed many of Utica's homes and buildings, but rebuilding began almost immediately. The town's new indoor waterpark is a testament to the success of that effort. South of town, Highway 178 intersects with Illinois Highway 71. Head east on Highway 71 from that point to reach Utica's major nature attractions, Starved Rock and Mathiessen State Parks, neither of which was greatly affected by the tornado.

Other Things to See and Do

JANUARY

Bald Eagle Watch Weekend, Ottawa; (815) 667-4054

Model Railroad Show, Dixon; (815) 288-6616

Illinois Snow Sculpting Competition, Rockford; (815) 987-8800

FEBRUARY

Teddy Bear Tea, Utica; (800) 868-7625 ext. 386

Cupid's Twist Gymnastics Meet, Elgin; (847) 458-2010

MARCH

Audrey Willmann's Doll & Bear Fair, St. Charles; (630) 264-0004; www.dollandbearshow.com

Farm Toy Show, Sublette; (815) 849-5929

Grundy County Environmental Fair, Coal City; (815) 942-2725

Festival of the Sugar Maples, Marengo; (815) 338-6223

APRIL

Antique Toy and Doll World Show, St. Charles; (847) 526-1645

MAY

Heritage Days Celebration, Streator; (866) 752-7255

Earlville Cruise Night; (815) 246-9545 or (815) 246-8412

Annual Kids' Fishing Expo at Baker Lake, Peru; (815) 223-2671

JUNE

Harvard Milk Days; (815) 943-4614

Ashton Summer Celebration; (815) 453-2331

Lake in the Hills Air Expo; (847) 960-7505

JULY

Seneca Summer Fest; www.senecasummerfest.com

Old Settlers Days, Rockton; (815) 624-7600

Petunia Festival, Dixon; (815) 284-3361

Sugar Grove Corn Boil; (630) 466-5166

AUGUST

Amboy Depot Days; (815) 857-3814

Mendota Sweet Corn Festival; (815) 539-6507

Sandwich Fair; (815) 786-2389; www.sandwichfair.com

SEPTEMBER

Illinois Storytelling Festival, Spring Grove; (815) 344-0181; www.storytelling.org

Morris Skyfest; (815) 942-0113

Watermelon Days, Thomson; (815) 259-5705

OCTOBER

Harvest Time Festival, Waterman; (815) 264-3652

Sycamore Pumpkinfest; (815) 895-5161

Annual Halloween Hoedown, Lemont; (630) 243-2700

NOVEMBER

On the Trail with Night Creatures, Romeoville; (815) 727-8700

Christmas in the Country, Sandwich; (630) 466-4546

Holiday Craft Show, Byron; (815) 234-8535

DECEMBER

Winter Bonfire, Willow Springs; (708) 839-6897

Dickens in Dundee; (847) 622-3848

Seasonal Sights and Sounds Parade, Sterling; (815) 625-2400

Christmas of Yesteryear, Richmond; (815) 678-4040

Illinois Waterway Visitor Center (all ages)

At Starved Rock Dam, 2 miles east of Utica on Dee Bennett Road; (815) 667-4054. Open year-round from 8:30 a.m. to 5 p.m. daily. Free. The visitor center is accessible for wheelchairs.

This visitor center overlooks the lock and dam, where you can see towboats push huge barges into the 110-foot-wide lock. The visitor center has a number of exhibits. Kids especially enjoy going inside the pilothouse from the Illinois Waterway towboat *John M. Warner,* which sank in a 1982 flood. They can see the boat's original steering console, radio, radar antenna, and spotlight. There is a display of pottery, arrowheads, and other tools and artifacts from the Native Americans who lived in the Illinois River Valley as long as 7,000 years ago. Another exhibit chronicles the history of the Illinois & Michigan (I & M) Canal, a 96-mile-long canal that linked Chicago with LaSalle and was completed in 1848.

Starved Rock State Park (all ages)

Highway 71, Utica; (815) 667-4726. Off Highway 71 to the north. Open year-round. Park hours are 5 a.m. to 10 p.m. daily. Visitor center hours are 9 a.m. to 4 p.m. daily. Admission to both the park and the visitor center is free. Tour boat rides on the *Belle of the Rock* paddle wheeler are offered from May through October, operating from 11 a.m. to 4 p.m. Monday through Friday and 10 a.m. to 5 p.m. Saturday and Sunday. Cost is $12 for anyone age 17 or older and $6 for kids age 16 or younger. For $15 per person, all ages, you can try the new Wild Goose 24-passenger airboat. Call (815) 434-9200 or check www.belleoftherock.com for more information. Rides on Rocky the Trolley depart from the Starved Rock Lodge at 1:30 and 3 p.m. Wednesday through Sunday. Cost is $10 for adults and $6 for kids. Call (815) 667-4211 or (800) 868-7625 for further information.

Highway 71 winds through wooded countryside south of Utica to Starved Rock State Park on the south side of the Illinois River. The park's name comes from a story of conflict between Native American tribes in the 1760s. An Illiniwek killed an Ottawa chief, provoking retaliatory attacks against his tribe by both the Ottawa and their allies, the Potawatomi. A group of Illiniwek retreated to a 125-foot sandstone butte overlooking the river, and the butte was promptly surrounded by their enemies. The Illiniwek eventually starved to death up on the rock. Today you can hike to the top of that same butte via a wide, paved walkway and wooden steps with railings. At the top are several observation platforms overlooking the river and dam. You can also meander along 15 miles of trails. The park boasts 18 stream-fed canyons and a variety of trees, flowers, and birds. It's a lovely place for a picnic lunch. The visitor center that opened in 2003 is air-conditioned and has restrooms, a nice gift shop, and a concession area offering burgers, hot dogs, popcorn, ice cream, sodas, and creamy fudge. There's also a historical exhibit room with artifacts in glass cases and a diorama showing Native American peoples and European explorers. The park has hiking and equestrian trails, and you can go fishing or boating in the Illinois River. Pets must remain on a leash at all times, and their owners are expected to clean up after them.

Mathiessen State Park (all ages)  

Highway 71, Utica; (815) 667-4868. Off Highway 71 to the south, across the road from Starved Rock State Park. Open year-round from 8 a.m. to sunset daily. Free admission.

This park has some interesting canyons and rock formations formed by waterfalls and erosion. A 5-mile trail accommodates hikers in temperate weather and cross-country skiers during winter. There is an equestrian trail, too. Bring a picnic basket and enjoy the natural beauty all around you. Swimming is not allowed in this park, however. Pets must stay on a leash at all times, and their owners must clean up after them. There is a vending machine area, but for any other food or information, you'll have to go over to Starved Rock State Park.

Starved Rock Stables (age 10 and up) 

Along Highway 71, west of Starved Rock State Park, Utica; (815) 667-3026. Look for two brown buildings and horse pastures. Open from May through October. One-hour trail rides depart at noon and 2 and 4 p.m. Wednesday through Sunday, with an additional 10 a.m. ride offered on Saturday and Sunday. There is a weight limit of 220 pounds per rider. Kids younger than 10 are not allowed on the trails. $$$$

This stable near the parks offers a leisurely ride along its own private trails, which wind through wooded areas and go up and down hills. No trotting is allowed, just gentle walking. It's a pleasant way to pass an hour, indeed.

Grizzly Jack's Grand Bear Lodge and Indoor Waterpark (all ages)

Highway 178, Utica; (866) 399-3866; www.grizzlyjacksresort.com. Waterpark is for guests of the lodge only; no day passes available. Call or check online for package deals and specials. $$$$

In striking contrast to the nature attractions of the area is this amazing new and still evolving commercial facility. Its cavernous 24,000-square-foot waterpark is four stories tall, the height from which you can ride a twisting water slide. Older kids will get a kick out of the surging wave pool, while younger children can play more safely in a shallow pool filled with playground apparatus and spray jets. Waterfalls spill over rock formations that separate the various sections and add to the ambience. Adjacent to the waterpark is the Cave Arcade full of electronic and skill games for which you can earn prizes. Grizzly Jack's Forest is a nearby separate indoor amusement park with bumper cars and eight other adult-size rides; at press time, plans were in the works to add the Snowball ride with giant snowman from the now defunct Santa's Village, which Grizzly Jack's bought when the venerable Dundee amusement park went out of business in 2006. Outdoors, an 18-hole miniature golf course on the lodge grounds is open when weather permits, and the Grizzly Bear Express, a mock train on regular rubber tires, tours the grounds carrying both kid and adult riders. Plans were in the works to add some outdoor amusement park rides as well. The lodgings all have rustic-looking decor but are thoroughly modern in their comfort and amenities; even the "basic" Vacation Suites are spacious. If you want to do your own cooking, you can rent a Vacation Villa or Log Cabin with full kitchen. The lodge offers nightly storytime for children if you're too tired to read to them before bed.

Where to Eat

Starved Rock Lodge, In Starved Rock State Park; (815) 667-4211 or (800) 868-7625. Open from 8 a.m. to 9 p.m. daily. Serving breakfast, lunch, and dinner. Reservations strongly recommended for dinner, especially on weekends. You don't have to be an overnight guest to dine in the lodge restaurant. Dinner items include steak, chicken, and pasta dishes. $$

Country Cupboard Ice Cream, Sandwich and Pizza Shoppe, 402 Clark Street; (815) 667-5155. Hours are 11 a.m. to 9 p.m. daily. In addition to the ice cream, you can have a light meal of burgers, sandwiches, or soup. $

Cajun Connection, 897 East U.S. Highway 6; (815) 667-9855; www.ronscajunconnection.com. Open from 4 to 9 p.m. Wednesday through Saturday and noon to 6 p.m. Sunday. "A Taste of Louisiana" is what chef Ron McFarlaine offers at this lively eatery in a remodeled house. Spice up your life with gumbo, jambalaya, or even batter-fried alligator. The kids' menu includes the usual chicken nuggets and grilled cheese plus something you probably won't find on any other kids' menu anywhere else in Illinois—frog legs! If you're lucky, you might be able to catch live music, for example, when they celebrate Mardis Gras in July.

Where to Stay

Starved Rock Lodge, In Starved Rock State Park; (815) 667-4211 or (800) 868-7625; www.starvedrocklodge.com. The lodge is a good choice for convenience. The area around here is quite rural, and there aren't a lot of other options nearby. This stone-and-log lodge, which was built in the 1930s by the Civilian Conservation Corps, sits on a bluff southwest of the namesake rock and has 72 luxury hotel rooms, plus a great hall with stone fireplace. There are also 13 renovated cabin rooms (without TV, which can be a plus). Kids age 11 or younger stay **free** with their parents. $$$–$$$$

Starved Rock Family Campground, In Starved Rock State Park; (815) 667-4726. Tent camping is available at 133 sites with

Other Helpful Regional Sources of Information

- **Blackhawk Waterways Convention and Visitors Bureau,** 201 North Franklin Avenue, Polo 61064; (815) 946-2108; www.bwcvb.com.
- **Lee County Tourism Council,** 113 South Peoria Avenue, Dixon 61021; (815) 288-1840; www.leecountytourism.com.

electrical hookup. The facility has showers and toilets. Fires are allowed in grill pits only. Pets must be kept on leashes at all times, and owners are expected to clean up after them. Alcoholic beverages are prohibited. $

For More Information

Heritage Corridor Visitor Bureau, 801 East US 6, Utica 61373; (815) 667-4356; www.heritagecorridorcvb.com.

If you keep driving west on I-80, you'll arrive at the Mississippi River and drop southward into Western Illinois, which is the subject of the next chapter.

Western Illinois

Rivers are the claim to fame for the 20 counties of Western Illinois. The mighty Mississippi forms the western boundary of the region (and the state), and the smaller but lovely Illinois defines its eastern edge. Floods during the 1990s made life along the waterways especially tough, but most of the people who live in the river towns sandbagged their way through the hard times and are still around to affirm the area's peaceful beauty. For information about the region, contact the **Western Illinois Tourism Development Office,** 581 South Deere Road, Macomb 61455; (309) 837-7460; www.visitwesternillinois.info.

In the upper west corner of Western Illinois, along the Mississippi River, lie the cities of Moline and Rock Island. Together with the Iowa cities of Davenport and Bettendorf on the other side of the river, they make up the Quad Cities. If you live in the Chicago area, the Quad Cities are only a two- to three-hour drive from home, easily accessible from Interstate 88 or 80. The route is less direct from the south, but you'll have an interesting drive up on U.S. Highways 67 or 51, the latter of which joins up with Interstate 74 around Bloomington and heads in via Peoria and Galesburg. Special events in the Quad Cities include the Quad Cities Jazz Festival in mid-May, Taste of the Quad Cities in Moline in late June, the Mississippi Valley Blues Festival in late June or early July, the Rock Island Summer fest in mid-July, the Rock Island County Fair in mid- to late July (both Moline and Rock Island are in Rock Island County), and the Bix Beiderbecke Weekend (Dixieland jazz) in late July; this last event actually takes place across the river in Iowa but may make hotel space tight on the Illinois side as well. For details about special events or for a useful visitor's guide or other information, contact the **Quad Cities Convention and Visitors Bureau,** 2021 River Drive, Moline 61265; (563) 322-3911 or (800) 747-7800; www.visitquadcities.com.

WESTERN ILLINOIS

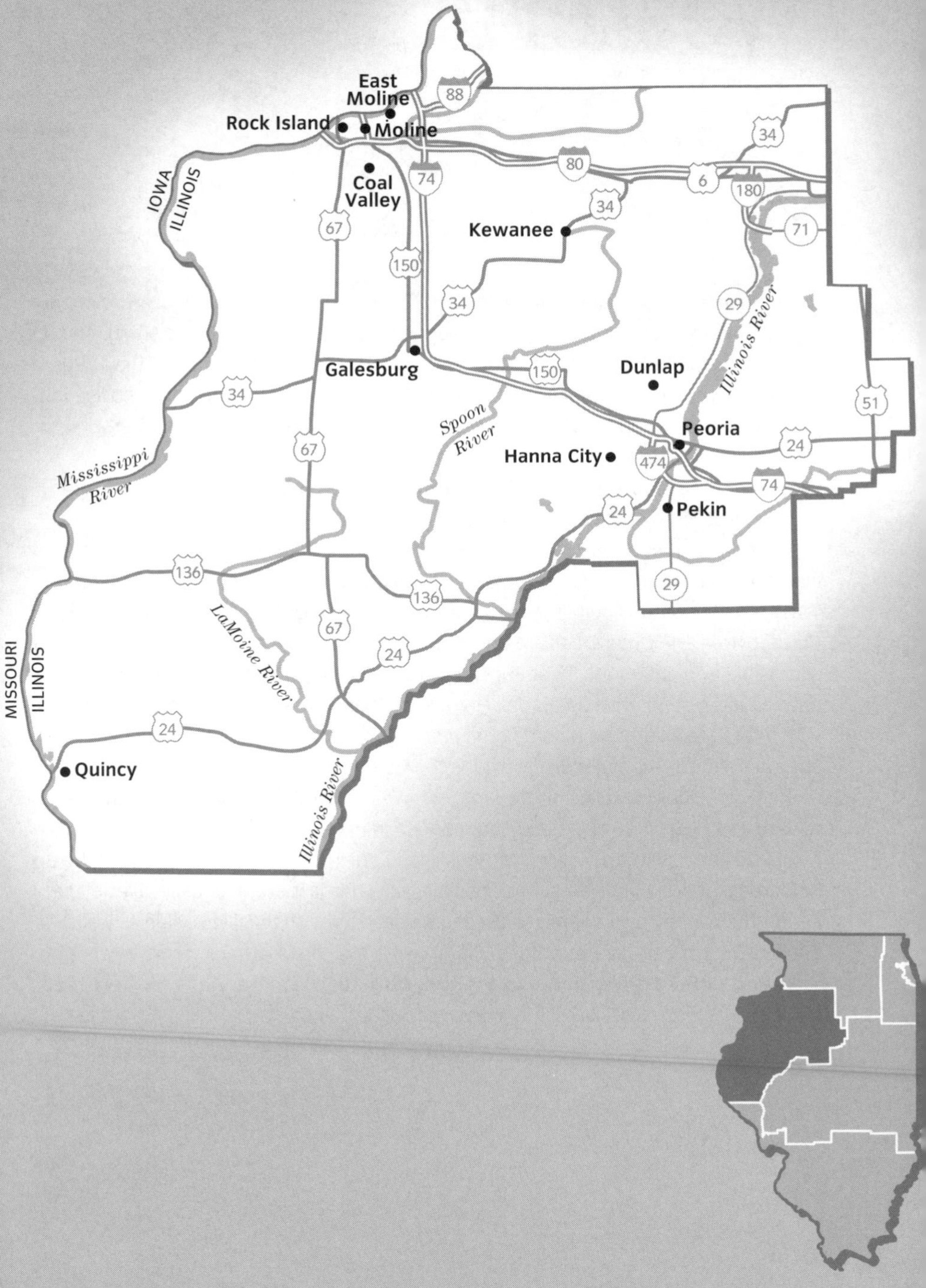

East Moline
88
Rock Island
Moline
34
80
6
180
74
Coal Valley
34
IOWA
ILLINOIS
67
71
Kewanee
150
34
29
Illinois River
Galesburg
150
Dunlap
34
51
Spoon River
Peoria
67
24
Mississippi River
Hanna City
474
74
24
Pekin
136
29
136
LaMoine River
67
24
MISSOURI
ILLINOIS
24
Quincy
Illinois River

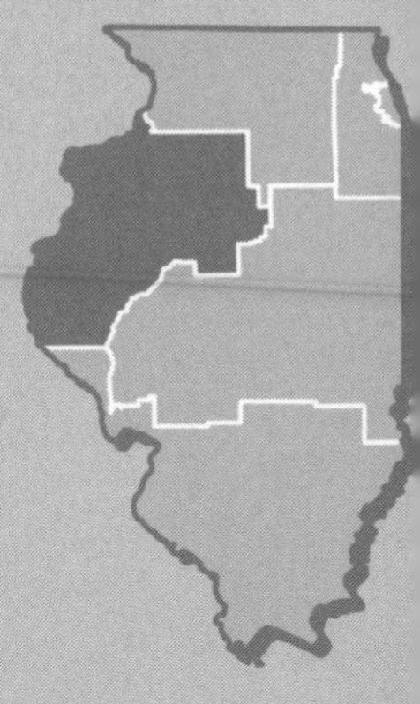

Moline

Population: 43,768. Let's start our Quad Cities visit in Moline. Most of the city lies between the Mississippi and the Rock Rivers, and I-74 cuts straight through. Under construction as this book went to press was a new attraction on the riverfront: Parakeet Island, a family-oriented amusement center with a tropical theme. The centerpiece Parrot Mountain Adventure Golf was to feature a 40-foot-tall volcano and an Albatross seaplane modeled after the one owned by Jimmy Buffett, the mellow crooner best known for his hit song "Margaritaville." Other attractions were to include electric go-karts, a video arcade, and a beach with sand volleyball, tiki huts, and an outdoor stage for live music. Concessions and a gift shop selling official Buffet merchandise also were planned. The entertaining Web site (www.parakeetisland.com) gives progress updates and plays cheery steel drum tunes. For further information contact Parakeet Island, 5420 River Drive, Moline 61265; (309) 736-9099.

John Deere World Headquarters (all ages)

One John Deere Place, off John Deere Road (Illinois Highway 5), Moline; (877) 201-3924 or (800) 765-9588. Open from 8 a.m. to 5:30 p.m. daily. Admission is free.

You'll be surprised at how much fun you'll have here. The facility was designed by the late Eero Saarinen, an acclaimed architect. You'll drive along a smoothly paved road through a wooded area (there's even a pond with swans and ducks) to reach the 20,000-square-foot product display building that is the center's family attraction. The two-story, glass-walled, rectangular building contains a collection of big, new, shiny green farm machines and yellow construction equipment that visitors can climb up into. Some of these rigs have tires that are about 6 feet in diameter, and the view from the cab of the mammoth combine conjures up visions of Stephen King run amok in a cornfield. Kids of all ages love it. Those with a historical bent will enjoy the long, glass-encased wall of memorabilia from the 1800s that includes advertising posters, folk art, and small farm implements and kitchen utensils. (Anyone who watches Roadrunner or Animaniacs cartoons will get a kick out of seeing a real anvil.) Because the center is the world headquarters for John Deere, you'll find plenty of brochures to pick up and helpful staff on the upper floor to answer questions. A small video station nestled under one staircase allows you to sit and watch the latest models of tractors and harvesters in action.

SouthPark Mall (all ages) 

4500 Sixteenth Street, off I-74 at John Deere Road, Moline; (309) 797-9070. Open from 10 a.m. to 9 p.m. Monday through Saturday and noon to 6 p.m. Sunday. The mall is accessible for strollers and wheelchairs.

If you're in the mood to shop, Moline has this indoor mall. JCPenney, Sears, Von Maur, and Younkers are the anchor department stores, with a wide array of specialty shops making up the balance. A 500-seat food court offers a place for respite. If you've never eaten a Maid-Rite, be sure to get one of these hamburger buns filled with loose, seasoned ground beef (plus cheese, if you like). The eatery also offers fries, shakes, and soft drinks to round out the meal. Yum! (If you don't want to visit the mall, Maid-Rite has shops all over the Quad Cities; check the local phone book for the nearest one.) Stores of particular interest to families with young children include Gymboree, Kay-Bee Toys, and the Children's Place.

MARK of the Quad Cities (all ages) 

1201 River Drive, Moline; (309) 764-2001. For Quad City Flames, call (309) 764-7825 or check www.qcflames.com. For Quad City Steamwheelers, call (866) 783-2684 or check www.steamwheelers.com.

This 12,000-seat indoor arena on the riverfront in downtown Moline opened in 1993. A spacious facility, it is clean and well lit. Elevators on both sides allow easy access to the upper level for people who have difficulty climbing stairs. Restrooms are conveniently located, and the women's rooms have changing tables. Concession locations are adequate, offering such standard fare as hot dogs, burgers, pizza, popcorn, soft pretzels, nachos, ice cream, sodas, and beer at average prices. The MARK hosts a variety of special events throughout the year. The facility also is the home of two sports teams: the Quad City Flames of the American Hockey League and the Quad City Steamwheelers of the Arena Football League 2. If you've never seen arena football, give it a try. The indoor field is about half the size of a regular outdoor field, and there are nets and bumpers off of which the players and the ball bounce around. The rules are a little different, too. It's just wacky!

John Deere Pavilion (all ages)

1400 River Drive, Moline; (309) 765-1000; www.johndeerepavilion.com. Hours are 9 a.m. to 5 p.m. Monday through Friday, 10 a.m. to 5 p.m. Saturday, and noon to 4 p.m. Sunday. Admission is free. No smoking inside the building.

This 15,000-square-foot exhibition hall with a glass front is across the street from the MARK of the Quad Cities in downtown Moline. Built in the late 1990s, it is literally a big part of the city's riverfront renovation project. Inside are antique tractors and exhibits related to agriculture. Although it also has some huge farm machines, this facility is more formal than the world headquarters building described earlier in this section; you can't run around and climb on everything here. The John Deere Store souvenir shop has some quality merchandise, including sturdy toy tractors and Ertl toys. The Planted Earth Cafe has food.

Celebration Belle (age 4 and up) 

2501 River Drive, Moline; (309) 764-1952 or (800) 297-0034; www.celebrationbelle.com. Operates year-round. Call or check the Web site for current schedule and prices of sightseeing and dinner cruises. Specialty cruises and package deals are also available. Cruises are not recommended for children age 3 or younger. $–$$$

Amid all the casino boats plying the rivers these days, here's a vessel without gambling that you can take for a family excursion along the scenic waterfront. Operated by Celebration River Cruises, the basic sightseeing cruise on the white, three-level *Celebration Belle* lasts one and a half hours, but longer excursions are also available.

Ben Butterworth Parkway (all ages) 

Along River Drive from 26th to 55th Streets, Moline; (309) 797-0785. Open from 6 a.m. to 11 p.m. daily. Admission is free.

This 2.2-mile paved bike path winds through a scenic park along the Mississippi River. There are three playgrounds and two picnic shelters in the park as well.

River Valley Golf (age 3 and up) 

5000 38th Avenue, Moline; (309) 762-7160. Open from May through September, weather permitting. Hours are 11 a.m. to 10 p.m. Sunday through Thursday and 11 a.m. to 11 p.m. Friday and Saturday. $

This 18-hole outdoor miniature golf course features rock gardens and waterfalls. There are no moving parts, but some tricky angles make the course a challenge.

Where to Eat

TGIFriday's, 1425 River Drive; (309) 764-6400. Along the riverfront, next to the MARK of the Quad Cities. Hours are 11 a.m. to 10 p.m. Sunday through Thursday and 11 a.m. to midnight Friday and Saturday. See Restaurant Appendix for description. $

Miss Mamie's Catfish House, 3925 16th Street (corner of 16th Street and Blackhawk Road); (309) 762-8336. Near SouthPark Mall. Open from 11 a.m. to 9:45 p.m. Monday through Thursday, 11 a.m. to 10:15 p.m. Friday and Saturday, and 11 a.m. to 9 p.m. Sunday. Items on the kids' menu—such as catfish sticks, chicken sticks, popcorn shrimp, and ribs—cost $3.95, including beverage. $

Rudy's Tacos, 2414 16th Street; (309) 762-3293. Hours are 11 a.m. to 10 p.m. Sunday through Thursday and 11 a.m. to 11 p.m. Friday and Saturday. Some Quad City natives swear by Rudy's Tacos, the namesakes of which are generously loaded with spicy meat and trimmings. These casual eateries also offer "Mexican burgers," hot dogs, salads, and—unlike Taco Bell—beer, wine, and full bar service in addition to soft drinks. $

Lagomarcino's, 1422 5th Avenue; (309) 764-9548. Hours are 9 a.m. to 5 p.m. Monday through Saturday; closed Sunday. Billed as a "turn-of-the-century ice-cream parlor and confectionery," Lagomarcino's offers ice-cream treats and homemade hand-dipped chocolates, plus sandwiches on homemade bread and salads if you want something besides dessert. $

Old Country Buffet, 3901 41st Avenue; (309) 797-8591. Hours are 11 a.m. to 8:30 p.m. Monday through Thursday, 11 a.m. to 9 p.m. Friday, 8 a.m. to 9 p.m. Saturday, and 8 a.m. to 8:30 p.m. Sunday. See Restaurant Appendix for description. $

Where to Stay

Radisson on John Deere Commons, 1415 River Drive; (309) 764-1000 or (800) 333-3333. Next to the MARK of the Quad Cities. This 6-story hotel has 163 rooms. Amenities include an indoor pool and hot tub on the ground floor in front. Dine in the adjoining TGIFriday's restaurant. Continental breakfast can be included in the room rate. $$$$

Comfort Inn Moline, 2600 52nd Avenue; (309) 762-7000 or (800) 424-6423. This 2-story motel has 62 rooms. Amenities include a small indoor pool and whirlpool. The room rate includes continental breakfast. $$$

Best Western Airport Inn, 2550 52nd Avenue; (309) 762-9191 or (800) 937-8376. This tan, 3-story motel received a 2-diamond rating from AAA. It has 50 rooms with cable TV. Amenities include an indoor swimming pool and hot tub. Continental breakfast is included in the room rate. $$$

Fairfield Inn, 2705 48th Avenue; (309) 762-9083 or (800) 228-2800. This 3-story, 63-room property has an indoor pool and whirlpool. The room rate includes continental breakfast. $$$

For More Information

Moline/Quad Cities Welcome Center, 2021 River Drive, Moline 61265; (563) 322-3911.

East Moline

Population: 20,333. This suburb east of Moline has a couple of fun attractions for active families.

EMPIRE Playground (all ages) 

In Mississippi Park on Illinois Highway 84, East Moline; (309) 752-1573. Near the East Moline–Hampton border. Open year-round from 7 a.m. to 10 p.m. daily. Admission is free.

The name of this huge outdoor wooden playground, EMPIRE, is an acronym for East Moline Playground Innovation Recreation Efforts. That's a fancy way of conveying that this was a community effort, built by hundreds of volunteers and financed entirely by donations. It's really something to be proud of—14,000 square feet of towers, tunnels, bridges, rope ladders, and slides. The official count is "48 play stations." The park where you'll find this playground is right on the banks of the Mississippi River. There are picnic tables and two pavilions with electricity, so you can bring lunch or supper to the park—if you can get the kids to stop playing long enough to eat. There's also a bike path.

Little Mississippi (age 3 and up) 

Highway 84, East Moline, at the East Moline–Hampton border; (309) 755-1212. Open daily from June through August and Saturday and Sunday only in May and September. Hours are noon to 8 p.m. $+

The 18-hole miniature golf course is just part of the fun at this outdoor amusement center adjacent to the EMPIRE Playground. It also has two more unusual games. The first, Bankshot, is sort of a cross between basketball, billiards, and miniature golf. You go around a course with 18 stations. At each one you shoot a basketball into a hoop—but the backboards are different sizes and shapes, and sometimes the only way to make the shot is to somehow carom the ball off the backboard. The second unusual game is Water Wars. For this one, two wooden cages or booths stand facing each other some distance apart. Each cage has an opening high up in the wall near the slatted roof. The person inside slings a water balloon out the opening toward the opposing cage. When the balloon splats against the cage, water drips through the roof and sides to dampen the opponent. If you have a really good aim, you might even douse him or her with a direct hit. You get a bucket of eight water balloons per game, and you can have up to three players inside each cage, so you can make it a family feud if you like. There is a concession stand for munchies to keep you going.

Where to Eat

Godfather's, 1347 42nd Avenue; (309) 792-3706. Hours are 11 a.m. to 10 p.m. Sunday through Thursday and 11 a.m. to midnight Friday and Saturday. The medium-thick, chewy-crust pizza here is loaded with cheese and your favorite ingredients. Round out the meal at the salad bar. $

Where to Stay

Super 8, 2201 John Deere Road; (309) 796-1999 or (800) 800-8000. This 2-story budget chain property has 60 rooms. Amenities include hot tub and exercise room but no swimming pool. Pets are allowed. The room rate includes continental breakfast. $$

Coal Valley

Population: 3,606. Just south of Moline is Coal Valley, which has one of the area's prime family attractions—the Niabi Zoo.

Niabi Zoo (all ages) 

13010 Niabi Road, Coal Valley; (309) 799-5107; www.niabizoo.com. The zoo is open from mid-April through Labor Day from 9:30 a.m. to 5 p.m. daily; after Labor Day through mid-October, hours are from 11 a.m. to 4 p.m. Monday through Friday and 9:30 a.m. to 5 p.m. Saturday and Sunday. The zoo is closed from mid-October through mid-April. The train departs the station every 15 minutes, and a ride costs $1.50 per person for anyone age 1 or older. Carousel tokens cost $1.50 per person. No smoking throughout zoo grounds. $

Driving along U.S. Highway 6 south of the Rock River, turn south onto East 11th Street, which runs into Niabi Road. The entrance area has a small parking lot and a low, one-story building housing the ticket sales area, main concession stand, and gift shop. The zoo grounds rest on 30 acres of Rock Island County Forest Preserve land. *Niabi* is reportedly an Oswego Indian word meaning "young deer spared from the hunter's arrow." Deer and other hooved animals are prominent among the approximately 160 species on display. You're also likely to see lions, camels, bobcats, wolves, wallabies, bears, monkeys, and Asian elephants. The author is particularly partial to the cute little multicolored birds called Lorikeets. Niabi Zoo is of a traditional style, with iron bars and fencing surrounding the animals' pens or pits. While this style looks rather like a prison, it nonetheless allows closer access to the animals than the more modern, open-spaces zoos do. Primates and birds have both indoor and outdoor display areas. The reptile house is interesting but very stuffy. Wide, paved pathways are easy to navigate with strollers or wheelchairs. The well-maintained grounds feature wildflowers and prairie grasses, and there are picnic tables and playgrounds when you're ready for a break. If the kids' feet get tired, you can take them for a ride around the zoo on the Mel McKay Express, a shuttle-size replica of an old steam engine, or give them a spin on the Endangered Species Carousel, a gilded merry-go-round featuring tigers, gorillas, elephants, and zebras.

Where to Eat and Stay

See entries for Moline and Rock Island.

Rock Island

Population: 39,684. The most prominent feature of Rock Island is Arsenal Island, which floats in the middle of the Mississippi River but has bridges connecting it to both the Illinois and the Iowa sides. The arsenal is an active U.S. Army factory, so you'll probably see some military personnel as you drive along. The Mississippi River Visitors Center at the west end of the island overlooks Lock and Dam 15 and has displays explaining how the process of "locking through" works so that you'll know what's going on when you see a barge down below. On the mainland the Rock Island Arts and Entertainment District, just called "the District" around town, handles special events and festivals; call (309) 788-6311 for details.

Rock Island Arsenal Museum (all ages) 

Building 60, Rock Island Arsenal, Rock Island; (309) 782-5021. Open from 10 a.m. to 4 p.m. daily except on Thanksgiving and the day after, Christmas Eve, Christmas Day, New Year's Eve, and New Year's Day. Admission is free.

Established in 1905, the Rock Island Arsenal Museum houses an extensive collection of vintage firearms among its historical displays. Its Children's Discovery Room has uniforms and helmets that kids (and parents) can try on.

Rock Island Arsenal Bike Trail (all ages) 

On Arsenal Island; (309) 794-5338. Open from dawn to dusk daily. Free.

This paved bike trail around the island is about 4 miles long, passing all the various sites. Helmets are required for all riders on the island.

Circa '21 Dinner Playhouse (age 3 and up) 

1828 Third Avenue, Rock Island; (309) 786-7733; www.circa21.com. Call for current schedule and ticket prices.

Housed in the historic Fort Armstrong Theatre, this dinner theater puts on some children's and family-friendly productions in addition to the usual shows geared toward adults.

Quad City Botanical Center (all ages) 

2525 Fourth Avenue, downtown Rock Island; (309) 794-0991; www.qcgardens.com. Hours are 10 a.m. to 5 p.m. Monday through Saturday and noon to 5 p.m. Sunday. Babies age 1 or younger get in free. $

Three square arches frame the walls and roof of glass in this spacious facility opened in 1998. It houses colorful tropical plants and garden greenery. There are some hands-on activities for kids.

A Night in the Slammer

About 30 miles southwest of the Quad Cities, in the little town of Aledo (population 3,613), is a fun place to stay overnight. The Slammer is a bed-and-breakfast inn housed in the former town jail. The three-story building has nine guest rooms, each with shared bath. You also can share the sauna and Jacuzzi on the third floor or take a stroll through the preserved cell block. For a family, a room with two queen-size beds costs $85 per night, which includes a full breakfast the next morning. No smoking and no pets are allowed on the premises. For recreation the town has a movie theater and a public swimming pool. To reach the Slammer take US 67 south to Viola and turn right onto Illinois Highway 17, heading west into downtown Aledo. The Slammer stands at 309 South College Avenue, across from the courthouse. For further information or reservations, call (309) 582-5359 or check www.theslammer.net.

Whitewater Junction (all ages) 

In Longview Park, 1601 Longview Drive, Rock Island; (309) 732-7946. Open from late May through late August. Hours are 11 a.m. to 5 p.m. and 6 to 8 p.m. Monday through Friday and 10 a.m. to 6 p.m. Saturday and Sunday. $$

This railroad-themed water park opened in 2003. It has a play area for children that includes zero-depth pool, fountains, and kiddie water slide. For older kids and adults, there's a deeper pool with lap lanes, spiral slide, and tube slide. Tables in the concession area have big umbrellas for shade.

Hauberg Indian Museum (age 5 and up) 

1510 46th Avenue, Rock Island; (309) 788-9536; www.blackhawkpark.org/hauberg.htm. Open daily from 9 a.m. to noon and 1 to 5 p.m. from March through October; closing time is 4 p.m. from November through February. Admission is free, although there is a suggested donation of $2 per adult and $1 per child.

On a wooded hill above Blackhawk Road in Rock Island stands the Hauberg Indian Museum. Nestled in a corner of a stone lodge built by the Civilian Conservation Corps in 1939, this museum is small but interesting if you're willing to take the time to examine it carefully and talk with the guide; kids below grade-school age would probably get bored quickly. Life-size dioramas show day-to-day life among the Sauk and Fox Indians throughout the four seasons during the period of 1750 to 1830. The dioramas contain authentic artifacts, and the summer and winter houses were constructed by residents of the contemporary Mesquakie Reservation. A bronze bust of the famous Sauk chief Black Hawk was made from an original plaster cast of his face.

Black Hawk State Historic Site (all ages) 

1510 46th Avenue, Rock Island; (309) 788-0177; www.blackhawkpark.org. Open from sunrise to 10 p.m. daily. Admission is free.

The Hauberg Indian Museum takes up only a fraction of the 208 acres composing the Black Hawk State Historic Site, which was first occupied by Native Americans as long as 12,000 years ago. The area was home to the powerful Sauk Nation from about 1730 to the late 1820s, when white European settlers began moving in following the questionably legal cessation of the Indian lands to the U.S. government two decades earlier. It is easy to see why anyone would want to live in this forested area along the Rock River, and the Illinois Historic Preservation agency that manages the site has taken care to maintain the indigenous wildflowers, trees, and birds. Please take care to leave them undisturbed when hiking along the site's 4 miles of marked trails.

Where to Eat

Huckleberry's, 223 18th Street; (309) 786-1122. Hours are 11 a.m. to 2 p.m. Monday, 11 a.m. to 9 p.m. Tuesday through Thursday, 11 a.m. to 11 p.m. Friday, 4:30 to 11 p.m. Saturday, and 4:30 to 9 p.m. Sunday. This local pizzeria offers both hand-tossed and deep-dish varieties. $

Poor Boy's Pizza, 4500 Blackhawk Road; (309) 786-2400. Open from 10:30 a.m. to midnight Sunday through Thursday and 10:30 a.m. to 1 a.m. Friday and Saturday. The tasty pizza here is another local treat. $

Rudy's Tacos, 2716 18th Avenue; (309) 794-1678. Hours are 11 a.m. to 10 p.m. Sunday through Thursday and 11 a.m. to 11 p.m. Friday and Saturday. This one's a brother to the Rudy's in Moline. $

Where to Stay

Holiday Inn, 226 17th Street; (309) 794-1212. This 8-story hotel has 172 rooms. Amenities include indoor swimming pool and exercise room. There is a restaurant on-site. No meals are included in the room rate. $$$

For More Information

Mississippi River Visitors Center, West End of Arsenal Island, Rock Island 61204; (309) 794-5338.

Kewanee

Population: 12,944. U.S. Highway 34 and Illinois Highways 78 and 81 converge in this Western Illinois town. It's easy to reach from I-80, too—just head south about 10 miles on Highway 78. Kewanee is famous for the huge Good's Furniture House downtown (200-220 Main Street North; 309-852-5656; www.goodsfurniture.com), but two other, less commercial attractions may be of greater interest to families.

Celebrating Agriculture, Swedish-Style

In late September you can celebrate Jordbruksdagarna, or Agricultural Days, in the historic village of Bishop Hill near Kewanee (look for signs along Highways 81 or 17 that direct you down the county roads leading to it). Religious dissidents from Sweden formed a communal society here in the mid-1800s, and many of the original buildings have been restored. Local artisans make traditional crafts such as pottery, jewelry, woven baskets, and wooden wares. For further information contact the Bishop Hill Arts Council, P.O. Box 47, Bishop Hill 61419; (309) 927-3345; www.bishophill.com.

Woodland Palace (all ages)

In Francis Park, off Illinois Highway 34, Kewanee; (309) 852-0511. Open from mid-April through mid-October. Hours are 1 to 5 p.m. daily. $

Frederick Francis, a 35-year-old inventor who had become wealthy from his patented watch springs, built this unusual house for himself and his wife in 1890. He kept adding handmade features and furniture to it until his death from a hernia at age 70 in 1925. A combination of wood, bricks, and stone, the house has no electricity, yet Francis was able to design an air-cooling system to keep the house comfortable in summer and install radiant-heat deflectors in the fireplace chimney to warm the home in winter. Pocket doors that slide into the wall seem to "disappear." Similarly, screens that retract into the walls above and below the window frames create a now-you-see-it, now-you-don't effect. Although you can wander around by yourselves, you'll enjoy your visit more if you let one of the enthusiastic guides take you through. These guys will point out some of the interesting things you might otherwise miss. Although the posted hours for the home are in the afternoon, guides may be on the premises as early as 8 a.m. or as late as 6 p.m. Tours take roughly an hour but can be abbreviated for families with restless youngsters.

Johnson-Sauk Trail State Park (all ages)

28616 Sauk Trail Road, Kewanee; (309) 853-5589. Open from 6 a.m. to 10 p.m. daily. Admission is free.

This 1,361-acre state park is just off Highway 78 about 5 miles north of town. Fifteen miles of trails through the woods are used for hiking in spring, summer, and fall and for cross-country skiing in winter. The park has a 58-acre artificially created lake in which anglers can fish for bass and muskie. Paddleboat rentals are available from the park's concession stand, which is open from May through September. You can get soda pop and snacks, fishing bait, and camping supplies there, too. The park has 10 picnic areas with tables and grills, two of the areas with shelters as well. You'll also notice a huge round barn in the park. Standing more than 80 feet tall and with a diameter of about 85 feet, it was built in 1910 and today contains antique farm equipment and historical displays. The barn is open for tours occasionally; call the park number to find out if there's one coming up around the time you wish to visit. The park was named after Frank Johnson, the Illinois senator who worked to get it established, and the Sauk Indians, whose trail from Lake Michigan to the Mississippi River passed through this area.

Where to Eat

Waunee Farm, South Tenney Street; (309) 852-2481. About a mile south of Super 8. Hours are 5 to 9 p.m. Wednesday and Thursday and 5 to 11 p.m. Friday and Saturday; closed Sunday through Tuesday. Ask about dinner specials. Friday and Saturday you can either order from the menu or opt for the smorgasbord. $

Where to Stay

Johnson-Sauk Trail State Park Campground, in the park; (309) 853-5589. There are 68 campsites here. Electrical hookups are available for RVs. Tent campsites are nestled among the pine trees. There is a building with showers. $

Super 8, 901 South Tenney Street; (309) 853-8800. This 2-story motel has 41 rooms with cable TV. Reserve a roll-away bed or crib for $5. The room rate includes a continental breakfast of coffee with toast, English muffin, or bagel. No pool. Pets allowed. $$

For More Information

Kewanee Chamber of Commerce, 113 East Second Street, Kewanee 61443; (309) 852-2175; www.kewanee-il.com.

Galesburg

Population: 33,706. About midway between the Quad Cities and Peoria off I-74 is historic Galesburg. U.S. Highways 34 and 150 and Illinois Highways 41 and 164 all feed into the city as well. Galesburg was founded in 1837, and many stately homes from the late 1800s and early 1900s remain. If you care about architecture, get out your list and check off Federal, Georgian, Gothic Revival, Italianate, Neoclassical, Prairie, and Romanesque as you find them—they're all here. The Seminary Street Historic Commercial District along 2 blocks of South Seminary Street in Galesburg is notable both for its restored buildings and for the specialty shops they contain. You'll find jewelry, pottery, stained glass, wall coverings, crafts, antiques, cosmetics, educational toys, chocolates, crepes, and bakery goodies among the items offered here.

Carl Sandburg State Historic Site (age 10 and up) 

331 East Third Street, Galesburg; (309) 342-2361. Open Wednesday through Sunday from 9 a.m. to 5 p.m.; closed Monday and Tuesday. Admission is free, but donations are welcome.

American poet and historian Carl Sandburg was born in Galesburg on January 6, 1878, in a three-room cottage that is now the Carl Sandburg State Historic Site. A visitor center stands next to the birthplace-museum, and Sandburg's ashes lie beneath Remembrance Rock (so named after his 1948 historical novel with that title) in a little wooded park behind the cottage. Sandburg grew up in Galesburg, dropping out of school at the age of 13 and doing odd jobs around town. At 18 he left to travel and, in 1898, served briefly in the U.S. Army during the Spanish-American War. He returned to Galesburg to attend Lombard College, although he never graduated. The lack of a degree didn't keep him from becoming first a newspaper writer, then a poet and biographer. Sandburg became a member of the "Chicago School" of influential writers who lived in Chicago from about 1912 to the late 1920s. He won the 1940 Pulitzer Prize for history for his comprehensive, six-volume biography of Abraham Lincoln and the 1951 Pulitzer Prize for poetry—not bad for a boy from Galesburg. Sandburg died in 1967.

Stockdale Soldier Citizen Museum (age 5 and up) 

1001 Michigan Avenue, Galesburg; (309) 342-1181. Hours are 9 a.m. to 2 p.m. Monday through Friday and 9 a.m. to 4 p.m. Saturday. Admission is free.

This museum contains military artifacts from many wars, starting with the War of 1812 and continuing up through the 1991 Persian Gulf War. The museum is open on Memorial Day and Veterans Day, two especially fitting occasions for a visit.

"Old Main" (age 7 and up) 

Cherry and South Streets, Galesburg; (309) 343-0112. Open from September through May. Hours are 8 a.m. to 4:30 p.m. Monday through Friday; closed major holidays. Admission is free.

Galesburg is the home of Knox College, and the college's main administration building, "Old Main," is a National Historic Landmark—it is reportedly the only remaining original structure of the 1858 Lincoln-Douglas debate sites. Two bronze plaques bearing the faces of Abraham Lincoln and Stephen Douglas are mounted on the east wall, the site of the debate. The Gothic Revival building is still in use, so it's typically open whenever school is in session.

Galesburg Railroad Museum (age 4 and up) 

211 South Seminary Street, Galesburg; (309) 342-9400; www.galesburgrailroadmuseum.org. Open from Memorial Day through Labor Day. Hours are 10 a.m. to 4 p.m. Tuesday through Saturday and noon to 4 p.m. Sunday; closed Monday. Admission is free, but suggested donation is $2 per adult or $5 per family.

This museum has a collection of stationary railroad cars and equipment from the early to mid-1900s. A passenger engine built in 1930 is open for tours; it has a caboose, too. Memorabilia are exhibited inside a 1923 Pullman parlor car. There are also two inspection cars from the 1950s that are outfitted with track maintenance tools.

Discovery Depot Children's Museum (all ages) 

128 South Chambers Street, Galesburg; (309) 344-8876; www.discoverydepot.org. Hours are 10 a.m. to 5 p.m. Monday through Saturday and 1 to 5 p.m. Sunday. Closed Monday during the school year. $.

This facility near the Galesburg Railroad Museum has loads of fun things to do for children of all ages—there's even a special area for "crawlers." Children can serve their parents plastic food in the mock-up cafe, sit in the cab of a corn combine with DVD player that simulates a ride through a cornfield, or play doctor in the medical-dental area. Be sure to check out the jumping area.

Where to Eat

Maid-Rite, 2250 Grand Avenue; (309) 342-2426. Hours are 10:30 a.m. to 6:30 p.m. Monday through Friday and 10:30 a.m. to 2 p.m. Saturday; closed Sunday. Order one of the namesake loose-meat ground beef sandwiches for a tasty lunch. $

Happy Joe's Pizza and Ice Cream Parlor, 1964 North Henderson Street; (309) 344-3121. Open from 11 a.m. to 10 p.m. Sunday through Thursday and 11 a.m. to 11 p.m. Friday and Saturday. A miniature train runs along a track that winds through this cheery eatery decorated in red-and-white barbershop motif. $

Where to Stay

Best Western Prairie Inn, I-74 at East Main Street; (309) 343-7151 or (800) 285-8637. This 2-story inn opened in 1982 as a Jumer's and was recently remodeled. There are 109 rooms here. Amenities include indoor swimming pool, fitness center, and whirlpool. Pets are allowed. Room rate includes continental breakfast. $$$

Fairfield Inn, 901 West Carl Sandburg Drive; (309) 344-1911 or (800) 228-2800. This economy chain property in the Marriott family has 3 floors and 56 rooms. Amenities include heated indoor pool and whirlpool. Continental breakfast is included in the room rate. $$

For More Information

Galesburg Area Convention and Visitors Bureau, 2163 East Main Street, Galesburg 61401; (309) 343-2485; www.visitgalesburg.com.

Peoria

Population: 112,936. I-74 takes an eastward turn beyond Galesburg and heads toward (and through) Peoria. You can reach Peoria from the south via Interstate 155. A scenic route from the north runs along the Illinois River, down Illinois Highway 26 on the east side or Illinois Highway 29 on the west. Both feature lush green foliage in summer and spectacular color in fall. From the north-northeast you can zip down Interstate 55 or Interstate 39, both of which connect with I-74 a bit south of the Peoria area around Bloomington-Normal; each also earlier intersects U.S. Highway 24, which provides a straight shot in from the east.

Peoria often has been the butt of comedians' jokes, but the joke's on you if you don't come and see all the family attractions this area has to offer—there are more than you'd expect. Try to visit during the milder seasons, when you can partake of the many outdoor activities. A good street to use as a focal point is War Memorial Drive: Coming from the east, US 24 turns into War Memorial Drive after you cross the steel-girder bridge over the Illinois River, and the street curves through the middle of town (but a ways north of downtown) until it becomes US 150 as you leave to the west. Most of the way it's two lanes wide in each direction.

You can tour the city in a historic trolley for $5 per person. Call the Peoria Area Convention and Visitors Bureau at (309) 672-2860 for details.

Lakeview Museum of Arts and Sciences (all ages) 

1125 West Lake Avenue, Peoria; (309) 686-7000; www.lakeview-museum.org. Hours are 10 a.m. to 5 p.m. Tuesday, Thursday, Friday, and Saturday; 11 a.m. to 8 p.m. Wednesday; and noon to 5 p.m. Sunday; closed Monday. Children age 3 or younger get in free, but the planetarium show is not recommended for this age. Call for descriptions of current special exhibits and planetarium shows. The planetarium is closed in September and October. $–$$

The Lakeview Museum of Arts and Sciences displays a variety of special exhibits. The exhibit *Grossology: The (Impolite) Science of the Human Body,* scheduled for the summer of 2008, is based on the popular book and is a don't-miss for kids. Permanent features at the museum include the Children's Discovery Center, the Natural Sciences Gallery, the Illinois Folk Art Gallery, and the West African Art Gallery. Children may be especially interested in the dinosaur display. The museum also has a planetarium.

Owens Recreation Center (age 5 and up) 

1019 West Lake Avenue, Peoria; (309) 686-3368. One block north of War Memorial Drive between University Street and Sheridan Road. Open year-round. Public skating hours available on recorded info line, (309) 686-3366. $

This facility has two full-size indoor ice rinks. Public skating is offered here even in summer, which is a different way to cool off if you're tired of swimming. The center has concessions.

Northwoods Mall (all ages) 

2200 West War Memorial Drive, Peoria; (309) 688-0443. Hours are 10 a.m. to 9 p.m. Monday through Saturday and 11 a.m. to 6 p.m. Sunday.

This indoor shopping mall is the largest in the Peoria area, with more than 100 stores. JCPenney, Sears, and Macy's are the anchor department stores. Kids may want to look around in the Disney Store or Kay-Bee Toys or play arcade games in Aladdin's Castle. Snack on Karmelkorn or cookies. For heartier food there's a pizza place and an A&W.

Mt. Hawley Bowl (age 4 and up) 

8200 North Hale Avenue, Peoria; (309) 692-7555. Open from 9 a.m. to 10:30 p.m. daily. $

This alley has 24 lanes, all with computerized scoring. You can bowl the regular way, in full light and with bumpers filling up the gutters for the children, or come during the Cosmic Bowling session, when bowling is by black light and the pins and balls glow.

Mt. Hawley Castle Golf (age 4 and up) 

8200 North Hale Avenue, Peoria; (309) 692-7555. Hours are 9 a.m. to 10:30 p.m. daily. $$

This outdoor facility next to the bowling alley has a 30-foot-tall castle. The attractive course features waterfalls and sand traps that make the play perhaps a bit too challenging for the youngest children.

Peoria's Glen Oak Zoo (all ages) 

2218 North Prospect Road, Peoria; (309) 686-3365; www.glenoakzoo.org. Open from 10 a.m. to 4:30 p.m. daily except Thanksgiving, Christmas Eve, Christmas Day, New Year's Eve, and New Year's Day. $

South off War Memorial Drive on Prospect Road is the tiny Glen Oak Zoo—watch carefully, because the small wooden signs blend in a bit too well with the park surroundings. You could easily see everything at a leisurely pace within an hour. However, that may change. At press time, the zoo was in the midst of a major expansion project. The following description was written before the renovation began.

The zoo layout cleverly forces visitors to pass through an indoor curving walkway lined with glass-walled cases containing reptiles, birds, and small mammals—displays you might otherwise skip—in order to reach the outdoor areas. The meerkats are especially cute, even if you haven't seen *The Lion King,* and it's worthwhile to be able to show your kids the real thing upon which the Disney movie character Timon was based. Reasonable-size monkey cages are at the end of the walkway just inside the doors leading outside; both the primates and the cages are clean and well maintained. There is a larger monkey pen outdoors, too.

Perhaps the nicest outdoor exhibit at the zoo is the lion enclosure, which has tall prairie grass resembling that of the African veld. Vines trail along the high fence, softening the effect of confinement. A glass wall along one section of the enclosure allows visitors to safely observe the felines close-up; on a hot day you may even find a lion lying right up against the cool glass. There is a "Contact Area," a barnlike structure with goats and assorted other critters, but the animals are behind fences, and kids can pet them through the wooden slats but are not allowed in with them. Kids of all ages enjoy the timber playground area; as they run and climb, they bear an eerie resemblance to the monkeys. The outdoor Safari Cafe has a limited but reasonably priced menu, including soda, popcorn, ice cream, hot dogs, and chicken sandwiches. There is a changing table in the women's restroom, which is located inside near a few educational displays.

George H. Luthy Memorial Botanical Garden (all ages) 

2218 North Prospect Road, Peoria; (309) 686-3362. Open year-round. Hours between Memorial Day and Labor Day are 10 a.m. to 5 p.m. daily. Hours during the rest of the year are 10 a.m. to 5 p.m. Monday through Saturday and noon to 5 p.m. Sunday. Closed Thanksgiving, Christmas, and New Year's Day. Admission is free; there is an unobtrusive donations box with suggested donation of $2 per person or $5 per family.

Adjacent to the zoo is the George H. Luthy Memorial Botanical Garden. It's worth a stroll, especially in peak blooming season—May through July, when you'll see an explosion of color. The specialty flower is the rose, and you'll find row after row of the aromatic blooms. The paved aisles are wide enough for baby strollers or wheelchairs. A fountain in the center of this four-acre herb and perennial garden provides pleasant ambient noise as well as visual appeal, and along the perimeter there are plenty of benches where you can rest your feet and still feast your eyes. The Conservatory building on the grounds houses tropical plants that will give you a hint of summer on a winter day. The gift shop offers garden-related items for sale.

Kartville (age 3 and up) 

919 Swords Avenue, just off Farmington Road, Peoria; (309) 676-3628. Open from spring through about October. Hours are 10 a.m. to 10 p.m. daily. $+

If you crave action, head over to Kartville. As the name suggests, go-karts are among the offerings here. Kids must be at least 9 years old to ride, and the price covers three laps. Dune buggies bounce along dirt trails beyond the kart track. There is no official age limit for the dune buggies, but common sense dictates that you wouldn't send a grade-schooler out on one alone. The bumper boats are a bit tamer, and you could probably let your kindergartner pilot one as long as the other riders weren't all rowdy teenagers. The ride lasts about five minutes. The miniature golf course is sparingly decorated and not too tricky, so little kids can play without getting totally frustrated. Prices are calculated per person per attraction, and the cost can mount quickly if you aren't careful. Ask about the occasional specials in which you get unlimited play for one price. In addition to the aforementioned attractions, Kartville has batting cages, for which you plunk in two quarters. Concessions are reasonably

Splashdown for Family Fun

This lively, family-oriented waterpark in nearby East Peoria is like a playground, only wet. The centerpiece Splashdown Island includes a giant wooden bucket that fills with water and then tips over, pouring a torrent of water on anyone standing below. The tamer Splash 'n' Play pool is designed for younger children. You can float on an inner tube along the chlorinated Lazy River or take the tube down a curvy water slide on the aptly named Wild Ride. The park claims to be "100% accessible to persons with disabilities." Snacks are available in a concession area on-site. From Peoria, take I-74 east over the Illinois River and exit at Camp Street (exit 95C). Continue to the second stoplight at Meadow Street, also US 150, and turn right, heading east for about 2 miles to Eastside Drive. Turn left toward the Eastside Centre; the road also leads to the waterpark. The address is 1 Eastside Drive, East Peoria; (309) 694-1867. The waterpark is open during summer from 11 a.m. to 6:30 p.m. Monday through Friday and 11 a.m. to 7 p.m. Saturday and Sunday. Call for current admission prices.

priced and include popcorn, soda, ice-cream bars, miniature tacos, and other goodies. Families with young children probably would have more fun earlier in the day when it's not as busy; the crowd can get a little rougher later at night, too.

African-American Hall of Fame Museum (age 5 and up) 

309 DuSable Street, Peoria; (309) 673-2206. Call ahead to check hours, which generally are 11 a.m. to 2:30 p.m. Monday through Friday. Admission is free, but donations are gladly accepted.

Permanent exhibits here are from the collection of Dr. Romeo Garrett, the first black professor at Bradley University, who died in 2000 at the age of 90. Special exhibits vary; a recent one featured black inventors and their inventions.

Spirit of Peoria (age 3 and up) 

100 Water Street, on the downtown Peoria Riverfront; (309) 637-8000 or (800) 676-8988; www.spiritofpeoria.com. Summer sightseeing cruises depart at 1 p.m. Wednesday, Saturday, and Sunday and last about an hour and a quarter. Buy tickets at the Gazebo Gift Shop, and be at the boat at least 15 minutes before departure time. $–$$

For a view of Peoria from the Illinois River, go to the foot of Main Street and board the *Spirit of Peoria,* a working replica of a century-old stern-wheeler that was built in 1988 and can hold up to 350 passengers. This boat is huge, with three levels of ornately decorated decks. The trim and the paddle wheel are both red, making an eye-catching contrast to the white boat and the blue-gray river. You'll see a number of historic and modern sights.

Peoria Chiefs (age 4 and up) 

Home games are played at O'Brien Field, 730 Southwest Jefferson Avenue, Peoria; (309) 688-1622, (309) 680-4000; www.peoriachiefs.com. Season runs from early April through early September. Check schedule for promotional giveaways such as caps or bobble-head dolls. Facility is accessible for wheelchairs and strollers. Parking in lot across the street costs $4. $$

Nestled in the heart of downtown Peoria, close enough to the river that you can feel its moisture in the air, is a pleasant ballpark for a family outing. O'Brien Field is the home of the Peoria Chiefs, the 2002 Midwest League minor-league baseball champions and Class A affiliate of the Chicago Cubs. In 2007, the Cubs' legendary Hall of Fame second baseman Ryne Sandberg became the Chiefs manager, reinforcing the team's connection to the parent organization.The Peoria ballpark has wide concrete walkways, ordinary but ample concessions at average prices, and adequate restrooms situated at regular intervals along the concourse, including two "family" restrooms behind sections 108 and 109. An electronic scoreboard in center field has a giant screen that shows crowd shots between innings, and fireworks shoot from the top of the board during the seventh-inning stretch. Beyond center field you'll find a playground and a couple of inflated enclosures for jumping, one of them topped by a head with googly eyes and toothy mouth that jiggle manically when the kids are bouncing around inside—it's quite a sight from the stands. Entertainment between innings seems a little lame compared with other minor-league ballparks in the state (for example, a contest for cracking frozen T-shirts), but some days there are special attractions that liven up the atmosphere. A word of caution: The "berm" (lawn) seating areas at the far ends of the stands are rather steeply sloped and might not be the best choice with small children.

Where to Eat

Fairview Farms Restaurant, 5911 Heurmann Road; (309) 697-4111. Hours are 4:30 to 8 p.m. Tuesday through Saturday and noon to 5 p.m. Sunday; closed Monday. At this restaurant in a converted farmhouse, you can buy a regular dinner or opt for the family-style menu, which entitles you to a choice of 2 out of the 5 meat entrees on the menu plus side dishes served in big bowls that you pass around the table. Reservations are recommended on weekends. $

Bob Evans Restaurant, 4915 North Big Hollow Road; (309) 692-3600. Hours are 6 a.m. to 10 p.m. Monday through Saturday and 7 a.m. to 10 p.m. Sunday. See Restaurant Appendix for description. $

Godfather's Pizza, 618 West Glen Street; (309) 688-5007. Hours are 11 a.m. to 10 p.m. Sunday through Thursday and 11 a.m. to midnight Friday and Saturday. The medium-thick, chewy-crust pizza here is loaded with cheese and your favorite ingredients. Round out the meal at the salad bar. $

Olive Garden, 6828 North War Memorial Drive; (309) 691-5975. Hours are 11 a.m. to 10 p.m. Sunday through Thursday and 11 a.m. to 11 p.m. Friday and Saturday. See Restaurant Appendix for description. $$

Perkins Family Restaurant, 4019 North War Memorial Drive; (309) 682-8616. Open 24 hours a day. This chain carries a wide array of breakfast, lunch, and dinner foods, including freshly baked cinnamon rolls and muffins. Expect a hearty meal in a clean, wholesome atmosphere. There is a children's menu with the usual assortment of choices. $

Where to Stay

Baymont Inn, 2002 West War Memorial Drive; (309) 686-7600 or (877) 229-6668. Get off War Memorial at the "exit" for Scenic Drive and drive around the perimeter of the Northwoods Mall onto Teamster Drive to reach the inn, a 3-story tan building with royal blue roof. It has 135 rooms and a heated outdoor swimming pool. Pets are allowed. Continental breakfast is included in the room rate. $$$

Ramada Inn, 4400 North Brandywine Drive; (309) 686-8000 or (800) 272-6237. This 4-story chain property has 250 rooms with cable TV. Amenities include game room, fitness center, indoor pool, and whirlpool. Pets are allowed, but add an extra $10 to the room rate. $$$

For More Information

Peoria Convention and Visitors Bureau, 56 Fulton Street, Suite 300, Peoria 61602; (800) 747-0302; www.peoria.org or www.peoriariverfront.com.

Dunlap

Population: 926. This little town north of Peoria has a fun family attraction you won't want to miss.

Wheels O' Time Museum (all ages) 

11923 North Knoxville Avenue, Dunlap; (309) 243-9020; www.wheelsotime.org. Open from May through October from noon to 5 p.m. Wednesday through Sunday. The buildings are accessible for wheelchairs except for the upstairs balcony in the main building. Coupons available online. $

The Wheels O' Time Museum is a treat to visit. The museum is 8 miles north of downtown Peoria on Illinois Highway 40 (formerly Highway 88). A gas station almost obscures the sign for the entrance on the left, but you can see the Rock Island Locomotive No. 886 parked on a piece of track in front of the peach-colored, two-story building that looks like a windowless warehouse or an airplane hangar. A German-style clock, with dwarves who strike a bell on the hour, breaks the monotony of the facade and gives a hint of the treasures inside. After you enter and pay the admission fee, you are immediately greeted by a cacophony of music from a player piano and from a miniature circus parade inside a glass-walled wagon. Nearby is a roomful of ticking clocks, from delicate miniatures to massive grandfathers.

The most eye-catching aspect of this first-floor showroom is the collection of vintage cars, all lined up and quietly gleaming an invitation to look. A 1916 Glide was manufactured by Peoria's own Bartholomew Company; it originally sold for $1,095—a bargain by today's standards but a sizable investment when you consider that the federal minimum wage didn't go into effect until 1938 and was 25 cents an hour, so a working-class mope in 1916 probably was lucky to make even $5 a week. Parents and grandparents of all ages are likely to find at least one model that brushes against their own past: a 1925 Star Model F, a 1933 Packard and Pierce Arrow, a 1941 Lincoln-Zephyr, a 1956 Bentley, a 1957 Nash Metropolitan, a 1967 Lincoln Continental convertible, a 1972 Datsun 240Z, a 1981 Delorean (anyone who's seen the movie *Back to the Future* will recognize this one). In a back corner there's a kid-size antique car that girls and boys can sit in—no, it doesn't move, but imagination is the best fuel, anyway. There are antique bikes, too, such as the F. E. Ide bicycle manufactured in Peoria in 1894.

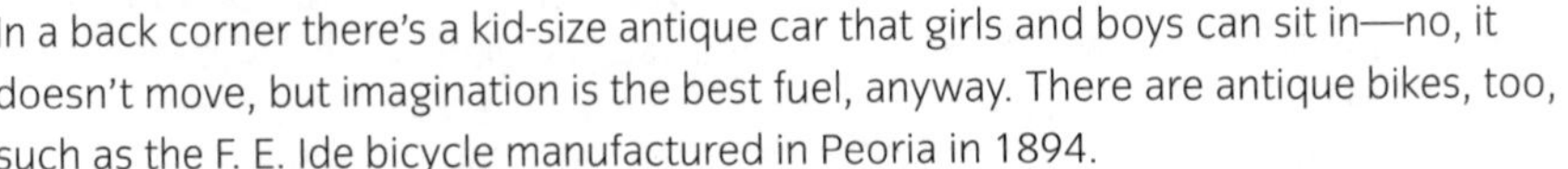

Along the periphery of the first floor and in a series of rooms along the balcony upstairs, you'll find a marvelous collection of vintage gadgets. The really great thing about them is that they all work. Plunk a nickel into an old jukebox to watch the arm pull out a 45 rpm record (ignore the kids' queries of "What's a record?") and play a tune by Tommy Dorsey, Duke Ellington, or Artie Shaw (for the wee ones, choose Patti Page's "How Much Is That Doggie in the Window?"). Try to tap out a message in Morse code on a telegraph, or tune in to the airwaves on a homemade crystal radio set from the 1920s. Press a button to activate a display of sturdy old electric trains (no cheap plastic on these models). Take the multiple-choice quiz to see how well you can identify kitchen utensils from great-grandma's day. You'll really show your age if, like this writer, you enjoy the resounding clatter of the Royal and Underwood manual typewriters more than the quiet click of a computer keyboard. Then there are numerous displays, including cameras—some accordion-like box models, some more "modern" ones with flash cubes (remember those?)—and dolls, from antiques to the Nancy Ann Storybook Dolls of the 1950s to original *Star Wars* figurines from the late 1970s and early 1980s, long before the first three movies were rereleased in 1997 and a whole new set of toys came on the market.

Head out the back door and down a flower-lined path to reach three more buildings. The first of these houses tractors and farm machinery, plus a nifty collection of old washing machines dating from 1800 through 1940. Push a button to start them gyrating. If Grandma's along, she might be able to explain from firsthand experience how the clothes were fished from the tub below and squeezed through the wringer rolls above. An item that kids will love but some parents will cringe at is the row of steam whistles you can toot with the pull of a chain. One sounds like a calliope;

another would signal quitting time for factory workers (or Fred Flintstone). Be warned, however: They are loud. The second building contains more vintage cars, plus gas pumps and a horse-drawn doctor's buggy from the late 1800s. The third building is the Firehouse, with fire engines and equipment. You can also climb up inside the engine of that locomotive you saw outside. You can pass a lot of time at Wheels O' Time.

Where to Eat and Stay

See entries for Peoria.

Hanna City

Population: 1,013. To the west of Peoria you'll find the small community of Hanna City and its Wildlife Prairie State Park, a wonderful place for families.

Wildlife Prairie State Park (all ages) 

3826 North Taylor Road, Hanna City; (309) 676-0998; www.wildlifeprairiestatepark.org. Off I-74 take exit 82 and head south about 2½ miles (or half a mile south off Illinois Highway 8). There are numerous signs, so you shouldn't miss it. Hours from May through August are 8 a.m. to 8 p.m. daily and in September are 9 a.m. to 6:30 p.m. daily; in April and from October through mid-December, hours are 9 a.m. to 4:30 p.m. daily. Call ahead to confirm the hours and rates before you drive all the way out there. You can get an overview of the place for an extra $2 per person to ride the miniature steam train. $–$$

This facility brings nature all together—animals, plants, fresh air. Come here when you have plenty of leisure time to enjoy it. The park has numerous well-marked trails for walking. Some of them pass over unobtrusively fenced areas containing such wildlife as cougars, wolves, foxes, otters, birds of prey, and bears. Heed the warnings and stay on the trails. Bison and elk have their own pasture, which you can see from an overlook terrace with tables and chairs. The Pioneer Farmstead area has a working water pump (but don't drink the green-tinted stuff) and various antique farm implements. Little kids will like the petting area, with its goats, horses, and other farm animals. The timbered visitor center looks rustic from the outside, but inside it's all modern and air-conditioned. It features an exhibit hall chronicling the history of the park, but the taxidermy animals here seem an unsettling juxtaposition with the live specimans so close by. The souvenir shop inside the visitor center has pretty stained-glass window hangings and other finely crafted items. A second gift shop on the other side of the parking lot also has fine wares. Open-air buildings near the visitor center feature hands-on and interactive displays that help kids learn about the habitat and its occupants. You can get a bite to eat at the Prairie View Snack Shop.

For a real adventure you can spend the night in the Wildlife Prairie State Park in one of four refurbished red cabooses. Each caboose contains a trundle bed, a bunk bed, and two futons to sleep up to six people. Other amenities include a small fold-down table with chairs, a minifridge, a microwave oven, a coffeemaker, and a tiny bathroom with sink, toilet, and shower. Baseboard heaters and an overhead air-conditioning unit will make the interior comfortable in any weather. Light switches are well labeled; one of the lights is a replica lamp. There's also a specially marked dial you can turn to activate a motor under the caboose that simulates the sound and feel of train movement—major cool. Outside there are several picnic tables and barbecue grills. You'll want to do your own cooking, because you're out in the middle of nowhere—besides, it's fun! Just remember to bring a can opener, because the caboose furnishes only plastic cutlery and paper cups and plates. Try to resist the temptation to watch the recently added TV set and instead enjoy such old-fashioned pastimes as reading, playing games, and even talking to one another. There is a pond close by where you might try your luck at fishing, although the lines and bobbers tangled in the trees offshore will give you a clue that others before you have not always been successful. If you're a city dweller, you may be surprised at the night sounds you hear: frogs, waterbirds, wailing peacocks, maybe even a far-off cougar growl. You'll also be amazed at how bright the stars look and how dark your surroundings are without streetlamps.

Down the road a bit from the cabooses are newer lodgings built in the late 1990s. A converted stable contains five two-room suites, and a cluster of converted grain silos stands nearby. While they lack the seclusion and old-fashioned charm of the cabooses, they are cute in their own way and contain similar amenities. The silos are billed as "cottages by the lake," which makes for better marketing than "corrugated metal silos by the fetid pond." A recreation room near the silos and stables was added in the early 2000s and features Ping-Pong and foosball tables, arcade games, and vending machines. Another lodging choice is the very secluded cabin on the hill, which is just what it sounds like. Drive up a hill and climb some narrow stone steps to reach this one-room log cabin with a scenic overlook of trees. The climate-controlled interior features high ceiling fan, double bed, futons, table and chairs, refrigerator, sink, and TV. A bathroom with a door is tucked in one corner.

Caboose lodging costs $70 (Sunday through Thursday) or $80 (Friday and Saturday) per night for two people. The corresponding rates for the stable units are $80 and $90, those for the silo cottages are $90 and $100, and those for the cabin on the hill are $100 and $125. For all four lodgings, tack on another $10 for each additional person age 3 or older. Depending on how large your family is, the rate compares favorably to that at a mid-range motel, and it's a more memorable experience. Call (309)

676-0998 to make a reservation. Be prepared to guarantee it with a credit card, although you can pay cash instead once you get there. If you prefer to pay by check in advance, write to Wildlife Prairie State Park, Rural Route 2, 3826 North Taylor Road, Hanna City 61536. Either way, you'll get a written confirmation of your reservation, and you should bring that letter along when you check in between 2 and 4 p.m. Check-out time is 11 a.m.

Where to Eat

Bring your own food if you're staying overnight in the Prairie Park. Otherwise, see entries for Peoria.

Where to Stay

If you don't want to try the Wildlife Prairie State Park lodging (awww!), see entries for Peoria.

Pekin

Population: 33,857. Highway 29 goes straight into this town, situated southeast of Peoria. You can also reach Pekin off Interstate 474.

Rockin' P Public Riding Ranch (age 8 and up) 

217 McNaughton Park Road, Pekin; (309) 382-1268. Open from April through late September or early October. The 1-hour trail ride departs at 9:30 and 11 a.m. and 12:30, 2, 3:30, 5, and 6:30 p.m. Monday and Wednesday through Sunday. The 2-hour trail ride departs at 9:30 a.m. and various other times Monday and Wednesday through Sunday. Riders must be at least 8 years old. The facility is closed Tuesday and when the weather's bad. Call ahead to schedule your ride. $$–$$$

Introduce your older children to the pleasure of horseback riding. This stable in McNaughton Park offers a gentle 2½-mile trail ride that passes through grasslands and forest, sometimes even through a cornfield or across a creek—the route varies.

Dragonland Water Park (all ages) 

1701 Court Street, in Mineral Springs Park, Pekin; (309) 347-4000; www.pekin.net/pekinparkdistrict/dragonland.htm. Open from Memorial Day through mid-August. Hours are 11:30 a.m. to 6 p.m. daily. $

For a family with young children, Dragonland Water Park is the ideal place to cool off on a hot summer day. From Peoria take Highway 29 and turn east onto Margaret Street, which merges with Court Street. You'll know you're getting close when you pass Mineral Springs Park pond with a fountain and paddleboats to the left and the "World's Greatest Sundial" to the right. Look for the sign for Memorial Arena, and turn left onto Mineral West Shore Drive. Being there at opening time is a good idea if you want to snag a chaise lounge; otherwise, there's a nice lawn area that even has a

A Trip Back in Time

About an hour's drive south of Peoria is the **Dickson Mounds State Museum** near Lewistown. The *mounds* part of the museum's name refers to the 800-year-old burial sites of the Mississippian American Indian people. The *Dickson* part is in honor of Dr. Don F. Dickson, who began excavating at his family farm in 1927. Archaeologists from the University of Chicago came to the area in the 1930s, and Dickson Mounds became first a state park in 1945, then a part of the Illinois State Museum in 1965. Today it concentrates on the plentiful archaeological artifacts that provide clues about the prehistory of the Illinois River Valley. The museum was renovated in 1994 to provide state-of-the-art exhibits and multimedia presentations. There are numerous hands-on activities in which visitors can touch objects, turn pages, or look through a microscope, for example. The museum's Discovery Center is geared toward kids. They'll especially enjoy the Discovery Drawers, a set of 32 drawers underneath a counter, each labeled with a picture and title. Kids can take out what's in the drawer and do something with it, such as "excavating" a fossil from dirt or dressing up in a costume of the past. Special programs are offered throughout the year, so call to find out what's coming up; you could participate in a hide-tanning workshop or enjoy folk music at a coffeehouse. A picnic area is on the 162-acre grounds, as are the remains of three early Mississippian buildings that you can look at. Museum shops offer snacks and souvenirs.

The contact information for Dickson Mounds is Rural Route 1, 10956 North Dickson Mounds Road, Lewistown 61542; (309) 547-3721; www.museum.state.il.us/ismsites/dickson. Heading southwest on US 24, turn south (before you reach the town) onto Illinois Highway 78/97 and proceed a few miles; signs will guide you to the museum. Coming from the south up Highways 78 or 97 or from the east on Illinois Highway 136, cross the bridge over the Illinois River at Havana, and then proceed north on the joined Highway 78/97, where you'll find signs to direct you in. Dickson Mounds is open from 8:30 a.m. to 5 p.m. daily except New Year's Day, Easter, Thanksgiving, and Christmas. Admission is **free.**

few trees to protect burn-prone people who don't worship the sun. There are no lockers in the locker room; they are located instead outside along a wall facing the pool area.

The pool has a zero-depth area so that even the tiniest tots can tiptoe in the water. For toddlers and young grade-schoolers, the shallow end features Dude the Dragonslide, a green fiberglass guy perhaps 10 feet tall; the children climb a vertical ladder up his back and whiz down the straight, water-slicked slide in front. The deep end of the pool is only 5 feet, making the swimming area less appealing for teens, but they may like the sand beach volleyball area or the two giant water slides. The narrower red slide is for people alone, while the wider blue one allows sliders to ride huge plastic inner tubes, colored mustard yellow for a single passenger and hot pink for a pair. Little kids can ride with bigger people, but the kids must wear life jackets (available there; no extra charge for life jackets or tubes). The prices in the concession area are reasonable. The menu includes soda, ice-cream bars, candy, popcorn, pretzels, hot dogs, and hot snacky items such as "pizza sticks."

Putt the Magic Dragon (age 4 and up) 

In Mineral Springs Park, near Dragonland Water Park, Pekin; (309) 353-1244; www.pekin.net/pekinparkdistrict/minigolf.htm. (Follow directions in Dragonland entry.) From June through mid-August hours are 11 a.m. to 10 p.m. daily. From mid-April through May and mid-August through late September, the minigolf course is open weekends only; hours are 6 to 10 p.m. Friday, 11 a.m. to 10 p.m. Saturday, and 11 a.m. to 8 p.m. Sunday. $

This 18-hole miniature golf course carries over the dragon theme of the nearby water park. It's also rather scenic thanks to the surrounding park, with greenery and a stream. Kids like the little caboose at the fourth hole. The on-site concession stand offers soda and snacks. There's a video game room near the golf course.

Eastcourt Village Mall (all ages) 

3500 Court Street, Pekin; (309) 999-1700. Hours are 10 a.m. to 9:30 p.m. Monday through Saturday and 11 a.m. to 7:30 p.m. Sunday.

This one-story indoor shopping mall is anchored by Bergner's department store. Shops offer an assortment of clothing and gifts. Hobby Lobby has craft kits and supplies.

Where to Eat

Bob Evans, 3440 Court Street; (309) 477-3020. Hours are 6 a.m. to 10 p.m. daily. See Restaurant Appendix for description. $

Steak n Shake, 3205 Court Street; (309) 347-5191. Open 24 hours a day. See Restaurant Appendix for description. $

Where to Stay

Concord Inn and Suites, 2801 Court Street; (309) 347-5533. This 4-story hotel has 124 rooms with cable TV. Amenities include an outdoor pool. Restaurant on-site. Pets allowed; $25 deposit. $$

Comfort Inn, 3240 North Vandever Avenue; (309) 353-4047 or (800) 424-6423. The inn has 48 rooms and an indoor swimming pool. Pets are allowed. Continental breakfast is included in the room rate. $$$

For More Information

Pekin Chamber of Commerce, 402 Court Street, Pekin 61554; (309) 346-2106; www.pekin.net.

Pekin Visitors Bureau, 111 South Capitol Street, Pekin 61554; (309) 477-2300 or (877) 669-7741; www.pekintourism.com.

Quincy

Population: 40,366. Quincy overlooks the Mississippi River. From the south or east, you can zip in on Interstate 172 from Interstate 72. From Peoria your best bet is to meander down US 24. The site was originally home to Native Americans from the Sauk, Fox, and Kickapoo tribes. They were displaced in the early 1800s by settlers from New England and immigrants from Germany. Quincy was the largest of the seven cities in which Abraham Lincoln and Stephen Douglas conducted their famous debates in 1858. Mark Twain, whose hometown of Hannibal, Missouri, is not far from Quincy to the south, visited Quincy in the late 1800s. During the 1900s the city built a reputation as an architectural center. Uptown Quincy, the central business district, offers a variety of shopping, dining, and entertainment; call (217) 228-8696 for details.

Villa Kathrine (age 5 and up) 

532 Gardner Expressway, Quincy; (217) 224-3688. Quincy's Tourist Information Center is here as well. To see the rest of the building, you must take a guided tour; you can't just go in and wander around. Call ahead to make sure a guide will be available. $

One of the most unusual buildings in Quincy is Villa Kathrine, which claims to be the only example of Mediterranean architecture in the Midwest. It was made out of local materials in 1900 by George Metz, a world-traveling Quincian who modeled the residence on Islamic structures he had seen. Its courtyard surrounds a reflecting pool. Restoration is ongoing. Volunteer guides take visitors through the home.

Quincy Museum (all ages) 

1601 Maine Street, Quincy; (217) 224-7669; www.thequincymuseum.com. Open Tuesday through Sunday from 1 to 5 p.m.; closed Monday. $

Housed in a fancy old converted mansion, this museum includes a "discovery center" room for kids. A dinosaur theme dominates, with fossils, books, and computer games on the subject. Other exhibit areas feature Illinois wildlife, Native American culture, and space exploration.

All Wars Museum (age 5 and up) 

1707 North 12th Street, Quincy; (217) 222-8641. Hours vary; call for current schedule. Admission is free, but donations are welcome.

Military buffs will want to check out the All Wars Museum. It is located on the grounds of the Illinois Veterans Home, one of the largest and oldest veterans' homes in the United States. Exhibits in the museum span the American Revolution through the Iraq War.

Quincy Community Theatre (age 4 and up) 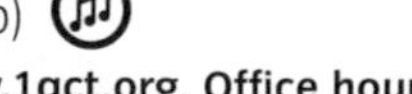

300 Civic Center Plaza, Quincy; (217) 222-3209; www.1qct.org. Office hours are 10 a.m. to 5 p.m. Monday through Friday; call for current shows and ticket prices.

The QCT organization dates back to 1923, and it moved into its current state-of-the-art facility in 1995. Many of the shows are appropriate for families. For example, the 2007–2008 season featured productions of *Footloose, The Adventures of Nate the Great,* and *A Year with Frog and Toad.*

Wavering Aquatic Center (all ages) 

In Wavering Park on North 36th Street, Quincy; (217) 228-9220. Open Memorial Day weekend through Labor Day. Hours are 1 to 8 p.m. daily. $

This facility features a 230-foot water slide, a diving well, and a sand volleyball court. There is a concession area as well.

Batting Cage and Miniature Golf Complex (age 3 and up) 

In Upper Moorman Park on North 36th Street, Quincy; (217) 228-1261. Open from early April through Labor Day. Before Memorial Day weekend, hours are 3:30 to 9 p.m. Monday through Friday, 10 a.m. to 9 p.m. Saturday, and noon to 9 p.m. Sunday. The rest of the season, hours are 10 a.m. to 10 p.m. Monday through Saturday and noon to 10 p.m. Sunday. $+

Like the two city pools, this complex also is run under the auspices of the Quincy Park District. It boasts Quincy's only 18-hole miniature golf course. The batting cages include two baseball and two slow-pitch softball pitching machines. Feed tokens into the machine to play; two tokens give you 10 pitches. Up to four people can ride in a paddleboat on Moorman Lake. Concessions are available.

Other Things to See and Do

JANUARY

Bald Eagle Days, Rock Island; (309) 788-5912

Quad-City Cat Club Show, Moline; (309) 755-9839

FEBRUARY

Eagle Days Festival, Havana; (800) 747-0302

Quad City Antique Toy, Doll, Petroleum, and Advertising Show, Milan; (563) 391-3579

MARCH

Bistate St. Patrick's Day Parade, Rock Island; (309) 788-2341

Windmill Follies, Golden; (217) 696-4672

APRIL

In-Fisherman Swap Meet, Rock Island; (309) 788-5912

MAY

Hornucopia, Rock Island; (309) 988-6311 or (800) 747-7800

Pekin Derby Days; (877) 669-7741; www.pekintourism.com

Sunset by the Mississippi, Nauvoo; (217) 453-6434

JUNE

Elmwood Strawberry Festival; (800) 747-0302

Rhubarb Festival, Aledo; (309) 582-5373 or (800) 747-7800

Railroad Days, Galesburg; (309) 343-2485

Tremont Turkey Festival; (800) 747-0302

JULY

Rock Island Summerfest; (309) 788-6311

Chilli Corn Fest, Chillicothe; (800) 747-0302

Most communities have a Fourth of July celebration, and many county fairs are in July and August.

AUGUST

Great River Tug Fest, Port Byron; (309) 523-3734; www.tugfest.org

New Windsor Fair and Rodeo; (309) 667-2503; www.nwrodeo.org

SEPTEMBER

Macomb Balloon Rally; (309) 833-1315

Morton Pumpkin Festival; (309) 263-2491

OCTOBER

Barry Apple Festival; (217) 335-2108

Milan Improvement Project Arts and Crafts Fair; (309) 786-7430

Fright Night, Rock Island; (309) 788-6311

NOVEMBER

Santa Claus Parade, Peoria; (800) 747-0302

Carthage Christmas Open House; (217) 357-3024

DECEMBER

Christmas Home Tours and Festival of Lights, Barry; (217) 285-2971

Julmarknad Christmas Market, Bishop Hill; (309) 927-3345

Quincy Mall (all ages)

On Broadway between 30th and 36th Streets, Quincy; (217) 223-8713. Hours are 10 a.m. to 9 p.m. Monday through Saturday and noon to 5 p.m. Sunday.

This one-story indoor shopping mall features 70 stores, including Kay-Bee Toys, and five restaurants. JCPenney, Sears, and Bergner's are the anchor department stores.

Where to Eat

Elder's Family Restaurant, 1800 State Street; (217) 223-7790. Hours are 11 a.m. to 11 p.m. Tuesday through Sunday; closed Monday. This is a meat-and-potatoes sort of place that serves steaks, burgers, and what it asserts is the "best fried chicken in town." $

Tower of Pizza, 1221 Broadway; (217) 224-6030. Open from 4 to 11:30 p.m. daily. This eatery's claim to fame is that it "serves Quincy's original thick crust pizza," with the dough and sauce made from scratch, along with sandwiches and drinks. Don't let the name fool you into looking for a tower—the restaurant is in a 2-story brick building with a cozy brick interior and lots of memorabilia on the walls. There's a drive-up window, or you can order carry-out, or they'll deliver to your hotel—they're definitely flexible. $

Where to Stay

Comfort Inn, 4122 Broadway; (217) 228-2700 or (800) 424-6423. This comfortable, 3-story chain property has 58 rooms. Amenities include indoor pool. The room rate includes continental breakfast. Minimum stay of 2 nights required. $$$

Holiday Inn, 201 South Third Street; (217) 222-2666 or (800) 465-4329. This 4-story hotel has 155 rooms. Amenities include an indoor pool in the atrium, an exercise room, and a game room. Rates include breakfast. Pets allowed, $10 extra. $$$

For More Information

Quincy Convention & Visitors Bureau, 300 Civic Center Plaza, Suite 237, Quincy 62301; (800) 978-4748; www.quincy-cvb.org.

Central Illinois

To drive into Central Illinois from the northeast is to plunge into the heart of the heartland. The sprawl of the suburbs and exurbs thins out until you're surrounded by nearly uninterrupted stretches of prairie—snow-covered, barren, and windswept in the dead of winter but verdantly carpeted with cornfields, wildflowers, and waving grasses during the warmer months. It was into this pastoral setting that Abraham Lincoln moved at the age of 21 and embarked on the long career path that would eventually lead him to the White House. Lincoln lore and historic sites abound in the 28 counties of Central Illinois. For general information about the region, contact the **Central Illinois Tourism Development Office,** 700 East Adams Street, Springfield 62701; (217) 525-7980; www.visitcentralillinois.com.

Springfield

Population: 111,454. From Quincy, where we ended the previous chapter, a drive east on U.S. Highway 36 takes you to the Illinois state capital, Springfield. Interstate 55 is the major north-south artery into the city, while Interstate 72 comes in from the east. Smaller highways, such as Illinois Highways 125, 97, 29, 124, 54, and 4, also feed into the area. Amtrak (800-231-2222 or www.amtrak.com) and Greyhound (800-229-9424 or www.greyhound.com) serve Springfield as well.

Springfield has tons of historic sites, and you'll want to make a judicious selection so as not to overload your kids (and yourself). Teenagers especially will complain if they think the trip is getting too "educational," so be sure to sprinkle in some purely fun activities amid all those museum visits. With the bicentennial of Lincoln's birth coming up in 2009 and the sesquicentennial (150-year anniversary) of the Civil War from 2011 through 2015, sites in Springfield are already planning special exhibits and activities for visitors.

CENTRAL ILLINOIS

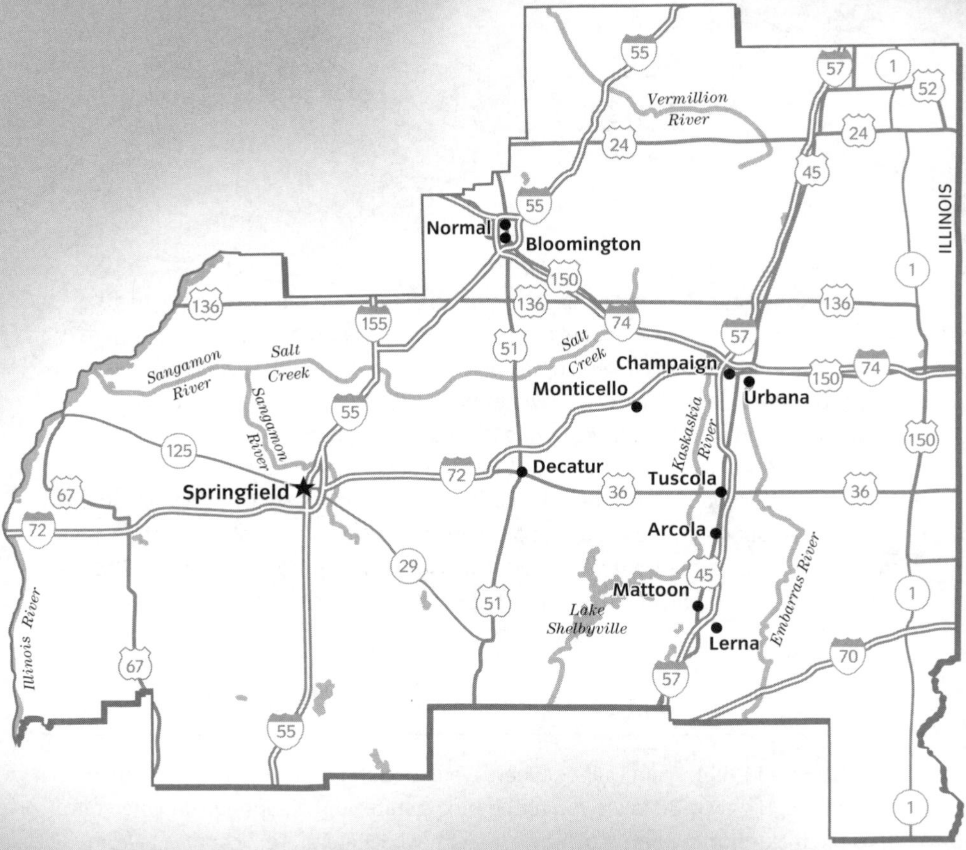

Vermillion River
Normal
Bloomington
ILLINOIS
INDIANA
Sangamon River
Salt Creek
Sangamon River
Salt Creek
Champaign
Urbana
Monticello
Springfield
Decatur
Kaskaskia River
Tuscola
Arcola
Mattoon
Lake Shelbyville
Lerna
Embarras River
Illinois River

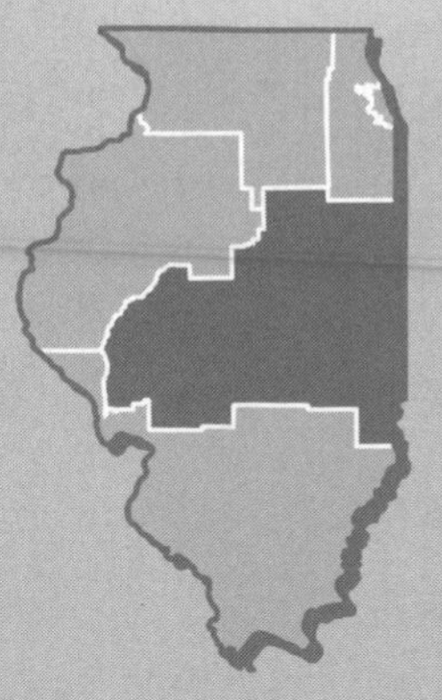

Illinois State Capitol (age 7 and up) 

Second and Capitol Streets, Springfield; (217) 782-2099. The capitol is open from 8 a.m. to 4:30 p.m. Monday through Friday and 9 a.m. to 3 p.m. Saturday and Sunday; closed major holidays. Admission is free. Tours are given on the hour and half hour. The building is accessible for strollers and wheelchairs. No smoking allowed in the building. If the legislature is not in session, you may be able to park within a block of the building at a metered space along the street; otherwise, the visitor center 1 block west of the capitol has a parking lot.

Let's start downtown with a must-see for adults and school-age children, the Illinois State Capitol. This ornate, silver-domed building is gorgeous, both inside and out. The old adage is true: "They just don't make 'em like that anymore." This one took 20 years to complete—it was finished in 1888—but it was worth the wait. A 1986 restoration of the interior succeeded in bringing out the grandeur of old. Marble floors and columns shine, giant painted tableaux look clean and crisp, and the stained glass in the dome sparkles. No matter what your political persuasion, you can't help but feel as though something really important and special must happen here. State house and senate visitor galleries on the fourth floor (accessible by original stone staircases trimmed with wrought iron or by more modern, utilitarian elevators) flank the chambers at each end of the building, so you can watch the action below. The legislators get to sit in oversize leather armchairs at polished desks of dark wood, with heavy draperies and crystal chandeliers adorning the windows and ceiling. If only the level of discourse were as noble as the surroundings.

Illinois State Museum (age 2 and up) 

Spring and Edwards Streets, Springfield; (217) 782-7386; www.museum.state.il.us. Open from 8:30 a.m. to 5 p.m. Monday through Saturday and noon to 5 p.m. Sunday; closed Thanksgiving, Christmas, and New Year's Day. A Place for Discovery is open from about 9:30 a.m. to 5 p.m. Tuesday through Saturday and 1 to 5 p.m. Sunday; closed Monday. Admission is free. The building is accessible for strollers and wheelchairs. No smoking.

In stark contrast to the lustrous capitol is the Illinois State Museum, a plain, squarish, flat-surfaced edifice a block away. Of the building's three stories, probably the most interesting for families is the lower level, where you'll find A Place for Discovery, a hands-on room geared most strongly toward grade-schoolers. They can grind corn with stones as the Indians did, listen to native birdcalls through headphones, or pull out drawers filled with fossils and bones to examine the contents. The main floor's natural history exhibits are composed of taxidermy and dioramas, which seem rather dated and hokey these days. Except for extinct species, you're better off skipping this floor and looking at live animals in the zoo instead. The top floor features an art gallery and an exhibit worth seeing called At Home in the Heartland. This display uses a combination of artifacts (including diaries, letters, and ledgers) and video screens to tell the stories of real Illinois people who lived over the course of the past century or so. The catch is that after conveying some initial information about a given person's life, the narrative stops at a point of decision and asks the viewer to choose from among several options what course of action the person should take (for example, which house or farm equipment to buy or whether to look for work in another city). The viewer's choice is then compared to what the person actually decided and how the alternative options might have turned out. Older kids as well as adults would enjoy this exhibit.

Lincoln Home National Historic Site (age 7 and up) 

Eighth and Jackson Streets, Springfield; (217) 492-4241, ext. 266; www.nps.gov/liho. Open year-round from 8:30 a.m. to 5 p.m. daily. Closed Thanksgiving, Christmas, and New Year's Day. Admission is free, but you must pick up a ticket at the Lincoln Home Visitors Center a block away at 426 South Seventh Street. Your ticket will be stamped with the starting time of your 20-minute tour (yes, you have to take the tour—you can't just walk in and browse around). Tours start every 5 to 15 minutes. Stop by early in the day, because the tickets for that day are usually gone by 3 p.m. Stairs leading to the front door and to the upper floor make touring the home difficult for visitors who have trouble walking. The visitor center has ways of making accommodations if you call in advance. The visitor center also is open from 8:30 a.m. to 5 p.m. daily. No smoking at the visitor center or the site.

One of the places visitors to Springfield tend to remember the longest is the Lincoln Home National Historic Site. It was the only home Abraham Lincoln ever owned, and he and his family lived there for 17 years before he was elected president and moved to Washington, D.C. The two-story tan frame house is furnished as it looked in 1860. Downstairs are the living room, the kitchen, and the family room. Upstairs are the bedrooms for the Lincolns, their children, and their live-in maid. No bathrooms—the outhouse is out back. About 50 items in the house are original Lincoln pieces, most notably the banister and the shaving mirror in his bedroom, and the rest are period pieces. (Lincoln sold all his furniture when he moved to the White House, so it was tough finding any of the original pieces.) Wallpaper in the Lincoln bedroom suite is an exact reproduction copied from a scrap of the original paper that was found during restoration. Guides give a good description of how the Lincolns lived, enlivening the basic facts with anecdotes, such as the time Papa Lincoln had to chase his naked youngest son down the street after the boy escaped from a bath in the kitchen. The Lincoln site includes not only this house but also neighboring homes in a 4-block area. Wooden-plank sidewalks like the kind that existed in 1860 have been installed, and ongoing restoration work makes the area continue to more closely resemble the period. The visitor center, by the way, has an especially nice gift shop with no tacky souvenirs. You'll find postcards, slides, books, coins, and interesting wooden games of the period.

Fun at the **Illinois State Fair**

If you visit Springfield in mid-August, you can take in the Illinois State Fair at the fairgrounds at Sangamon Avenue and Peoria Road. The fair has been going on annually for more than 140 years, and the stately grounds with their big brick buildings reflect that traditional charm. Once you are inside, you'll find a lot of free activities and displays; it's great fun just to wander around and see what you stumble across—maybe harness racing, a ponytail contest, a demonstration of an ethanol-powered vehicle, an art exhibit, a reggae concert, or a sheep show with judges squeezing the animals' sides like rolls of Charmin (to feel for the ribs; it's legit, but it looks funny). Be sure to bring some cash for all the good junk food—this is the place to forget about fat and calories for a few hours and snarf some corn dogs, cotton candy, and other tasty-but-naughty stuff; you can take an extra walk around the block tomorrow. The kids will probably beg for some tacky souvenirs, too, and your life will be easier if you plan to fork over a couple bucks and indulge them a little. For info on this year's fair, call (217) 782-6661 or check www.illinoisstatefair.info.

Oliver Parks Telephone Museum (age 3 and up) 

529 South Seventh Street, Springfield; (217) 789-5303. Hours are 9 a.m. to 4:30 p.m. Monday through Friday; closed major holidays. Admission is free. Accessible for strollers and wheelchairs. No smoking.

If you're already downtown, drop in at the Oliver Parks Telephone Museum, right off the street near the lobby of the big brick SBC building. This museum is tiny (one room) and sort of hands-on—you can turn a dial or pick up a receiver, but nothing is hooked up. The phones on display are from the personal collection of namesake Parks (1904-1983), a Decatur native who worked for the phone company his whole life and started amassing the phones in 1949. Most are original, though some are replicas. They date from the late 1800s to the present, so just about every parent will be able to find one that looks like what she or he had as a kid. Were you around in 1954, when the first colored phones came out (they were all black before then), or 1959, when the Princess phone was introduced? How about 1962, for the first touch-tone phones? There are even a couple of those phone-with-TV models that were floated in the 1970s and received a thoroughly tepid public response. Your visit here won't take long, but it will be interesting.

Old State Capitol (age 7 and up) 

Fifth Street between Adams and Washington Streets, Springfield; (217) 785-7960. Open from 9 a.m. to 5 p.m. daily from April 16 through Labor Day and 9 a.m. to 5 p.m. Tuesday through Saturday from the day after Labor Day through April 15. Closed Sunday and Monday and some holidays. Admission is free, although there is a box for suggested donations of $2 per adult and $1 per child. The building is accessible for wheelchairs. No smoking.

The Old State Capitol was the statehouse from 1839 until 1876, when the state offices were moved to the capitol that is still in use today. The Old Capitol was the first statehouse in Springfield, following the legislators' vote to move the capital there from Vandalia. It also was the first capitol building in Illinois to house all three branches of state government together—the executive (the governor, treasurer, secretary of state, and other officers), the legislative (the House of Representatives and the Senate), and the judicial (the Supreme Court). After the government moved to the new capitol, the Old Capitol was used for other purposes until 1961, when the governor signed legislation allowing the state to buy and renovate the Greek Revival building. It was totally dismantled in 1966 and then put back together three years later, after a below-ground parking ramp and offices were added and the walls rebuilt. It was restored to look the way it did in Abraham Lincoln's time. The House, where Lincoln served his final term as a representative in 1840–41, has a coat and top hat placed at the seat he probably occupied. He returned to this very chamber in 1858 for his famous "House Divided" speech, and his body lay in state here before burial at the Lincoln Tomb. The Senate chamber is more ornate, with a chandelier hanging from the high ceiling. White pillars stand in a semicircular arc across the back to support a gallery where the women sat. (Women didn't win the right to vote until the Nineteenth Amendment was passed in 1920, so they certainly were not allowed to run for elected office, and they were not allowed on the floor with the men.) They made their opinions clearly known by clapping their hands in approval or stomping their feet in disapproval. Behind a railing at the back of the main floor, called a lobby, stood people who shouted to their senator and tried to persuade him to vote their way. Such people came to be known as lobbyists, and they're still at it today, although in subtler ways.

Abraham Lincoln Presidential Library and Museum (age 5 and up)

1 Old State Capitol Plaza, Springfield; (217) 782-5674 or (800) 610-2094; www.alplm.com. Library and museum are open from 9 a.m. to 5 p.m. daily; closed Thanksgiving, Christmas, and New Year's Day. Free admission to library; admission charge for museum. Both buildings are accessible for wheelchairs and strollers. $–$$

Occupying a whole block at the corner of Sixth and Jefferson Streets is a huge complex comprising the Abraham Lincoln Presidential Library and Museum. Under the supervision of the Illinois Historic Preservation Agency, the library portion opened in

2003, and the museum was completed in 2005. The new library houses the collections of the Illinois State Historic Library—about 46,000 documents and artifacts relating to Lincoln, including his famous *Gettysburg Address* and the *Emancipation Proclamation*. The museum has one exhibit with a specific tie-in to the library. Called *Ghosts of the Library*, it uses eye-catching special effects to explain the importance of preserving historical documents. It is housed in one of several exhibition halls accessible from the central rotunda, where some natural light filters in through high windows. The two main exhibit galleries—*The Journey, Part I*, and *The Journey, Part II*—chronicle Lincoln's life before and after he entered the White House, respectively. The displays are basically dioramas gone high-tech; the figures are fairly lifelike, and the sound and lighting enhance the mood of the tableaux. While the museum's goal reportedly is to make visitors feel immersed in Lincoln's world, that isn't really possible given the anachronism of a bank of TV screens broadcasting mock campaign ads for the candidates in the 1860 presidential race. Younger children who have little sense yet of historical perspective wouldn't realize that television didn't even exist in Lincoln's time, so accustomed are they to seeing political ads on TV, and most don't pay attention to them anyway. Similarly, the four-minute video presentation of a multicolored map showing the progression of the Civil War (1861-1865) and its mounting body count is a compelling special effect but in no way representative of how news traveled in those days. That said, however, if through their use of familiarly modern technology the museum planners can succeed in their effort to spark further interest in Lincoln lore so that kids will want to see the real stuff elsewhere in Springfield, then it works. The few genuine articles to be found in the museum are mostly housed in the *Treasures Gallery*. There is a hands-on area, *Mrs. Lincoln's Attic*, where children can play with toys like those used in Lincoln's day and try on clothing or do chores in 1800s style.

Nelson Recreational Center (all ages)

1601 North Fifth Street, Springfield; (217) 753-2800. The pool is open from Memorial Day through Labor Day, from 1 to 5 p.m. Monday through Friday and 1 to 6 p.m. Saturday and Sunday. The indoor ice rink is open year-round; call for current open skating hours and admission prices. $

If you're ready for something more active after all that downtown culture, head north to the Nelson Recreational Center in Lincoln Park. You can take a dip in the pool during summer or go ice-skating year-round. The ice rink was remodeled in 2003. The park grounds also have a picnic area, a playground, and a pond.

Adventure Village (ages 2 to 12) 

Sangamon Avenue and Peoria Road, Springfield; (217) 528-9207. Hours are noon to 3 p.m. Saturday and Sunday from early May through mid-September; closed during the Illinois State Fair. $$$

Adventure Village is an active option especially appropriate for younger children. This family amusement park with about a dozen rides is located just inside the main gate of the Illinois State Fairgrounds. Choose from among the regular-size Ferris wheel, merry-go-round, Tilt-A-Whirl, or YoYo or the kid-size Himalaya, Spider, helicopters, or little duckies. There are a couple of attractions that kids can bounce around in, one inflated and the other filled with plastic balls, and a miniature train travels the perimeter of the park (but seats can accommodate adults as well). Some rides have height restrictions: For example, children must be at least 36 inches tall for one but not more than 48 inches tall for another. A wrist ticket allows unlimited rides.

Lincoln Tomb (age 7 and up) 

1500 Monument Avenue, off North Grand Avenue in Oak Ridge Cemetery, Springfield; (217) 782-2717; www.illinoishistory.gov/hs/lincoln_tomb.htm. Open from 9 a.m. to 5 p.m. daily from March through October and 9 a.m. to 4 p.m. daily from November through February. Also open from 7 to 8 p.m. Tuesday year-round except in July. It is closed New Year's, Martin Luther King Jr., Presidents, Veterans, general election, Thanksgiving, and Christmas days. Admission is free.

Here you'll find the 117-foot-tall Lincoln Tomb. Bronze statuary groups flank the four corners at the base of the granite obelisk, and a statue of the president stands in front. Below, outside the entrance to the tomb, is a bronze bust of Lincoln; his nose is a shiny gold from all the visitors who have rubbed it for good luck. Abraham and his wife, Mary Todd Lincoln, plus three of their four sons, Eddie, Willie, and Tad, are in crypts here. (Fourth son Robert Todd Lincoln is buried in Arlington National Cemetery with his wife and son.) Construction of the tomb began in 1869, four years after the president's assassination, and it was dedicated in 1874. Reconstructions were done in 1899 and 1930. Today you can go inside the cool marble tomb and walk in a circular path past bronze statues of Lincoln at various stages of his life to the chamber in back where the family is interred. A rectangular red marble headstone marks the spot where the president is buried. There is a simple elegance and dignity to this place.

Illinois Vietnam Veterans Memorial (age 7 and up) 

In Oak Ridge Cemetery near the Walnut Street entrance, Springfield; (217) 782-2717. The memorial is open the same hours as the cemetery itself, 8 a.m. to 8 p.m. daily from the first Sunday in April through the last Sunday in October and 8 a.m. to 5 p.m. daily the rest of the year. Free.

The Illinois Vietnam Veterans Memorial is about half a mile west of the Lincoln Tomb. Modeled after the national monument, this one features slanted black marble slabs fanning out from a white circular memorial to the various branches of the armed forces. Each of the slabs is engraved with the names of Illinois service personnel who died in or are still missing from the Vietnam War (1957–1975), a total of 2,970 lives sacrificed. Words on paper do not do justice to how moving this memorial is. It is a worthwhile stop for families: The Vietnam War is recent enough to have touched many parents' lives in some way, and a visit here is more valuable than a chapter in a history book in spurring discussion of this controversial war and its continuing repercussions.

Washington Park Botanical Gardens (all ages) 

In Washington Park, accessible from both South Grand Avenue and Chatham Road; (217) 753-6228. Mailing address: P.O. Box 5052, Springfield 62705. Open year-round, from noon to 4 p.m. Monday through Friday and noon to 5 p.m. Saturday and Sunday; closed Thanksgiving, Christmas Eve, and Christmas Day. Admission is free, although there is a donation box should you wish to support upkeep of the gardens. No smoking in the conservatory.

Because of its domed conservatory, the Botanical Gardens are open year-round. The conservatory contains tropical plants, and outside gardens are filled with roses and perennials during the temperate months.

Thomas Rees Memorial Carillon (age 2 and up)

In Washington Park, accessible from both South Grand Avenue and Chatham Road; (217) 753-6219 or (217) 544-1751; www.carillon-rees.org. Mailing address: P.O. Box 5052, Springfield 62705. The carillon is open from noon to 8 p.m. Wednesday through Sunday during June, July, and August and noon to dusk on weekends only during spring and fall; closed December through March. No charge to look around outside or in the room at the base; two-part tour includes video presentation and elevator ride to see the bells. $

Washington Park and Lincoln Park are the largest of Springfield's 30 parks. The most obvious attraction in Washington Park rises above the treetops—the Thomas Rees Memorial Carillon. Free concerts ring out every Sunday afternoon from the 66 bronze bells that span a range of five and a half octaves. The bells, cast in the Netherlands, have a total weight of nearly 74,000 pounds, with the smallest a mere 22 pounds and the largest a whopping 15,000 pounds. The carillon was dedicated in 1962 and renovated in 1987. Visitors can watch a short video presentation in a room inside the base of the carillon, then ride an elevator up to the bell tower. A small gift counter in the base of the tower offers souvenirs, including small bells.

White Oaks Mall (all ages) 

2501 West Wabash Avenue (corner of Wabash Avenue and Veterans Parkway), Springfield; (217) 787-8560; www.white-oaks-mall.com. Hours are 10 a.m. to 9 p.m. Monday through Saturday and 11 a.m. to 6 p.m. Sunday.

Serious shoppers will want to head to White Oaks Mall, where the slogan is, "Shop like you mean it." Anchored by department stores Bergner's, Macy's, and Sears, this two-story enclosed mall contains a variety of specialty stores. Of particular interest to kids are GameStop and Fluff n Stuff (where you make your own stuffed toys). Aladdin's Castle features arcade games. The food court has a McDonald's and also offers pizza, hot dogs, ice cream, and cookies, among other taste treats. For a restaurant meal, try the MCL Cafeteria. The White Oaks Cinema shows first-run movies.

Jungle O Fun (age 2 and up) 

3031 Koke Mill Road, Springfield; (217) 787-0707; www.jungle-o-fun.com. Open from 10 a.m. to 6 p.m. daily; closed major holidays. $–$$

About a quarter mile west of the mall, this indoor children's playground has an unusually large "play apparatus"—21 feet high—with slides, ball pits, bounce area, and all the good stuff you expect from this type of facility. There's a game room, too, plus a concession area where you can sit down for a cold soft drink or a meal of pizza or hot dogs.

Knight's Action Park and Caribbean Adventure (age 6 and up)

1700 Recreation Drive (US 36 south bypass and Chatham Road), Springfield; (217) 546-8881; www.knightsactionpark.com. Open from 9 a.m. to 10 p.m. daily from April through October; water attractions start in mid-May and end on Labor Day. $$$–$$$$

This sprawling complex has both wet and dry activities to keep the family busy. The water attractions include swimming pools, water slides, bumper boats, pedal boats, and the Caribbean Wild River action ride. A wave pool was added in 2000. The miniature golf course includes a green dragon peering out over a stone wall as you putt. Older kids may enjoy go-karts and laser tag. You can spend even more money in the batting cages or the arcade game room. Come only if you're prepared to drop a bundle and spend the better part of the day here to get the maximum bang for your buck. It's not the best value for little kids, who tire more quickly and can't handle all the offerings, but you'll probably have to drag your teenager out at the end of the visit.

Henson Robinson Zoo (all ages) 

1100 East Lake Drive, Springfield; (217) 753-6217; www.hensonrobinsonzoo.org. From March through October, the zoo hours are 10 a.m. to 5 p.m. Monday through Friday and 10 a.m. to 6 p.m. Saturday and Sunday. During June, July, and August, the closing time is extended to 8 p.m. on Wednesday. From November through February, hours are 10 a.m. to 4 p.m. daily. Stroller rental available. The building and grounds are accessible for strollers and wheelchairs. $

You'll have a scenic drive skirting Lake Springfield to get to the Henson Robinson Zoo. This facility was expanded and renovated in 1996, and the building through which you enter has a classroom, a gift shop and concession area, and clean restrooms with changing tables and low sinks. Walkways are paved with smooth asphalt that's great for strollers and wheelchairs. The general atmosphere here is relaxed and pleasant. Spider monkeys frolic on an island in the middle of a pond, and free-roaming fowl wander the grounds, the more unusual specimens being a turkey and a pure-white peahen. An American desert exhibit contains American kestrels, a burrowing owl, and sand tortoises. (It used to have a roadrunner, too, but that's been moved to the bird section.) Cacti dot the pen's landscape, and a painted mural across the back wall re-creates the colors of the American Southwest. A number of exhibits are labeled Vanishing Animals, including the blackfooted penguin, river otters, Asiatic black bears, and Galapagos tortoises. Other highlights are the prairie dog colony, the prowling cheetah, the majestic bald eagle, and the fruit bats in the nocturnal animals exhibit. One element that shows mixed results is the Zoo Key, a plastic tab that you can buy or rent and which is inserted into a slot on an electronic box at various points around the grounds to elicit additional information, quizzes, and songs—wonderful for children in the 2-to-6 age range. The problem is that there's also a button you can push that simply plays a little tune urging you to go get a "zoo-key, zoo-key," in the same sort of syrupy-sweet tone as the songs on the *Barney* TV show. Naturally, preschoolers love this ditty and will go around pushing the button on every box they see; after a while, it will drive everyone else bananas.

Where to Eat

Saputo's, 801 East Monroe Street; (217) 544-2523. Open from 10:30 a.m. to 10:30 p.m. Monday through Friday, 5 to 10:30 p.m. Saturday, and 5 to 9:30 p.m. Sunday. This downtown restaurant has been owned and operated since 1948 by "Springfield's first family of Italian cooking." Pasta dishes reflect the specialties of southern Italy: ravioli, rigatoni, mostaccioli, manicotti, fettucine Alfredo, and linguine with clam sauce, for example. Steaks and seafood also appear on the menu. $$

The Old Lux, 1900 South 15th Street, between Laurel and Ash Streets; (217) 528-0503. Open from 4:30 to 10 p.m. Friday and Saturday and 4:30 to 9 p.m. Tuesday, Wednesday, Thursday, and Sunday; closed Monday. This downtown establishment dates back to 1941 and boasts that it was "voted best filet in Springfield"—as in filet mignon. Steaks, chicken, and seafood entrees dominate the menu, which also features sandwiches. Be sure to check on the nightly specials. $$

Cozy Dog Drive In, 2935 South Sixth Street; (217) 525-1992. Hours are 8 a.m. to 8 p.m. Monday through Saturday; closed Sunday and holidays. This local eatery claims to have invented the batter-dipped, deep-fried hot dog on a stick, later copied by others and dubbed "corn dog." Here it's called a Cozy Dog. Located on the historic old Route 66, you'll find related memorabilia on the walls. $

Sonic Drive-In, 2000 North Dirksen Parkway; (217) 789-1000. Open year-round from 7 a.m. to 10 p.m. Monday through Thursday and 9 a.m. to 10 p.m. Sunday; closing time extended to midnight daily in summer. See Restaurant Appendix for description. $

Gallina's Pizza, 3133 South Dirksen Parkway; (217) 529-0649. In Capitol City Shopping Center, near Hampton Inn. Hours are 11 a.m. to 11 p.m. Monday through Saturday; closed Sunday. This casual, family-operated eatery serves a hot, cheesy, thin-crust pizza that is *delizioso!* Deep-dish pizza, pasta dinners, and sandwiches are also on the menu. Blowups of family snapshots in Italy line the brick walls, and half the selections in the jukebox are in Italian, the other half assorted American classic rock. $

Rock 'n' Roll Hardee's, 2501 Stevenson Drive; (217) 529-1331. Hours are 5:30 a.m. to 10:30 p.m. Monday through Friday, 5:30 a.m. to 11 p.m. Saturday, and 6 a.m. to 10 p.m. Sunday. The roast beef sandwiches, burgers, fried chicken, tasty breakfast biscuits, and other reasonably priced menu offerings are the same as those at most Hardee's, but the red-white-and-black decor is filled with neon, chrome, and such nostalgic features as an authentic Texaco gas pump and a Wurlitzer jukebox (not original—it plays CDs). $

Old Country Buffet, 2733 Veterans Parkway; (217) 787-2202. Hours are 10:30 a.m. to 8:30 p.m. Monday through Friday and 8 a.m. to 8:30 p.m. Saturday and Sunday. Serving breakfast, lunch, and dinner. See Restaurant Appendix for description. $

Where to Stay

Despite being in the Land of Lincoln, you're not likely to find many log cabins for lodging. Most of the motel chains are on the east side of the city, clustered along I-55, with another clump on the west along Highway 4.

Comfort Inn, 3442 Freedom Drive; (217) 787-2550 or (800) 424-6423. This property has 66 rooms and an indoor swimming pool and whirlpool. The room rate includes continental breakfast. Pets are allowed for an extra $25 per stay. $$$

Days Inn, 3000 Stevenson Drive; (217) 529-0171 or (800) 325-2525. This 2-story chain property has 153 rooms. There is an outdoor swimming pool. Pets are allowed, $5 per day extra. Room rate includes continental breakfast. $$

Fairfield Inn, 3446 Freedom Drive; (217) 793-9277 or (800) 228-2800. This 3-story, 63-room economy member of the Marriott family has an indoor swimming pool and whirlpool. Continental breakfast is included in the room rate. $$$

Hampton Inn, 3185 South Dirksen Parkway; (217) 529-1100 or (800) 426-7866. This 4-story, 123-room hotel has comfortable rooms with coffeemaker and cable TV. Amenities include heated indoor pool and whirlpool. Free cookies and lemonade are available in the lobby in the afternoon. The room rate includes a generous continental breakfast. $$$

Super 8 East, 1330 South Dirksen Parkway; (217) 528-8889 or (800) 800-8000. This 4-story mock-Tudor hotel has 63 rooms with cable TV. No pool. Pets allowed. Continental breakfast is included in the room rate.$$

For More Information

Springfield Convention & Visitors Bureau, 109 North Seventh Street, Springfield 62701; (217) 789-2360 or (800) 545-7300; www.visit-springfieldillinois.com.

Decatur

Population: 81,860. About an hour's drive east of Springfield (I-72 and US 36 are the same road on this stretch) is Decatur. Incorporated as a city in 1836, it became a rail hub for the Great Western and Illinois Central Railroad starting in 1854. In 1900 R. R. Montgomery reportedly invented the fly swatter in Decatur. In 1920 the Decatur Staleys became a charter member of the National Football League. Coached by George Halas, the team later would become the Chicago Bears. Throughout the 1900s affluent Decatur families adopted a variety of architectural styles for their homes. Today the city's Historic District features Gothic Revival, Second Empire, Italianate, Queen Anne, Classic Revival, Romanesque Revival, and Frank Lloyd Wright's Prairie styles. But many of the ordinary citizens here live in basic bungalows.

Scovill Children's Zoo (all ages) 

71 South Country Club Road, Decatur; (217) 421-7435; www.decatur-parks.org. Open from 10 a.m. to 7 p.m. daily between Memorial Day and Labor Day. From mid-April to Memorial Day and from Labor Day to mid-October, hours are 10 a.m. to 4 p.m. Monday through Friday and 10 a.m. to 6:30 p.m. Saturday and Sunday. $

This local zoo is small but quite nice. A real effort has been made to integrate indigenous plant life into the animal exhibit areas, and multicolored flower beds brighten the well-tended grounds. The collection of about 500 animals includes kangaroos, a capybara, emus, Chilean flamingos, toco toucans, Amazon parrots, ring-tailed lemurs, a ring-tailed coati, bobcats, and a whole "town" of prairie dogs. A petting zoo contains goats, donkeys, piglets, a calf, ducklings, and chicks. For an extra $1.50 for adults or $1 for kids or seniors, you can ride a little train that's a one-quarter-scale replica of an 1863 C. P. Huntington steam engine. The train even has a wheelchair lift.

Project Playground (ages 2 to 12) 

71 South Country Club Road, Decatur, next to the zoo. Hours are 6 a.m. to 10 p.m. daily, year-round. Free.

Since it's right next door to the zoo, you can count on this sprawling, wooden outdoor playground to add at least half an hour to your visit. It has towers, bridges, ladders, slides, swings, you name it.

Children's Museum of Illinois (all ages) 

55 South Country Club Road, Decatur; (217) 423-5437; www.cmofil.com. Open from 9:30 a.m. to 4:30 p.m. Tuesday through Friday, 10 a.m. to 5 p.m. Saturday, and 1 to 5 p.m. Sunday; closed Monday. The museum is within walking distance of the zoo. You can park your car in the zoo lot and walk over if the museum lot is full; parking is free in both lots. $

You'll easily spot this two-story white building with red and green trim. Little children will have a good time just pointing out the squares, triangles, and diamond shapes in the facade. One of the special features at this children's museum is the Shadow Wall, a wall covered with phosphorescent (glow-in-the-dark) vinyl opposite a black wall with a bright flashlight at the top—the only light in the room. You stand up against the vinyl wall, striking a pose if you like, and when the flash goes off, your body blocks the light behind it on the wall, creating the appearance of a dark shadow against the lightened wall. Definitely cool. The museum also has giant bubble makers, whisper disks, a plasma sphere, a tandem bike with a skeleton rigged up as the second rider, a fire truck, and a toddler play area with blocks. A kid-size bank, grocery store, and post office offer a chance to role-play. In the Handicapped Area, able-bodied kids can expe-

Lincoln's New Salem

About 20 miles northwest of Springfield, up Highway 97, is Lincoln's New Salem Historic Site, a reconstruction of the village of New Salem, where Abraham Lincoln lived and worked for six years as a young man during the 1830s. You can stroll down the "main drag" and stop to look into the cabin-style shops and houses on either side of the street; the total distance is about three quarters of a mile. If your toddler (or you) can't make it that far, you can hitch a free ride in a horse-drawn wagon, which will save you some steps. Perhaps you can walk in and ride out, or vice versa. The Onstot Cooper Shop is the only original building. The others were rebuilt during the 1930s by the Civilian Conservation Corps at the original sites. All are filled with authentic furnishings and artifacts of the 1830s. Guides in period costumes are posted in many of the two dozen buildings to help explain what went on there. Sometimes you'll see a demonstration of craftwork or music. Hours are 9 a.m. to 5 p.m. daily from mid-April through Labor Day and 9 a.m. to 5 p.m. Wednesday through Sunday from the day after Labor Day through mid-April; closed some holidays. Days and hours of operation are subject to change, however, especially during winter months, so call (217) 632-4000 to double-check before driving out there. Admission is free, with a suggested donation of $2 per adult and $1 per child. You can watch a free 10-minute orientation film in the visitor center auditorium before setting off. The climate-controlled center also contains exhibits and restrooms. Souvenirs are in another nearby building, along with a McDonald's. These two modern buildings are accessible for wheelchairs and strollers, but most of the historic buildings are not. There is a picnic area if you want to bring your own lunch. Further information is available at www.lincolnsnewsalem.com.

rience firsthand the challenge of getting around on crutches or in a wheelchair. Lucky's Climber is a two-story climbing structure lined with carpeting and including sturdy nets. A Water Table play area was added in 2003. This museum is a lot of fun for the young and the young at heart.

Rock Springs Nature Center (all ages)  

3939 Nearing Lane, Decatur; (217) 423-7708; www.maconcountyconservation.org. Open year-round. Visitor center hours are 8 a.m. to 5 p.m. Monday through Friday, 9 a.m. to 4:30 p.m. Saturday, and 1 to 4:30 p.m. Sunday. Homestead Prairie Farm is open from 1 to 4 p.m. Saturday and Sunday from June through October. The bike trail is open from 8 a.m. to dusk daily. Admission to all areas is free, although donations are accepted. There are fees for some special events.

This conservation education complex has numerous features to enhance the relationship between human beings and nature. The visitor center and museum are a good place to start. From there, head outside to the Homestead Prairie Farm, a farmstead that has been restored to represent the lifestyle of the 1860s. Gaze over the expansive grounds from the lookout tower. There are ponds for fishing and numerous trails, one a 10-foot-wide trail accessible to wheelchairs as well as hikers and bicyclists. A bikeway originating on the property goes across a 224-foot-long bridge over the Sangamon River.

Hickory Point Mall (all ages) 

I-72 at U.S. Highway 51, north of Decatur; (217) 875-0080; www.hickorypoint.com. Mailing address: 1146 Hickory Point Mall, Forsyth 62535-1006. Hours are 10 a.m. to 9 p.m. Monday through Saturday and noon to 5 p.m. Sunday.

A modernistic building houses this one-story indoor mall anchored by Von Maur, JCPenney, Kohl's, Sears, and Bergner's department stores, with about 70 shops.

Where to Eat

Old Country Buffet, 3194 North Water Street; (217) 875-0525. Hours are 11 a.m. to 8 p.m. Monday through Thursday, 11 a.m. to 9 p.m. Friday, 8 a.m. to 9 p.m. Saturday, and 8 a.m. to 8 p.m. Sunday. See Restaurant Appendix for description. $

Where to Stay

Holiday Inn Select Decatur, 4191 US 36 and Wycles Road; (217) 422-8800 or (800) 465-4329. This 4-story property, renovated in 2001, contains 383 guest rooms, and it has a banquet room that can hold 2,000 people. Amenities include an indoor swimming pool, whirlpool, fitness center, and games. Pets are allowed. There are 4 restaurants on the premises. Breakfast is not included in the room rate. $$$

Ramada Limited, 355 Hickory Point Road; (217) 876-8011 or (800) 272-6232. Opened in 1997, this 3-story property has 62 rooms with cable TV, coffeemaker, and hair dryer. Amenities include an indoor swimming pool and whirlpool. Roll-away bed available at extra charge. Continental breakfast is included in the room rate. $$

For More Information

Decatur Area Convention & Visitors Bureau, 202 East North Street, Decatur 62523; (800) 331-4479; www.decaturcvb.com.

Bloomington

Bloomington and Normal are like Minneapolis and St. Paul—you can hardly mention one without the other, and the two communities indeed seem as one when you're driving around in them. Roughly an hour's drive from Peoria (Interstate 74 from the northwest), Springfield (I-55 from the southwest), Decatur (US 51 from the south), or Champaign-Urbana (I-74 from the southeast; another linked pair we'll be exploring later in this chapter), it is easy to combine a stop here with a visit to other cities in the area.

Bloomington (population 64,808) is on the western side. It is home to Illinois Wesleyan University and has some interesting family attractions.

Miller Park (all ages) 

Off South Morris Avenue, Bloomington; (309) 434-2260. The park is open from sunrise to sunset daily, and admission is free.

Miller Park has an old locomotive on display that you can climb up into, a band shell, and a concession booth as well. When you add these attractions to the zoo (see next entry) and the miniature golf course (see subsequent entry) that are situated here, you can easily spend a whole summer day at this one park.

Miller Park Zoo (all ages) 

1020 South Morris Avenue, Bloomington; (309) 434-2250; www.millerparkzoo.org. Hours are 9:30 a.m. to 4:30 p.m. daily; closed Thanksgiving and Christmas Day. Take Veterans Parkway to Morris Avenue and turn north; brown signs will help direct you. The zoo is nestled among the Miller Park grounds. $

Well-paved pathways make it easy for strollers to navigate this small, well-established zoo. It opened in 1891, but only the lion house looks anywhere near that old, and it's in good shape. The big cats have large, rock-walled and fenced outdoor pens connected to the house, so they are in open air during temperate weather. Alas, the last of the zoo's lions have died, but Miller Park claims to be the only zoo in Illinois with Sumatran tigers. These are majestic felines, yet when you see one lolling in a doze on its back with its paws up, it looks just like an oversize house cat. The zoo also has beautiful snow leopards. You'll find sun bears in this area as well. Glass cases containing amphibians and other small animals are placed low enough for little kids to see into them easily. An indoor tropical rain forest exhibit is small but pleasant. Goats and sheep roam the contact area for youngsters to pet. Feeding schedules are posted at the entrance if you want to pick a time when you can watch the animals eat. They definitely perk up then; for example, the two lemurs go ape when the staffer comes in with their tray of fresh fruit and veggies.

The Miller Park Zoo has a number of unusual specimens in its collection: a reindeer; an endangered red wolf; a forest genet, a mammal that looks like a cat but is related to the mongoose and civet; and, from Papua New Guinea, a singing dog whose name is earned from its melodic howl. The Wallaby Walkabout is a fenced-in area visitors can stroll through (staying on the pathway, mind you) to see free-roaming wallabies and other small creatures from the Land Down Under. Zoo Lab has hands-on activities and a butterfly garden. The gift shop here is especially good, with jewelry and high-quality stuffed animals—including such offbeat ones as lemurs and platypuses—at prices that aren't totally outrageous.

Chucky's Caddy Club (age 3 and up) 

In Miller Park, Bloomington; (309) 434-2651. Open from 10 a.m. to 8 p.m. daily during summer. $

Decorated with flowers and a little wishing well, this miniature golf course is rather plain and straightforward, making it popular with kids. The prices are fairly reasonable, so it won't break the bank to stay and play a while.

Grady's Family Fun Park (age 3 and up) 

1501 Morrissey Drive (U.S. Highway 150), Bloomington; (309) 662-3332; www.gradysfunpark.com. Open from April through September. Summer hours are 10:30 a.m. to 9 p.m. Monday through Thursday, 10:30 a.m. to 10 p.m. Friday and Saturday, and 10:30 a.m. to 8 p.m. Sunday. Grounds are accessible for strollers and wheelchairs. $+

There's something for everyone here. There's no charge to get in; you pay only for what you play. A sign also gives fair warning to potential troublemakers, who are noticeably absent: GRADY'S IS A FAMILY FUN PARK. NO DRUGS, ALCOHOL, PROFANITY, PETS OR LOITERING. UNRULY BEHAVIOR WILL NOT BE TOLERATED. The facility is clean, colorful, and well lit. The 18-hole miniature golf course features a Statue of Liberty, a working windmill, and a barn, all the proper scale, and the holes aren't so tricky as to frustrate younger players. An arcade adjacent to the minigolf course has the usual sorts of video games, plus genuine pinball machines for those who love the physical satisfaction of leaning forward and pumping the flippers; you get three balls for a quarter. At seven minutes the bumper-boat ride is longer than usual for this type, and nearly two dozen boats can be in the water with space left over. Life jackets are provided for the kiddies. Tots age 2 or younger are not allowed in the boats. Older kids may enjoy the go-karts; they must be at least 12 to drive one and at least 4 to be a passenger. In the batting cages you can choose from among fast- or slow-pitch softball or slow-, medium-, or fast-pitch baseball. You of course are expected to wear a helmet (provided free along with the bat). Tiny tots will get a kick out of the kiddie carnival, a collection of eight junior-size rides, such as Ferris wheel, airplanes, Himalaya, and choo-choo.

Prairie Aviation Museum (age 4 and up) 

2929 East Empire Street, at Bloomington-Normal Airport, Illinois Highway 9 East, Bloomington; (309) 663-7632; www.prairieaviationmuseum.org. Hours are 11 a.m. to 4 p.m. Tuesday through Saturday and noon to 4 p.m. Sunday; closed Monday. $

Here you'll find two old airplanes—a 1942 Douglas DC-3 and a 1963 Corsair—that you can examine up close. Go into the cockpit and imagine yourself as the pilot. Also part of the outdoor and hangar displays are a 1958 Cessna 310B, a Marine Corps Sea Cobra helicopter, a huge UH-1 "Huey" helicopter, and other aircraft. Indoors the main museum has a flight simulator and displays of model airplanes, real engines, an escape capsule, old uniforms, and memorabilia from the now-defunct Ozark Airlines, which operated flights around the Midwest. Maybe you're old enough to remember that carrier or even (like this author) flew on one of its planes.

Where to Eat

Lucca Grill, 116 East Market Street (corner of Market Street/Highway 9 and US 51 North); (309) 828-7521. Open from 11 a.m. to 10 p.m. Monday through Saturday and 3 to 9 p.m. Sunday. Serving lunch, mid-afternoon sandwiches, and dinner. This casual little Italian restaurant is loaded with atmosphere, from the ornate ceiling to the memorabilia-covered walls to the dumbwaiter in the back that brings food down from the second-floor kitchen. It's noisy, so you won't have to worry about your kids getting too loud, and it can get pretty crowded, so try to come before or after the main dinner hour if you don't want to wait for a table. The thin-crust pizza is cheesy and delicious. The thick, spicy meat sauce available for the assorted pasta dishes makes them taste almost like goulash (which is good or bad, depending on how you feel about goulash). You can get marinara or Alfredo sauce instead, if you prefer. Pasta entrees come with salad and bread. Steaks, chicken, and seafood dishes also appear on the menu. One caveat for parents of wee babes: The restrooms are tiny, each barely big enough for a toilet and a sink—forget about trying to change a diaper here. $$

Bakers Square, 321 Veterans Parkway; (309) 454-5555. Open from 6 a.m. to 11 p.m. Sunday through Thursday and 6 a.m. to midnight Friday and Saturday. See Restaurant Appendix for description. $

Where to Stay

Days Inn West, 1707 Market Street; (309) 829-6292 or (800) 329-7466. Off I-55/74 at Market Street exit. This economical 3-story chain property has 58 rooms. Amenities include an indoor heated pool with spa.

Pets are allowed in smoking rooms only. Continental breakfast is included in the room rate. $$

America's Best Inns, 1905 Market Street; (309) 827-5333 or (800) 237-8466. This 106-room budget property has an outdoor pool, allows pets, and includes continental breakfast in the price of the room. This motel also has a special parking lot for trucks, but the rooms are fairly well insulated against the interstate traffic. $$

For More Information

Bloomington-Normal Area Convention and Visitors Bureau, 3201 Circa Drive, Suite 201, Bloomington 61704; (309) 665-0033; www.bloomingtonnormalcvb.org.

Normal

Population: 45,386. Normal lies to the east of Bloomington and is the home of Illinois State University (ISU) and Illinois Wesleyan University. The Children's Discovery Museum moved to Normal from Bloomington in 2005. Among the city's other attractions, Normal has a mall, which can be a comfortable place to push the stroller around for a couple hours, and lots of eateries.

Illinois State University Planetarium (age 5 and up)

School Street and College Avenue, Normal; (309) 438-8756; www.phy.ilstu.edu/~trw/planetfiles/skyline.html. Show days and times vary, typically Monday and Wednesday evenings during summer.

The white-domed, 100-seat Illinois State University Planetarium, at the east end of Femley Hall on the ISU campus, offers public programs while the university is in session. During fall and spring sessions, shows are given on weekends. During the summer session both weekday and weekend shows are offered. The Spitz A-3P star projector can beam more than 2,300 stars onto a 30-foot dome, and the shows are designed to appeal to kids. Tickets may be purchased at the door beginning 15 minutes before the show. Use your best judgment about whether your preschooler is ready for this kind of show—you don't want your child to get scared or bored and thus be turned off to this fascinating science before ever giving it a fair chance.

Ecology Action Center (age 5 and up) 

202 West College Avenue, Normal; (309) 454-3169; www.ecologyactioncenter.org. Hours are 9 a.m. to 5 p.m. Monday through Friday and by appointment Saturday; closed Sunday. Admission is free.

An old house is home to this small facility opened in 1995 and dedicated to environmental education. Free tours take 15 to 30 minutes, and visitors learn about recycling, composting, and saving energy. Recycled products are on display in one room; another room features live fish and a nature mural. The center hosts many school groups and community workshops.

Children's Discovery Museum (ages 2 to 11) 

101 East Beaufort Street, Normal; (309) 433-3444; www.childrensdiscoverymuseum.net. Call or check online for directions; part of Beaufort Street near the museum was scheduled to be closed through December 2008 due to hotel construction. Hours are 9 a.m. to 5 p.m. Tuesday, Wednesday, and Saturday, 9 a.m. to 8 p.m. Thursday and Friday, and 1 to 5 p.m. Sunday; closed Monday during the school year. Additional summer hours June through August from 9 a.m. to 5 p.m. Monday. The facility is accessible for wheelchairs and strollers. $

This three-story, glass-walled children's museum will delight kids with varying interests in its brightly colored, hands-on activity centers. Artistic types can paint on a wall or make artwork out of recycled materials, which they can take home. Athletic types can enjoy the maze of ropes and nets in the Lucky Climber apparatus that extends the height of the top two floors. Railroad buffs can assume the role of conductor in the area with the model train. Children who like to play doctor can check out the medical center. The AgMazing area has a tractor to ride in and lots of farming-related things to do. The Toddler Backyard is a small playground designed for the littlest visitors. Kids of all ages are drawn to the Sugar Creek Waterplay area, which provides all sorts of wet ways to have fun. Consider packing a spare set of clothes for the kids to change into after they're done there, or maybe just let them blow-dry in the ImagineAir area. You can bring your own snacks and drinks to enjoy in the Landings refreshment room when the kids (and you) need a break. There are restrooms with changing stations on all three levels, including a family restroom on the ground floor. Lockers and coathangers are available next to the gift shop near the entrance.

Fairview Family Aquatic Center (all ages) 

800 North Main Street, Normal; (309) 454-9555. Open from Memorial Day through Labor Day. Hours are noon to 8 p.m. daily. $

There are actually two swimming pools at this facility. The "activity pool" is the better one for families with young children. It is zero-depth along one edge, with water sprays, arched water jets, a water "mushroom" fountain, and a polar bear slide. A 5-foot-deep area at the other end has six lanes for lap swimming. The "plunge pool" has much deeper water, a 1-meter diving board, and two drop slides. Sand volleyball and a concession area round out the amenities.

Normal Theater (age 3 and up) 

209 North Street, downtown Normal; (309) 454-9722; www.normaltheater.com. Call for current schedule of films and other entertainment. $

This restored art deco movie house originally opened in 1937 and reportedly was the first theater in Bloomington-Normal built specifically for sound films. Today it shows "classic" (that is, old) movies, some suitable for families, as well as live theatrical and musical performances.

Illinois Basketball Coaches Association Hall of Fame (age 8 and up) 

8 Traders Circle, in the Holiday Inn North, Normal; (309) 452-8300. Open all day, every day. Free.

This exhibition room honors coaches, players, and other people related to basketball. It probably wouldn't be of much interest to little children, but older kids who've played the game or followed a team may enjoy a brief visit, especially if you're staying in the motel anyway.

Eastland Mall (all ages) 

1615 Empire Street, off Veterans Parkway, Normal; (309) 663-5361. Open from 10 a.m. to 9 p.m. Monday through Saturday and noon to 6 p.m. Sunday.

This one-story indoor shopping mall is anchored by Sears, JCPenney, Kohl's, and Bergner's. Gap Kids features children's clothing. Electronics Boutique stocks video games among its inventory. Hat World has cool caps. Snacks and light meals can be purchased in the food court.

Where to Eat

Bakers Square, 321 South Veterans Parkway near the malls; (309) 454-5555. Hours are 6 a.m. to 11 p.m. Sunday through Thursday and 6 a.m. to midnight Friday and Saturday. See Restaurant Appendix for description. $

Steak n Shake, 325 South Veterans Parkway; (309) 454-2899. Also 614 West Raab Road; (309) 451-3721. Although neither of these is the chain's founding restaurant (the original is closed), they are both open 24 hours a day. See Restaurant Appendix for description. $

Where to Stay

The Chateau, 1601 Jumer Drive; (309) 662-2020. Off Veterans Parkway in Normal. This beautiful 4-story hotel does indeed look like a château, and the Old World opulence reflects its former affiliation with the Jumer hotel chain. Opened in 1988, it has 180 guest rooms and suites, each elegantly furnished. Amenities include indoor swimming pool, whirlpool, saunas, and game room. The level of refinement here is not appropriate for little children, who would not appreciate it, but a Chateau visit makes a memorable treat for older grade-schoolers and teens with taste. Breakfast is not included in the room rate. Breakfast, lunch, dinner, and room service are provided by the on-site restaurant. Be sure to ask about package deals and discounts for AAA; you might be able to keep the price below $100. $$$$

Motel 6, 1600 North Main Street; (309) 452-0422. At the opposite end of the economic spectrum from The Chateau, this budget property has 98 rooms and an outdoor pool. Pets are allowed. $

Super 8, 2 Traders Circle; (309) 454-5858. Exit at Business 51 south off I-55. This budget property has 52 rooms with cable TV. Pets are allowed at extra charge. Room rates include continental breakfast. $$

Holiday Inn North, 8 Traders Circle; (309) 452-8300 or (800) 465-4329. At I-55 and US 51. This 5-story hotel has 160 rooms. Amenities include indoor pool, hot tub, sauna, exercise room, and game room. Pets allowed. $$$

Best Western University Inn, 6 Traders Circle; (309) 454-4070 or (800) 937-8376. This 2-story brick motel received a 2-diamond rating from AAA. It has 100 rooms plus indoor swimming pool and video games. You can also go fishing at this property. Small pets are allowed but may not be left in room unattended. Continental breakfast is included in the room rate. $$$

For More Information

Town of Normal, 100 East Phoenix Avenue, Normal 61761; (309) 454-2444; www.normal.org.

Sonic Boom

Remember the good old days of summer when you were growing up and everyone piled into the car to go get burgers and milkshakes at the drive-in? Or maybe the closest you ever came to that experience was watching old reruns of *Happy Days* on TV or renting the 1973 movie *American Graffiti.* Well, your chance is coming. The southern chain of Sonic Drive-In restaurants is moving northward, now extending across much of southern and central Illinois, with plans for further expansion toward Chicago. Pull into a parking space, place your order at the speaker box below the menu board, and a carhop on roller skates will deliver it. There's also a small outdoor patio with picnic tables if you'd rather not eat in the car. Don't ask how they're going to wheel through the snow come winter—just enjoy! (See the Restaurant Appendix for a list of current locations in Illinois.)

Champaign

Champaign-Urbana, our other twin city in Central Illinois, is roughly an hour's drive southeast of Bloomington-Normal via I-74 or US 150. From Decatur it's less than an hour's drive northeast on I-72. Coming from the north or south, Interstate 57 will be the fastest route. Champaign-Urbana has a combined population of about 100,000, not counting the student body at the University of Illinois—another 36,000 people. The U of I campus straddles the boundary between Champaign and Urbana and is a dominant presence in the life of the community. For general information about the university and its offerings, call (217) 333-4666 or check www.uiuc.edu. Let's look first at some family activities on the Champaign side.

Market Place Shopping Center (all ages) 

2000 North Neil Street (at I-74), Champaign; (217) 356-2700. Open from 10 a.m. to 9 p.m. Monday through Thursday, 10 a.m. to 10 p.m. Friday and Saturday, and 11 a.m. to 6 p.m. Sunday. Stroller and wheelchair rentals are available.

This one-story indoor shopping mall is the biggest and best in the area. With white walls and ceilings, it's not the most colorful mall you've ever seen, but skylights augment the artificial lighting to make it bright and airy. The marble-look floors provide a smooth rolling surface for strollers or wheelchairs. Two fountains, one in front of JCPenney and the other in front of Sears, add pleasing ambient noise and visual appeal. Those two department stores plus Bergner's are the anchors, and the floor plan is roughly cross-shaped. (A Kohl's store is nearby but not attached to the mall.) A number of stores here are of particular interest to kids. Those on a hunt for the newest Beanie Babies can check in either of two Hallmark stores, Kirlin's or Marian's. Hat World carries an amazing inventory of caps bearing the logos of professional sports teams and schools. At World of Science, you can buy experiment kits with biology or dinosaur themes or a Make Your Own kit for soap, hot sauce, or a medieval clock. The store carries a fascinating array of toys, games, puzzles, and books, and it even has a music listening station. Grade-schoolers especially will think World of Science is really cool. There is an arcade called Tilt lit in yellow and orange neon, but it caters more to teens and adults than children. The mall has no food court, but there's one pizza place, and you can buy a bunch of sweets to snack on: caramel corn, cookies, chocolates, and other candy.

Orpheum Children's Science Museum (all ages) 

346 North Neil Street, Champaign; (217) 352-5895; www.m-crossroads.org/orpheum. Hours are 9 a.m. to 6 p.m. Tuesday and 1 to 6 p.m. Wednesday through Sunday. $

Housed in a 1914 theater building, this museum opened in the late 1990s and underwent further expansion in 2000 and 2001. Inside are a variety of hands-on exhibits that make learning about science fun. For example, kids can walk a 14-foot plank or operate a block and tackle to experience the amazing scientific principles of such simple machines as the lever and the pulley, which enable people to lift objects much heavier than their own weight. The Bernoulli Blower suspends a ball in midair, and the Ghost Images exhibit plays tricks with light. Younger children will be drawn to the plastic human torso model, the cardboard blocks, and the PVC pipe organ. In the outdoor Dino Dig area, visitors use paleontologists' tools to unearth mock dinosaur bones. Kids can sift through sand to find little polished rocks in Kiki's Gem Mine.

William M. Staerkel Planetarium (age 5 and up)

2400 West Bradley Avenue, on the Parkland College campus, Champaign; (217) 351-2568; www.parkland.edu/coned/pla. Open year-round on Friday and Saturday evenings. Planetarium shows are not recommended for children younger than preschool age. Light shows are not recommended for preteens; children age 5 or younger will not be admitted to a light show. $

You'll have stars in your eyes after a visit to the planetarium, viewing projections of heavenly bodies onto the interior dome to create a night sky indoors. Each year there are special shows geared toward children; recent titles included "Zubenelgenubi's Magical Sky," "Rusty Rocket's Last Blast," and "In My Backyard." Younger children may get scared of the dark or simply bored, so don't rush them into a planetarium show at too early an age; use your best parental judgment in determining whether your youngster is ready for this fascinating medium. For teens and adults there is also a "light show" that blasts loud rock music and throws in all sorts of special effects—flashing lights, fog, video-style pictures—for a total sensory overload. Popular light shows have featured Pink Floyd, The Who, Led Zeppelin, U2, and others.

Putt-Putt (age 3 and up) 

815 Dennison Drive, Champaign; (217) 356-6121; www.puttputtcu.com. Off Prospect Avenue, 1 block north of Bradley Avenue. Summer hours are 10 a.m. to 11 p.m. Monday through Thursday, 10 a.m. to 11:30 p.m. Friday and Saturday, and 10 a.m. to 11 p.m. Sunday. The hours are cut back in fall, and the place closes after the last weekend in September, reopening in late spring. Call ahead or check the Web site for specials and coupons that can cut the cost. $+

This is not the most exciting course in the world, but it's the only game in town if you want to play miniature golf in Champaign. There are actually two courses, one a bit more difficult but more fun than the other and still possible to make par. Each green is framed in bittersweet-orange metal trim. Any skill you have at shooting pool will come in handy on some holes where you'll need to carom the ball off the metal borders (which makes an amusing "doink" sound) to get around obstacles such as wooden blocks or steel posts and reach the cup. Some of the greens have rolling hills that make the shot a bit trickier. But there are no moving parts and no tunnels, and the decor and landscaping are fairly minimalist—a full-size giraffe statue on one course, a baby elephant on another, a few yellow daylilies, and a lot of grass. There's a pop machine but no concession stand.

Rudolph's Cousins

The ones here don't have red noses, but you'll find a herd of reindeer imported from Alaska at this family ranch north of Champaign near Rantoul, a town just east of I-57 along U.S. Highway 136. Admission to **Hardy's Reindeer Ranch** is **free,** although there are charges for a couple of other attractions here. To enter the six-acre corn maze—which features a different elaborate design each year—you pay $5 for anyone age 13 or older and $4 for kids age 3 through 12; tots age 2 or younger get in free, but you better keep a tight grip on their hand! You can also enjoy Indy-style pedal race carts for $3 per person, all ages; $1 off if you do both the maze and the carts. In the fall you can pick a pumpkin. The gift shop offers a variety of souvenirs as well as homemade fudge and cookies. From August through the end of September, hours are 10 a.m. to 8 p.m. Wednesday through Saturday and 1 to 8 p.m. Sunday. Hours in October are 8 a.m. to 8 p.m. Monday through Saturday and 1 to 7 p.m. Sunday. Hours in November and through December 28 are 10 a.m. to 7 p.m. Monday through Saturday and 1 to 7 p.m. Sunday; closed Thanksgiving and Christmas. Closed from December 29 through July. For further information, contact Hardy's Reindeer Ranch, 1356 CR 2900N; (217) 893-3407; http://reindeerranch.com.

In 2004 the facility added five batting cages and a Jump Shot basketball game. The latter features a two-sectioned padded cage with a trampoline floor. Players shoot basketballs over the netted wall separating the two sections. The action is wild and bouncy; teens love it.

Ants in Their Pants (ages 2 to 12) 

125 South Mattis Avenue, Champaign; (217) 351-2687. At the south end of a strip of stores in the Country Fair Shopping Center, just south of University Avenue. Hours are 3:30 to 7:30 p.m. Monday through Friday, noon to 7:30 p.m. Saturday, and noon to 5 p.m. Sunday. Babies too young to play on the equipment and all accompanying adults get in free. Kids must wear socks (available for sale if they didn't wear any). $

You won't have to worry about the weather if you take the kids to this indoor amusement center. The biggest attraction is a giant play apparatus with tubes, slides, nets, and clear-bubble observation ports. The thing is a riot of color—it has a padded purple metal framework, with other plastic parts in pink, yellow, orange, blue, and green. Nearby is a smaller apparatus in black and white. Within a square metal framework, two layers of bouncy elastic webbing crisscross above a ball pit. Kids have a blast

playing spider in it. You'll also find two rows of arcade games for varying ability levels. For the littler kids there are a couple of "bop" games that elicit giggles. Grade-schoolers go for basketball, Bozo buckets, the Barbie-and-Ken surf race, and youth-oriented video games. And everybody likes Skeeball. Most games cost only one token (25 cents) to play. Ditto the little horsie, helicopter, and choo-choo for the tots. The Ninja Turtles amusement park ride costs two tokens, but it goes up and down and around and around. At no extra charge is the toddler play area for those age 3 or younger. Enclosed by a 2-foot-high wall, it has a padded slide; a shallow, open ball pit; and an assortment of Little Tikes cars, shopping carts, and kitchen appliances. The restrooms are clean and have changing tables. The only on-site refreshments are pop and juice in a vending machine.

Centennial Park (all ages) 

2202 West Kirby Avenue, off Mattis Avenue between Sangamon Drive and Kirby Avenue, Champaign; (217) 398-2550. Open daily from 8 a.m. to 11 p.m. Free admission.

Centennial Park is a good place for outdoor relaxation. Here you can have a picnic, hike a fitness trail, or release the kids on the playground. The Sholem Pool and the Prairie Farm are both in this park, too (see next two entries).

Sholem Pool and Waterworks Waterslide (all ages) 

2200 Sangamon Drive, Champaign; (217) 398-2581. At the north end of Centennial Park. Open from Memorial Day weekend through Labor Day. Hours are 11:30 a.m. to 8 p.m. Monday through Friday and 10 a.m. to 8 p.m. Saturday and Sunday. $

Enter the pool complex at the sandy brick building with pink and yellow flower beds in front. There is a huge rectangular pool for regular swimming. It has a diving well with boards off to the side at one end. Children age 6 or younger, accompanied by parents, can swim in the separate kiddie pool. Depth is about 1 to 2 feet all the way around, so parents of toddlers should stay within arm's reach at all times. The water slide is in a separate area connected by a gate. Long wooden staircases lead up and up and up to a platform at the top of two long, twisting white flumes. Kids must be at least 3 feet tall and able to swim one width of the pool to be allowed on the slides, the latter requirement a wise precaution. The pool can get temporarily crowded during the week with busloads of day campers who get an hour or two to swim. The concession area has tables with umbrellas where you can enjoy a soda and a snack such as chips, candy, ice cream, nachos, or a hot dog.

Prairie Farm (ages 1 to 8) 

2202 West Kirby Avenue, at Mattis Avenue, Champaign; (217) 398-2583. At the south end of Centennial Park; parking is along Kirby Avenue. Open from Memorial Day through Labor Day. Hours are 1 to 7 p.m. Monday through Friday and noon to 7 p.m. Saturday and Sunday. Petting area is open from 3 to 5 p.m. daily. Admission is free, although there is a cute donation box that looks like a miniature barn if you feel like contributing to the upkeep. Paths are paved and accessible for strollers and wheelchairs. No smoking allowed.

This small, simple facility is especially appealing for younger children. There are little red barns and pens with pigs, cows, horses, and chickens to look at. If the tots want a more hands-on experience, they can go in the fenced-in petting area and get acquainted with goats, ponies, and a calf. A pop machine is the only concession on-site, but you can bring a picnic basket and enjoy your own food at one of several picnic tables (which is a better deal for toddlers anyway). There are a couple of old wooden wagons on the grounds that add atmosphere but are not for playing on. Big shade trees keep the area comfortable on a warm, sunny day.

Curtis Orchard and Pumpkin Patch (all ages)

3902 South Duncan Road, Champaign; (217) 359-5565; www.curtisorchard.com. East of I-57 and south of I-72. Open from late July through mid-December. Hours are 9 a.m. to 6 p.m. Monday through Saturday and 11 a.m. to 6 p.m. Sunday. Admission is free, but naturally you would be expected to pay for the apples or pumpkins you pick. Fees are charged for some of the kids' attractions.

South of town is this family-oriented orchard with 4,000 trees from which you can pick your own apples. You can also tour a working farm that produces corn and soybeans. Kids can play in the barn, take a pony ride, wind their way through a maze, knock a golf ball into the cup on the putting greens, or visit goats, bunnies, and chicks in the petting farm. The sales area has delicious cobbler, pies, and doughnuts plus bags of fruit you can buy if you don't feel like picking it yourself. The orchard sells Halloween pumpkins and Christmas trees, too.

Where to Eat

Famous Dave's, 1900 Round Barn Road, off Mattis Avenue; (217) 403-1166. Across the street from Ants in Their Pants. Hours are 11 a.m. to 9:30 p.m. Monday through Thursday, 11 a.m. to 10:30 p.m. Friday and Saturday, and 11 a.m. to 9 p.m. Sunday. Formerly the Round Barn Steakhouse, this casual, family-oriented chain restaurant specializes in barbecued ribs and pork. Children's menu prices range from $2.50 to $3.50, including drink. Kids' choices include cheeseburger, chicken strips, roasted chicken, and peanut butter and jelly sandwich. $

Sonic Drive-In, 601 North Mattis Avenue; (217) 356-1230. Open year-round from 7 a.m. to 10 p.m. Sunday through Thursday and 7 a.m. to midnight Friday and Saturday;

closing time extended to midnight daily in summer. See Restaurant Appendix for description. $

Bob Evans, 1813 North Neil Street; (217) 356-1006. Hours are 6 a.m. to 10 p.m. daily. See Restaurant Appendix for description. $

TGIFriday's, 101 Trade Center Drive; (217) 352-5595. Hours are 11 a.m. to 10:30 p.m. Sunday through Thursday and 11 a.m. to 11 p.m. Friday and Saturday. See Restaurant Appendix for description. $$

Where to Stay

Comfort Inn, 305 Marketview Drive; (217) 352-4055 or (800) 424-6423. There are 66 comfortable rooms in this 2-story motel. It has an indoor pool with whirlpool. Continental breakfast is included in the room rate. $$

Fairfield Inn, 1807 Moreland Boulevard; (217) 355-0604. This 3-story property has 62 rooms, 8 suites, and an indoor heated pool and spa. The room rate includes continental breakfast. $$$

Super 8, 202 Marketview Drive; (217) 359-2388 or (800) 800-8000. This economy property has 61 rooms with cable TV. Pets are allowed. Continental breakfast is included in the room rate. $$

For More Information

Champaign County Convention and Visitors Bureau, 1817 South Neil Street, Suite 201, Champaign 61820-7269; (217) 351-4133 or (800) 369-6151; www.cucvb.org.

Urbana

The Urbana half of Champaign-Urbana is more closely connected with the university and has fewer attractions of interest to families with young children, but there are a couple here to check out.

Spurlock Museum (age 8 and up) 

600 South Gregory Street, Urbana; (217) 333-2360; www.spurlock.uiuc.edu. From I-74, exit south onto Lincoln Avenue and continue south onto the University of Illinois campus. Turn right, heading west, onto Oregon Street and go 1 block to Gregory Street; museum is at the corner of Oregon and Gregory Streets. (Note: Do not confuse Gregory Street with Gregory Drive, which is across the campus.) Metered street parking available; additional parking in metered lot on south side of building. Hours are noon to 5 p.m. Tuesday, 9 a.m. to 5 p.m. Wednesday through Friday, 10 a.m. to 4 p.m. Saturday, and noon to 4 p.m. Sunday. Closed Monday. Admission is free, but there is a suggested donation of $3 per person, which may be placed in a glass-walled, wooden-framed box near the entrance to the exhibit halls. The facility has an elevator and is accessible for wheelchairs. No smoking, food, or drink in the building.

Opened in 2002, this museum explores various cultures of the world. In each of its five exhibit halls, the materials are well displayed, mainly in glass cases. There are not too many items per case, and there are written explanations on laminated notebook-style pages below each case. The halls are pleasantly lit, have an appealing color balance, and allow ample space to maneuver between display cases. This museum is not really appropriate for small children, however; visitors should be able to read and have some concept of the larger world, and they must be mature enough not to run around wildly and bang on the glass cases or touch other items on display, thus the suggested minimum age of 8. That caveat aside, this is a lovely place for older children to visit. Two exhibit halls are on the first floor. The Ancient Mediterranean hall includes beautiful plaster-cast reproductions of large marble and bronze statues from Greece and Italy (some of which you should be aware are male nudes, if you have a problem with that) and genuine artifacts including jewelry, utensils, pots, urns, and oil lamps. The American Indian hall features musical instruments, ceremonial clothing, statues and figurines, and a full-size tepee. Walk up a gently curving staircase (or use the elevator) to reach the three exhibit halls on the second floor. The highlight in the Southeast Asia and Oceania hall is a *barong ket,* a gorgeous dragonlike figure paraded out during religious festivals in Bali. A bamboo frame is covered with red fur and hundreds of gilded mirrors, and a mask with a fierce face is attached to the front. In its original use, two male dancers underneath the beast would manipulate it during the festival. At the Spurlock Museum, this one hangs suspended from the ceiling. Also of interest to children are the authentic Indonesian shadow puppets and the ceramic reproductions of the 2,000-year-old giant terra-cotta soldiers found in the tomb of the Chinese emperor Ying Zheng in 1974. Other displays include batik cloth and paper currency from colonial and postcolonial times. The Europe hall covers the period from the Middle Ages to modern times. Kids would likely enjoy the German hunting crossbow, the suits of armor, a World War I helmet riddled with what look like bullet holes, and the huge ancient book of music from the medieval period that has square notes. Be sure to show them the 100-year-old copy of *Magna Carta* and the little chunk of the Berlin Wall that fell in 1989. This hall also has tasteful presentations of religious texts and relics from Islam, Judaism, and Christianity. The final hall, showcasing Africa and the Middle East, contains a real Egyptian mummy and sarcophagus in a back corner, along with plaster casts of ancient statues including a pharaoh. A nearby case contains a fragment of a carved stone tablet and related artifacts from Mesopotamia. Other appealing exhibits feature kente and raffia cloth, drums and other musical instruments, and ceremonial masks and carvings. One of the more moving displays focuses on the slave trade. A visit to the Spurlock Museum can help families broaden their horizons and appreciate the wonderful diversity of human culture.

Crystal Lake Park and Pool (all ages) 

1311 North Broadway, at Park Street, Urbana; (217) 328-2321. The park is open year-round, from sunrise to 11 p.m. daily. Park admission is free. Pets must be kept on leashes, and alcoholic beverages are not allowed. The pool is open during summer only, from 1 to 8 p.m. Monday through Friday, 11 a.m. to 8 p.m. Saturday, and noon to 7 p.m. Sunday. $

Crystal Lake Park is a nice place to relax and enjoy the great outdoors here in Urbana. It's the biggest park in the Champaign-Urbana area and the only one with a lake. You can fish for largemouth bass, channel catfish, bluegill, and redear from shore or from one of several overlook decks. If you want to go out onto the lake, you can rent a rowboat, canoe, or two-seater paddleboat for $3.50 per half hour or $5 per hour. Arrange the rental at the Lake House, where you can also find soft drinks and light snacks. The Lake House Cafe is open from 11 a.m. to 6 p.m. daily from late April through early September. The T-shaped swimming pool also has a concession area. Or you can have a picnic at the park using the picnic tables and grills scattered throughout the grounds. You can take a hike along the nature trails, or turn the kids loose on the playground. You can skate on the frozen lake for some winter fun.

Where to Eat

Garcia's Pizza, 803 South Lincoln Avenue; (217) 359-1212. Open from 11 a.m. to 11 p.m. Sunday through Thursday and 11 a.m. to midnight Friday and Saturday. This campus-area pizza place is a favorite of students. Both thick- and thin-crust types are offered. If your kids are the type who'll eat anything, try the "gut-buster" with the works. (There are several Garcia's outlets in Champaign as well.) $

Where to Stay

Eastland Suites, 1907 North Cunningham (I-74 and U.S. Highway 45); (217) 367-8331. Despite its name, this property has about 150 regular hotel rooms, each with microwave and minifridge, as well as several types of suites. A $2 million renovation in 2000 gave the place a nearly brand-new look. Amenities include indoor pool and exercise room. Pets are allowed with $50 deposit, $35 of which is refundable. Breakfast is included in the room rate: continental Saturday and Sunday, hot breakfast weekdays. $$$

Hampton Inn, 1200 West University Avenue; (217) 337-1100. This 92-room property has an exercise room but no swimming pool. Continental breakfast is included in the room rate. $$$$

Monticello

Population: 5,138. About 18 miles west of Champaign-Urbana is the town of Monticello. You'll find a couple of pleasant family attractions here.

Monticello Railway Museum (all ages) 

Off I-72 at exit 63, Monticello; (217) 762-9011; www.prairienet.org/mrm. Open only weekends and holidays from May 1 through October 31. Board at 11 a.m. or 12:30, 2, or 3:30 p.m. Saturday or Sunday at the museum's restored Illinois Central Depot or at 11:30 a.m. or 1, 2:30, or 4 p.m. Saturday or Sunday at the restored 1899 Wabash Depot in downtown Monticello. $–$$

Here you'll see historic railroad cars and equipment on display, including both steam engines and electric railcars. You can take a 50-minute train ride through the countryside in one of the museum's vintage coaches or cabooses. A uniformed conductor will punch your ticket and remain on hand to answer any questions you may have.

Allerton Park and Retreat Center (all ages) 

515 Old Timber Road, near the railway museum, about 4 miles southwest of Monticello—look for signs; (217) 333-3287; www.conted.uiuc.edu/allerton. Open daily from 8 a.m. to sunset. Admission is free. A visitor center on the grounds is open from 9 a.m. to 5 p.m. daily from April through November and 8 a.m. to 4:30 p.m. Friday and Saturday only from December through March.

This lovely 1,500-acre park features flower gardens, greenhouses, sculpted hedges, and statues and sculptures from Cambodia, Thailand, and China. The park has been named a National Natural Landmark.

Where to Eat

Pizza Hut, 777 West Bridge; (217) 762-8585. Hours are 11 a.m. to 10 p.m. daily. See Restaurant Appendix for description. $

Where to Stay

Best Western Monticello Gateway Inn, 805 Iron Horse Place, I-72 at exit 166; (217) 762-9436 or (800) 937-8376. This 41-room property received a 3-diamond rating from AAA. It is just a quarter mile south of the railway museum and about 5 miles from Allerton Park. Amenities include indoor swimming pool. Continental breakfast is included in the room rate. $$

For More Information

Monticello Chamber of Commerce, Old Wabash Depot, P.O. Box 313, Monticello 61856; (217) 762-7921 or (800) 952-3396; www.monticello.net or www.monticellochamber.org.

Tuscola

Population: 4,448. This town bills itself as "Your First Stop in Amish Country." You won't see many buggies until you get a bit farther south, but there are several attractions here for the family to enjoy.

Tanger Outlet Center (all ages) 

I-57 at US 36, Tuscola; (217) 253-2282; www.tangeroutlet.com. Open from 10 a.m. to 9 p.m. Monday through Saturday and 11 a.m. to 6 p.m. Sunday.

This outdoor factory outlet mall has more than 60 stores. The triangular design of the main sign is repeated along the rooftops of the strip. OshKosh B'Gosh and Carter's Childrenswear have cute children's clothes, and older kids can pick out brand-name sneakers at bargain prices at the Reebok store. The Kay-Bee Toy Outlet may be tempting. Samsonite Company Store can provide luggage for your next family vacation. You'll find burgers, tacos, and pizza among the food court offerings.

Douglas County Museum (age 8 and up) 

700 South Main Street, Tuscola; (217) 253-2535. Hours are 9 a.m. to 4 p.m. Monday through Wednesday only; other hours by appointment. Admission is free, but donations are appreciated.

This small museum emphasizes local history through its changing exhibits. For example, one recent display featured old photographs and antique cameras, another was a collection of toys spanning the 20th century. The exhibit Every Day Should Be Veterans Day featured World War II memorabilia. Because many of the glass display cases contain books and papers, young visitors will find it more interesting if they are able to read.

Prairieland Pride Playground (ages 1 to 12) 

In Ervin Park, off Main Street, Tuscola; (800) 441-9111. Open during park hours, 7 a.m. to 9 p.m. daily. Admission is free.

The community built this magnificent outdoor playground in 1996. Kids of all ages, but especially the younger ones, will love to run and jump and climb all over this wooden apparatus that has towers, bridges, and slides.

Where to Eat

Tuscany Steak and Pasta House, US 36 at Main Street; (217) 253-1030. Open from 11 a.m. to 10 p.m. daily. Serving lunch, dinner, and Sunday buffet. The name should tip you off about what kind of food to expect at this local favorite. A children's menu for those age 10 or younger includes spaghetti, ravioli, tortellini, pizza, burgers, and chicken strips, at about $4, not including drink. $$

Red Barn Buffet, I-57 at US 36, behind Tanger Outlet Center; (217) 253-9022. Open from 11 a.m. to 8 p.m. daily. Sample Amish-style cuisine in this spacious restaurant. $$

Where to Stay

Baymont Inn, 1006 Southline Drive (I-57 at US 36); (217) 253-3500 or (877) 229-6668. Near Tanger Outlet Center. This 2-story, tan brick motel has 59 rooms with in-room coffeemaker and cable TV. Amenities include heated indoor pool and fitness center. Pets allowed. Continental breakfast is included in the room rate. $$$

Holiday Inn Express, 1201 Tuscola Boulevard; (217) 253-6363 or (800) 465-4329; www.hiexpress.com/tuscolail. Near Tanger Outlet Center. There are 82 rooms at this 3-story motel. Amenities include indoor heated pool and whirlpool. The room rate includes continental breakfast bar. Pets allowed. $$$

Super 8, 1007 East Southline Drive (I-57 at US 36); (217) 253-5488 or (800) 800-8000. Near Tanger Outlet Center. This 2-story budget property has 63 rooms with cable TV. No pool. Pets allowed. $$

For More Information

Tuscola Visitors Center, 502 Southline Road (US 36), Tuscola 61953; (800) 441-9111; www.tuscola.org.

Arcola

Population: 2,652. Near the intersection of US 45 and Illinois Highway 133 is Arcola. This town lies at the eastern edge of an area known as Illinois Amish Country, which stretches to the west for 10 to 15 miles, extending north as far as US 36 and south roughly to the border between Douglas and Coles counties. This area contains numerous homes and businesses belonging to members of the Old Order Amish, a Protestant religious group (part of the Pennsylvania Dutch) that believes in living a simple life separate from the rest of the world. The Amish are easy to recognize by appearance: Men wear wide-brimmed hats and typically dress in black or blue, the married ones sporting a beard but no mustache, while women wear plain, solid-color long dresses and white bonnets called prayer caps. Amish clothes are fastened with straight pins—no buttons, zippers, or snaps. Amish rules forbid the use of electricity and telephones, and they do their plowing with animals rather than machines. They usually travel in horse-drawn black buggies.

In reality, it's hard to live completely separated from the rest of the world, and Amish businesses do serve non-Amish patrons as well as members of their own community. But don't plan to visit if you just want to gawk and take pictures—save that for the zoo. No person appreciates being stared at as an oddity, and it is against Amish religious beliefs to be photographed. Just exercise the golden rule and treat them with the same respect and courtesy with which you would want others to treat you. With that attitude, you probably will find the Amish quite hospitable. (You also

The Big Cheese in Arthur

If you're in Amish Country in early September, you can see and taste a sample from a 1,000-pound cheese wheel at the annual **Amish Country Cheese Festival** in Arthur. Flea markets, a dog show, a petting zoo, and buggy rides are also part of the two-day celebration. The biggest concentration of Amish, about 3,500 people, is in and around the town of Arthur, west of Arcola along Highway 133. Here you'll find shops specializing in handmade wood furniture, custom-built cabinets, upholstery, textiles, health foods, and baked goods. (You can also get horseshoes, leather harnesses, or wagon repair services if you happen to have a horse and buggy.) Special events in addition to the cheese festival are scheduled throughout the year. Contact Amish Country Information Center, 106 East Progress Street, Arthur 61911; (800) 722-6474; www.illinoisamishcountry.com.

will find some telephones and electrical service in the area; not everyone around here is Amish.) Be aware that Amish businesses are usually closed on Sunday.

The Historic Depot, a redbrick building in downtown Arcola, has helpful tourist information provided by friendly people. Redbrick streets add a quaint touch to the 3-block-long downtown. Main Street is lined with interesting shops selling crafts, antiques, and memorabilia. The Amish are famous for their handmade brooms, and there is an annual **Broom Corn Festival** in mid-September, featuring crafts, entertainment, food, and a parade highlighted by the Lawn Rangers, a drill team with lawn mowers.

If you notice quite a bit of Raggedy Ann memorabilia around here, there's a good reason. You can see the gravestone of Johnny Gruelle, author of the charming children's books, near the depot. The Johnny Gruelle Raggedy Ann and Andy Museum is downtown. An annual festival honors the floppy celebrities the weekend before Memorial Day weekend.

Johnny Gruelle Raggedy Ann and Andy Museum (all ages) 

110 East Main Street, Arcola; (217) 268-4908; www.raggedyann-museum.org. Open from mid-March through December. Hours are 10 a.m. to 4:30 p.m. Tuesday through Saturday; closed Sunday and Monday. Admission is free, but there is a suggested donation of $1 per person age 12 or older. The building is wheelchair accessible.

Johnny Gruelle was born in Arcola in 1880. In 1915 he created and patented Raggedy Ann, a rag doll with black button eyes and red yarn hair. He published *Raggedy Ann Stories* in 1918 and continued to write books about Raggedy Ann and later Raggedy Andy until his death in 1938 in Miami Beach. This museum opened in 1999, although building and expansion continued into the 2000s. There are three permanent installations so far. Johnny's Studio is a re-creation of the author's Miami Beach workshop of the early 1930s. Marcella's Room is an imagined interpretation of a bedroom used by Gruelle's daughter, Marcella, from about 1908 to 1912, based on Gruelle's drawings in *Raggedy Ann Stories*. The third permanent exhibit area contains 10 display cases highlighting the chronological development of the Raggedy Ann dolls and story characters. The special exhibit *For the Heart's Sake* shows the history of five generations of Gruelle family artists. Another special exhibit is *Hands across the Water: The Raggedys in Japan*. If you and your kids grew up loving Raggedy Ann and Andy, you won't want to miss this treasure trove of memorabilia. You can buy dolls and other souvenirs in the gift shop and reprints of the original books in the bookstore.

Rockome Gardens (all ages) 

125 North County Road 425E, Arcola; (217) 268-4106 or (800) 549-7625; www.rockome.com. Season begins in late April and runs through mid-October. Days of operation are somewhat limited until the peak season, late May through early September, when the facility is open daily from 10 a.m. to 6 p.m. Be sure to call ahead if you plan to visit during the off-peak times. Most parts of the park are accessible for strollers and wheelchairs, but there are a few places reachable only by stairs. $–$$

Arcola's most famous attraction is Rockome Gardens. Formerly an Amish farm and homestead, in 1958 it became a sprawling complex of rock and flower gardens, craft and food shops, and entertainments. The original farmhouse was preserved and is presented as a museum showing how the Amish live. With their prohibition on electricity, the Amish use wood or gas cookstoves, gas-operated refrigerators, and propane gas to heat their homes. Rooms are plainly furnished.

If you're willing to spend a few extra dollars per person, you can take a tour of the grounds in a genuine horse-drawn Amish buggy. The friendly driver will point out the attractions and answer questions as you clop along. The ride offers a good overview so that you can decide which parts you want to walk back to later. The grounds are large enough that youngsters' feet may tire, so set your priorities at the beginning (looking at the rocks and flowers may not be the most thrilling thing for them, so save that for farther down the list). There is also a "train" ride on a wheeled wagon that goes out into the cornfields rather than around the grounds. Newer attractions include a wooden "tree house," reachable by stairs, and an interesting model train layout. Some of the older attractions have perennial appeal. The Haunted Cave, where things pop out at you accompanied by spooky voices and sound effects, is fun but a bit too scary for younger or more nervous children. JIn 2007, Rockome added fishing, kayaking, and horseback riding tours.

A unique attraction for kids in the 3-to-12 age range is the horse-powered sawmill. It costs $2, but it's worth it. The kid sits atop a horse whose harness is attached to an elaborate network of gears and belts to power a rotating sawblade about 10 feet away. As the kid rides the horse around in a circle, the gears turn and the sawblade whirs away to slice a half-inch-thick round off the end of a log. Then the kid goes to the blacksmith shop, where, for 10 cents per letter, the young smithy will use a glowing-hot iron to emblazon the kid's name into the wood. This personalized keepsake makes a great souvenir. There are demonstrations throughout the grounds of other skills as well; a favorite among families is the candy making, with samples of the finished product.

Antique farm implements are on display in one barn, room displays with period furnishings in another. Craft shops feature quilts, dolls, candles, and jewelry. If you want a snack, you'll have to forget about fat, carbs, and calories to indulge in Amish-made sausage, cheese, fudge, ice cream, or a rich, buttery-tasting iced cinnamon roll.

Where to Eat

Dutch Kitchen Family Restaurant, 127 East Main Street, downtown; (217) 268-3518. Open from 7:30 a.m. to 7 p.m. daily. Amid decor with country charm, you can eat a sandwich, a plate lunch, or a full dinner. Save room for the homemade pie. $

Rockome Family-Style Restaurant, at Rockome Gardens; (217) 268-4106 or (800) 549-7625. Open from 11 a.m. to 7 p.m. on days when Rockome Gardens is open. "Family-style" means that food at each table is served from communal bowls and platters. $$

Where to Stay

Arcola Inn, 236 South Jacques Street; (888) 729-9137. This one-story brick motel has comfortable, modern rooms with telephone and cable TV. The room rate includes continental breakfast. $$

Comfort Inn, 610 South Ridge Street; (217) 268-4000 or (800) 229-5750. The 41 rooms in this chain property have cable TV and recliners. Outdoor pool. Pets allowed. Continental breakfast is included in the room rate. $$

Arcola Camper Stop, 472 Davis Street; (217) 268-4616. A quarter mile west of I-57 off exit 203. Open year-round, but more limited service in winter. This RV park has water and electrical hookups, hot showers, restrooms, pay phone, and dump station. $

For More Information

Arcola Depot Welcome Center, 135 North Oak Street, Arcola 61910; (800) 336-5456; www.arcola-il.org.

Mattoon

Population: 18,291. I-57 skirts this town, and several other throughfares pass through it: US 45 and Illinois Highways 121 and 16. The main drag is Broadway Avenue, which parallels Highway 16 a block north. This Broadway doesn't quite live up to its New York namesake, however. The marquee of the old downtown movie theater no longer lights up because the cinema is closed. (The Showplace 8 between Mattoon and Charleston handles the movies nowadays.) Still, there are a few family-oriented spots around town, plus baseball and softball tournaments each summer and Bagelfest in July.

Lake Shelbyville Area

Southwest of Amish Country along Highway 16 is the 11,000-acre Lake Shelbyville. The United States Army Corps of Engineers began construction of this artificial lake on the Kaskaskia River in 1963, and water was impounded to begin filling it in 1970. Several towns that border the lake have related attractions of interest to families, including Findlay, Sullivan, Windsor, and the lake's namesake, Shelbyville.

The **Lake Shelbyville Visitor Center,** on Dam Road just east of Shelbyville, is open year-round. Hours between Memorial Day and Labor Day are 9 a.m. to 4:30 p.m. daily. Days of operation are more restricted the rest of the year. Call (217) 774-3951 for details.

The Army Corps of Engineers offers free tours of the **Lake Shelbyville Dam,** which is visible off Highway 16, just east of Shelbyville. Call the visitor center for the current schedule, and take one of the tours if you can—it goes right under the sluice gates. If you can't be there at tour time, the Spillway East Recreation Area, just off the highway below the dam, has picnic tables and grills, a playground for the kids, and restrooms. You'll likely see someone fishing in the waters beyond the spillway.

Two state parks, **Eagle Creek** and **Wolf Creek,** offer a variety of outdoor activities year-round. For both parks you can contact Superintendent, Eagle Creek State Park, Route 1, P.O. Box 198-B, Findlay 62534; (217) 756-8260.

For more information about the area, contact the Shelby County Office of Tourism, 315 East Main Street, Shelbyville 62565; (217) 774-2244; www.lakeshelbyville.com.

Other Things to See and Do

JANUARY

Teeny Tiny Tea Party, Palestine; (618) 586-9418 or (618) 586-2427

Annual Midwest Elvis Presley Impersonators Competition, Springfield; (217) 793-3733

FEBRUARY

Mardi Gras, downtown Decatur; (217) 423-7000

Maple Syrup Time, Springfield; (217) 529-1111; www.lmgnc.org

MARCH

Illinois Food Products Expo, Springfield; (217) 782-6675; www.agr.state.il.us

Spring Bloom Arts Festival, Bloomington; (800) 433-8226

Home, Lawn & Garden Expo, Decatur; (217) 422-7300

APRIL

Community Wide Yard Sale, Carlinville; (217) 854-2141

Lincoln's Ghost Walk, Springfield; (309) 221-5579; www.springfieldwalks.com

MAY

Woofstock, Decatur; (217) 875-1910

Heyworth Hey Days; (800) 433-8226

Springfield Highland Games and Celtic Festival; (217) 787-1093

Springfest, Oblong; (618) 592-4355

JUNE

Le Roy Summerfest; (800) 433-8226

Saybrook Freedom Festival; (800) 433-8226

Turtle Races, Danville; (217) 446-5327

Pana Mid-State Classic Car Show; (217) 562-5721

JULY

Chatham Jaycees Sweet Corn Festival and Illinois Championship Cow Chip Throw, Chatham; (217) 483-2109

Most communities have a Fourth of July celebration, and many county fairs are in July and August.

AUGUST

Apple Dumpling Festival, Atwood; (217)-2734

World FreeFall Convention, Rantoul; (217) 222-5867

Fairbury Fair; (815) 692-3899; www.fairburyil.org

Cowden Pioneer Days; (217) 783-2121

SEPTEMBER

National Sweetcorn Festival, Hoopeston; (800) 383-4386

Apple and Pork Festival, Clinton; (217) 935-3364

Taste of Country Fair and Festival, Lexington; (800) 433-8226

Casey Popcorn Festival; (217) 932-5951

Honey Bee Festival, Paris; (217) 465-4179

OCTOBER

Scarecrow Daze, Shelbyville; (217) 774-4723

Indian Summer Festival, Springfield; (217) 529-1111

Heath Harvest Festival, Robinson; (800) 445-7006

NOVEMBER

Annual Greater Downstate Indoor Bluegrass Music Festival, Springfield; (217) 243-3159; www.bluegrassmidwest.com

Forest of Lights, Downs; (800) 433-8226

DECEMBER

Festival of Trees, Jacksonville; (800) 593-5678

Holiday Open House, Bement; (217) 678-8184

Pontiac Holiday Basketball Tournament; (815) 844-6692 or (815) 844-6113

First Night Celebration, Danville; (217) 328-4500

Peterson Park (all ages)

Broadway Avenue east of North Sixth Street, Mattoon. Open from 5 a.m. to 11 p.m. daily. Free admission.

You can have a picnic in the park. There are picnic tables, or you could spread out a blanket on the grass. A vintage army tank makes an interesting conversation piece. Children will enjoy the newer playground equipment made of sturdy plastic in bright colors. You can play a round of miniature golf, too (see next entry).

Pla-Mor Golf (age 3 and up) 

500 Broadway Avenue, in Peterson Park, Mattoon; (217) 235-9711. Open from noon to 9:30 p.m. daily during summer. $

This 18-hole miniature golf course features red, yellow, and blue borders around each of the greens, and a working stoplight adds another flash of color. Some of the holes are a little tricky, but fun. You'll try to drive the ball between the blades of a windmill, under some dangling bowling pins, and around a loop-the-loop.

Lytle Park Pool (all ages) 

3320 Western Avenue, in Lytle Park, Mattoon; (217) 258-9801. Open from 11:30 a.m. to 8 p.m. daily in the summer. $

This local swimming hole claims to be the largest outdoor public pool in the state, holding a million gallons of water. Water levels range from zero-depth to 10 feet. The pool has water slides and diving boards. The surrounding park has playground equipment and basketball and tennis courts.

Silver Star Skate Center (age 4 and up) 

US 45 North, Mattoon; (217) 234-6667; www.silverstarskatecenter.com. Call or check Web site for current open skating hours and prices. $

Claiming to be "Central Illinois' Premier Roller Rink," this facility opened in the 1930s and was renovated in the late 1990s. The smooth, spacious rink can accommodate a lot of skaters. Bring your own skates or rent them here. An arcade features video games and air hockey. Concessions are available, and there is a party room for birthday and other celebrations.

Where to Eat

McHugh's Double Drive Thru, South Eighth Street and Charleston Road (Highway 16); (217) 234-7565. Open year-round. Hours are 10 a.m. to 10 p.m. Sunday through Thursday and 10 a.m. to 11 p.m. Friday and Saturday. This burger joint decorated in a red-and-white checkerboard design has been in business since the early 1990s. Yes, it does have 2 drive-through lanes, but there also are 6 round tables with umbrellas outside if you want to eat on the premises during summer. Burgers are cooked to order and look like McDonald's but taste better. The fries look and taste much like Mickey D's. Be sure to ask about the day's special flavor of milk shake; the blackberry is delicious! Or you can stick with vanilla, chocolate, or strawberry. $

Lee's Famous Recipe Chicken, South Eighth Street and Charleston Road (Highway 16); (217) 235-3731. Hours are 10 a.m. to 9 p.m. daily. While McHugh's across the street challenges McDonald's, Lee's gives KFC a run for the money. Choose your chicken fried or baked, and a dinner comes with two side items. The already reasonable prices are even lower on Tuesday. $

Where to Stay

All three of these economical chain properties opened in the mid-1990s and are located just off I-57 at exit 190B.

Baymont Inn, 206 McFall Road; (217) 234-2355 or (800) 228-2800. Formerly a Fairfield Inn, this 3-story, 63-room inn has an indoor pool and whirlpool. Continental breakfast is included in the room rate. $$

Hampton Inn, 1416 Broadway Avenue East; (217) 234-4267 or (800) 426-7866. Winner of the Symbol of Excellence award for top-quality Hampton hotels as rated by guests throughout the chain, this 3-story, 61-room property features an indoor pool. Room rates include continental breakfast bar. $$$

Super 8, 205 McFall Road; (217) 235-8888 or (800) 800-8000. This basic budget motel has 61 rooms with cable TV and recliners. Pets are allowed with advance notice. No pool. Continental breakfast is included in the room rate. $$

For More Information

Mattoon Welcome Center, 500 Broadway, Mattoon 61938; (800) 500-6286; www.mattoonillinois.org.

Lerna

Lincoln Log Cabin State Historic Site (age 6 and up) 

400 South Lincoln Highway, Lerna (accessible off Illinois Highway 130 between Charleston and Greenup, or I-57 between Mattoon and Effingham); (217) 345-1845; www.lincolnlogcabin.org. Open from 8:30 a.m. to dusk Wednesday through Sunday; closed Monday and Tuesday; also closed New Year's, Thanksgiving, and Christmas days. Free.

The Lincoln Log Cabin State Historic Site preserves the last home of Thomas and Sarah Bush Lincoln, Abraham Lincoln's father and stepmother. Thomas Lincoln purchased a farm in 1840 and worked the land, using traditional methods to grow corn, oats, and wheat. The family also raised livestock, including hogs, sheep, milk cows, chickens, and geese. Their own food garden included potatoes and other vegetables. Today an accurate replica of the Lincolns' cabin, reconstructed from old photographs and affidavits, stands on the original site. (The original cabin had been moved to Chicago in 1892 for the World's Columbian Exposition and was subsequently lost—and don't ask how you can lose a whole cabin.) A garden, orchard, and crop field have been planted with varieties from the 1800s. During summer the site becomes even more of a living-history farm, with costumed interpreters playing the roles of the Lincoln family and their neighbors. They work in the fields, do housework, and (for the kids) play games of the period, and they speak in the Southern Upland dialect used on the farm (yes, it's still English). Food is prepared using recipes from 1840s cookbooks. Costumed interpreters are on-site from May through October.

Adjacent to the Lincoln farm on the historic site is the **Sargent Farm,** a reconstruction containing the original frame house purchased in 1840 by the Lincolns' more prosperous neighbor, Stephen Sargent. Whereas the Lincolns practiced traditional subsistence farming, Sargent was considered a "progressive" farmer who took advantage of the latest agricultural innovations. His farm was originally located 10 miles east of the Lincoln farm but was moved to the Lincoln Log Cabin State Historic Site in 1985 to allow visitors to observe in closer proximity the contrast between the two farming styles.

The **Reuben Moore Home,** 1 mile north of the Lincoln log cabin, was the home of Abe Lincoln's stepsister, Matilda Hall, who married Reuben Moore and moved with him into the house in 1856. Lincoln was a dinner guest at this frame house. Special events are held throughout the year.

Where to Eat and Stay

See entries for Mattoon.

Southern Illinois

You'll know you're heading down into Southern Illinois when you begin to notice the flat stretches of central prairie giving way to a gentle undulation of wooded hills and valleys. Forests cover about 10 percent of the state, and most of them are here (the Shawnee National Forest spans the width of far Southern Illinois, stretching for about 70 miles). Get ready to slow down and enjoy the natural beauty that surrounds you. For information about this part of the state, you can contact the **Southernmost Illinois Tourism Bureau,** P.O. Box 378, Anna 62906; (618) 833-9928 or (800) 248-4373; www.southernmostillinois.com.

Effingham

Population: 12,384. OK, so Effingham isn't Rome, but it sure seems like all roads lead here. Interstates 57 and 70, U.S. Highways 40 and 45, and Illinois Highways 32 and 33 all converge in this town. It is estimated that 25,000 vehicles a day pass through Effingham. Amtrak and Greyhound stop here, too. However you arrive, you'll find some attractions of interest for families in this area.

The biggest attraction in the area is **Lake Sara,** located 5 miles northwest of Effingham along Highway 32/33; take exit 160 off I-57/70. Along the 27 miles of picturesque shoreline, you'll find a swimming area with water slide, sandy beach, and modern bathhouse, an 18-hole golf course (217-868-2860), campgrounds (217-868-2964), and a marina, J & J Marina (217-868-2791). Buy an Illinois state fishing license at the marina and get a boat permit from the Effingham Water Authority and you're ready to fish for black bass, bluegill, crappie, walleye, and channel catfish.

Effingham's lively downtown is well maintained and attractive, with neat awnings in blue, red, and green overhanging brick storefronts. The two-story redbrick Effingham County Courthouse stands in the center, at Jefferson Avenue and Third Street. Effingham, reportedly named after a British lord who refused to fight against the colonists during the American Revolution, has been the county seat since 1859.

SOUTHERN ILLINOIS

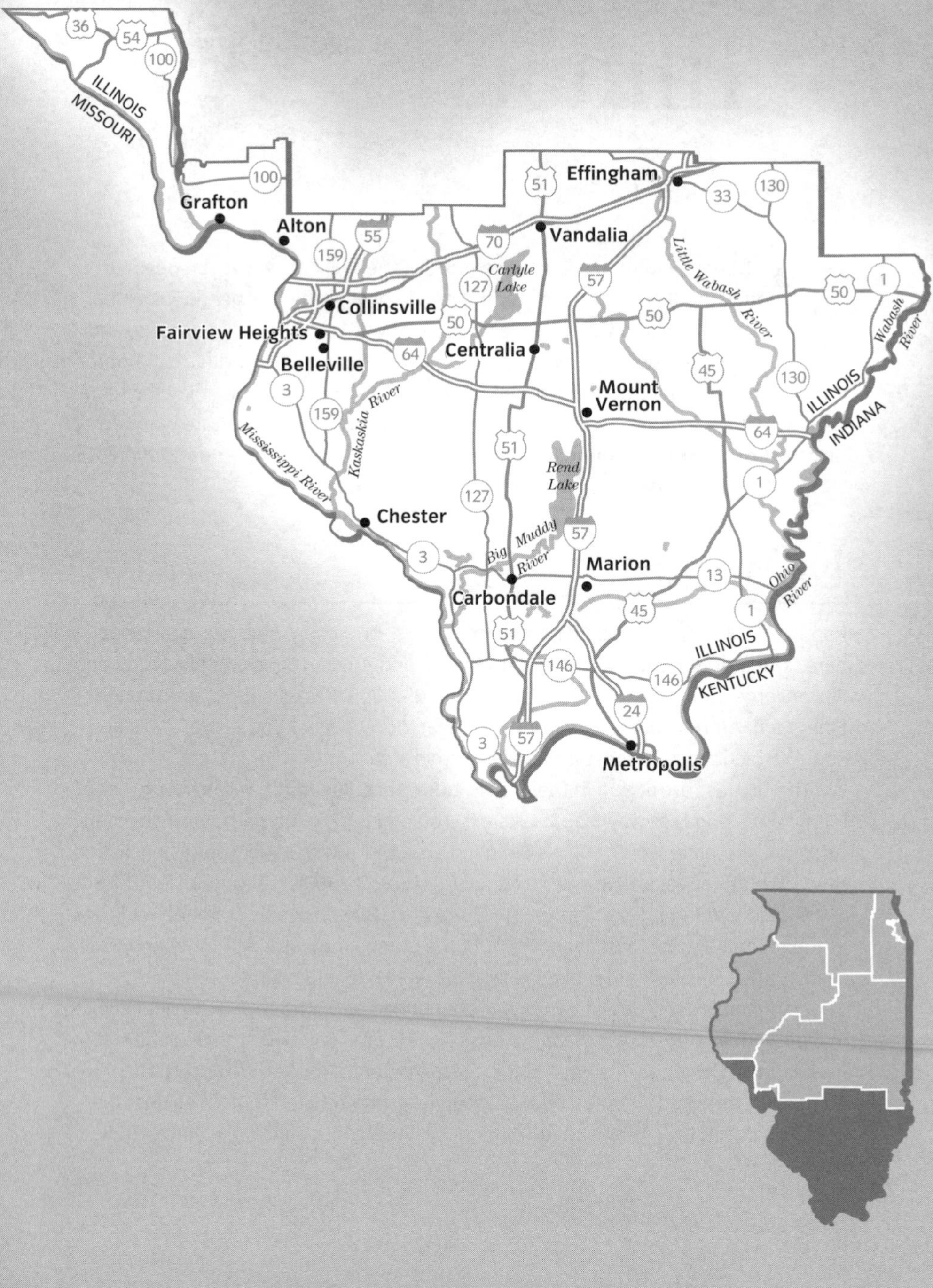

Grafton
Alton
Collinsville
Fairview Heights
Belleville
Effingham
Vandalia
Centralia
Mount Vernon
Chester
Marion
Carbondale
Metropolis
ILLINOIS
MISSOURI
INDIANA
KENTUCKY
Carlyle Lake
Rend Lake
Mississippi River
Kaskaskia River
Big Muddy River
Little Wabash River
Wabash River
Ohio River

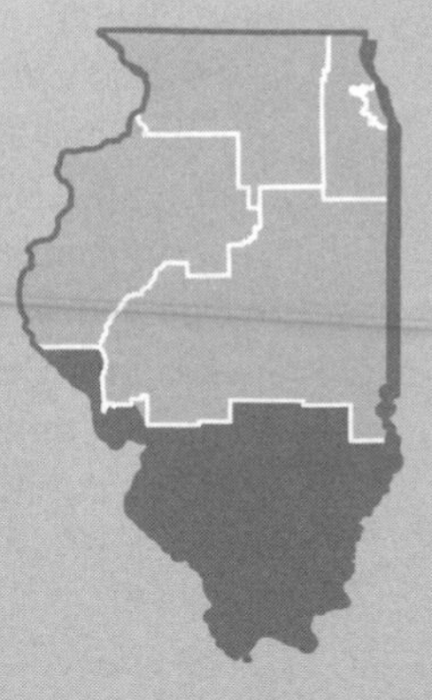

You'll feel as though you're farther west than Illinois if you visit Effingham during a three-day period in June—that's when students from around the state converge here for the Illinois High School Rodeo Association State Rodeo Finals. You'll see these gutsy teenagers compete in such events as roping, steer wrestling, and bull and bronco riding.

MY Garage Corvette Museum (age 2 and up) 

At Mid America Designs, One Mid America Place, North US 45, exit 162, Effingham; (217) 590-4200 or (800) 500-1500. Open from April through October, Monday through Friday from 8 a.m. to 5 p.m. and Saturday from 9 a.m. to 3 p.m.; closed Sunday. Admission is free.

Anyone who likes cars will enjoy a visit to MY Garage, a museum of vintage Corvettes. Situated on the grounds of the Mid America Designs company, in a long, green building to your right after you've entered off US 45, the facility has more than 30 of these classic cars exhibited. The ambience is 1950s–1960s nostalgia, from the rock and roll background music to the mock storefronts that attempt to re-create the era. You'll find a variety of related Corvette memorabilia on display as well.

K Bowl (age 4 and up) 

1208 North Keller Drive (North Highway 32), Effingham; (217) 342-4145. Regular hours are noon to 10 p.m. Sunday through Thursday and noon to midnight Friday and Saturday. $

This 32-lane bowling alley is under the same roof as TGIFriday's (see Where to Eat) and an off-track betting parlor (not for families). It has automatic computerized scoring, and gutter bumpers are available for families with younger children. A game room has video games and pool tables. Carryout pizza is available at K Bowl, or you can hold out for a full meal at Friday's next door.

Choo-Choos!

A fun place for train buffs is the Ben Winter Museum in Altamont, about 12 miles southwest of Effingham off US 40. Here you'll find about two dozen steam- and gasoline-powered engines, all reportedly in working order. Two of them are set up on a track to take a short trip into the surrounding countryside. The museum also houses a couple of Linotype machines from the 1890s (my great-grandfather used one like it in his family printing business) and an 1881 threshing machine. The museum is open from mid-April through mid-October; call ahead for current hours. Admission is free, but donations are appreciated. Contact Ben Winter Museum, 1815 East 900th Avenue, Altamont; (618) 483-6665.

Evergreen Hollow Park (all ages) 

Off Evergreen Avenue, Effingham; (217) 342-4415. Off I-57/70, take exit 160. Turn south onto Keller Drive and then almost immediately east onto Evergreen Avenue. Open from 5:30 a.m. to 11 p.m. daily. Free admission.

Here's a good place for a picnic on a nice day. There's a playground for the kids, too. The park covers 27 acres and also includes four tennis courts that are lit at night, and three baseball and softball diamonds.

Kluthe Memorial Swimming Pool (all ages) 

On Evergreen Avenue, in Evergreen Hollow Park, Effingham; (217) 342-4415. Off I-57/70, take exit 160. Turn south onto Keller Drive and then almost immediately east onto Evergreen Avenue. Open from Memorial Day through Labor Day. Hours are 12:30 to 8:30 p.m. daily. $

There are actually two pools here, one for swimming laps and one for just hanging out. The latter is great for wee ones, with a zero-depth end and a 4-foot maximum on the other end, plus a play area with frog slide. Older kids and teens will enjoy the big water slide. Pop and snacks are available from vending machines.

Evergreen Mini Golf (age 3 and up) 

On Evergreen Avenue, in Evergreen Hollow Park, Effingham; (217) 342-2544. Off I-57/70, take exit 160. Turn south onto Keller Drive and then almost immediately east onto Evergreen Avenue. Open from April through September. Hours are 11 a.m. to 10 p.m. Monday through Thursday, 11 a.m. to 11 p.m. Friday and Saturday, and noon to 9 p.m. Sunday. $

This 18-hole miniature golf course benefits from its setting in Evergreen Hollow Park. The course includes a waterfall (which doesn't always work), a wishing well, and assorted animals. Soft drinks and snacks are offered at the concession counter.

Heart Theatre (age 3 and up) 

133 East Jefferson Avenue, Effingham; (217) 342-6161. Call for current show titles and times. $

This downtown theater stands across the street from the county courthouse. Its big, brightly lit marquee spells out tonight's bargain second-run feature film. Buy your ticket at the booth outside, open the beveled glass doors, and walk into this art deco palace. They just don't make 'em like that anymore.

Village Square Mall (all ages) 

US 45 South, Effingham; (217) 347-0623; www.shopsatvillagesquare.com. Take exit 160 off I-57/70. Open from 10 a.m. to 9 p.m. Monday through Saturday and noon to 5 p.m. Sunday.

Effingham's only indoor mall is very basic: one rectangular strip with stores on both sides. But the fact that it has few frills—no boutique carts or potted plants—makes its open aisles great for strollers and wheelchairs. Bring along a few quarters, and your tot can ride on a tiny motorcycle, Noah's Ark, or merry-go-round. JCPenney anchors the mall at one end. Merchandise for sale in 30 stores includes clothing, shoes, music, and gifts. There's no food court, so don't plan on a meal; an ice-cream cone will tide you over. You can catch a movie at the adjacent RMC Cinema multiplex; call (217) 347-5997 or check www.rmccinemas.com/effshow.htm for showtimes.

Silver Dollar Lanes (age 4 and up) 

2300 South Banker, off US 45 South, Effingham; (217) 342-3939. Near Village Square Mall. Call for current open bowling hours and prices. $

This nondescript building has 24 lanes. For families with young children, there are lightweight balls, small shoes, and bumpers to fill the gutters. A game room has five pool tables.

Where to Eat

Flying J Cafe, in the Flying J Auto Truck Plaza on north Highway 32/33; (217) 347-7161. Open 24 hours a day. As you might expect with all the roads crisscrossing Effingham, the town has a number of truck stops. They can be surprisingly good places to eat, serving hearty meals and often pies and other desserts with a homemade taste. This is one of the most well known. $

Pizza Man, 604 West Jefferson Avenue; (217) 347-7766. West of downtown. Hours are 11 a.m. to 10 p.m. Monday through Saturday and 4 to 10 p.m. Sunday. This place is a local favorite. If you have a really big family, there's a 28-inch pizza on the menu. $

TGIFriday's, 1208 North Keller Drive (Highway 32/33); (217) 342-9499. In the same building as K Bowl lanes. Open from 11 a.m. to 9:30 p.m. daily. See description in Restaurant Appendix. $$

Where to Stay

Anthony Acres Resort, Beach Road; (217) 868-2950; www.anthonyacres.com. Off Highway 32, turn south at the BP Gas station onto Lake Sara Road and continue about half a mile. Turn west onto Moccasin Road and continue about 1.5 miles, and then turn south onto Beach Road, a gravel road, and follow the signs to the resort office. If you'd like to stay in something more comfortable than a tent, you can rent a furnished "cabin" in a long row of peach-colored cinder-block units at this casual resort that's right next to the lake—great for fishing. Each cabin has a fully equipped kitchen, so you can cook up all those fish you catch, along with other food you bring along (hot dogs are a handy backup when the fish aren't biting). The resort has a little sand beach and small roped-off swimming area, a playground, a game room, a hiking area, and boat docks. The grounds are tidy and the accommodations very basic but nice. $$$

Holiday Inn Express, 1103 Avenue of Mid-America; (217) 540-1111 or (888) 232-2525. This 3-story hotel has 122 rooms, each with a coffeemaker and cable TV. Amenities include indoor pool and health club. Pets allowed. Room rate includes continental breakfast delivered to your room. $$

Ramada Limited, 1205 North Keller Drive (Highway 32/33); (217) 347-7131 or (800) 272-6232. Across from Avenue of Mid America. This property has 74 rooms with cable TV. It features an indoor pool, sauna, whirlpool, and exercise room. Pets allowed. Breakfast is included in the room rate. $

For More Information

Effingham Convention and Visitors Bureau, 201 East Jefferson Avenue, Effingham 62401; (217) 342-5310 or (800) 772-0750; www.visiteffinghamil.com.

Greater Effingham Chamber of Commerce and Industry, 903 North Keller Drive, Effingham 62401; (217) 342-4147; www.effinghamchamber.org or www.effinghamil.com.

Vandalia

Population: 6,975. From Effingham, keep going west about 30 miles along US 40 or I-70 to where they intersect with U.S. Highway 51 and you'll reach Vandalia. This lovely town was the Illinois state capital from 1819 to 1839, before the capital moved to Springfield. It was in Vandalia that Abraham Lincoln was enrolled as a practicing attorney and assumed the first statewide office of a political career that eventually took him to the White House. Even before that, Vandalia was the western terminus of the nearly 600-mile-long Cumberland Road, the main route taken by pioneers from the East to the West in the 1800s. The marble *Madonna of the Trail* statue, a memorial to the pioneer mothers of covered wagon days, stands on the northwest corner of the Vandalia Statehouse square to mark the spot where the Cumberland Road ended.

Vandalia Statehouse (age 5 and up) 

315 West Gallatin Street, at the corner of Kennedy (US 51), Vandalia; (618) 283-1161. About 1 mile south of I-70 on US 51. Open daily from 8:30 a.m. to 5 p.m. from March through October and 8 a.m. to 4 p.m. from November through February. Closed many holidays. Admission is free, but there is a clear plastic box for donations, with a suggested amount of $2 per adult and $1 per child. Accessible for wheelchairs in all areas except the restrooms. No smoking inside the building.

The white, Federal-style Vandalia Statehouse is the oldest existing capitol building in Illinois, dating back to 1836. The two-story building has legislative chambers on the upper floor and state offices on the lower floor. The cross-shaped interior design allows for great cross breezes with the doors open in milder weather. Friendly guides in period costume will gladly give you a personal tour, or you can just wander at leisure. Some original furnishings remain, along with other period pieces. (Explain a spittoon and watch your kid's face for the "ewwww!" reaction.) The guides may let your children sign their names with a quill pen on a piece of paper for a memorable souvenir. While all ages are admitted, a historical site such as this one will be of limited interest to kids who haven't yet started school and begun to hear about Abe Lincoln, thus the recommended minimum age of 5.

This statehouse was actually Vandalia's third capitol. The first, a two-story frame structure, was destroyed by fire in 1823. The second, hurriedly erected in 1824 so that the capital would not be moved to another town, was poorly constructed and by 1834 suffered from hazardously sagging floors and bulging walls. It was there that newly elected state legislator Abraham Lincoln first took his seat in 1834. The building was abandoned after the legislature adjourned in 1835. With workers salvaging what they could from the second building, the third capitol was constructed quickly (over a period of four months) but carefully and was opened in time for the legislative session that convened in December 1836, Lincoln's second term as a state representative. In 1837 Lincoln made his first protest against slavery here, a relatively mild statement asserting that "the institution of slavery is founded on both injustice and bad policy." The slavery issue was further debated by legislators, however, most notably Lincoln and Stephen Douglas. Amid charges of corruption (some things never change), the legislature in 1837 voted to move the capital to Springfield in 1840. And so it remains to this day. The Vandalia Statehouse served as the Fayette County Courthouse until 1933. Restoration from the 1930s through the 1970s brought the capitol back to its appearance during Lincoln's time.

Fayette County Museum (age 8 and up) 

Main Street at Kennedy Boulevard, Vandalia; (618) 283-4866 or (618) 283-1534. Behind the Vandalia Statehouse, half a block north. Open from 9:30 a.m. to 4 p.m. Monday through Friday. Admission is free, although donations in any amount are welcome.

This brick building with bell tower was the First Presbyterian Church a hundred years ago, but now the pews are gone, and its roomy interior is a museum chock-full of Lincoln-era and other historical memorabilia. Two items actually used by Lincoln are here: his letter cabinet and an ax with his initials carved into the head. A mural painted across one wall shows what Vandalia looked like during Abe's time as a state legislator. There are shackles that were once used to restrain American slaves, a rusted testament to the degradation forced upon one group of human beings by another. Then there are farm implements and kitchen gadgets from everyday life in the mid-1800s, many of which are curiosities to us today. If you'd like an explanation of what some of these things are, a volunteer guide will be glad to provide explanations and show you around. If you're visiting in summer, you'll be glad to know that air-conditioning was installed in the museum in 1998. This museum will fascinate older kids, but it's too small to navigate a stroller through, and there are too many delicate items on open display that would pose a temptation for younger children to grab without any appreciation of their historical significance, thus the recommended minimum age of 8.

Vandalia Bowl (age 4 and up) 

2605 VanTran Avenue, Vandalia; (618) 283-9294. Open bowling hours vary; call ahead to check. $

This cozy bowling alley refurbished its 12 lanes in the summer of 1998, so your ball is likely to have a smooth roll toward the pins. For families it's helpful to have the gutters blocked with the soft bumpers (everyone's score improves that way!). Computerized scorekeeping makes it easy to keep track of the strikes and spares.

Vandalia Lake (all ages)   

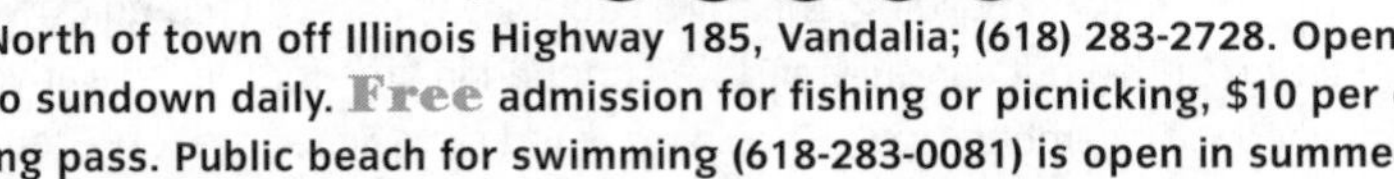

North of town off Illinois Highway 185, Vandalia; (618) 283-2728. Open from sunup to sundown daily. Free admission for fishing or picnicking, $10 per day for a boating pass. Public beach for swimming (618-283-0081) is open in summer from noon to 6 p.m. Monday through Thursday, noon to 7 p.m. Friday, 10 a.m. to 7 p.m. Saturday, and 11 a.m. to 6 p.m. Sunday. $

This 660-acre lake north of town was constructed in 1967. Visitors can walk in the woods that border the lake's 12 miles of shoreline or go fishing for largemouth bass, bluegill, and channel catfish. There is a marina for boaters. You can swim at the public beach or have a home-packed lunch at one of the picnic tables nearby. There's a campground if you'd like to stay the night.

Where to Eat

McDonald's, 820 Veterans Avenue; (618) 283-2711. Accessible off I-70. Open from 5:30 a.m. to 11 p.m. Sunday through Thursday and 5:30 a.m. to midnight Friday and Saturday. Here you'll find the burger chain's usual fast-food fare, but this particular eatery is worth mentioning because it has an indoor playground for the kids, which is open from 8 a.m. to 8 p.m. daily. $

Pizza Hut, 1620 North Eighth Street; (618) 283-0530. Hours are 11 a.m. to 10 p.m. Sunday through Thursday and 11 a.m. to 11 p.m. Friday and Saturday. See description in Restaurant Appendix. $

Ponderosa Steakhouse, I-70 and U.S. Highway 41; (618) 283-4559. Take exit 61 off I-70. Open from 11 a.m. to 9 p.m. Monday through Thursday, 11 a.m. to 10 p.m. Friday, 7 a.m. to 10 p.m. Saturday, and 7 a.m. to 9 p.m. Sunday. Lunch and dinner daily featuring steaks, of course, plus chicken, seafood, and sandwiches. Entrees include salad bar and buffet of hot side dishes. Breakfast buffet served Saturday and Sunday only. $

Where to Stay

Days Inn, 1920 Kennedy Boulevard, I-70 and US 51 North; (618) 283-4400; www.daysinnvandalia.com. Take exit 63 off I-70. This 1-story motel has 91 rooms with cable TV and an outdoor pool. Restaurant on premises. Pets allowed. Room rates include deluxe continental breakfast. Big parking lot for trucks and RVs. $$

Ramada Limited, 2707 Veterans Avenue; (618) 283-1400 or (800) 272-6232; www.ramadavandalia.com. This property has 60 rooms with cable TV and outdoor pool. Pets allowed with deposit. Room rates include continental breakfast. $$$

Travelodge, 1500 North Sixth Street, I-70 and US 51 North; (618) 283-2363 or (800) 515-6375. Take exit 63 off I-70. You'll recognize this 2-story 45-room property by the mock St. Louis arch and metal rocket slide out front. Rooms have cable TV and coffeemakers. There's also an outdoor pool. Pets welcome. Ask about Sleepy Bear's Den rooms. Room rates include continental breakfast. $$

For More Information

Vandalia Tourist Information Center and Chamber of Commerce, 1408 North Fifth Street, Vandalia 62471; (618) 283-2728; www.vandaliaillinois.com.

Now let's take a look at the southern area along the Mississippi River, starting with Grafton.

Grafton

Population: 609. Founded in the 1800s, Grafton is reportedly the oldest town in Jersey County. A record flood in 1993 caused a great deal of destruction, but Grafton has kept on going. The Shafer Wharf Historic District has a variety of shops and historic buildings. Probably the biggest claim to fame here, however, is Pere Marquette State Park.

Pere Marquette State Park (all ages) 

Illinois Highway 100, also called Great River Road, Grafton; (618) 786-3323. Open from 7 a.m. to 9 p.m. daily. Admission is free.

This scenic 7,900-acre park is the largest state park in Illinois. It was named after the French missionary priest Jacques Marquette (*père* is the French word for "father"), who accompanied the French-Canadian explorer Louis Jolliet on a canoe trip down the Mississippi in 1673. Today the park has 12 miles of hiking trails and 12 miles of equestrian trails that you can use to conduct your own expedition. To rent a mount, call Pere Marquette Riding Stables at (618) 786-2156. The park also has picnic areas and a boat dock. Interpretive programs are available, and there are concessions. Overnight accommodations are available in the park at the lodge or at a campground for tents and RVs.

Raging Rivers Water Park (all ages)

100 Palisades Parkway (just off Highway 100/Great River Road), Grafton; (618) 786-2345; www.ragingrivers.com. Open from late May through early September. Hours are 10:30 a.m. to 6 or 7 p.m. daily, the earlier closing time applying at the beginning and end of the season. The rates drop after 3 p.m. Parking costs $5 per vehicle. No glass containers or alcoholic beverages allowed. $$$

White-water rapids and two 500-foot-long body flumes earn this sprawling complex its name. The 45-foot Shark Slide ends through the mouth of a toothy, fiberglass *Jaws* look-alike. There's a 4-foot wave pool, too, which is a fun experience but not recommended for small children. Ditto the swishing Swirlpool. Tots can play instead in the Itty Bitty Surf City pool area with small water slides. The Treehouse Harbor is like a playground in the water—but watch out for the giant water bucket that will tip over and dump its contents on anyone standing below. Visitors of all ages can float on an inner tube along the 600-foot Runaway Rafts Ride.

Where to Eat

Fin Inn, Highway 100/Great River Road; (618) 786-2030. Open from 11 a.m. to 9 p.m. daily. This restaurant specializes in river fish. You can also get steaks, seafood, and chicken. Twenty-three of the tables are alongside viewing windows that allow diners to peek in at river fish and turtles swimming in four 2,000-gallon aquariums. $$

O'Jan's Fish Stand, 101 West Main Street; (618) 786-2229. Open year-round. Hours are 11 a.m. to 6:30 p.m. daily, although it may close as early as 6 p.m. in winter. This casual eatery overlooks the river. Sit outside on the open deck if the weather permits. Otherwise, there are about 10 tables inside, but the room is glassed in to retain the view. The food is mainly fish, of course. $

Where to Stay

Pere Marquette Lodge, Highway 100, also called Great River Road; (618) 786-2331. You can stay overnight in the state park in its spacious lodge, which has a 700-ton stone fireplace in the main hall. There are 50 rooms in the main lodge, plus 22 guest cabin rooms. Don't let the rustic look fool you, though—you'll also find an indoor pool with sauna and Jacuzzi and a restaurant that serves steaks, seafood, fried chicken, and a Sunday buffet, so you won't exactly be roughing it. $$$

For hotels and motels, see subsequent entry for Alton.

Alton

Population: 30,496. Highway 100 continues south along the Mississippi River from Grafton to Alton, a historic river town founded in 1818. If you're driving along during fall, keep your eyes open for the 200 to 400 bald eagles that spend the winter in the area each year. Around Alton the state highways also carry street names. As you may already know, Highway 100 is Great River Road. Illinois Highway 3 is Homer Adams Parkway or Beltline, Illinois Highway 140 is College Avenue, and Illinois Highway 143 is Berm Highway.

Along Highway 143, which parallels the Mississippi River, you'll find the **Melvin Price Lock & Dam No. 26.** Stop here and watch barges pass through; it's **free.** Farther south, where Highway 143 intersects Illinois Highway 67, the **Clark Bridge** looms. This cable-stay bridge spanning the Mississippi looks like a giant pair of silver inverted Vs. There's no charge to drive across.

Sam Vadalabene Bike Trail (all ages) 

Along Great River Road between Alton and Grafton; (800) 258-6645. Open from sunrise to sunset daily. Free.

If you start at the Alton end, about 1 mile northwest of town, there's a free parking area. This paved trail extends for 15 miles along the Great River Road and ends at Pere Marquette State Park.

Alton Museum of History and Art (age 6 and up) 

2809 College Avenue, Alton; (618) 462-2763. Hours are 10 a.m. to 4 p.m. Monday through Friday and 1 to 4 p.m. Saturday and Sunday. $

This museum has a fine display on the Underground Railroad, the network of hiding places used by runaway slaves on their passage north to freedom. Alton was a key station for slaves who escaped from St. Louis while en route to auction. Local citizens hid the slaves in their attics, cellars, or barns, or even in local caves, to keep them safe from the trackers and bounty hunters who pursued them. (The Visitors Bureau offers a guided tour of some of these sites; call 800-258-6645.) Another museum exhibit of interest to kids concerns Robert Wadlow, known as the "Gentle Giant," whom the *Guinness Book of World Records* cites as the tallest man in history. Wadlow was born in 1918 and reached an adult height of 8 feet, 11.1 inches—just shy of 9 feet!—before his death in 1940. Even today's tallest NBA players would have had to look up to him. A life-size bronze statue of Wadlow stands outdoors across the street from the museum.

Looking for **Lewis and Clark**

Two hundred years ago, a pair of U.S. Army officers named Meriwether Lewis and William Clark arrived in Illinois and set up a winter camp in preparation for a historic journey up the Missouri River. At **Camp River DuBois,** established at the confluence of the Mississippi and Missouri Rivers in December 1803, Lewis and Clark trained their crew and planned their trip. They set off in May 1804 and made it all the way to the Pacific Ocean before returning in September 1806, a round-trip of about 8,000 miles. The Lewis and Clark expedition would eventually enable the United States to claim the Oregon region and continue its westward expansion. You can see where it all began at the **Lewis and Clark Interpretive Center** in Hartford, 10 miles south of Alton off Highway 3 at New Poag Road. Exhibits at this museum, which opened in 2002, include a 55-foot-tall, 150-foot-long scale replica of Lewis and Clark's vessel, a wooden, flat-bottomed keelboat with full mast and sail. Near the interpretive center is a re-creation, opened in 2003, of Camp River DuBois. Costumed interpreters here will show you around the five log cabins and stockade fortress. Frontier activities help you further imagine what life was like in Lewis and Clark's time. The interpretive center and Camp River DuBois are open from 9 a.m. to 5 p.m. Tuesday through Sunday; closed Monday. Admission is **free.** Also at this 60-acre site, the Lewis and Clark Confluence Tower was completed in 2007 and rises 150 feet above the point where the Mississippi and Missouri rivers meet. Call (618) 251-5811 for further information about the site.

Alton Square Mall (all ages) 

200 Alton Square Mall Drive at Homer Adams Parkway, Alton; (618) 465-5500. Hours are 9 a.m. to 9 p.m. Monday through Saturday and noon to 6 p.m. Sunday. The mall is accessible for strollers and wheelchairs, but there are no ramps from one level to the other; you must use elevators in the department stores.

This two-story indoor shopping mall is anchored by Macy's, JCPenney, and Sears department stores and has numerous specialty shops. Kids are most likely to be interested in Kay-Bee Toys or the novelties in Spencer Gifts and Kirlin's Hallmark. Teens will find plenty of clothing and music stores. A food court features pizza, pasta, cookies, and ice cream.

Bowl Haven Lanes (age 4 and up) 

3003 Humbert Road, Alton; (618) 465-2695. Facility opens at 11 a.m. Monday through Saturday and at 4 p.m. Sunday; call for open bowling times. $

Children are welcome here. They have lighter (6-pound) bowling balls for kids and will place bumpers in the gutters. Automated scoring makes things easier for Mom and Dad, too.

Where to Eat

Joe K's Family Restaurant, 2530 State Street; (618) 466-9796. Open from 6 a.m. to 2 p.m. daily. Remodeled in 2007, this friendly, family-oriented restaurant serves breakfast and lunch only. $

Pizza Hut, 3096 Homer Adams Parkway; (618) 465-6600. Hours are 11 a.m. to 10 p.m. Monday through Thursday, 11 a.m. to midnight Friday and Saturday, and noon to 10 p.m. Sunday. See Restaurant Appendix for description. $

Red Lobster, 170 Homer Adams Parkway; (618) 465-6554. Hours are 11 a.m. to 10 p.m. Sunday through Thursday and 11 a.m. to 11 p.m. Friday and Saturday. See Restaurant Appendix for description. $$

Steak n Shake, 80 Homer Adams Parkway; (618) 466-7006. Open 24 hours a day. See Restaurant Appendix for description. $

Where to Stay

Comfort Inn, 11 Crossroads Court; (618) 465-9999 or (800) 424-6423. This 3-story chain property has 62 rooms and a heated indoor pool. Pets are allowed. Continental breakfast is included in the price of the room. $$$

Holiday Inn, 3800 Homer Adams Parkway; (618) 462-1220 or (800) 465-4329. This 4-story hotel has 137 rooms. Amenities include Holidome recreation center with indoor pool, whirlpool, sauna, and fitness center. Pets are allowed. Ask about the package deal including Raging Rivers Water Park. $$$

Budget Inn, 1900 Homer Adams Parkway; (618) 463-0800. This 115-room property, formerly a Days Inn, features indoor swimming pool and fitness center. Pets are allowed. $$$

For More Information

Alton Regional Convention and Visitors Bureau, 200 Piasa Street, Alton 62002; (618) 465-6676 or (800) 258-6645; www.visitalton.com.

Collinsville

Population: 24,707. Along Illinois Highway 159 south of Interstate 55/70, you'll come to Collinsville. Look for the **World's Largest Catsup Bottle,** a 170-foot-tall steel water tank and tower. It was built in 1949 and restored in 1995, and it's now on the National Register of Historic Places. (For merchandise or memorabilia, call 618-345-5598 or visit www.catsupbottle.com.) If you arrive in early June, you'll be just in time for the **International Horseradish Festival** (www.horseradismfestival.com). Maybe you'll want to enter the root toss or the horseradish-eating (on hot dogs) contest. You'll also find the more typical crafts and a petting zoo at this free event. Another popular celebration in Collinsville is the **Italian Fest** in mid-September; there's no admission charge for that one, either (www.italianfest.net). Probably the most famous attraction in the Collinsville area—and one you shouldn't miss—is Cahokia Mounds.

Cahokia Mounds (all ages) 

30 Ramey Street, Collinsville; (618) 346-5160; www.cahokiamounds.com. Take Interstate 255 south from I-55/70 (or north from Interstate 64) to the Collinsville Road exit. The site is open daily in summer. Head 2 miles west on Collinsville Road to the interpretive center, which is open from 9 a.m. to 5 p.m. Admission is by donation; the suggested rate is $2 for adults and $1 for kids. A free picnic area on the grounds is open from 8 a.m. to dusk. Call ahead or check the Web site for special events including craft demonstrations, storytelling, and dance and music performances.

This state historic site, which covers nearly 4,000 acres, contains the remains of the central section of what is reportedly the only prehistoric Indian city north of Mexico. The area was first inhabited around AD 700 and reached a population of nearly 20,000 at its peak in 1100 before declining over the next couple of centuries and finally being abandoned by the 1400s. Scholars don't know exactly why this once-thriving walled city with temples, plazas, rows of thatch-roofed houses, and sprawling agricultural fields died out; theories include disease, war, social unrest, and a climatic shift in the 1200s that could have reduced crop production and depleted resources needed to sustain the population. When French explorers arrived in the late 1600s, they found the Cahokia Indians, a subtribe of the Illini, living there and named the region after them. In 1982 Cahokia Mounds was designated a United Nations World Heritage Site for its importance in the study of North American prehistory, joining the illustrious company of such other World Heritage Sites as the Great Wall of China, the Taj Mahal, the Egyptian Pyramids, and the city of Rome.

The prehistoric earthen mounds were built in platform, conical, and ridgetop formations, the shape and size depending on the mound's intended use. The larger, flat-topped platform mounds served as bases for ceremonial buildings and homes for the wealthy elite. The other two kinds were used as markers or as burial plots for prominent people. Although the buildings are long gone, 68 of the original 120 mounds have been preserved, as has Woodhenge, a 410-foot-diameter circular sun

Carlyle Lake

Carlyle Lake is the largest artificially created lake in Illinois. The 15-mile-long lake covers about 26,000 acres within an area bordered by I-70 and US 40 to the north, US 51 to the east, U.S. Highway 50 to the south, and Illinois Highway 127 to the west. Seven recreation areas and two state parks are clustered around its shores. There are swimming beaches, nature trails, picnic areas, camping areas, and boat ramps and rentals. Call (618) 594-2484 for details.

calendar akin to England's Stonehenge. Little kids will like the open spaces, while students can mentally re-create the great cultures that once existed at the very spot on which they stand.

Splash City Family Waterpark (all ages) 

10 Gateway Drive, off Highway 159 in Eastport Plaza, Collinsville; (618) 346-7529; www.collinsvillerec.com. Open daily from late May through mid-August and Friday, Saturday, and Sunday only from mid-August through Labor Day; hours are 11 a.m. to 7 p.m. All children age 7 or younger must be accompanied in the water by an adult. Nonswimming adults supervising older children may pay a lower "just watching fee" in lieu of regular admission. $$

This facility features two twisting water slides, Crystal Creek for inner-tube floating, several swimming areas (including a four-lane lap pool), a wet sand play area, and concessions. The zero-depth "spray area" has water jets, slide, and playhouse. The Lily Pad Walk of floating green plastic "pads" you walk across is pretty wacky. A separate baby pool is enclosed by a gate. Older kids may want to try simulated surfing on the Flow Rider; lessons are available. On a clear day, you can see the St. Louis Gateway Arch in the distance.

Gateway Fun Park (all ages) 

8 Gateway Drive, off Highway 159 in Eastport Plaza, Collinsville; (618) 345-7116; www.gatewayfun.com. Open from 11 a.m. to 10 p.m. Sunday through Thursday and 11 a.m. to midnight Friday and Saturday. The two-hour wristband good for "unlimited fun" is a good bet. $$

This indoor-outdoor family entertainment center near the waterpark has something to do no matter what time of year you visit. Indoors you'll find bumper cars in bright neon colors, a Max Flight roller coaster simulator, and a bunch of arcade games that spit out tickets you can redeem for cheesy prizes. The outdoor area features two 36-hole miniature golf courses on a pretty layout with waterfalls and a little mill with waterwheel. If you're really into water, go play Water Wars, where you launch water balloons at an opponent, or ride the bumper boats, armed with squirt guns that can shoot a 20-foot stream. There's a standard-size go-kart track that appeals to adolescents itchy for a license, but the younger kids aren't left out—there's also a separate track just for kids ages 4 through 9 with little cars that are sooo cute!

Where to Eat

Bob Evans, 600 North Bluff Road; (618) 344-1131. Hours are 6 a.m. to 10 p.m. Sunday through Thursday and 6 a.m. to 11 p.m. Friday and Saturday. See Restaurant Appendix for description. $

Wendy's, 401 North Bluff Road; (618) 345-7999. Open from 10 a.m. to 10 p.m. Sunday through Thursday and 10 a.m. to 11 p.m. Friday and Saturday. See Restaurant Appendix for description. $

Where to Stay

Drury Inn, 602 North Bluff Road; (618) 345-7700; www.druryhotels.com/properties/collinsville.cfm. This 123-room property has an indoor pool. It also allows pets. The room rate includes continental breakfast. $$

Holiday Inn, 1000 Eastport Plaza Drive; (618) 345-2800 or (800) 551-5133; www.hicollinsville.com. This huge chain property has 229 rooms and 34 suites. Amenities include indoor pool, whirlpool, and fitness center. Pets allowed. Room rate may include continental breakfast; be sure to check. $$$

Super 8, 2 Gateway Drive; (618) 345-8008 or (800) 800-8000. This 63-room budget property near Splash City and Gateway Fun Park includes continental breakfast in the room rate. $$

For More Information

Collinsville Chamber of Commerce, 221 West Main Street, Collinsville 62234; (618) 344-2884; www.discovercollinsville.com.

Fairview Heights

Population: 15,034. This town reportedly is one of the fastest-growing communities in southwestern Illinois. And where there's growth, there are families.

Recreation Station Playland (all ages) 

Longacre Drive at South Ruby, in Longacre Park, Fairview Heights; (618) 489-2040. Open year-round from 8 a.m. to sunset daily. Free.

At 16,000 square feet, this outdoor wooden playground structure is one of the biggest in the United States. In addition to the usual slides and ladders, it has a castle and a sunken pirate ship.

St. Clair Square (all ages) 

I-64 at Highway 159 East, Fairview Heights; (618) 632-7566; http://stclairsquare.com. Hours are 10 a.m. to 9:30 p.m. Monday through Saturday and noon to 6 p.m. Sunday.

This two-story indoor shopping mall has more than 140 stores, anchored by JCPenney, Sears, and Dillard's department stores. Parents can buy clothing for their young children at Children's Place and Gymboree. The mall has a food court.

Where to Eat

Old Country Buffet, 10850 Lincoln Trail, in Crossroads Center; (618) 398-4702. Hours are 10:30 a.m. to 8:30 p.m. Monday through Thursday, 11 a.m. to 9 p.m. Friday, 8 a.m. to 9 p.m. Saturday, and 8 a.m. to 8:30 p.m. Sunday. See Restaurant Appendix for description. $

Olive Garden, 25 Ludwig Drive; (618) 397-8727. Hours are 11 a.m. to 10 p.m. Sunday through Thursday and 11 a.m. to 11 p.m. Friday and Saturday. See Restaurant Appendix for description. $

Where to Stay

Best Western Camelot Inn, 305 Salem Place; (618) 624-3636 or (800) 937-8376. Near the mall, this 2-story tan motel has 55 rooms with cable TV. Amenities include indoor swimming pool, hot tub, and game room. Pets weighing less than 15 pounds and kept in carriers allowed for extra $15 a night. $$

Fairfield Inn, 140 Ludwig Drive; (618) 398-7124 or (800) 228-2800. This 63-room chain property in the Marriott family has an indoor pool. Continental breakfast is included in the room rate. $$$

For More Information

Fairview Heights Chamber of Commerce, 10003 Bunkum Road, Fairview Heights 62208; (618) 397-3127; www.fairviewheightschamber.org or www.fairviewheights.com.

Southwestern Illinois Tourism, 10950 Lincoln Trail, Fairview Heights 62208; (800) 442-1488; www.thetourismbureau.org.

Can You **Bear It?**

If you're Cubs fans but can't make it all the way up to Chicago, the next best thing in Southern Illinois is the **Gateway Grizzlies.** This Frontier League baseball team plays in a ballpark built in 2002 with capacity for 6,000 fans among reserved seats, bleachers, and lawn sections; tickets cost $5 to $9. Izzy the Grizzly is a cute mascot with great kid appeal. The Grizzlies season runs from late May through early September. The ballpark is accessible off I-255, exit 15; detailed directions appear on the Web site. Contact Gateway Grizzlies, 2301 Grizzlie Bear Boulevard, Sauget 62206; (618) 337-3000; www.gatewaygrizzlies.com.

Belleville

Population: 41,410. This community traces its roots to the mid-1800s, when more than 6,000 German immigrants came to the area. Every day, so the story goes, the baker's wife walked around town delivering gingerbread and other baked goods from a basket balanced on her head. Today Belleville celebrates that heritage with the annual "Gingerbread Walk" festivities between Thanksgiving and New Year's Day.

Eckert's Country Store and Farms (all ages) 

951 South Greenmount Road, Belleville; (618) 233-0513; www.eckerts.com. Store open from 8 a.m. to 8 p.m. daily, year-round. Call ahead for field hours and fruit availability.

At this farmstead you can pick your own fruit, including strawberries in spring and apples in fall. Pumpkins are available in October. You'll get to ride out to the fields in a farm wagon. You can cut your own Christmas tree between Thanksgiving and Christmas. For the kids there's a small petting zoo on the grounds. You can have a light meal in the restaurant and buy jams and jellies and fresh produce in the Country Store.

Fun Spot (age 5 and up) 

1400 West Boulevard, Belleville; (618) 234-4502. Call for current skating times and prices. Closed in July. $

This family-oriented roller rink's name says it all. If it doesn't run past your kids' bedtime, the Wednesday evening session—called "Cheapskate Night"—is a bargain. Other sessions have special activities or wacky promotional themes; check it out.

Skyview Drive-In (all ages) 

5700 North Belt West, Belleville; (618) 233-4400. Open from spring through fall. First show starts around sunset. Call for current schedule of films and show times. Bring a portable FM radio to hear the sound; speakers are no longer in use.

Have some old-fashioned fun by taking the family to the drive-in for a movie—or two. Each of the two screens plays a double feature of first-run films. Pay attention to the ratings, however, because sometimes the PG movie you want to see is paired with an R-rated second feature that you should skip.

Where to Eat

Ryan's Family Steakhouse, 4850 North Illinois Street; (618) 236-0579. Hours are 10:45 a.m. to 9:30 p.m. Sunday through Thursday and 10:45 a.m. to 10 p.m. Friday and Saturday. In addition to the specialty steaks, the highlight here is the Megabar, a buffet of carved meats, salad, vegetables, and other side dishes. The Megabar alone is plenty for some diners. $

Sonic Drive-In, 6208 West Main Street; (618) 222-7152. Open year-round from 7 a.m. to midnight Sunday through Thursday and 7 a.m. to 1 a.m. Friday and Saturday; closing times are earlier during the school year. See Restaurant Appendix for description. $

Where to Stay

Super 8. 600 East Main Street; (618) 234-9670 or (800) 800-8000. Recently remodeled, this 42-room property also offers hot tub suites. No pool on-site, but guests can use the one at the nearby YMCA. Continental breakfast is included in the room rate. $$

For More Information

Belleville Tourism, 216 East A Street, Belleville 62220; (618) 233- 6769 or (800) 677-9255; www.bellevillechamber.org or www.belleville.net.

Centralia

Population: 14,136. Centralia was named by the Illinois Central Gulf Railroad for its location at about midpoint in south-central Illinois. During the 1990s downtown development around the intersection of US 51 and Illinois Highway 161 and a $1.6 million streetscape improvement project gave the city a face-lift. There's a story behind the Egyptian motif you may notice on some of the buildings: Back in 1831 a late spring and an early killing frost left many northern Illinois counties with virtually no corn to harvest. Milder weather in the south left that region with plenty, so northerners "went down to buy corn in Egypt," a reference to the biblical Genesis story with Joseph and his brothers. So if you hear people around these parts talking about Egypt, they probably don't mean the country in Africa.

Centralia Carillon (all ages)

114 North Elm, Centralia; (618) 533-4381. Tours are available upon advance request and conducted for a fee. The bell tower can be reached only by stairs.

The most prominent feature of Centralia's refurbished downtown is the Centralia Carillon. Built during the early 1980s, it stands 160 feet tall and has 65 bells, which you can see through the clear glass windowpanes that enclose the belfry. Nearly all the bells are inscribed on their outer surface. The smallest weighs 20 pounds and has a diameter of 8 inches; the largest weighs 5½ tons and measures nearly 80 inches in diameter; the total bell weight is 30½ tons. The bells are played by a local carillonneur who climbs 173 steps to reach the 7½-foot, 5½-octave keyboard. Tunes range from classical to pop. There's a small museum in the base of the tower. A small park with a fountain surrounds the carillon.

Foundation Park (all ages)  

Private Park Driveway, off East McCord Street (Highway 161), Centralia; (618) 532-6789. Open year-round from dawn to 11 p.m. daily. Admission is free. Alcoholic beverages are prohibited.

On the east side of the city is a 235-acre nature park called Foundation Park. It has a picnic area, a fitness trail, two stocked ponds for fishing, and a wintertime ice rink. Engine 2500, a preserved classic steam engine, is on display in the park. You might catch an outdoor concert in the Joy Bowl, a 5,000-seat amphitheater. There's no admission charge to the park—unless you visit during the Annual Balloon Fest in mid-August. Then it costs $2 per person age 7 or older (age 6 or younger free) to get in, plus another $3 for nearby lot parking. But you'll probably think it's worth it to see more than 40 hot air balloons making a mass ascension each morning and evening. A few unusual ones show up, too—one year they included a three-tier birthday cake, a clown, a jester, a bald eagle, and Tony "They're GRRRREAT!" the Tiger. Artisans demonstrate such skills as woodworking and dulcimer playing, and you can choose from among about two dozen concessionaires if you get hungry. Fireworks top off the festivities. The crowd ranges from 50,000 to 75,000, so you'll have company.

Fairview Park Pool (all ages) 

Off West McCord Street between Brooks Avenue and Buena Vista Terrace, Centralia; (618) 533-7676. The park is open year-round, and park admission is free. The swimming complex is open daily from June through mid-August from noon to 6 p.m. every day except Tuesday and Thursday. $

Another park in Centralia is Fairview Park, which has a swimming complex with three pools. The main swimming pool measures 60 feet by 80 feet and is 4 to 5 feet deep; the wading pool is 30 feet by 50 feet and 1 to 2 feet deep; and the diving pool has 1- and 3-meter boards and is 13 feet deep. There are bleachers where you can watch the action.

Where to Eat

Long John Silver's, 1161 West Broadway; (618) 532-9313. Open from 11:30 a.m. to 9 p.m. daily. Sit-down restaurant with drive-thru for carryout. See Restaurant Appendix for description. $

Pizza Hut, 725 West Broadway; (618) 532-2782. Hours are 11 a.m. to 10 p.m. Sunday through Thursday and 11 a.m. to 11 p.m. Friday and Saturday. See Restaurant Appendix for description. $

Sonic Drive-In, 1000 West Broadway; (618) 532-0519. Open daily, year-round. Summer hours are 7 a.m. to midnight; closing time is earlier during school year. See Restaurant Appendix for description. $

Where to Stay

Bell Tower Inn, 200 East Noleman; (618) 533-1300. This local lodging half a block from the carillon has 58 rooms and an indoor pool. Small pets are allowed. $

For More Information

Greater Centralia Chamber of Commerce, 130 South Locust, Centralia 62801; (618) 532-6789 or (888) 533-2600; www.seecentralia.com or www.centraliail.com.

Mount Vernon

Population: 16,269. Southeast of Centralia is Mount Vernon, which, like Effingham, lies at the crossroads of numerous thoroughfares: I-57 and I-64 and Illinois Highways 15, 37, 142, and 148. Mount Vernon was established in 1819 and is the seat of Jefferson County.

Cedarhurst Center for the Arts (age 3 and up) 

2400 Richview Road, west off Highway 37, Mount Vernon; (618) 242-1236; www.cedarhurst.org. Hours are 10 a.m. to 5 p.m. Tuesday through Saturday and 1 to 5 p.m. Sunday; closed Monday and all national holidays. General admission is free, but donations are appreciated. There are fees for the craft fair and for some special programs and special events.

One of the most interesting places in town is the Cedarhurst cultural facility. Cedarhurst displays paintings by American artists from the late 19th and early 20th centuries. Its Children's Gallery offers changing exhibitions and special programs and activities. Outdoors you can wander among 30 artworks in the Sculpture Park or stroll the half-mile Juniper Ridge Nature Trail. The popular Cedarhurst Craft Fair takes place here the first weekend after Labor Day.

Jefferson County Historical Village (all ages)

1411 North 27th Street, Mount Vernon; (618) 246-0033. Open from first weekend in May through last weekend in October. Hours are 10 a.m. to 4 p.m. Saturday and 1 to 4 p.m. Sunday. Admission is free.

Structures dating from 1873 to the 1920s stand here. They include log cabins, a one-room schoolhouse, a church, a print shop, a blacksmith's shop, and a general store featuring antique tools. Costumed guides give demonstrations to show what village life was like around the turn of the *last* century.

Rend Lake Area

Due south of Mount Vernon is Rend Lake, a huge recreation spot and a habitat for great blue herons and assorted other waterfowl and shorebirds. With 19,000 acres of water contained within 162 miles of shoreline, it is the second largest artificially created lake in Illinois; only Carlyle Lake is bigger. The Army Corps of Engineers operates six major recreation areas around Rend Lake, with campgrounds, beaches, picnic and wildlife areas, and a marina. Facilities and fees vary, so for detailed information write: Management Office, U.S. Army Corps of Engineers, Rural Route 3, Benton 62812, or call the Rend Lake Visitor Center at (618) 439-7430; www.rendlake.com.

A good place to start your trip to the area is at the Rend Lake Environmental Learning Center, at the east end of Main Dam Road.

Where to Eat

Lone Star Steakhouse, 122 Outlet Avenue, off I-57; (618) 244-7827. Hours are 11 a.m. to 10 p.m. Sunday through Thursday and 11 a.m. to 11 p.m. Friday and Saturday. Steaks are the obvious specialty at this family-oriented chain restaurant. $$

Pizza Hut, 3519 Broadway; (618) 244-3848. Open from 11 a.m. to midnight Sunday through Thursday and 11 a.m. to 1 a.m. Friday and Saturday. See Restaurant Appendix for description. $

Where to Stay

Holiday Inn, 222 Potomac Boulevard (I-57/I-64 and Highway 15); (618) 244-7100 or (800) 243-7171. This 5-story hotel has 223 rooms with cable TV. Amenities include indoor pool, sauna, and whirlpool. Pets are allowed. Ask about the package deal for Cedarhurst Craft Fair. $$

Motel 6, 333 South 44th Street (I-57 and Highway 15); (618) 244-2383 or (800) 466-8356. This budget chain motel has 78 rooms and an outdoor pool. Pets are allowed. $

For More Information

Mount Vernon Convention and Visitors Bureau, 200 Potomac Boulevard, Mount Vernon 62864; (618) 242-3151 or (800) 252-5464; www.mtvernon.com.

Marion

Population: 16,035. South of Rend Lake and east of I-57 is the pleasant community of Marion. If you're coming from the north down I-57, there's a rest area just before exit 77 where you can enjoy a picturesque view of the lake. There are attractions both natural and commercial in Marion, and the town square is charming. A carillon towers at the center, and the new civic center stands in modern contrast to an older brick building displaying the year 1900 in its masonry.

Illinois Centre Mall (all ages) 

Off I-57 (exit 59) west at Illinois Highway 13, Marion; (618) 997-5377; www.illinoiscentre mall.com. Open from 10 a.m. to 9 p.m. Monday through Saturday and noon to 5:30 p.m. Sunday. The mall is accessible for wheelchairs and strollers, which are available for rental, as are lockers.

Billed as "Southern Illinois' largest shopping mall," Illinois Centre opened in 1991 and contains about 60 businesses anchored by Target, Sears, and Dillard's department stores. Skylights in the high, pale green ceilings and gray-and-white floor tiles in the wide aisles help give the one-story mall its airy, spacious feeling. A fountain with palm trees in the center of a large food court adds to the ambience. Of special interest to kids are the Learning Zone and the Fish Tales Pet Store. The Family Fun Arcade has a variety of electronic and skill games. Smaller children may enjoy the coin-operated little rides scattered throughout the mall. You can catch a movie at the nearby Century 8 multiplex. A Kidz Fest is held at the mall in April, with clowns, puppets, magic shows, face painting, and a carnival in the parking lot; call (618) 997-5377 for details.

Southern Illinois Miners (age 4 and up) 

Games are played at Rent One Park, off I-57 (exit 59) west at Highway 13, then take Halfway Road north off Highway 13 and turn right onto Fairmont Drive; ballpark is on the north side of the street. Business office is in Illinois Centre Mall, Suite 750, P.O. Box 1207, Marion 62959; (618) 998-8499; www.southernillinoisminers.com. Season runs from late May through early September; game time is 7:05 p.m. Monday through Saturday and 2:05 p.m. Sunday. Call or go online for the current schedule and ticket prices. Facility is accessible for wheelchairs and strollers. Parking costs $2. $–$$

Rent One Park (named after the rent-to-own business that paid for naming rights through 2016), home of the Southern Illinois Miners minor-league baseball team, opened in 2007 not far from the Illinois Centre Mall. The 4,000-seat stadium has a wide, open concourse and an upper deck with 14 enclosed skybox-style suites, plus a lawn section for those who prefer to bring a blanket and sit on the grass. In recognition of the region's heritage as coal-mining country, the team mascot is a beefy miner wielding a pickax. The Miners belong to the 12-team Frontier League that also includes the Rockford River Hawks and the Windy City Thunderbolts. If the kids get restless with the game, they can check out the Funzone play area on the left-field side, but be aware there's a $5 admission charge.

Crab Orchard National Wildlife Refuge (all ages) 

8588 Highway 148, south of Marion; (618) 997-3344; www.fws.gov/midwest/Crab Orchard/. From I-57, take exit 54B onto Highway 13 west and continue to Highway 148; turn left and head south for a couple miles to the refuge. Grounds are open 24/7, year-round. Visitor center is open from 8 a.m. to 4:30 p.m. daily. Visitors must pay one-day federal fee of $2 per vehicle; additional fees apply for boats. No alcohol allowed anywhere in the refuge; dogs must be kept on leashes at all times. $

This is the place for nature lovers in the Marion area. Nestled within the Shawnee National Forest, the 44,000-acre refuge has three artificial lakes and 5 hiking trails, one of which (the paved Woodland Trail loop) claims to be wheelchair accessible though it is a bit rugged nonetheless. If walking's not your thing, you can still get some sense of the place with the nine-mile auto tour. Maps for both the drive and the hikes are available at the visitor center. Camping and fishing also are offered at the refuge. So is hunting, though not within 50 yards of any "designated public-use facilities," which includes the roads, but make sure not to let the kids stray.

Where to Eat

Cracker Barrel, 2602 W. Main Street, (618) 993-6306. Hours are 6 a.m. to 10 p.m. Sunday through Thursday and 6 a.m. to 11 p.m. Friday and Saturday.

Sonic Drive-In, 2710 Walton Way (west off I-57, exit 54B), (618) 997-5005. Open daily, year-round. Summer hours are 7 a.m. to midnight; closing time is earlier during school year. See Restaurant Appendix for description. $

Where to Stay

Comfort Inn, 2600 West Main Street; (618) 993-6221 or (800) 424-6423. Near Crab Orchard National Wildlife Refuge, this 2-story redbrick motel has an outdoor heated swimming pool. Continental breakfast is included in the room rate. $$$

Fairfield Inn and Suites, 1400 Halfway Road; (618) 993-3011. Near the ballpark and the mall, this entire 3-story motel is nonsmoking. It has an indoor pool. Room rates include deluxe continental breakfast with hot breakfast sandwiches and waffles. $$$

For More Information

Marion Chamber of Commerce, 2305 West Main Street, Marion 62959; (618) 997-6311 or (800) 699-1760; www.marion illinois.com.

Carbondale

Population: 20,681. Carbondale sits atop the upper edge of the Shawnee National Forest along Highway 13. US 51 runs straight south through town. Carbondale has a number of historic homes, many of them still private residences, dating back to the turn of the 20th century. Drive along Poplar, Walnut, and Main Streets to catch a glimpse of some. If you're into architecture, look for Victorian, Italianate, and Queen Anne styles.

Carbondale is the home of Southern Illinois University. The SIU mascot is the *saluki,* a breed of dog, so don't be surprised if you see that word crop up in the names of stores and restaurants. Call (618) 453-2121 for information on university-related attractions and events.

Woodlawn Cemetery (all ages) 

405 East Main Street, Carbondale; (800) 526-1500. Open daily; free.

The first Memorial Day service reportedly was observed in Carbondale's Woodlawn Cemetery in 1866. The cemetery has more than 60 graves of Civil War soldiers, and it is on the National Register of Historic Places. You can stop by anytime to pay your respects.

Poplar Camp Beach (all ages) 

At Cedar Lake, off US 51 south of Carbondale; (800) 526-1500. Open during summer. Hours are 9:30 a.m. to 5:30 p.m. Monday through Friday and 9 a.m. to 7 p.m. Saturday and Sunday. $

Here's a lovely place for a day at the beach. In addition to the lake, the area has restrooms, picnic tables, and concessions. Lifeguards are on duty in case of emergencies. Away from the beach area, Cedar Lake is also a popular spot for fishing. Anglers go after bass, bluegill, crappie, and catfish.

University Mall (all ages) 

1237 East Main Street, Carbondale; (618) 529-3681; www.myuniversitymall.com. Hours are 10 a.m. to 9 p.m. Monday through Saturday and noon to 5:30 p.m. Sunday. The mall is accessible for wheelchairs and strollers.

This one-story indoor shopping mall is anchored by Macy's and JCPenney department stores. It has about 70 shops. Kids are drawn to the Science Center. The mall has a food court. The Kerasotes Showplace 8 Theatre (618-549-6505) claims to be the only stadium seating movie theater in Southern Illinois.

Jefferson County Stage Company (age 3 and up) 

101 North Washington, Carbondale; (618) 549-5466. Call for current schedule.

Plays for children are presented occasionally by this nonprofit organization of amateur actors from the community. A "Summer Family Production" is staged each July.

Where to Eat

Denny's, 1915 West Sycamore; (618) 457-7196. Open 24 hours a day, serving breakfast, lunch, and dinner. $

Lone Star Steakhouse, 3160 East Main Street; (618) 529-2556. Open from 11 a.m. to 10 p.m. Sunday through Thursday and 11 a.m. to 11 p.m. Friday and Saturday. Adults can enjoy such beef cuts as rib eye, filet mignon, and prime rib. Fried chicken, fajitas, and other nonbeef items are also available. The children's menu price of about $4 includes beverage, fries, and ice cream along with the main dish; entrees include chicken tenders and grilled cheese. $$

Steak n Shake, 1365 East Main Street; (618) 457-1668. Open 24 hours a day. See Restaurant Appendix for description. $

Where to Stay

America's Best Inns, 1345 East Main; (618) 529-4801 or (800) 237-8466. This 82-room motel has an outdoor pool and allows pets for an extra $15 per pet per night. The room rate includes a Best Inns Breakfast of cold cereal, milk, juice, coffee, and toast. $$

Quality Inn, 1415 East Main; (618) 549-4244 or (800) 424-6423. This 64-room property has an indoor pool. The 2-bedroom suite has 3 double beds. Continental breakfast is included in the room rate. $$

Super 8, 1180 East Main Street; (818) 457-8822 or (800) 800-8000. Across the street from University Mall, this 63-room property is very basic (no pool) but includes continental breakfast in the room rate. $$

For More Information

Carbondale Convention and Tourism Bureau, 1245 East Main Street, Suite A-32, Carbondale 62901; (800) 526-1500; www.cctb.org.

Southern Illinois Visitor's Guide, 710 N. Illinois Avenue, Carbondale 62901; (618) 529-5454 or (800) 228-0429; www.thesouthern.com.

Chester

Population: 5,185. Along Highway 3, at the junction with Illinois Highway 150 near the Mississippi River, is the town of Chester. This historic river town was established in 1819. Elzie C. Segar, creator of the cartoon character Popeye, was a native son whose legacy lives on with the **Elzie C. Segar Memorial Park** downtown. You'll recognize it because of the giant Popeye statue. The Popeye's Picnic festival is held during early to mid-September, featuring a parade, a carnival, food stands, a flea market, music, and fireworks.

Four miles northeast of Chester on Highway 150 is **Mary's River Covered Bridge,** which was built in 1854 and has a 90-foot span. It was originally part of a planked road between Chester and Bremen.

Spinach Can Collectibles (all ages) 

1001 State Street, Chester; (618) 826-4567; www.popeyethesailor.com. Open from 9:30 a.m. to 4 p.m. Monday through Saturday; closed Sunday.

Located inside Chester's historic 1875 Opera House building, this is the place to be for all things Popeye. The store sells Popeye merchandise, is the headquarters of the Official Popeye Fan Club, and houses the Mini Popeye Museum full of Popeye collectibles from around the world. You can buy other kinds of collectibles here, too, including trading cards and comic books.

Randolph County Museum and Archives (age 7 and up) 

1 Taylor Street, Chester; (618) 826-2667. Open from 12:30 to 3:30 p.m. Sunday, Monday, Thursday, and Friday. Admission is free.

For a sampling of French colonial and Civil War memorabilia, check out the Randolph County Museum and Archives. The museum building itself is a piece of history, built in 1864. It is staffed entirely by volunteers, many of whom are retirees with personal stories to share about the area. Next door is the Randolph County Courthouse, whose glassed-in observation deck affords a panoramic view of the Mississippi River Valley. The county commemorated its bicentennial in 1995.

Randolph County State Recreation Area (all ages)   

Off Highway 150, 5 miles northeast of Chester; (618) 826-2706. Open year-round, from sunrise to about 10 p.m. daily. Admission is free. Pets must be kept on leashes at all times.

Randolph County Lake, an artificially created clear-water lake completed in 1961, is the centerpiece of this recreation area. The lake is stocked with bass, bluegill, channel catfish, rainbow trout, redear, and walleye, and several other kinds of game fish also have found their way in. Bring your own gear or rent tackle and buy bait at the on-site concession stand. You can also rent a boat there or bring your own; the lake has a boat ramp. Six picnic areas feature shelters, tables, grills, and water fountains, and there's a small playground. Hiking trails wind through the woods for visitors on foot, and there are 8 miles of equestrian trails if you have a horse. Campsites are available for overnight guests. Strictly regulated small-game hunting is allowed for properly licensed visitors who check in at the park office.

Where to Eat

Reids' Harvest House Smorgasbord, 2440 State Street; (618) 826-4933. Open from 7 a.m. to 8:30 p.m. Tuesday through Thursday and Sunday and 7 a.m. to 9 p.m. Friday and Saturday; closed Monday. About half a mile down the road from Reids' Inn is this restaurant serving buffet-style breakfast, lunch, and dinner. $

Where to Stay

Best Western Reids' Inn, 2150 State Street; (618) 826-3034, (877) 826-4701, or (800) 937-8376. This 2-story brick motel has 46 rooms with cable TV. Amenities include indoor hot tub and outdoor swimming pool. Small pets allowed with deposit. Room rate includes continental breakfast. $$

For More Information

Randolph County Tourism Committee, 1 Taylor Street, Chester 62233; (618) 826-5000.

Metropolis

Population: 6,482. US 45 will take you to Metropolis. As you might guess, Superman is a big deal here—literally. A 15-foot-tall painted bronze statue of the Man of Steel stands guard in front of the Massac County Courthouse on Superman Square downtown. The annual Superman Celebration takes place here in June, bringing in upwards of 100,000 visitors. If you come in from the east along US 45 off Interstate 24, however, you can't help but notice another giant figure on the south side of the road that's nearly as large as Superman—that's Big John holding those grocery bags outside the namesake supermarket. Once you're in town, US 45 is labeled East Fifth Street on the signs.

Super-Museum (age 3 and up) 

517 Market Street, on Superman Square, downtown Metropolis; (618) 524-5518; http://store.supermansuperstore.com. Open daily from 9 a.m. to 6 p.m. $

You can learn more about the caped hero in the Super-Museum. Its collection spans 60 years and is worth $2.5 million. The museum, for which there is a $3 per person admission fee, is housed at the back of a gift shop full of souvenirs that's almost a museum in itself.

Shawnee National Forest

Sprawling across the far-southern portion of Illinois, from the Mississippi River border on the west to the Ohio River border on the east, is the massive and beautiful Shawnee National Forest. The national forest encompasses many state parks, including Cave-in-Rock, Dixon Springs, Giant City, and Horseshoe Lake, and the Trail of Tears State Forest. Lake Thunderhawk and Little Grassy Lake also lie within it. You'll find hiking trails and spots for picnicking, fishing, and camping in these areas. Shawnee National Forest features such natural wonders as the Pomona Natural Bridge, the Burden Falls waterfall, and the Garden of the Gods. The Golconda Marina draws many boaters who come to enjoy the Ohio River Recreation Area. For a complete listing of Shawnee National Forest attractions—plus detailed information on hiking, backpacking, camping, and picnicking—contact the Shawnee National Forest Headquarters, 50 Highway 145 South, Harrisburg 62946; (800) 699-6637; www.fs.fed.us/r9/shawnee. Another helpful Web site is www.shawneetourism.com. A really useful, complete guide to the state parks can be obtained by writing to the Illinois Department of Conservation, Lincoln Tower Plaza, 524 South Second Street, Springfield 62701-1787.

Americana Hollywood (age 3 and up) 

On Ferry Street, several blocks south of US 45/East 5th Street; (618) 524-5518. Open daily from 9 a.m. to 6 p.m. $

This cousin of the Super-Museum focuses on movie memorabilia. Like the Super-Museum, a museum at the back of the store costs $3 to enter. But all the dolls, toys, posters, and kitsch in the rest of the store are fun to look at, too. Outside is a large, open area with benches, tables, and a life-size Marilyn Monroe statue in a white dress, striking the famous *Some Like It Hot* pose.

Fort Massac State Park (all ages) 

1308 East Fifth Street, Metropolis; (618) 524-9321. The park is open year-round from 7 a.m. to 10 p.m. daily. Museum hours are 10 a.m. to 5:30 p.m. daily. Admission is free for both.

Besides Superman, the other prime attraction in the area is Fort Massac State Park on the banks of the Ohio River, south off US 45. Dedicated in 1908 as the first Illinois state park, it features a reconstructed timber fort that's a replica of one originally built in 1794. The park's museum has a collection of uniforms and equipment used by

Other Things to See and Do

JANUARY

American Bald Eagle Tours, Alton; (800) 258-6645

International Goose Calling Invitational, Marion; (800) 433-7399

FEBRUARY

Sweetie Pie Festival, Mascoutah; (618) 566-7355

Annual Children's Art Show, Effingham; (618) 238-4497 or (618) 547-9055

MARCH

Frontier Days, Teutopolis; (217) 857-3111

March Madness Archery Shoot, Eddyville; (618) 672-4316

APRIL

Southern Illinois Irish Festival, Carbondale; (618) 549-3090; www.silirishfest.org

Southern Illinois Sheep and Craft Festival, Waterloo; (618) 939-8536

MAY

Mayfest, O'Fallon; (618) 632-2815

1820 Children's Day, Edwardsville; (618) 692-1818

Berry Bicycle Ride and Strawberry Festival, St. Jacob; (314) 416-9930

JUNE

Rendezvous at Fort de Chartres, Prairie du Rocher; (618) 284-7230; www.ftdechartres.com

Pinkstaff Ice Cream Social; (618) 943-3516

Heritage Days Festival, Okawville; (618) 243-5694

JULY

Annual Model Train Show, Altamont; (217) 536-6400

Most communities have a Fourth of July celebration, and many county fairs are in July and August.

AUGUST

Cobden Peach Festival; (618) 893-2777 or (800) 248-4373

Marissa Coal Festival; (618) 295-2562

Old Settlers Days, Sumner; (618) 943-3516

SEPTEMBER

Golconda Shrimp Festival; (618) 683-6246

Murphysboro Apple Festival; (618) 684-3200 or (800) 406-8774; www.murphysboro.com

Barnstorming Days, Watson; (217) 536-9990 or (888) 536-5352

OCTOBER

Carmi Corn Days; (618) 382-7606

Annual Oblong Follies; (618) 592-4355

Vulturefest, Makanda; (618) 549-5523

NOVEMBER

Veterans Day Parade, Anna; (618) 833-5182

Capital Classic Basketball Tournament, Lawrenceville; (618) 943-3516

Dog Show, Belleville; (217) 532-6478

DECEMBER

Crossville Winterfest; (618) 966-2237

Mouse House, Caseyville; (618) 345-6256

Christmas Memories and Tea with Mrs. Kringle, Freeburg; (618) 539-3665

soldiers who were stationed at the fort. You can enjoy the 1,450 acres of parkland for picnicking, hiking, boating, and camping.

The third weekend in October at the park is reserved for the Fort Massac Encampment, two days of reenactments of battles and military maneuvers from the period 1750-1812. Food is cooked over open fires, and crafts are handmade the old-fashioned way.

Elijah P. Curtis Home (age 8 and up) 

405 Market Street, Metropolis; (618) 524-5120. Open from April through September, by appointment only. Admission is free, but donations are welcome.

This historic home with unusual woodwork was built in 1870 and belonged to Major Elijah P. Curtis, who served in the Civil War. The Massac County Historical Society operates the home as a museum and includes it in home tours around Christmastime.

Bob's Bowling and Recreation Center (age 4 and up) 

US 45 East, Metropolis; (618) 524-9900. Open from noon to 11 p.m. Monday through Saturday and 2 to 11 p.m. Sunday. $

This local bowling alley has 16 lanes with automated scoring. It also features pool tables, video games, and a snack bar.

Bremer's Orchard (all ages)

5446 Orchard Road, Metropolis; (618) 524-5783. Open from 10 a.m. to 6 p.m. daily in season, June and July. Call ahead to check availability.

This peach orchard is on a family farm. It's not a pick-your-own place, however, and it doesn't have any other amenities, so come here if you just want to buy a box of fresh fruit to take home with you.

Where to Eat

Farley's Cafeteria, 613 Market Street; (618) 524-7226. Open from 3:30 to 7 p.m. Wednesday through Saturday; closed Sunday through Tuesday. Near the Super-Museum. Walk through the buffet line and select your preferred combination of entree, side dish, salad, dessert, and beverage. Prices are a la carte, so don't let your eyes be bigger than your stomach. $

The Buggy BBQ and Grill, 2125 East Fifth Street, US 45 at I-24; (618) 524-9290. Open from 4 to 9 p.m. Tuesday through Thursday, 4 to 10 p.m. Friday and Saturday, and 11 a.m. to 4 p.m. Sunday; closed Monday. Look for the bronze horse and buggy out front and you'll find hearty dinner fare inside. Kids' menu has the usual favorites. $

Pizza Hut, US 45 at I-24; (618) 524-3820. Hours are 11 a.m. to 10:30 p.m. Sunday through Thursday and 11 a.m. to 11:30 p.m. Friday and Saturday. See Restaurant Appendix for description. $

Montego's, 1201 East Eighth Street; (618) 524-4059. Across from Fort Massac State Park, on US 45. Hours are 11 a.m. to 9 p.m. Sunday through Thursday and 11 a.m. to 11 p.m. Friday and Saturday. This local restaurant features a pizza buffet on Thursday, Saturday, and Sunday nights and an all-you-can-eat catfish fry Friday night. At other times you can order steaks, ribs, and pizza off the menu and nibble from the salad bar. $

Where to Stay

Super 8, 203 East Fifth Street, US 45 at I-24; (618) 524-8200 or (800) 566-9970; www.super8metropolis.com. With all the "Super" stuff around town, the Super 8 fits right in. This 2-story redbrick property, nicer than most in this chain, has an indoor pool and spa tub and also features deluxe whirlpool suites in addition to the regular rooms. Pets under 30 pounds are allowed for an extra $7 per pet per night. Continental breakfast is included in the room rate. Pizza Hut is next door. $$$

Metropolis Inn, 2119 East Fifth Street, US 45 at I-24; (618) 524-3723, (800) 577-0707, or (800) 937-8376. This 57-room, 2-story property has an indoor pool and allows small pets. Room rate includes continental breakfast. $$

Comfort Inn, 2118 East Fifth Street, US 45 at I-24; (618) 524-7227 or (800) 424-6423. Take exit 37 off I-24. This chain motel has 52 rooms with cable TV. Amenities include an indoor heated pool. Pets weighing less than 20 pounds $5 per night; larger pets $10. Continental breakfast is included in the room rate. $$

For More Information

Metropolis Area Chamber of Commerce, 607 Market Street, P.O. Box 188, Metropolis 62960; (618) 524-2714 or (800) 949-5740; www.metropolischamber.com.

Appendix

Restaurants

You'll find a number of chain restaurants throughout Illinois. These are detailed descriptions of some that are most appropriate for families. While most restaurants in a chain are similar, there may be slight variations among individual restaurants. As of January 1, 2008, smoking is prohibited in all Illinois restaurants.

Bakers Square

(800) 800-3644; www.bakersquarerestaurants.com

This chain started out many years ago as Poppin' Fresh Pies, serving mainly pie and light soup-and-sandwich meals. Over the years it changed its name to Bakers Square and broadened both its menu and its hours. Now most locations serve both light and hearty fare for breakfast, lunch, and dinner. The kids' menu is about $3, not including drink or pie, and has such entrees as burgers, chicken strips, macaroni and cheese, and roast turkey. The Web site includes street maps and driving directions for each location. Locations include:

Alsip
Bolingbrook
Bourbonnais
Burbank
Champaign
Chicago
Crystal Lake
Deerfield
DeKalb
Downers Grove
Elk Grove Village
Glendale Heights
Gurnee
Hanover Park
Hoffman Estates
Homewood
Joliet
LaGrange
Lake in the Hills
Lansing
Libertyville
Matteson
Melrose Park
Mount Prospect
Naperville
Niles
Normal
Orland Park
Oswego
Palatine
Palos Heights
Peoria
Plainfield
Rockford
Rolling Meadows
South Elgin
Springfield
St. Charles
Villa Park
Westmont
Wheaton
Willowbrook
Wilmette

Bob Evans

(800) 272-7675; www.bobevans.com

Maybe you've seen his sausage in the supermarket. That's how ol' Bob began back in 1946. He started making his own recipe to serve at his truck stop in Ohio. Eventually he built a restaurant to serve the famous sausage, and other things, and then another, and another. There are now more than 500 Bob Evans restaurants in 20 states. They share a sort of red-barnish facade with the name emblazoned in yellow, and inside the decor is folksy. Sausage remains the centerpiece of the breakfast menu, surrounded by such hearty accompaniments as biscuits and gravy, eggs, or hotcakes. The lunch and dinner menus feature burgers and other sandwiches, and country-cookin' entrees such as chicken and noodles, meat loaf, turkey and dressing, and country fried steak. Sandwiches are typically less than $5; entrees in the $6 to $9 range. Only nonalcoholic beverages are served. The children's menu costs about $2, not including drink, and features pizza, hot dog, spaghetti, cheeseburger, chicken nibbles, chicken quesadilla, and a turkey dinner. Locations include:

Bloomington
Champaign
Collinsville
Decatur
East Peoria
Fairview Heights
Joliet
Marion
Mount Vernon
Pekin
Peoria
Plainfield
Springfield

Boston Market

(800) 365-7000; www.boston-market.com

This chain offers sit-down food at close to fast-food speed and prices. The most expensive individual meal shouldn't cost more than $6, not including the drink, and you can buy a family-style meal that drives the per-person cost down a bit more. Marinated rotisserie chicken is the specialty, but ham, turkey, and meat loaf are other meat options. Side dishes include potatoes, various tasty vegetables, stuffing, pasta, and a plethora of salads. Children's meals are junior versions of the adult choices, with smaller portions and smaller prices. Best of all, the entire chain is smoke-free. Locations include:

Arlington Heights
Aurora
Bolingbrook
Buffalo Grove
Chicago
Crestwood
Crystal Lake
Deerfield
Elgin
Elk Grove Village
Fairview Heights
Geneva
Glenview
Gurnee
Hanover Park
Homewood
Joliet
Lombard
Melrose Park
Mount Prospect
Naperville

Norridge
Oak Lawn
Orland Park
Palatine
Park Ridge
Schaumburg
Skokie
Waukegan
Westmont
Wheaton

Chuck E. Cheese's

(888) 778-7193; www.chuckecheese.com

This family-friendly chain is known more for its entertainment value than its food. But people don't usually come for the food, they come to play! Small children enjoy a playground of tubes, slides, and ball pits. Grade-schoolers will have a good time feeding tokens into all the arcade and skill games. And when you do sit down to eat, there is entertainment in the form of 6-foot-tall robotic puppets gathered on a stage to sing and play music for you. Head cheese Chuck E. is a big gray mouse, and if there's a birthday party, someone in costume will deliver the cake to the birthday girl or boy. Regular coupons in the newspapers can save you money if you buy a package deal with pizza, pitcher of soda pop, and game tokens. Redeem your arcade prize tickets for a plastic doodad at the souvenir stand. Locations include:

Arlington Heights
Batavia
Bloomington
Chicago
Crystal Lake
Darien
Fairview Heights
Gurnee
Joliet
Matteson
Melrose Park
Naperville
Oak Lawn
Peoria
Rockford
Skokie
Springfield
Streamwood
Tinley Park
Vernon Hills
Villa Park

Culver's

(608) 643-7980; www.culvers.com

Celebrating its 20th anniversary in 2004, this Wisconsin-based fast-food chain has been expanding southward into Illinois since the mid-1990s, with new locations opening every year. Calling Culver's a burger joint would be unfair—even though the specialty Butterburger (so named for its buttered bun) is a pretty tasty hamburger—because the menu has much more than burgers. Other sandwiches include breaded pork tenderloin, beef pot roast, fried cod, grilled chicken, and hot ham and cheese. You can also get a full meal platter with potatoes, coleslaw, dinner roll, and a choice of fried chicken, fish, or shrimp. On the lighter side, there's soup served in a bowl made out of bread. That option would leave plenty of room for Culver's other specialty: frozen custard, which is like soft-serve ice cream, only richer. It's offered in vanilla, chocolate, and the "flavor of the day," and you can get it in cones, sundaes, and shakes. Kids' meals come with a "free" ice-cream cone. Place your order at the counter, and it will be prepared fresh and delivered to your table in a few minutes. The restaurants' well-lit blue-and-white decor is bright and cheery. The dining room and the bathrooms nearly always look very clean, no matter how crowded the restaurant gets. For kids there are souvenirs with the mascot, Scoopie, which looks like an ice-cream cone with arms and legs. Sometimes a full-size Scoopie in character costume makes an appearance; call ahead if you want to catch one of those times. Locations include:

Addison
Antioch
Aurora
Belvidere
Bloomington
Bolingbrook
Bridgeview
Buffalo Grove
Carol Stream
Carpentersville
Champaign
Collinsville
Crystal Lake
Darien
Decatur
Dixon
Downers Grove
East Peoria
Edwardsville
Effingham
Frankfort
Freeport
Galena
Geneseo
Grayslake
Gurnee
Huntley
Island Lake
Joliet
Lake Zurich
Lansing
Libertyville
Lincoln
Lombard
Matteson
McHenry
Minooka
Moline
Morris
Morton
Mount Prospect
North Aurora
O'Fallon
Oswego
Palatine
Pekin
Peoria
Peru
Plainfield
Princeton
Rochelle
Rock Falls
Rockford
Romeoville
Roscoe
Schaumburg
South Elgin
Springfield
Sycamore
Tinley Park
Winnebago
Woodstock
Yorkville
Zion

Giordano's

(800) 982-1756; www.giordanos.com

This chain has been around since 1974 and is famous for its stuffed pizza, a thick concoction in which cheese and other ingredients of your choice are placed upon a layer of crust and then covered over with another layer of crust and tomato sauce. The menu also includes lasagna, fettucine Alfredo, mostaccioli, ravioli, spaghetti, chicken dishes, and a variety of sandwiches and salads. Entrees are generally less than $10. Beer and wine are offered in addition to soft drinks. Locations include:

Addison
Algonquin
Buffalo Grove
Chicago
Downers Grove
Elk Grove Village
Evanston
Glen Ellyn
Gurnee
Joliet
Lake Zurich
Morton Grove
Naperville
Niles
Oakbrook Terrace
Oak Park
Orland Park
Oswego
Plainfield
Rockford
Rosemont
South Elgin
St. Charles
Streamwood
Westchester
Willowbrook

HomeTown Buffet and Old Country Buffet

(800) 871-0956; www.buffet.com

At HomeTown and Old Country, two sister chains established in the 1980s, you pay one price up front and then take whatever you want from several buffet tables. Even drinks (nonalcoholic) and desserts are included. The adult price for dinner is about $9, and kids age 10 or younger typically pay 50 cents multiplied by their age. The salad bar has lettuce salads, macaroni, cottage cheese, and others. At least two kinds of soup are offered, too. Hot food includes beef, ham, fried and broiled chicken, fried and broiled fish, pasta, various types of potatoes, corn, carrots, and other vegetables, plus various types of breads and rolls. Desserts include ice cream, puddings, cobbler, and other sweets. It's a good value for the money. Locations include:

Arlington Heights
Bloomingdale
Bradley
Champaign
Chicago
Chicago Ridge
Countryside
Crystal Lake
Deerfield
Fairview Heights
Forest Park
Forsyth
Joliet
Lansing
Lombard
Matteson
Moline
Naperville
Niles
Northlake
Peoria
Rockford
Rolling Meadows
Springfield
Streamwood
Tinley Park
Vernon Hills
West Dundee

IHOP (International House of Pancakes)

(818) 240-6055; www.ihop.com

Most IHOPs are open around the clock, serving breakfast anytime and lunch and dinner at their appropriate times. Of course breakfast features pancakes, but you can get bacon and eggs, French toast, waffles, and other things as well. Lunch and dinner include a variety of sandwiches and meat-and-potatoes sort of entrees under $10. Children's menu prices fall in the $3 to $4 range. Frequent newspaper coupons make IHOP a bargain. Locations include:

Addison
Algonquin
Arlington Heights
Aurora
Belleville
Bloomington
Bolingbrook
Bourbonnais
Bridgeview
Buffalo Grove
Champaign
Chicago
Cicero
Crestwood
Crystal Lake
Decatur
Elgin
Evanston
Glendale Heights
Glenview
Gurnee
Hoffman Estates
Joliet
Lansing
Matteson
McHenry
Melrose Park
Moline
Oak Park
O'Fallon
Orland Park
Peoria
Peru
Rockford
Rosemont
Schaumburg
Skokie
Springfield
St. Charles
Vernon Hills
Waukegan
Westchester
Wheaton
Wood River

Long John Silver's

www.ljsilvers.com

A lot of little kids won't eat fish, but they probably will at this chain of nautically themed restaurants that started in 1969. Here mild-flavored cod is batter-dipped and deep-fried—delicious! For those who truly won't eat fish, chicken "planks" are prepared the same way. Kids can get a meal with fish or chicken, fries, small soda, and toy in a colorful bag for about $3. Adults can choose from a tantalizing assortment of platters that include combinations of fish, chicken, shrimp, and clams, served with fries, coleslaw, hush puppies (deep-fried balls of cornmeal dough), and beverage. Place your order at the counter and carry your food to the table or out the door. Some restaurants have a kids' play area. Many now share space with an A&W, a Taco Bell, or a KFC, thanks to a 2002 acquisition by Yum! Brands, which owns those chains as well. Locations include:

Arlington Heights
Aurora
Bartlett
Beardstown
Belvedire
Bensenville
Bloomington
Bolingbrook
Bradley
Calumet City
Carbondale
Centralia
Champaign
Chicago
Chicago Heights

Collinsville
Countryside
Crest Hill
Danville
Decatur
DeKalb
Downers Grove
East Peoria
Effingham
Elgin
Fairview Heights
Forest Park
Fox Lake
Frankfort
Freeport
Galesburg
Godfrey
Granite City
Gurnee
Hanover Park
Harrisburg
Homewood
Jacksonville
Joliet
Lincoln
Lincolnwood
Litchfield
Machesney Park
Macomb
Marion
Matteson
Mattoon
McHenry
Moline
Morris
Mount Carmel
Mount Vernon
Mundelein
New Lenox
Oak Lawn
Orland Park
Ottawa
Pekin
Peoria
Pontiac
Quincy
Rantoul
Romeoville
Round Lake Beach
Salem
Shorewood
South Chicago Heights
South Elgin
Springfield
Sterling
Streator
Taylorville
Vandalia
West Frankfort
Westmont
Wood River

McDonald's

(800) 244-6227; www.mcdonalds.com

The Oakbrook-based fast-food giant merits a brief mention here for its family-friendly atmosphere. Locations with a PlayPlace are especially helpful when traveling, because they provide a relatively safe environment for young children to work off some pent-up energy before getting back in the car. The food is familiar and consistent, and kids' Happy Meals with toys remain a bargain at about $3. High chairs are usually available. By 2007, about half the McDonald's restaurants nationwide had been renovated—or in some cases completely rebuilt—to incorporate more earth tones into both their interior and exterior appearance, partly in an attempt to compete with Starbucks for the young-and-hip clientele, but the chain is still plenty kid-friendly. Locations throughout Illinois.

Old Country Buffet

See previous listing for HomeTown Buffet.

Olive Garden

(800) 331-2729; www.olivegarden.com

This chain of sit-down restaurants, established in 1982, is good for families whose children are at least in grade school, because you do have to wait for your order to be taken, cooked, and delivered. Pasta entrees include such traditional favorites as lasagna, ravioli, and fettucine Alfredo, but the specials often provide variations on those themes to great success. There are some chicken and seafood entrees on the menu as well. Entree prices range from about $9 to $14, including a big communal bowl of salad from which you can take as many servings as you like. Children can order pasta or their own minipizza for about $4. Locations include:

Arlington Heights
Bloomingdale
Bloomington
Bolingbrook
Burbank
Champaign
Downers Grove
Fairview Heights
Gurnee
Lansing
Lincolnwood
Matteson
Naperville
North Riverside
Orland Park
Peoria
Rockford
Schaumburg
Springfield
St. Charles
Vernon Hills
West Dundee

Pizza Hut

(800) 948-8488; www.pizzahut.com

This chain provides consistent quality in thin-crust, hand-tossed, and thick pizzas. Sit-down locations also typically offer salads and pasta dishes. Beverages are all nonalcoholic. Coupons can cut the cost a bit; check your Sunday newspaper or go online. Locations throughout Illinois.

Popeyes Chicken

(877) 767-3937; www.popeyes.com

"Love That Chicken from Popeyes!" That's the company's slogan, and the Schuldt family agrees with it wholeheartedly—Popeyes is our favorite fried-chicken chain. The flavorful chicken (mild or spicy) is crispy on the outside and juicy inside, and the buttery buttermilk biscuits melt in your mouth. Most Popeyes restaurants have both sit-down and carryout service. The chain started in New Orleans in 1972, and its menu reflects the cuisine of that region: You can get Cajun rice or red beans and rice in place of french fries, and some restaurants also offer Cajun crawfish. The kids' meal costs less than $3 and includes drink and toy. Popeyes was named after Gene

Hackman's Popeye Doyle character in the film *The French Connection,* but Popeye the Sailor Man is featured in the advertising. Coupons from the newspaper or online can cut the cost of a family dinner. Locations throughout Illinois.

Portillo's

(630) 851-5151 in the Chicago metro area, (866) 986-2333 from elsewhere; www.portillos.com

This casual Chicago-area chain, established in 1963, offers burgers, hot dogs, and other sandwiches such as chicken or Italian beef, typically in a two-story restaurant with all sorts of interesting memorabilia and mannequins to look at. Themes are typically either 1920s–1930s Prohibition era or 1950s rock 'n' roll. The prices are low enough that no children's menu is offered. Locations include:

Addison
Arlington Heights
Batavia
Bloomingdale
Bolingbrook
Chicago
Crestwood
Crystal Lake
Downers Grove
Elk Grove Village
Elmhurst
Forest Park
Glendale Heights
Naperville
Niles
Northlake
Oak Lawn
Oswego
Rolling Meadows
Schaumburg
Shorewood
Skokie
St. Charles
Streamwood
Summit
Sycamore
Tinley Park
Vernon Hills
Villa Park

Red Lobster

(800) 562-7837; www.redlobster.com

This sit-down restaurant chain offers reasonable-quality seafood at reasonable prices. Dinners are served with crisp lettuce salad and hot, garlicky biscuits. You can Create Your Own Platter of two or three seafood choices. Entrees run about $10 to $18. Items on the children's menu cost about $4, including drink; among them are popcorn shrimp, chicken planks, and spaghetti. Locations include:

Alton
Aurora
Bloomingdale
Bloomington
Bolingbrook
Bradley
Champaign
Chicago
Danville
Downers Grove
Fairview Heights
Forsyth
Geneva
Gurnee
Joliet
Lincolnwood
Marion
Matteson

Norridge
Oak Lawn
Orland Park
Peoria
Peru
Rockford
Schaumburg
Springfield
West Dundee

Sonic Drive-In

(866) 657-6642; www.sonicdrivein.com

This Oklahoma-based southern burger chain—established in 1953, two years before Ray Kroc opened the first McDonald's in Des Plaines—is creeping northward and by 2007 had spread across much of southern and central Illinois, with future plans for expansion toward Chicago. The tricky part for Sonic will be figuring out how to survive a Midwestern winter when the dining area is all outdoors: drive-in stalls serviced by brightly clad carhops on roller skates, plus a patio with picnic tables. One carhop we spoke with simply shrugged and said, "I'll wear a parka." But before the snow falls, pile the kids in the car and show them how it was done in the "good ol' days," even if those days were before your time, too. The experience has greater appeal than the food itself: the flat, wide burgers, the french fries, and the corn dogs are rather ordinary, though the breading on the chicken strips is better than average. Complete the order with a milkshake, malt, or soft-serve sundae, or think outside the retro box and get a smoothie. The Wacky Pack kids' meal comes with any of the aforementioned entrees or a grilled cheese sandwich, plus fries, a fruity Slush, and a prize, all for about $3. By the way, the chain has no connection with Sonic the Hedgehog and instead has its own cartoon clan: four kids named Molly, Junior, Cherrie, and Pete, plus Coney the wiener dog. Locations include:

Anna
Belleville
Carbondale
Centralia
Champaign
Collinsville
Du Quoin
East Alton
Edwardsville
Godfrey
Harrisburg
Highland
Jacksonville
Jerseyville
Marion
Mattoon
Metropolis
Mount Vernon
O'Fallon
Pekin
Savoy
Springfield
Swansea
Vandalia
West Frankfort

Steak n Shake

(309) 827-8411; www.steaknshake.com

If you're looking for some atmosphere in an economical choice, Steak n Shake restaurants are done up in black-and-white ersatz art deco. The chain began in 1934 in Normal and for many years remained concentrated in central, western, and southern Illinois, but it began to reach northward into the Chicago suburbs in the late 1990s. The menu offers "steakburgers" (like hamburgers, only allegedly made with better-quality beef) and other sandwiches accompanied by thin french fries, salads, and other assorted side dishes. The dessert menu is heavy on mouthwatering ice-cream concoctions. Most Steak n Shake restaurants are open twenty-four hours a day, seven days a week, serving breakfast as well as lunch and dinner. Locations include:

Alton
Aurora
Batavia
Belleville
Bloomington
Bolingbrook
Bourbonnais
Carbondale
Champaign
Collinsville
Danville
Decatur
DeKalb
Downers Grove
East Peoria
Edwardsville
Effingham
Elgin
Elk Grove Village
Evanston
Fairview Heights
Forsyth
Galesburg
Glendale Heights
Gurnee
Hoffman Estates
Jacksonville
Joliet
Lake in the Hills
Lincoln
Machesney Park
Marion
Mattoon
McHenry
Moline
Mount Prospect
Mount Vernon
Naperville
Normal
O'Fallon
Pekin
Peoria
Peru
Quincy
Rockford
Rolling Meadows
Rosemont
Springfield
Streamwood
Tinley Park
Urbana
West Chicago
Wood River

TGIFriday's

(800) 374-3297; www.tgifridays.com

Here is a sit-down restaurant where you can bring the kids and not have to worry about them getting too loud. Chances are, the place is already loud. The restaurant exudes a party atmosphere, but the place also tries to seem homey and old-fashioned. A raised section in the center of the restaurant houses a bar. High chairs and booster seats are generally available. The menu is almost a book, it has so many pages. Sandwiches cost about $6 to $9 and are typically served with french fries. Entrees, most served with soup or salad, potato, and sometimes vegetables, fall in the $9 to $15 range for pasta, chicken, fish, and shrimp, and in the $15 to $20 range for steaks and ribs. A menu of smaller "right portion" entrees are in the $7 to $9 range, sparing both your diet and your wallet. The children's menu entrees for either lunch or dinner cost about $4, not including drinks. Open for lunch and dinner. Locations include:

Aurora
Batavia
Bedford Park
Bloomingdale
Bloomington
Bolingbrook
Bourbonnais
Carpentersville
Champaign
Cherry Valley
Chicago
Crystal Lake
Darien
Effingham
Fairview Heights
Glenview
Gurnee
Hoffman Estates
Joliet
Lake Zurich
Lombard
Moline
Naperville
Oak Lawn
Oak Park
Orland Park
Peoria
Quincy
Rockford
Schaumburg
Springfield
St. Charles
Vernon Hills
Wheeling

Wendy's

(614) 764-3100; www.wendys.com

Serving lunch and dinner; some locations are open late into the evening. High chairs and booster seats are generally available. Wendy's is one of the best fast-food buys around. The value menu features a variety of items for only 99 cents, so you can have a feast for only two or three bucks per person. There are kid meals with little prizes, if you want to go that route, usually under $3. Most adult combos with burger, fries, and drink are under $6. The hearty stuffed pitas fall in the $3 to $4 range. Most Wendy's restaurants tend to be clean and well lit. Locations throughout Illinois.

Lodging Appendix

The following is a list of some of the more family-oriented hotel and motel chains. Individual listings in each town include information on a particular property's size, amenities, and price category (prices do vary by location; for example, downstate properties are typically cheaper than those in the Chicago metro area). You'll take some of the anxiety out of your trip if you make your reservations in advance. Rates may vary by season, usually being higher in summer. At most of these chains, kids stay free in the same room with their parents, but the age cutoff may be 12 at one place and 18 at another, so check the specifics when you make your reservation. Be sure to ask about any special rates or package deals that are sometimes available. You'll also save money by staying at a hotel or motel that includes breakfast in the room rate. Note the following terms:

Continental breakfast: At least coffee and some sort of bread or pastry. Exactly what you get varies from one property to another. Many also include juice, milk, and cold cereal.

Full or American breakfast: Hot food such as bacon and eggs or pancakes. Rarely included in the price of a room at any hotel or motel.

If you plan to bring a pet along, be sure to call the hotel or motel in advance. Even among places that allow pets, there are usually some restrictions. For example, some properties allow only "small" pets, and you need to be sure yours would be what they, not you, consider small. You also may have to pay a fee, typically $5 to $10 per night but sometimes as much as $25, or leave a deposit when you check in. Finally, a responsible member of your party must be with the pet at all times.

*An asterisk indicates that there is a listing for a specific hotel or motel in that town's Where to Stay entry.

Baymont Inn and Suites

Reservations (877) 229-6668, TDD (800) 834-4410, Customer Service (866) 464-2321; www.baymontinns.com

Formerly Budgetel, most of these properties are three- or four-story rectangular concrete blocks. They have comfortable, nicely furnished rooms inside, and all that cement seems to help muffle outside noise. Rooms have coffeemakers and cable TV. Some Baymont Inns also have suites. Only a few of the Baymont Inns in Illinois have a swimming pool, but those that do are indoor pools. None of the Illinois properties has a restaurant on the premises, but there is usually one within walking distance, often next door. Nearly all the Illinois properties accept "small pets." It's best to check with the specific one you want to stay at to determine what they consider "small." All are willing to make special accommodations for nonsmokers or persons with disabilities. There's all sorts of stuff for business travelers, too. Locations include:

*Alsip
Bloomington
Calumet City
Champaign
Decatur
DeKalb
Glenview
Hoffman Estates
*Mattoon
North Aurora
O'Fallon
*Peoria
Peru
Rockford
Springfield
*Tuscola

Best Western

(800) 937-8376 English, (800) 332-7836 Spanish/Español, (800) 634-9876 French/ Français, TDD (800) 528-2222 for hearing impaired; www.bestwestern.com

Although Best Western claims to be "the World's Largest Hotel Chain," its properties are independently owned and operated, so there is a much greater variation in appearance, amenities, and quality than with many other chains. Most of the ones in Illinois are two-story motels, although there are a few high-rise hotels. Some have an indoor or outdoor swimming pool. Some allow pets. Some have a restaurant on the premises. Some include breakfast in the room rate. Some of the properties are beautiful and well maintained, some so-so, and a few downright divey. If you can, visit the particular motel you want before you book a room there. If that's not feasible, try to get the chain's current Travelers' Guide & Road Atlas, a detailed list for each location. At all U.S. Best Westerns, children age 12 or younger stay free in the same room with a paying adult. Locations include:

Antioch
Burbank
Charleston
*Chester
*Chicago
Collinsville
Danville
DeKalb
Des Plaines
Du Quoin
*Elk Grove Village
Evanston
*Fairview Heights
Flora
*Galena
*Galesburg
Grayville
Joliet
*Moline
Monee
*Monticello
Morton
Morton Grove
Naperville
Nashville
*Normal
Pontoon Beach
Rantoul
Robinson
Romeoville
Rosemont
Savoy
Springfield
*St. Charles
Ullin
Waukegan
Westmont
Wheeling

Comfort Inn

(800) 424-6423 English, (866) 291-9816 Spanish/Español, (800) 267-3837 French/ Français, TTY (800) 228-3323 for hearing impaired; www.comfortinn.com

Properties vary in appearance, but most are rectangular, light-colored buildings two to six stories high. Rooms are comfortable, most with cable TV. There are a few Comfort Suites, which feature partially divided living and sleeping areas (no door between them) and a coffeemaker and small refrigerator. Among the approximately 50 properties in Illinois, more than half have an indoor swimming pool; a few have an outdoor pool, and some have no pool at all. Be sure to check for the one you're interested in. Policies regarding pets also vary. A few Comfort Inns have a restaurant on the premises, but most do not. All include continental breakfast in the room rate. Locations include:

*Alton
*Arcola
*Aurora (Suites also)
Bloomington
Casey
*Champaign
*Chicago
Collinsville
Crystal Lake
Danville
*Des Plaines
Dixon
*Downers Grove
Edwardsville
Effingham (Suites also)
Elgin (Suites only)
*Elk Grove Village
Fairview Heights (Suites only)
Forsyth
Franklin Park
Galesburg
*Geneva
*Gurnee (Suites also)
Harrisburg
Harvey (Suites only)
*Joliet
*Lansing (Suites only)
Lincoln
Litchfield
Lombard (Suites only)
Manteno
*Marion (Suites also)
Markham
Mattoon (Suites only)
Mendota
*Metropolis
*Moline
*Morris
Morton
Mount Vernon
Mundelein
Normal (Suites only)
Oakbrook Terrace (Suites only)
O'Fallon
Orland Park
Ottawa
Palatine
Peoria (Suites only)
Peru
Pontiac
*Quincy
Rochelle (Suites also)
*Rockford (Suites also)
Romeoville
Salem
Schaumburg (Suites only)
Schiller Park (Suites only)
Skokie
South Jacksonville
*Springfield (Suites also)
Sycamore
Tinley Park (Suites only)
Waukegan

Days Inn

(800) 329-7466 English, (888) 709-4024 Spanish/Español; www.daysinn.com

The size and shape of the buildings varies, and so do the amenities offered. Some have an indoor heated pool, some have an outdoor pool, and some have no pool. Some have an on-site restaurant. Some include continental breakfast in the room rate. The main thing they have in common is comfortable rooms at economical prices. Locations include:

Addison
Alsip
Alton
*Barrington
Benton
*Bloomington
Burbank
Carbondale
Caseyville
Champaign
Charleston
Chicago
Danville
Decatur
Effingham
*Elgin
*Elk Grove Village
El Paso
Farmer City
Galesburg
Harvey
Lansing
Libertyville
Loves Park
Macomb
Marion
*Melrose Park
Morris
Morton
Mount Vernon
Naperville
Niles
Normal
North Chicago
Oglesby
Princeton
Quincy
Rantoul
Sheffield
*Springfield
St. Charles
*Vandalia
Waukegan
Woodstock

Fairfield Inn

(800) 228-2800; www.fairfieldinn.com

Fairfield Inn is the economy-class member of the Marriott family. The building is two to four stories high. Rooms have simple, comfortable furnishings and cable TV. All the Illinois inns have a heated swimming pool, most an indoor one with spa as well. All properties in the chain include continental breakfast in the price of the room. Locations include:

Bedford Park
Bloomington
*Bourbonnais
*Champaign
Chicago
Danville
Effingham
*Fairview Heights
Forsyth
*Galesburg
Glenview
*Gurnee
Joliet
Lombard
*Marion
*Mattoon
*Moline
Mount Vernon
Naperville
Peru
Quincy
*Springfield
Tinley Park

Hampton Inn

(800) 426-7866; www.hamptoninn.com

The inn is usually a white building, three to five stories high. Amenities include coffeemakers, irons and ironing boards, dataports, and a free movie channel on the TV. Nearly all of the more than 30 Hampton Inns in Illinois have a swimming pool, about half an indoor one. Room rates include a complimentary continental breakfast buffet. Locations include:

Addison
Aurora
Bedford Park
Bloomington
Bolingbrook
*Bourbonnais
Carbondale
Carol Stream
Chicago
Collinsville
Countryside
*Crestwood
East Peoria
Effingham
Elgin
Elk Grove Village
Fairview Heights
Forsyth
Freeport
*Gurnee
Hoffman Estates
Jacksonville
Joliet
Lincolnshire
*Lombard
Marion
*Mattoon
McHenry
Moline
Mount Vernon
Naperville
Ottawa
Quincy
*Rockford
*Schaumburg
Schiller Park
Skokie
*Springfield
Tinley Park
*Urbana
Westchester

Holiday Inn

(800) 465-4329; www.holiday-inn.com

Properties vary in appearance but usually have nicely furnished rooms, an indoor or outdoor pool, and a restaurant on the premises. They are pretty reliable in terms of cleanliness and competent staff. Typically breakfast is available in the restaurant or through room service, but the cost is not included in the room rate. The newer Holiday Inn Express properties are generally smaller and do not have an on-site restaurant (usually there's an independent restaurant nearby), but they typically do include a continental breakfast and unlimited local telephone calls in the room rate. They may or may not have a pool; it's best to double-check. Those with suites have a separate living-room area, and usually there's a door between it and the bedroom area. Locations include:

Algonquin
*Alton
Annawan
Arlington Heights
Aurora
Bedford Park
Beloit
Bloomington
Bolingbrook
*Bourbonnais
Bradley
Cahokia

Carlinville
Calumet Park
*Carol Stream
Champaign
*Chicago
*Collinsville
Countryside
*Crystal Lake
Danville
*Decatur
DeKalb
*Downers Grove
East Peoria
Edwardsville
*Effingham
Elgin
*Elk Grove Village
Elmhurst
Freeport
Galesburg
*Glen Ellyn
Granite City
Gurnee
Harvey
Highland
Hillside
Hinsdale
Itasca
Joliet
Kankakee
Lansing
Libertyville
Lincoln
Lisle
Litchfield
Lombard
Loves Park
Macomb
Marion
Matteson
Metropolis
Moline
Monee
*Morris
Morton
*Mount Vernon
*Naperville
*Normal
Oakbrook Terrace
Oak Lawn
O'Fallon
Oglesby
Oswego
Ottawa
Palatine
Pekin
*Peoria
Pontiac
Pontoon Beach
*Quincy
Riverwoods
Rochelle
Rock Falls
*Rockford
Rock Island
Rolling Meadows
Rosemont
Schaumburg
Shiloh
Skokie
Sparta
Springfield
*St. Charles
Sterling
Sycamore
Tinley Park
Troy
*Tuscola
Urbana
Vandalia
Waukegan
Wheaton
William Tell
Willowbrook
Woodstock

Motel 6

(800) 466-8356 English, (877) 467-7224 Spanish/Español; www.motel6.com

This budget chain offers low-cost lodging. The rooms may not be the largest or quietest you've ever stayed in, but they're usually reasonably clean and comfortable. About half the properties have an outdoor swimming pool. There are no meals included in the room rate, and only a few properties have a restaurant on-site, but food of some sort is nearby. "One well-behaved pet per room" is allowed at all Motel 6 locations but must be declared at registration and attended at all times. Book online with the "Click 6" feature and you'll knock about $5 off the room rate. Locations include:

Arlington Heights
*Aurora
*Bourbonnais
Carbondale
Caseyville
East Peoria
Effingham
Elk Grove Village
Glenview
Joliet
Marion
Minonk
*Mount Vernon
*Normal
Palatine
Rockford
Rolling Meadows
Schiller Park
Springfield
*Villa Park

Quality Inn

(877) 424-6423 English, (866) 291-9816 Spanish/Español, (800) 267-3837 French/ Français; TTY (800) 228-3323 for hearing impaired; www.qualityinn.com

Properties vary in appearance. A cousin of Comfort Inn, Quality Inn is geared more toward the economy-minded business traveler, but families can sometimes find a bargain on the weekend, when many business travelers have gone home. Most of the Illinois properties have an indoor or outdoor swimming pool. A few have a restaurant on the premises, and those that do not have one include breakfast in the price of a room. Some Quality Inns also include suites. Locations include:

Bloomington
Bradley (Suites also)
*Carbondale
Caseyville
Dixon (Suites also)
Elgin
Elk Grove Village
Elmhurst
Moline
Morton
Rockford (Suites only)
Schaumburg
Schiller Park
Springfield

Ramada

(800) 272-6232; www.ramada.com

The typical Ramada Inn has nicely furnished rooms, an indoor or outdoor pool, and a restaurant on the premises. Breakfast usually is available in the restaurant or through room service and is not included in the room rate, but some properties do include a continental breakfast. Ramada Limited properties have been cropping up—smaller motels that offer a continental breakfast with the room. Locations include:

Bloomington
Bolingbrook
Burr Ridge
Carbondale
*Chicago
Collinsville
*Decatur
*Effingham
Fairview Heights
*Freeport
Galesburg
Glendale Heights
Homewood
Joliet
Lansing

Mattoon
Mount Prospect
Mundelein
Oak Forest
O'Fallon
*Peoria
Pontoon Beach
Rockford
Rosemont
South Beloit
Springfield
Troy
Urbana
*Vandalia
Waukegan

Red Roof Inn

(800) 843-7663 English, (877) 733-7244 Spanish/Español; www.redroof.com

This is a fairly economical chain that offers clean, comfortable rooms. It's fine if you're just looking for a place to sleep. But if you want to hang out at the motel, this chain may not be your best choice because most have few amenities of interest to kids. None of the Illinois properties has a swimming pool or an on-site restaurant; only the Troy property offers breakfast with the room. Red Roof Inns allow one small pet per room. The pet must be declared at registration and attended at all times. Locations include:

Arlington Heights
Champaign
*Chicago
Deerfield
*Downers Grove
Hoffman Estates
Joliet
Lansing
Mount Vernon
Naperville
Peoria
Rockford
Springfield
Troy
Willowbrook

Sleep Inn

(800) 424-6423 English, (866) 291-9816 Spanish/Español, (800) 267-3837 French/Français; TTY (800) 228-3323 for hearing impaired; www.sleepinn.com

A cousin of Comfort Inn, Sleep Inn is more of a budget chain, with comfortable rooms and few amenities in one- or two-story buildings. Most of the Illinois properties do not have a swimming pool or a restaurant on the premises. (The Peoria one has an indoor pool and also offers suites.) All do include continental breakfast in the room rate. Locations include:

Bedford Park
Danville
Decatur
Harvey
Lake Bluff
Lansing
*Naperville
O'Fallon
Peoria
Rockford
Springfield
*Tinley Park
Urbana

Super 8

(800) 800-8000 English, (877) 202-8812 Spanish/Español; www.super8.com

This South Dakota-based budget chain continues to expand. Rooms tend to be clean and comfortable, the amenities minimal, although a few have a swimming pool. All offer free coffee in the lobby each morning, and some include continental breakfast in the room rate. Some of the properties allow pets. Locations include:

Altamont
Alton
Anna
Aurora
Beardstown
*Belleville
Benton
Bloomington
Bourbonnais
Bridgeview
Calumet Park
Canton
*Carbondale
Carlyle
*Champaign
Chenoa
Chicago
Chillicothe
*Collinsville
*Crystal Lake
Danville
Decatur
*DeKalb
Dixon
DuQuoin
Dwight
East Hazel Crest
*East Moline
East Peoria
Effingham
Elgin
Elk Grove Village
El Paso
Fairview Heights
Franklin Park
Freeport
Galesburg
Galva
Geneseo
Gilman
Glen Ellyn
Grayville
Greenville
Hampshire
Harrisburg
Jacksonville
Jerseyville
Joliet
*Kewanee
*Lansing
LeRoy
Lincoln
Litchfield
Macomb
Marion
Marshall
*Mattoon
McHenry
McLean
Mendota
Metropolis
Mokena
Moline
Monee
Monmouth
Morris
Morton Grove
Mount Carmel
Mount Vernon
Mundelein
Murphysboro
*Normal
Okawville
Olney
Ottawa
Paris
Pekin
Peoria
Peru
Pontiac
Pontoon Beach
Princeton
Quincy
Rantoul
River Grove
Rochelle
Rock Falls
Rockford
Romeoville
Salem
Savanna
*Springfield
Staunton
*St. Charles
Streator
Taylorville
Troy
*Tuscola
Urbana
Washington
Waterloo
Watseka
Waukegan
Wenona
Willowbrook
Woodstock
Yorkville

Travelodge and Thriftlodge

(800) 578-7878 English, (800) 372-6310 Spanish/Español; www.travelodge.com

Travelodge and Thriftlodge properties are a good choice for families on a budget. The properties are usually two-story buildings with 50 to 100 clean, comfortable rooms. The DeKalb, Effingham, and Springfield locations also offer the Sleepy Bear's Den guest room for families, which has bear decor and a VCR with kids' videos. Most of the Illinois properties have an outdoor swimming pool. About half the properties allow pets; check ahead of time. All the Illinois properties either have a restaurant on the premises or are located near one. A few of the properties include continental breakfast in the room rate. Locations are Travelodge unless otherwise indicated and include:

Chicago
*DeKalb
Effingham
Niles (Thriftlodge)
Peru
Rockford
Springfield
Urbana
*Vandalia

General Index

A

B

C

D

E

F

G

H

I

J

K

L

M

N

O

P

Q

R

S

T

U

V

W

Activities Index

Amusement Centers, Indoor Playgrounds, and Theme Parks

Children's Museums

Miniature Golf

Parks

Playgrounds (Outdoor)

Trains

Water Parks, Swimming Pools, and Beaches

Zoos and Animal Attractions

Free Attractions Index

There is no admission charge for the following attractions, although some of them have donation boxes for optional contributions.

About the Author

Lori Meek Schuldt is a freelance writer who has worked as a newspaper reporter and as an editor for academic publishers and *The World Book Encyclopedia*. She has spent much of her time in recent years exploring Illinois with her husband, Michael, and their daughter, Rachel.